Figuring Jerusalem

Figuring Jerusalem

Politics and Poetics in the Sacred Center

SIDRA DEKOVEN EZRAHI

The University of Chicago Press
Chicago and London

The University of Chicago Press, Chicago 60637
The University of Chicago Press, Ltd., London
© 2022 by The University of Chicago
Published 2022
Printed in the United States of America

31 30 29 28 27 26 25 24 23 22   1 2 3 4 5

ISBN-13: 978-0-226-78732-9 (cloth)
ISBN-13: 978-0-226-78746-6 (paper)
ISBN-13: 978-0-226-78763-3 (e-book)
DOI: https://doi.org/10.7208/chicago/9780226787633.001.0001

The epigraph on page vii is from Leah Goldberg, *Selected Poetry and Drama*,
trans. Rachel Tzvia Back (New Milford, CT: Toby Press, 2005), 168–69.
Reproduced with the permission of the translator.

Library of Congress Cataloging-in-Publication Data

Names: Ezrahi, Sidra DeKoven, author.
Title: Figuring Jerusalem : politics and poetics in the sacred center /
    Sidra DeKoven Ezrahi.
Description: Chicago : University of Chicago Press, 2022. | Includes bibliographical
    references and index.
Identifiers: LCCN 2021034620 | ISBN 9780226787329 (cloth) | ISBN 9780226787466
    (paperback) | ISBN 9780226787633 (ebook)
Subjects: LCSH: Hebrew literature—History and criticism. | Jerusalem—In literature.
Classification: LCC PJ5012.J4 E97 2022 | DDC 892.409—dc23
LC record available at https://lccn.loc.gov/2021034620

♾ This paper meets the requirements of ANSI/NISO Z39.48-1992 (Permanence of Paper).

To Bernie, who turns every journey into a homecoming

Break your bread in two,
Jerusalem, earthly and heavenly,
thorn jewels on your slopes
and your sun among the thistles.
A hundred deaths but not your mercy!
Break your bread in two:
one part for the birds of the sky
the other
for heavy feet to trample
at the crossroads.

[. . .]

Above my eyes
toward evening
in a city weary of wanderings
in the wayfarers' quarter
small and trembling
wings
trace circles of despair.

A Hebron-glass-sky.
First lamp that is lit.
A swallow with no nest.
Flight that has stopped.

What now?
　　　LEAH GOLDBERG,
"Jerusalem, Earthly and Heavenly"

Contents

Figures

Note on Hebrew Transliteration

For the convenience of the reader who knows Hebrew, I have included spellings and minimal diacritics that are fairly easy to follow, and I have tried to be consistent. The letter het [ח] is represented by an underdot (ḥ); the letter kaf [כ] as kh; ayin [ע] is indicated by ʿ before the letter. Where there are inconsistencies, they usually represent different spelling practices of sources that are quoted. Also, most names and common terms, such as Agnon, Yitzhak, or *akeda*, are presented without diacritics.

"Why Jerusalem?" The Politics of Poetry

Why, of all places, Jerusalem? Why not Babylon
with her Tower of Babel and her babbling tongues . . .
Why not Rome with her catacombs,
why not Mecca with her Black Stone,
why not Vancouver with her salmon
that ascend to her from the sea, crawling
on their bellies up the hard mountain slope
like atoning pilgrims, kosher pilgrims of fin and scale
that arrive at the blue heights, spawn, and die.[1]

YEHUDA AMICHAI

לָמָּה יְרוּשָׁלַיִם. לָמָּה לֹא בָּבֶל עִם מִגְדָּל בָּבֶל וְשָׂפוֹת רַבּוֹת,
. . . לָמָּה לֹא רוֹמָא עִם הַקַּטָּקוֹמְבּוֹת
לָמָּה לֹא מֶכָּה עִם הָאֶבֶן הַשְּׁחוֹרָה,
לָמָּה לֹא וַנְקוּבֶר עִם דְּגֵי הַסַּלְמוֹן
שֶׁעוֹלִים אֵלֶיהָ מִן הַיָּם וְזוֹחֲלִים
עַל גְּחוֹנָם בְּמַעֲלֵה הָהָר הַקָּשֶׁה
כְּמוֹ עוֹלֵי רֶגֶל מְכַפְּרִים, עוֹלֵי סְנַפִּיר וְקַשְׂקֶשֶׂת.
וְהֵם מַגִּיעִים לַמָּרוֹם וּמַשְׁרִיצִים וּמֵתִים.

יהודה עמיחי[2]

If, indeed, it is never quite clear, even to the city's serial inhabitants, *why Je-rusalem*, she may nevertheless be the most longed-for and fought-over city in the world. Architecture embodying layers of sacred memory and sacred promise sits atop the Temple Mount, at the vortex of the Holy Basin[3] which is the vortex of the Holy City and the tinderbox of history. Still: *why another book* on Jerusalem? She may also be the most written-about city in the world.[4] The historical accounts are, inevitably, long and heartbreaking, reflecting the haunting presence of this city as object of fantasy, pilgrimage, and conquest for all monotheists. In his book *Jerusalem, Jerusalem*, James Carroll sums it up succinctly:

[This is] the story of how humans living on the ridge about a third of the way between the Dead Sea and the Mediterranean have constantly been under-mined by the overheated dreams of pilgrims who, age in and age out, arrive at the legendary gates with love in their hearts, the end of the world in their minds, and weapons in their hands.[5]

Note how Carroll divides the inhabitants of this beleaguered city into "humans" and "pilgrims." Indeed, as soon as their ethnic and religious identities are occluded or stripped away, along with the garb that distinguishes them from each other, and the weapons by which they would kill one another, they stand in their human nakedness before the mercy of God. Jerusalem is both the fixed place that evokes a kind of insanity in many of its pilgrims—called, in the professional medical literature, "the Jerusalem syndrome"[6]—and the mobile reference for utopian visions of human collectivity and redemption.

For Jews who "returned" to this city after two millennia of self-described "wandering," the apocalyptic frenzy is constitutive. Held at bay for the first half century of Zionist thought and praxis, and then for the first twenty years of Israel's existence, the frenzy has erupted predictably and ominously since 1967 and gathered momentum since the turn of the third millennium. Now, the Israeli enterprise probably stands or falls on the little hill that contains the history and the remnants of ancient Jerusalem. Yet Jewish traditions, deriving from the Bible, and evolving through continents and centuries beyond the destruction of each of the Temples, provided alternatives to physical proximity to the sacred and, thus, keys to the ethics and poetics of Jewish survival. It is my ambition to present a convincing argument for using those keys to open up the space between the Hill and all who approach it. It of course remains to be seen whether Jews who have returned to the Hebrew spawning ground can apply the keys to a higher intelligence and a stronger life force than those poor salmon, those "atoning pilgrims, kosher pilgrims of fin and scale / that arrive at the blue heights, spawn, and die."

Sacred Space

At least since recorded memory, Jerusalem has been claimed by more than one people or religious community, and claims to sovereignty have typically been proprietary and exclusive, based either on *precedence*—"we" were there "first"—or on *supersession*—"we" are the "capstone." But even the supersessionist model can produce forms of coexistence. Think of the Jebusites (*ha-yevusim*) who, according to the biblical account, were living in the city when David declared it his capital; they are referred to variously as the "inhabitants of the land" or the "inhabitants of Jerusalem" (*yoshvei ha-aretz; yoshvei yerushalayim*, II Sam. 5:1–10; Judg. 1:21). There is ample evidence in the biblical text and elsewhere that David's conquest of the city did not involve genocide or even expulsion of the local people; the Jebusites did not exactly welcome the king and his tribe, but they eventually lived in harmony with them (II Sam. 24:16; II Chr. 3; II Sam. 5:6; Judg. 1:21; Josephus, *Antiquities of the Jews*,

VII:3).[7] In later versions of such impulses, Muslim thinkers represent their edifices, physical and theological, as constructed on Jewish and Christian foundations, rendering Islam the truest, because the most inclusive, iteration of monotheism, and the Dome of the Rock the culmination or palimpsest of the ultimate religious shrine.[8]

Even if proximity to the sacred center and exclusivity and conquest have been the preferred mode of resolution for all three monotheistic religions (and the worst may be yet to come), I shall argue that there are actually *two* models of Jerusalem that are grounded in scriptures and in history. The first is the unmediated approach, with its built-in dangers to life and limb. But there is also a mediated, capacious, and inclusive approach to sacred space. Beneath the rubble of war and the blood of sacrifice, there persist forms of interpolation between the self and the center or object of holiness, Jewish versions of the world-embracing, compassionate engine of the human imagination. They take the shape of Abraham's lesson on "one of those hills" in the Land of Moriah, where he was told to sacrifice a *ram in place of his son*. They are inherent in the Shulamite's instructions to her lover in Song of Songs, where she harnesses extravagant similes and metaphors to sing of human love rather than transcendental holiness, of a garden bower rather than a Temple in Jerusalem.

Figuring Jerusalem

To speak of mediation, then, is to speak of literature and liturgy. For postbiblical Jews, reading and replica became powerful diasporic compensations for the absence of a Temple and its sacrificial cult, and these in turn became the foundation of a life-affirming aesthetic and ethical stance in the world.[9] *Figuring Jerusalem* has always been as natural as fighting for her, or as pledging vengeance for ancient wrongs to be exacted in the time of return. If it was poetry, and the mimetic impulse, that saved the ancient Hebrews in Jerusalem and the Jews throughout history, then perhaps it will be poetry that will save the modern Hebrews and their neighbors in the Age of Return. What will defeat us is the *literalization* of what has remained in a state of metaphoric suspense for thousands of years. If we lose the city, it will be for having turned a deaf ear to poetry, to the very human, self-conscious, compassionate exercise of the imagination.

Archaeology and Architecture

The volume before you sends a plumb line through classical texts that constitute its archaeological foundations. These, in turn, anticipate transformations

that the mimetic muscle would undergo as the sources of Hebrew power reunited with the gravitational pull of sacred sites. The introduction traces the
evolution of sacred space and lingers at some of its major inflection points
throughout the biblical corpus, until it settles on one mountain in Jerusalem.
But even as scattered altars, ziggurats, burning bushes, shrines, tents of meeting, and tabernacles appear to coalesce in the "House" that Solomon built to
the "Name of God," close attention to these texts actually reveals a dichotomy
that persists to this day: between divine presence or immanence perceived as
confined to physical space, and as invoked in human acts of hypostasis, appellation and representation.

The following three chapters explore two biblical texts and one medieval
treatise that will shape the representation of Jerusalem and the apprehension
of divine presence throughout Jewish history—and will largely determine the
liberties and strictures of the Hebrew imagination. Chapter 1 focuses on the
narrative cycle in Genesis 17–22, which incorporates the Binding of Isaac or
the *akeda*. Chapter 2 explores the Song of Songs. As I have already suggested,
these texts constitute the two primary sites of substitution, mediation, and exchange in the Hebrew Bible, providing the classical prooftexts for the premise
that the mimetic imagination can serve as moderating force between the self
and the sacred.

In parsing the narrative that surrounds the *akeda*, I attempt to return it to
its primary, generic state. Jews and Christians often forget that Isaac wasn't sacrificed, overlooking the comedy that structures the narrative and suffuses the
rhetoric of Gen. 17–22. As we will see, not only does the aborted tragedy—
the divine intervention that saves the designated sacrifice from the knife at
the last minute—conform to the classical definition of the comic, but the language surrounding the core chapter (Gen. 22) is also replete with comic allusions and set pieces.

The ongoing, though generally implicit, dialogue between early Christians and early Jews might have induced certain rabbis and medieval Hebrew poets to defensively "kill" Isaac and present his "ashes" and his "rebirth"
as offerings to match those of that other crucified and risen Jew; the *akeda*
would, indeed, become the primary topos of martyrdom from early antiquity
through the present.[10]

Song of Songs, a poetic cycle set in King Solomon's Jerusalem, presents
other challenges. The Song is replete with many references to royal accouter-
ments and pleasures. The rich metaphors and similes that abound in this text
constitute extravagant acts of imagination that foreground human love and
play while effacing the most significant "fact" of Jerusalem in the time of King
Solomon. Salient by its absence in the plain text is any reference to the Temple

or other sites of holiness connected with the city under the great king's reign. Shir ha-shirim is perhaps the most profane (i.e., that which is outside sacred time or place) text in the entire Hebrew Bible, which is why it has been subjected to ingenious acts of exegetical acrobatics.

If the rescue of Isaac had somehow to be suppressed to conform to a more preemptive sacrificial mindset as part of the implicit interdenominational dialogue, it is easy to imagine that it was the absence of holy sites in Song of Songs that kept the rabbis, and the early Church fathers, up at night constructing elaborate parables for this rather naked love song. That is, in both traditions, the peculiar exercise of the imagination that produced parable or allegory was intent on occluding the imagination's other muscle: that which generates the comic spirit and revels in similes and metaphors.

Each of these texts, in my reading, valorizes a poetic and political posture that is radical in both senses of the word: true to the ancient roots and also a challenge to their prevailing iterations in centuries of exegesis and appropriation. From the time of its canonization to the present, the story of the *akeda* provided a tragic-sacrificial response to history while hiding its comic structures and rhetoric in plain sight; restoring the lost comic muscle can, then, provide the antidote to tragic-sacrificial impulses in contemporary Israel. Similarly, poetic tropes and erotic encounters in Song of Songs still struggle to be liberated from exegetical camouflage.

The first chapters of this book will highlight these biblical texts, both located in Jerusalem (or proto-Jerusalem), and both nurturing the poetic and the political soul of the city from its foundation in early Hebrew consciousness. Reading them against the grain of traditional exegesis and fifty-plus years of Jewish sovereignty over the Temple Mount, I argue that beneath the exclusive claims and implacable connections made between text and territory lie two primary examples of the mimetic imagination that can serve as mediating forces in modern Jerusalem.

Which brings me to chapter 3. The peculiar danger of the centripetal pull enabled by proximity to the sacred is revealed in another classical text: Maimonides's *Guide of the Perplexed*. This monumental medieval treatise, which composes the third foundational layer for my study, is an elaborate exhortation to respect the freedom of imagination in relation to an unimaginable God by acknowledging that language is a human tool that must be applied with its own controls. Chapter 3 explores the complex analysis by the philosopher, known by his Hebrew acronym as "the Rambam," of the anthropomorphic dangers inherent in any spatial apprehension of, or approach to, the Divine. I argue that this methodical treatise, inflected by medieval Hebrew and Arabic philosophical and poetic discourses, has particular relevance to contemporary Jerusalem, that Maimonides's nuanced endorsement of poetic tropes along with advisories against the dangers of proximity speaks loudly to today's temptations.

The journey of these classical texts through time and space is also a story of dialogue among the three monotheistic religions as they parse—both explicitly and implicitly—their scriptures in conversation and competition with each other. Interdenominational tensions have led to some of the bloodiest confrontations over two millennia; when it comes to Jerusalem, the struggle is, again, between exclusivist messianic expectations of return to and redemption for only one people in the place itself and claims that Jerusalem belongs to everyone and can even become the model for utopian fantasies of replication. The American Puritans who built their "city on a hill," like the late nineteenth-century Methodist minister and his followers who built a model of the Holy Land and Jerusalem in Chautauqua, New York,[11] were behaving not unlike Jews who for centuries had built their "mikdash me'at" or miniature temple in a synagogue or even in their own soul.[12]

The Storyteller and the Poet of Jerusalem

The second half of this book follows the three classical texts as they resonate in the prose and poetry of the two writers who are celebrated by all who live in or love Jerusalem as the quintessential storyteller and poet of the modern city. Between them, Shmuel Yosef Agnon and Yehuda Amichai cover the entire twentieth century and the efflorescence of modern Hebrew literature. Agnon was born in Buczacz, Galicia, in 1888, arrived in the yishuv (prestate Israel) in 1908, and died in 1970;[13] Amichai was born in 1924 in Würzburg, Germany, arrived in the yishuv in 1936, and died with the twentieth century.

Between them they also enact the polarity between unmediated and mediated approaches to the sacred. The prose of Agnon and the poetry of Amichai are informed by the classical Jewish library with overlapping resonances, though over the decades they would each evolve distinct ways of narrating and "figuring" Jerusalem. Amichai's platform becomes, I shall argue, a more direct, "unfettered" encounter with the Bible; Agnon engages the biblical text largely through the rabbinic prism that potentially transforms diasporic liberties into constraints in the era of Return and within the force field of Redemption.

Chapter 4 explores Agnon's poetics of space in two of his canonic stories, "Agunot" and "Aggadat ha-sofer" (The Tale of the Scribe). Constructing an imaginary dialogue between the Rambam and modern Israel's Nobel laureate, I examine the strictures, dilemmas, and opportunities probed in *The Guide of the Perplexed* as they appear through the physical manifestations or simulacra of holy objects and paradigms in these Hebrew fictions. And the layered resonances of Song of Songs open another window onto the work of the storyteller who imports diasporic mediations that offset yearnings for proximity to the sacred.

In chapter 5, focusing on Agnon *in* Jerusalem, I trace the rather obscure ways in which the "Binding of Isaac" wends its way through his magnum opus, *Tmol shilshom* (Only Yesterday), and through the life of its main protagonist, Isaac (Yitzhak) Kumer. In some ways this modern narrative actually follows the biblical pattern, providing many instances of mediation and substitution—the human comedy embedded in the quotidian. Finally, however, Isaac's story succumbs to the tragic arc inscribed in his name, murdering him, along with the comedy that he managed to live, as it were, under the radar. The chapter concludes by arguing that the two geographical poles in Agnon's life and work—Jerusalem and his native town of Buczacz, or its fictional surrogate—rhyme in ways that provide him with a template for different resolutions to his own existential struggle. In stories written over a lifetime, Jerusalem and Buczacz are rendered as, essentially, nonpolitical entities, protected from the usual transactions that characterize multicultural urban spaces. But this would become especially consequential in Jerusalem in the brief period between the war of 1967 and Agnon's death in 1970, when his profound ambivalence about newly acquired access to the sacred center was expressed in posthumously published prose—as well as in his tentative personal behavior vis-à-vis the Wailing Wall and the Temple Mount.

While both Agnon and Amichai are heir to millennial yearnings for proximity to the sacred, and both recognize the perils of proximity, Agnon and his characters remain for the most part caught in the unresolved dilemma, while Yehuda Amichai enacts a poetic resolution to the dilemma—a resolution consistent with the deepest comic and poetic secrets imported from the Diaspora. As I have indicated, the midrashic impulse was not unavailable to the poet of Jerusalem, who had marinated in a traditional home and classroom. But the license to invent, to create endless similes and metaphors combining and recombining all aspects of the physical and metaphysical world, is enabled more by biblical poetics and diasporic freedoms, informed but unencumbered by rabbinic strictures. This was true even—or especially—in the presence of Mount Zion, where the poet's last home was located.

Personally Speaking

And this is where my project becomes personal. I am aware that in claiming that Amichai's poetry and presence interact with my own biography, I am repeating a claim that most of his readers would make. He is every Hebrew reader's personal poet, available, it seems, for all private and public occasions.[14] But there are other intersections and lines of affinity.

Having arrived in Palestine with his family in 1936, Ludwig Pfeuffer would become Yehuda Amichai and would fight in the Jewish Brigade with the British Army during the Second World War and in three of Israel's wars (1948, 1956, and 1973). I immigrated to Israel several years before the Six Day War, when the State and I were both relatively young: she was fourteen and I was nineteen. Amichai and I each lived on Rehov Metudela before 1967. Though Holy Jerusalem was very old, she was out of sight, remaining infinitely imaginable because she was infinitely inaccessible. This "new" city in which we both lived was youthful. More important, she was slim.

After 1967, both Amichai and I moved into the renovated areas of south Jerusalem. I lived in a structure that dated back to the early twentieth century and contained layers of tragic history;[15] Amichai's home in Abu Tor was located in "No Man's Land," also identified as the biblical Valley of Gehenna.[16] His last home, in "Mishkenot sha'ananim," faced Mount Zion, on the other side of the valley known variously as Birket es Sultan, Brekhat ha-Sultan, or "Sultan's Pool"—a liminal place where, as the poet demonstrates, religious war can be preempted, or ignited, if the Jewish father's lost son and the Arab shepherd's stray goat get caught up in the "terrible had gadya machine."[17]

Even as we briefly shared the intoxication of the post-'67 years, many of us came to realize the disastrous potential of the engorged entity that Jerusalem had become. After 1967, along with dwindling hopes for reconciliation and peace, Amichai's invocation of a formerly divided Jerusalem would challenge the public euphoria:

> They're burning the photos of the divided Jerusalem
> and the beautiful letters of the beloved,
> who was so quiet.
> The noisy old dowager, all of her,
> with her gold and copper and stones,
> has come back
> to a fat legal life.
>
> But I don't like her.
> Sometimes I remember the quiet one.[18]

Like the poet, I too don't like the "noisy old dowager" and have come to miss the "old longing."[19] The real problem may be that Amichai, and many of us, grew wiser as we aged—and she didn't. That fat old dowager not only lives with an insatiable appetite but remains in the childish grip of utopian blueprints and literalized metaphors, such as the vengeful pledge to total recall spelled out in Psalm 137: "O daughter of Babylon, happy is he who will repay you for what you have done to us. Happy is he who shall seize and dash thy babies against the rocks" (Ps. 137:8–9). Returning to such iron-age impulses, wreaking on today's enemies the wrath of the ages, may be a way of reclaiming the past by eschewing the wisdom of age and the humor and humanity of distance.[20] But in his later verses, the modern poet of Jerusalem insists on bringing that wisdom, that humor, and that distance to bear on present longings:

> Longing for Jerusalem, for childhood in Jerusalem in another faraway time:
> the children of the Levites longing, now that they are old, in exile
> by the waters of Babylon. They still remember singing
> in the Temple when their voices had just begun to change.
> At night they remind one another of their childhood:
> Remember how we played hide-and-seek behind
> the Holy of Holies,
> in the shadow
> of the embroidered mantle of the holy Ark,
> between the cherubim?[21]

Hide-and-seek behind the Holy of Holies? Precisely! In maturity, the remembered games of our collective childhood, the laughter and the freedom, can detoxify the dangers of unmediated proximity to the sacred. But like the noisy old dowager, there are those whose longing is of a different order: a return to the place of childhood without recalling the games of childhood; a righteous vengeance putatively acquired by the waters of Babylon. As Ariel Hirschfeld writes, "the destruction of the Temple . . . [like] the breaking of the tablets constitute[s] historical and developmental truth with profound implications. The maturation and survival of the Jewish people, tragic as the circumstances may have been . . . brought about a separation of meaning from place. The reconnection to place, to The Place, the Wailing Wall and the Temple Mount, is the ultimate test of its maturity."[22]

Indeed, the default of this reconnection to "The Place," to "Jerusalem in another faraway time," will reappear as forms of anxious messianism that punctuate the Exile at transitional moments. The messianic undercurrents of the Zionist enterprise centered on the Temple Mount—occluded from sight after the establishment of the State but maintained at the forefront of underground movements—would emerge as powerful forces around the turn of the millennium. "Jewish redemption," explains Tomer Persico, "classically founded on renewed Jewish sovereignty in the Holy Land," would entail the "establishment of a Temple and a monarchical government descended from the house of David."[23]

For those of us, then, who lived in Jerusalem between 1948 and 1967, the Sacred Center was out of sight and out of reach, and a kind of diasporic ethical distance could be replicated even in this City of Cities under Israeli sovereignty. If post-'67 reconnection to The Place eschews the maturity, the sanity, the wit, and the deferments achieved through endless acts of substitution, then a relentless literalism has defeated the hard-won wisdom and humanity of a long tradition of negotiating distance. When Prime Minister Benjamin Netanyahu insists that Jerusalem is the "bedrock of our existence,"[24] compared to nothing but herself, he indulges unselfconsciously in metaphor while acting as if metaphor-making is not a crucial feature of free-thinking people; he purports to abolish self-conscious comparison and substitution, those very acts of world-embracing compassion. But without this self-consciousness, and this compassion, we are all doomed to kill or be killed on, and for, the altar.

I could not have anticipated, when I began this inquiry into what happens when the Hebrew imagination "comes home," how urgent the topic would become. How close we are to recapitulating another murderous chapter in human history because we have forgotten or suppressed the lessons we learned along the way, because we have come to ignore the fact that all those who live on the "ridge about a third of the way between the Dead Sea and the Mediterranean" are, beneath the visions of the "end of the world in their minds, and weapons in their hands," also—simply—"humans."

What, then, happens to Hebrew letters when the messianic genie, held within the diasporic fluid of distance for two thousand years after the destruction of the "Second Temple" and for twenty years after the declaration of Israeli statehood, escapes from the bottle? The short answer, elaborated in the second half of the volume before you, is that S. Y. Agnon remained, until the very end, torn between the temptations and the perils of living and writing in proximity to the sacred. Yehuda Amichai, on the other hand, evolved a clear set of resolutions, in his person and his poetry, forging a language in which he could perform both a literary and an existential mediation from the sacred. He lived to witness the greatest agony of his time; the Second Intifada, bubbling beneath the surface for years, broke out just days after his death. His last will and testament might well be read as a radical interrogation of that explicitly poetic platform on which he and his readers had stood for half a century—the similitudes and the precarious "makaf," or hyphen,[25] that protected the space between two humans and between the human and the Divine. He seemed to lament that bringing the Hebrew imagination "home" meant, for many, literalizing what had been held in the allegory of suspicion for millennia, occluding the human love being enacted in that open wound "on the border between Jerusalem / and Jerusalem." For Amichai, the "Singer of the Song of Songs" dare not ignore the overloaded inflections of his own images.[26] And yet, like the aging Prospero, who understood the human limits of even his own art and felt compelled to "drown [his] book," Amichai had already bequeathed to his audience a lifetime of magic.

The Wailing Wall

I wrote the last draft of this book during the coronavirus lockdown of the spring of 2020, when the plaza in front of the "Wailing Wall" was devoid of its usual crowds. Yet the empty space revealed a profound truth. As with all religious shrines, what has made this site holy is the procession of worshippers over the centuries who have desperately poured out their hearts and their prayers; it became sacred not because of the presence of divine grandeur but by the accumulation of human pathos. No one put it better than Mark Twain, in his irreverent version of one pilgrim's progress. Toward the end of *Innocents Abroad*, after visiting the Church of the Holy Sepulchre in Jerusalem, he allowed his Protestant American skepticism to fall away briefly in the face of the generations that have sanctified the place: "for fifteen hundred years its shrines have been wet with the tears of pilgrims from the earth's remotest confines."[27] Imagining the Wall, wailing in its loneliness, provided me with a forlorn hope, that we too might yet learn something about how to heal the wounds at the center of our being—though that is not likely to happen in my lifetime. The final editing of these pages was accompanied, once again, by the noise of war, as unrest in the Sheikh Jarrah area of east Jerusalem bled into violence on (where else?) the Temple Mount/Haram al Sharif, which led to the latest hostilities between Hamas in Gaza and the Israeli military. One of the saddest aspects of this latest war, which has claimed hundreds of lives, and which Israel calls, euphemistically, "Shomer ha-ḥomot" (Guardian of the Walls), was the explosion of urban violence in the mixed Arab-Israeli cities inside Israel. As I write these words, it appears that the oldest fraternal rivalry in the monotheistic world shows no signs of abating, and that the world's most precious thirty-seven acres of real estate may always remain the site of ultimate sacrifice.

"This House, which is called by My Name"

The nights I used to spend with devout and pious men beside the Wailing Wall . . . gave me eyes to see the land of the Holy One, Blessed be He—the Wall which He gave us, and the *city upon which He established His name.*

      s . y . a g n o n , Nobel Prize acceptance speech, 1966 (emphasis mine)[1]

Jerusalem is a port city on the shore of eternity.
The Temple Mount is a huge ship, a magnificent
luxury liner. From the portholes of her Western Wall
cheerful saints look out, travelers. Hasidim on the pier
wave goodbye, shout hooray, hooray, bon voyage! She is
always arriving, always sailing away. And the fences and the piers
and the policemen and the flags and the high masts of churches
and mosques and the smokestacks of synagogues and the boats
of psalms of praise and the mountain-waves. The shofar blows: another one
has just left. Yom Kippur sailors in white uniforms
climb among ladders and ropes of well-tested prayers.

And the commerce and the gates and the golden domes:
Jerusalem is the Venice of God.

      y e h u d a a m i c h a i , "Jerusalem 1967," no. 21[2]

The two writers of modern Jerusalem reference the same Wall at nearly the same moment—though on two sides of the historical divide that would give Jews access to and sovereignty over that site after two thousand years. For S. Y. Agnon, whose recollection of access predates the war of 1948—when the city was under the control of the British Mandate—but was uttered a year before the war of 1967, the Wall is the eternal source of the centripetal force that focuses vision, the center of the City and of the Land that defines and confines holiness and the mortar that congeals all the disparate parts of the Diaspora and of each ragged Jewish soul. For Yehuda Amichai, in the euphoric aftermath of the Six-Day War, it is the launching pad for a centrifugal and ecumenical reach, generating unfettered similes and metaphors that carry messages to the far corners of the universe.

What is it about the Wall itself that enhanced and narrowed the vision of Jerusalem's storyteller—while enlarging and widening the vision of Jerusalem's poet? The Western, or Wailing, Wall is the most magnetic place in the

Jewish world. Synagogue life evolved with orientation toward the Temple—whether by physical pilgrimage while one of the Temples still stood, or by prayer directed westward or eastward depending on where the worshipper resided in the millennia since the destruction of the "Second" Temple and the exile of its Jewish inhabitants. Its centrality is cemented in the daily practice and eschatology of Jews worldwide and in the politics of modern Israel.

But the Wall itself is only a remnant of a retaining wall that surrounded the Temple that King Herod rebuilt and fortified around the turn of the Common Era (Herod, vassal of the Roman empire, already represents the layered reality and ecumenical potential of the site).[3] For the messianists of today, the Wall provides mere stepping stones to the Place Itself: the once (and future) Temple. The real difference between the scribe of Jerusalem and the poet of Jerusalem, between narrowed and expansive visions of holiness, was there from the moment redemptive endings were projected onto edenic origins and the now-time had to be negotiated in the interstices. As we shall see, this template was in place even before the destruction of the Temples generated a culture founded on ruins and desire, on remnants of a remembered state of perfection and visions of completion pasted onto a putative future. Traces of this template and the perils of proximity are contained in an ancient story that is ritually reenacted every year.

The Perils of Proximity

The Torah reading for Yom Kippur, the holiest day in the Jewish calendar, is from Leviticus 16, and begins: "And the Lord spoke to Moses after the death of the two sons of Aaron." We are reminded here laconically of the passage related six chapters earlier, one of the most painful in the Torah, where God instructs Aaron and his sons as to the priestly procedures they are to follow to prepare the atonement sacrifice for the altar at the Ohel Moed, the Tent of Meeting. Having meticulously followed these instructions, Aaron's sons, Nadav and Avihu, then inexplicably "brought forward alien fire [esh zara] before the Lord, which He had not charged them. And fire came out before the Lord and consumed them" (Lev. 10:1–2).

ויקחו בני אהרון נדב ואביהוא איש מחתתו ויתנו בהן אש וישימו עליה קטורת ויקריבו לפני יהוה אש זרה אשר
לא צוה אותם: ותצא אש מלפני יהוה ותאכל אותם וימותו לפני יהוה.

Six chapters later, in the reading adopted for Yom Kippur, this event is succinctly recalled as the sin of—and punishment for—drawing "too close to the presence of the lord" (be-korvatam lifnei adonai va-yamutu, בקרבתם לפני יהוה וימותו, Lev. 16:1).[4]

Although this incident becomes ingrained in the mind of every observant Jew as recalled not only in the lectionary cycle but also on the holiest day of the year, there are additional examples in the Hebrew Bible of instant punishment meted out to those who, unscripted, come too close to the source of holiness. Think of poor Uzzah: King David and his entourage were triumphantly accompanying the Ark of the Covenant to Jerusalem on an ox-driven cart; when the oxen stumbled, Uzzah put up his hand to steady the ark—and was instantly struck down (II Sam. 6:5–15). That was enough to terrify the king into sequestering the ark for three months before he finally found the courage to bring it to the "City of David."

The City is just as toxic—and intoxicating—now as it was three thousand years ago. Its toxicity spreads throughout the body politic, infecting every attempt at civic resolution that is not based on exclusive, inscrutable, and peremptory divine promise. If, as I am arguing, the antidote to the lure, and the danger, of proximity to the sacred can come from the accumulated wisdom of two thousand years of negotiating distance through compensatory practices and ersatz spaces, we must nevertheless note, even before we enter the City, that in both instances just cited, there is an assumption that holiness resides in or hovers over a place or an object. But it turns out that that presumption was implicitly interrogated and refined throughout the history and the journeys of the Jews.

In their annual acknowledgment of both ancient temptations and diasporic compensations, Jews worldwide not only read the object lesson of Aaron's poor sons, but also mimic the pageant of the High Priest entering the Holy of Holies and performing the sacred rite that could be executed only by him and only once a year. After the final destruction of the Temple in the first century CE, that act could no longer be ritually performed and could only be dramatically recalled. It therefore differs from all other rites in the Jewish liturgy: not a prayer from the individual or community to God, but rather a theatrical reenactment of an ancient ritual. But the reenactment itself is flawed, since the central element has been forgotten or suppressed—or was suppressed and then forgotten.

What is that element? It is the pronunciation of the full name of God, the "Tetragrammaton" in all its inflections.[5] That is, even in that holiest of all places and holiest of all times, it was not the divine *presence* that was encountered by the High Priest—but the divine *name* that was evoked, by an all-too-human, if exalted, agent.[6] Indeed, the Name of God becomes the link between space and speech in the constitutive moments of Hebrew monotheism. Even more poignantly, the divine-human encounter takes place in language that preempts or supersedes the spatial dimension even before the loss of correct

pronunciation that will necessitate a series of circumlocutions. The antecedents of the Temple and its rituals already anticipate an evolution in faith and
practice that will eventually substitute *nomination* for *revelation*. The "amnesia" that will later set in can be seen, then, as even further protection from
the shamanistic powers of naming itself as well as from the presumption of
physical proximity.

The covenantal site of revelation and sacrifice—the meeting place, as it
were, between the human and the Divine—will begin, in the Hebrew Bible,
with a vague designation, "one of those mountains in the Land of Moriah,"
where the first patriarch, Abraham, was commanded to sacrifice his son as a
burnt offering (Gen. 22:1). Later, in the dreamscape of Abraham's grandson,
Jacob, there appears a ladder, ramp, or ziggurat that reaches from earth to
heaven and is visited by heavenly hosts, capped by the appearance of the Deity. Upon waking, Jacob designates this place the "house of God":

> And Jacob awoke from his sleep and he said, "Indeed, *the Lord [YHWH] is in*
> *this place*, and I did not know." And he was afraid and he said, "How fearsome
> is this place! This can be but the *house of God [beit elohim]*, and this is the gate
> of the heavens." (Gen. 28:16–18, emphases mine)

The House of God first appears, then, as a rather abstract index of divine
presence ("this place").[7] Jacob goes on to name the town where his vision
took place "Bethel," literally House of God (Gen. 28:19), which establishes an
etiological connection between revelation and location[8]—but also elides the
unselfconscious uses of singular and plural designations of God (*beit el, beit
elohim*).[9]

Consider, again, Jacob's revelation: "Indeed, the Lord [YHWH] is in this
place, and I did not know." In rabbinic Hebrew, the word *makom*, or place,
would come to refer to God. In 1993, as Chancellor of the Jewish Theological
Seminary, Ismar Schorsch ruminated on the many names for the Divine, and
on the tension between any specific designation of divine habitation and the
more capacious notion that God's glory fills the universe, that God is Place
itself:

> William Blake caught the spirit of Judaism perfectly when he wrote: "*To see*
> *a World in a grain of sand, And a Heaven in a wild flower; Hold Infinity in the*
> *palm of your hand, And Eternity in an hour.*" Behind the plethora of divine
> names that came to mark Judaism, there resonates but one defiant conviction:
> "that the Lord alone is God in heaven above and on earth below; there is no
> other (Deut. 4:39)." All that exists flows from a single source, even if no one
> name comes close to illuminating it, though Ha-makom is a daring and lofty
> creation of the religious imagination.[10]

Within the confines of the Hebrew Bible, however, the most dramatic and direct dialogue over the physical confines of the Divine takes place, not in dreams or poetic or even prophetic projections, but in the intimate encounters between Moses and God, who first manifests Himself in the burning bush (Ex. 3:2ff.). From the beginning, Moses is not content with abstraction and insists on details: in order to establish his own credibility with the Children of Israel, he asks for God's name. The tetragrammaton *YHWH* (s.) is here articulated in what would be interpreted as a kind of futuristic promise—*ehyeh asher ehyeh, I will be what I will be*[11]—immediately followed by an elaboration and proliferation of names in first-person singular and plural pronouns: "God [*elohim* (pl.)] said moreover to Moses, 'Thus shalt thou say to the children of Israel, the Lord God of your fathers [*YHWH* (s.) *elohei avotekhem* (pl.)] has sent me to you'" (Ex. 3:13–14). It is in His attributes, manifest through the working of history, and not in or limited to physical presence, that God is known from the beginning of the narrative that will consolidate ragtag tribes into a nation. Moses, however, not content anymore to know God "by name" (Ex. 33:17), persists in demanding to know his "Interlocutor" through visual apprehension. The Lord's response is to partially conceal Moses in the cleft of a rock and then pass by so that only His "backside" is revealed: "You will see My back, but My face will not be seen . . . for no human can see Me and live" (Ex. 33:23, 20).[12]

All subsequent debates about the monotheistic turn and claims to proximity to and attributes of the Divine are founded in these constitutive moments.

Revelation and Nomination

Moses is to supervise the construction of the mobile Ark of the Covenant in which, it is presumed, God's "presence" will dwell, along with the tablets of the law: "Let them make me a sanctuary, that I may dwell among them," the Lord instructs the newly minted leader. Having already "met" the Divine in the Burning Bush (Ex. 3:2), in the cleft of the rock, and on Mount Sinai, Moses will continue to "meet" Him at the Ark of the Covenant: "And in the Ark you shall set the tablets of the Covenant that I shall give you. And I shall meet you there and speak with you" (Ex. 25:21–22). The term *ohel mo'ed*, or tent of *meeting*, will inform the designation of the feast days as *mo'adim*, the appointed times in which such meetings between the human and the Divine are reenacted, performed, or recalled.

But it turns out that within the covenantal framework solidified in the Book of Exodus, Moses is the *only one* to encounter God directly and live: "And the Lord would speak to Moses face-to-face, as a man speaks to his fellow" (Ex. 33:11). The Ark becomes so radioactive with divine presence that, as we have seen, anyone who touches it or brings "strange fire" to it pays with his life. Recall that in this earliest arid moment in the evolution of Hebrew monotheism, even a slight delay in Moses's descent from the mountain at Sinai prompts the Israelites to build a physical manifestation of the Divine in the shape of a Golden Calf. However, as their nomadic existence gives way to greater permanence, the notion of an invisible, incorporeal God also grows, and forms of appellation come increasingly to replace direct encounter.

Passing through a number of extemporaneous altars and dramatic encounters with Moses to a movable ark accompanying a people in the wilderness, the site of revelation and sacrifice—the meeting place, as it were, between the human and the Divine—will, finally, congeal into one fixed shrine in Jerusalem. But David's radioactive ark and poor Uzzah's fate, like Nadav and Avihu's unscripted behavior at the Tent of Meeting, remain as a warning. Even after King David consolidates his dominion over Jerusalem, whose indigenous biblical name is "Yevus," and over its "local inhabitants," the "Yevusim" or Jebusites (*yoshvei ha-aretz*, I Chr. 11:4),[13] even as he purchases Arauna's threshing floor and establishes the city's status as Sacred Center by placing the Ark of the Covenant in its precincts, even as his son Solomon commences building a "house" for the Lord meant to match his own lavish quarters, and finally even as, in the concluding chapters of the Hebrew scriptures, this "house" will be identified with the very first covenantal spot where Abraham prepared to sacrifice his son, seemingly tying up all the loose ends, still an ambivalence persists about confining the Divine in physical space.

In the process that culminates in the construction of the Temple, David first points out to Nathan the prophet the anomaly between his own dwelling and that of God: "See, pray, I dwell in a cedarwood house while the Ark of God dwells within curtains" (II Sam. 7:1–2). Later, his son will boast that "I indeed have built You a lofty house, a firm place for You to dwell in forever" (I Kings 8:13).[14]

Although it appears that God agrees to limit the place of encounter to the confines of a specific edifice, this promise is made contingent on the behavior of the children of Israel:

This house that you build—if you walk by My statutes and do My laws and keep all My commands to walk by them, I shall fulfill My word with you that I spoke to David your father, and I shall dwell in the midst of the Israelites, and I shall not forsake My people Israel. (I Kings 6:12–13)

Then, only two chapters later, when Solomon boasts that he has built a house for the Lord, His eternal dwelling place—"Then did Solomon say: 'the Lord

meant to abide in thick fog. I indeed have built You a lofty house, a firm place
for Your dwelling forever'" (I Kings 8:12–13)—he is implicitly chastised by the
Lord, Who, while appearing to address the issue of succession and vocation
between David and Solomon, is subtly redefining the space of the human-
divine encounter:

> And the king turned his face and blessed all the assembly of Israel with all
> the assembly of Israel standing. And he said: "blessed be the Lord the God of
> Israel, Who spoke with *His own mouth* to David my father, and with *His own
> hand* has fulfilled it, saying: 'From the day that I brought out My people Israel
> from Egypt, I have not chosen a town from all the tribes of Israel to build *a
> house for My name to be there*, but I chose David to be over My people Israel.'
> And it was in the heart of David my father to build a *house for the name of
> the Lord God of Israel*. And the Lord said unto David my father: 'Inasmuch as
> it was in your heart to build a *house for My name*, you have done well, for it
> was in your heart. Only you will not build the house, but your son, who is-
> sues from your loins, he will build the *house for My name*.'" (I Kings 8:15–19,
> emphases mine)

Mouth of God, hand of God, house of God . . . name of God. The danger of
anthropomorphism is matched by the presumption of physical confinement—
and both are challenged and superseded by nomination. Further, as the tribes
consolidate, as the city is chosen, and finally as holiness is centralized and,
seemingly, confined to one "house" on one mountain, traces persist throughout
Scriptures of the struggle between *presence* and *designation* of, or address to, the
Divine. The ancient Solomonic temple was built, according to biblical accounts
rendered by scholarship into temporal eons (since no physical remains have
been found), in the tenth century BCE (II Samuel; I Chronicles; I Kings) and
stood for nearly four hundred years before being destroyed by the Babylonians
(II Kings; II Chronicles). Increasingly, ambivalence about the physical confines
of divinity turns into resistance, particularly among the later prophets of Israel,
who experienced the upheavals of destruction and exile. Located in the volatile
time just before the destruction of the Temple of Solomon, God's speech, as filtered through the prophet Jeremiah, refers to *divine action* and *human response*
as supplanting the premise of *divine confinement*:

> "Has this house, *on which my name has been called*, become an outlaws' cave
> in your eyes? . . . I spoke to you constantly and you did not listen, and I called
> you, and you did not answer. [Therefore] I will do to this house, on *which
> my name has been called*, in which you put your trust, and to the place that I
> gave to you and to your fathers, as I did to Shiloh." (Jer. 7:11, 13–14, emphases
> mine)[15]

God's words are similarly ventriloquized by Isaiah—the so-called Third Isaiah, a figure placed in the eighth century BCE, when the Temple would have stood in its glory, but who in all likelihood lived in the Land of Israel after the return from the Babylonian exile. His injunctions insist on the abstract and ubiquitous nature of the divine presence: "The heavens are My throne, and the earth is My footstool. What house would you build for Me and what place for My resting?" (Is. 66:1).

Not only, then, does God instruct the kings of Israel to erect a temple to His *name*; the instruction proceeds in altered and augmented form to the later prophets. What emerges from all these exchanges, though it is an axiom that will be consistently deflected, is that the Temple that is to be built, and that will become the holiest place in Judaism, is *not the dwelling place of the Deity but the site where the human voice can call to, can name, can invoke, the Deity—or, by vile action, take the Name in vain.*[16]

Jerusalem: A City without Walls

Moreover, before the dust had settled on its ruins, and before physical reconstruction had commenced under the new Persian regime, the Temple was rebuilt as a vision or figment of the imagination. Presumably prophesying within living memory of the Temple itself, during or shortly after the destruction of the city and the exile of its inhabitants, both Ezekiel and Zechariah provide blueprints that are suffused with precise measurement and, at the same time, hint at the beginning of a mimetic culture premised on unbound flights of imagination.

Ezekiel, in exile in Babylonia, is instructed by a divine voice to create a model of Jerusalem—to incise the city on a brick or tile and playact the coming retribution that will befall its wayward inhabitants:

> "And you, man, *take you a brick and put it before you and incise on it the city of Jerusalem.* And you shall lay a siege against it and build against it a siegework and throw up a ramp against it and set an armed camp against it and put against it battering rams all round. And you, take you an iron pan and make it an iron wall between you and the city. *And you shall set your face toward it*, and it shall be besieged, and you shall lay siege against it. *It is a sign* for the house of Israel. *And you, lie down on your left side* and put the guilt of the house of Israel upon it. For the number of days that you lie on it you shall bear their guilt." (Ezek. 4:1–4, emphases mine)

Subsequently, an otherworldly figure appears, lifts the prophet up and brings him "in visions of God to Jerusalem," where he reveals to him the Temple in great detail, though with "small" revisions of the natural landscape—such as water gushing from under the platform of the Temple and flowing eastward in streams and rivers, turning the Dead Sea sweet and forming an eschatological topography (Ezek. 46:21–47:13).[17]

The prophet has been commanded to become both storyboard artist and actor in a bizarre pageant, and then the primary audience for a mystical tableau. Further, both Ezekiel and, presumably a few decades later, Zechariah have visions of a man with a measuring cord or rod. "Where are you going?" Zechariah asks the man. "To measure Jerusalem," he replies, "to determine its width and its length." But the surveyor is preempted by an angel who assures him that "Jerusalem shall be peopled as a city without walls, so many shall be the men and cattle it contains. And I Myself—declares the Lord—will be a wall of fire all around it, and I will be a glory inside it" (Zech. 2:5–9; see also Ezek. 40:1–43:9).[18]

Jerusalem incised on a brick; the Temple suspended between heaven and earth. A city without walls; the Lord Himself as a wall of fire. At this early hour, Jerusalem and its holy center have already become infinitely compressive, infinitely expandable—and the site of infinite flights of fancy.[19] "Across the centuries, 'rebuilding the Temple' has remained an inspirational clarion call for a spiritual idealism more even than for a real building," observes Simon Goldhill.[20]

What may seem like a trivial distinction could be the most significant move in the protracted dawn of Hebrew monotheism, though it is a move that is undermined periodically when people act on the desire to draw near to, to possess or merge with, the divine presence. The seesaw between the presumption of unmediated presence and forms of mediation—calling, naming, imagining—will continue to haunt and shape Judaism from its inception in ancient Hebrew impulses to the present moment.

After discussing the complex idea of the divine *kavod* or glory through the prophetic books, Victor Avigdor Hurowitz relates it to the long period of the Second Temple, during which this splendid edifice was understood to be "devoid of its Divine resident." The logically unresolvable internal contradictions are resolved only by a theological leap of faith, as Hurowitz demonstrates in summoning the builder and architect of the First Temple:

> To be sure, the concept that God is not restricted to the Temple is complementary to the concept that God is found everywhere and can be worshipped anywhere and everywhere, and this is the concept which permits the existence of synagogues, the Jewish institution which eventually inherited and replaced the Temple ... But were one to ask the builder of the First Temple and the architect who designed it the rhetorical question "Will God really dwell with Man upon the earth?" he would be likely to answer "But of course, for the Temple is Heaven on Earth."[21]

The pendulum continues to swing, and with it the knot that binds site and story, space and speech, presence and representation tightens or loosens. The narrative of sacred space that opened in Genesis 22 with God's directing Abraham to take his son to a vague destination—*"one of the mountains* [in the land of Moriah]"—concludes in II Chronicles by consolidating all the loci and vessels of holiness, from the first to the last book of the Hebrew Bible:

> And Solomon began to build the *house of the Lord* in Jerusalem on *Mount Moriah* where He had appeared to *David his father* at the place that David had readied at the *threshing floor of Ornan the Jebusite.* (II Chr. 3:1, emphases mine)

The elasticity built into the vision of Jerusalem from the beginning is then, by the end of the Hebrew Bible, confined to Mount Moriah, which would in turn become known as the Temple Mount.[22] But over time, this very elasticity will gesture outward toward the city, its environs, and Zion as a whole—whose boundaries, henceforth, are the protean demarcations of an imagination informed by, and at the same time uncannily liberated from, memory. And that's even before the other monotheistic religions put their stakes in this hallowed ground: the ground on which Queen Helena was said to have discovered the crosses on which Jesus and the thieves had been crucified;[23] the site from which Mohammed ascended to heaven, leaving his footprint in the rock that became the Dome of the Rock. In turn, the rock where Isaac was nearly sacrificed, referred to already in Ezekiel as *tabur ha-aretz,* the *omphalos* or "navel of the world" (Ezek. 38:12),[24] would be identified in rabbinic and mystical traditions as *even ha-shtiya,* or the foundation stone, from which the world was created and which continues to hold back the churning waters at the fundament of the universe.[25] Such acts of consolidation concentrate the mind and create the centripetal pull that will exert its power for millennia, along with infinite possibilities for interdenominational cooperation—or strife.

Moreover, this process is facilitated by a radical and sustained poetic conceit. For some two thousand years after the second destruction in 70 CE, in the absence of a Temple, a republic, or any form of territorial or political sovereignty, and at variable distances from the ruined shrine, the Hebrew poet managed to preserve Jerusalem in its symbolic state. In this project he drew upon one of the earliest acts of the biblical poetic imagination: the personification of Jerusalem as woman.

"To what shall I compare thee?"

The prevailing image that would inspire the poetry of the long centuries of exile was that of the static, remote other. Perhaps the most radical expressions of such psycholiterary impulses are elaborated in the prophetic discourses themselves. "To what shall I *compare thee that I may comfort thee?*" the poet, whom we imagine as Jeremiah, asks the personified city of Jerusalem, which has just been destroyed by the Babylonians (Lam. 2:13).[26] That is, the right metaphor, the right simile, will, presumably, provide ultimate consolation.

And it seems that the only image that could contain all images is that of the woman. In fact, the woman is both the *substance* and the *vessel*, or the "tenor" and the "vehicle," of the most powerful metaphors of Jerusalem. Tikva Frymer-Kensky and other scholars have shown that the feminized city was a common trope in the ancient Near East; this may appear less surprising to modern Hebrew readers, given the gendered nature of the language. Jerusalem is always addressed in the feminine—the generic Hebrew word for city, *'ir*, is, indeed, feminine—and neighboring cities were sometimes referred to as her "sisters."[27] But the conceit goes further and becomes more elastic: the prophets Micah, Isaiah, Jeremiah, and Zechariah envision Jerusalem alternately as confined within her walls *and* as peripatetic spirit of the city, an immanence that can separate itself from the place and wander with the people of Israel. So although the feminization of cities was common in the ancient Near East, the poetic gendering of Jerusalem may also signify its special status as the religious and political capital of the united kingdom of ancient Israel, God's beloved daughter—*bat yerushalayim*—signaling maternal care and nurturing *and* a peripatetic sympathy with the scattered tribes of diasporic Israel.[28]

What would continue to inspire the poetry of the centuries was the static, remote beloved, the female *other*, forever beautiful, even in her ruin. So ubiquitous was the primary act of personification that hardly anyone remarks anymore on Jerusalem's appearance in Jewish memory as that of the desired female, or on the common posture toward Jerusalem as that of longing, and the common persona of the poet as that of her lover. But at some level, the fact that there is slippage between the epithets of lover and daughter throughout the Scriptures and beyond implicitly acknowledges that these images are, after all, simply simulacra.

And these simulacra extend far beyond the sacred precincts. Many of medieval poet Yehuda Halevi's poems of longing for Jerusalem, with the erotic intensity of his images and the intertwining of love and death, are almost indistinguishable from his "secular" love poems. Referring to himself en route to the Holy Land as "captive of desire," the poet says: "It would delight my heart to walk naked / and barefoot among the desolate ruins where your shrines once stood . . ."[29]

One is tempted to say that the female Jerusalem recurs throughout the history of Hebrew poetry and prayer as a dead metaphor—object of an almost necrophilic obsession.[30] But perhaps Jerusalem was really only asleep, awaiting the moment when the return of the exiles would arouse her from her millennial repose? At that moment, would the metaphoric enterprise that has come full circle, wither away—or would it, could it, begin all over again?

Mimicking the Sacred: Importing the Secret of Diaspora

Between 70 and 1967 CE, Jewish practice and poetics were premised on collective distance from the physical site of sacred transactions and on compensatory practices performed in the "meantime" between Destruction and Redemption. The mimetic cultures that developed in far-flung diasporas have been the subject of much interest in recent decades, including my own study of the aesthetics of exile, *Booking Passage*.

The genius of the rabbinic imagination may have been in providing both an exegetical platform and an existential license for a development that had, as we have seen, already begun in Scriptures: substitution of texts and prayer for sacrificial acts, of nomination for immanence as the essence of the divine-human encounter. It was, indeed, the mimetic impulse that inaugurated the long Jewish journey into Exile: for Jews from the earliest days of their dispersal, the synagogue was a miniature Temple—*mikdash me'at*.[31]

The Babylonian exiles were early practitioners of this form of mimetic compensation. Here, from Tractate Megillah, is the rationale for this practice. Recounting God's commandment to Abraham that if his descendants sin, they can achieve atonement through sacrificial offerings, the Patriarch says:

> Master of the Universe, this works out well when the Temple is standing and offerings can be brought to achieve atonement, but when the Temple will no longer be standing, what will become of them? God said to him: I have already established for them the order of offerings, i.e., the verses of the Torah pertaining to the halakhot of the offerings. *Whenever they read those portions, I will deem it as if they sacrificed an offering before Me, and I will pardon them for all of their iniquities.* (Tractate Megillah 31b, emphasis mine)

כל זמן שקוראין בהן מעלה אני עליהן כאילו מקריבין לפני קרבן ומוחל אני על כל עונותיהם[32]

We need not dwell on the anachronism of Abraham anticipating the destruction of a Temple that hasn't even been built yet . . . That fiction—כאילו or *as if*—is the basis not only of diasporic mobility but also of the ethical imagination that Jews evolved at a distance from the sacred. Even if the worshipper only genuflected in the direction of the absent Temple, acts of nomination had replaced presumption of presence in all the byways of Jewish civilization.

And yet, during the long years officially defined as Exile, at least three major forms of proximity to the sacred emerged in different diasporic centers, each one undermining the principle of substitution and distance—as well as the doctrine of deferred messianism. The Karaite movement is premised on prolonged grief enacted through pilgrimage to the ruined shrine and rites of mourning performed there, while eschewing the rabbinic culture of accommodation and substitution.[33] Various expressions of mysticism have transferred the encounter with the Divine from a geographical place to the human body.[34] And periodic outbursts of messianic fervor have been accompanied by pilgrimage to and/or settlement in the Holy Land and claims to exclusive sovereignty over the holy shrines.[35] The most prolonged and consequential of these, which is ongoing since the Israeli conquest of East Jerusalem and the West Bank in 1967, is the conflation of a military-political victory with the theological end of exile.

Resonances of the dilemma between acts of substitution—the basic premise of diasporic culture—and the opportunities presented by a return to the sacred permeate the entire culture of post-'67 Israel. Commentaries on the weekly Torah portion in the liberal Israeli newspaper *Haaretz* can provide an insight into the contemporary overlap between religion and politics within the gravitational pull of the Temple Mount. In his gloss on Ex. 35–40 (Parashat Vayakhel-Pekudei, the concluding chapters of the Book of Exodus), Yakov Z. Meyer describes Moses as the "contractor" for the tabernacle or *mishkan*, the first presumably confined space of divine immanence:

> The end of Exodus marks the end of the depiction of the tabernacle's construction. *God enters his designated dwelling place*, and Moses, as contractors always do after they have completed a project, stands outside: "Then the cloud covered the tent of meeting, and the glory of the Lord filled the tabernacle. And Moses was not able to enter into the tent of meeting, because the cloud abode thereon" (Exodus 40:34–35). The first verse of Leviticus, the next book in the Pentateuch, opens with God speaking from within the tabernacle to Moses; the newly erected structure, meanwhile, begins to fulfill its function as a mediating space. (Emphasis mine)

But then, drawing his conclusions from a number of midrashic elaborations and retellings of the construction of the tabernacle, Meyer describes Moses also as a *literary* contractor:

> Whereas the Torah describes how God's glory fills the entire tabernacle, the midrash does not relate to that structure per se *but rather depicts how God's glory fills the Torah* . . . In this week's reading, Moses is mentioned, but, in the beginning of Leviticus . . . the Torah tells us, "And the Lord called unto Moses, and spoke unto him out of the tent of meeting" (Lev. 1:1). Here the

Torah—the same Torah that Moses has written—is *calling upon its author to come inside . . . The only "pillars" Moses builds and on which he writes God's name are the passages in the Torah*—that is, the text under discussion here, which describes erection of the tabernacle and the fashioning of its components, tools and utensils. (Emphases mine)

Two weeks later, Meyer writes in his commentary on Lev. 6:8:

We can also assume that the destruction of the Temple in Jerusalem facilitated a *further transformation* in the system of sacrifices: the *presentation of textual sacrifices—that is, offerings made in the course of studying the relevant laws governing sacrifices. The Book of Leviticus can be understood not as a "memorial book," but rather as a new temple*, one that can enable us to continue, within its boundaries, to worship God through the presentation of sacrifices. But this mode of worship has undergone a transformation, becoming an *intellectual activity. It has evolved into the study of texts*—involving a struggle for the preservation of the significance of sacrifices, a *struggle wherein the study of the text has replaced the actual offering itself.* (Emphases mine)[36]

From his exegesis, it remains unclear to most readers, I suspect, whether Meyer embraces this culture of textual substitution as a form of progress or, at the very least, as a viable step in Jewish civilization—or whether he is leaving the door open to the reinstatement of sacrifice if/when the Temple is rebuilt . . .

The basic conundrum—whether the text supplants the sacrifice for all time or only until Redemption, whether God's presence fills the universe or resides in one confined space—extends easily, almost seamlessly, to the political realm. The State of Israel is defined in most modern Jewish prayerbooks—not only in orthodox communities—as the first beat of redemptive time (*reshit tzemiḥat geulateinu*).[37] The implication is that the rabbinic genius provided the authoritative license for a mobile mimetic culture; their own practice of midrashic exploration and transformation of biblical texts such as Song of Songs into stories and images must yield, by this logic, to literalizing impulses, to a grounding of the imagination in implacable claims to physical proximity to and sovereignty over divine space. The talmudic *mashal* itself, the parable or story, becomes, then, really only a placeholder, meant to surrender not to the original poetic image but to the *nimshal*, the territorialized meaning, when the Hebrew imagination "returns home."

It is in that conundrum that the entire argument of this volume rests. My exploration of the elastic Jewish claim to Jerusalem, and within Jerusalem, to the Temple Mount, focuses on the written word as an elaboration of the insight that the symbolic status of the city was born not subsequent to but at the same time, and claims the same legitimacy, as the material edifice. Acts of imagination, which would become the default mode for Jews in a prolonged state of exile, the very "secret of Diaspora," are, I submit, the original antidote to idolatrous impulses that have returned in our time and gained momentum in post-'67 Israel. Indeed, the transformations that the mimetic imagination has undergone as the sources of Hebrew power reunited with the gravitational pull of sacred sites and holy land over the past half century recapitulate, in crucial ways, the earliest iterations of the sacred in relation to space.

From King David, the putative author of the Book of Psalms, who in turn invoked the Levites singing and plucking on the steps of the Temple, through the *paytanim* (liturgical poets) of the Middle Ages, whose intricate poems were incorporated into Jewish liturgy, to Yehuda Amichai, poetry has been an essential and consequential part of the Hebrew self. But there is inherent tension between its power as liturgical and as profane utterance, particularly in its situational status vis-à-vis the holy mountain—never more so than in our time. In his Nobel speech, Agnon declared himself a *paytan* manqué whose historical belatedness changed his craft:

> As a result of the historic catastrophe in which Titus of Rome destroyed Jerusalem and Israel was exiled from its land, I was born in one of the cities of the Exile. But always I regarded myself as one who was born in Jerusalem . . . I belong to the Tribe of Levi; my forebears and I are of the minstrels that were in the Temple . . . In a dream, in a vision of the night, I saw myself standing with my brother-Levites in the Holy Temple, singing with them the songs of David, King of Israel, melodies such as no ear has heard since the day our city was destroyed and its people went into exile. I suspect that the angels in charge of the Shrine of Music, fearful lest I sing in wakefulness what I had sung in dream, made me forget by day what I had sung at night; for if my brethren, the sons of my people, were to hear, they would be unable to bear their grief over the happiness they have lost. To console me for having prevented me from singing with my mouth, they enable me to compose songs in writing.[38]

I will enlarge on this in my discussion of Agnon, but I want to emphasize here that it is not only the generic difference between poetry and prose that is at stake, but the very freedom of the imagination in the presence of sacred temptations. Mimicking the sacred not only does not reduce its grandeur; it magnifies its reach.

This book is meant to bolster the knowledge that lurks in the deep recesses of the Hebrew imagination: the liberating, inclusive, and subversive forces of naming, of poetry and storytelling as a wedge against murderous, exclusive, literalized claims to ownership of divine presence and divine promise.

PART ONE

Literary Archaeologies

"Yes, you did laugh!": The Secret of the *Akeda*

Why do lines of poetry and aggadah stick to this landscape, to this city? Ancient, decorated with distant memories and death, she carries within her the first layers, the foundation stones of poetry, of literature.

LEAH GOLDBERG[1]

The insight that launched this book is anchored in evidence stretching from
the rich biblical record and scant archaeological traces of the ancient world to
modern forms of recall and reincarnation of that world: that stories compete
with stones and that human acts of nomination, appellation, and imagination
soften or even undermine the presumption of physical proximity to a defined
and confined divine presence. Furthermore, where the holiest site in Jerusalem is concerned, the nomenclature, interpretative postures, and iconography reveal an ongoing dialectic among (and within) the three monotheistic
traditions: between synchrony or homage and supersession or effacement.
These currents, in their periodic eruptions, form two thousand years of alternately shared and contested history. And in our time, from a debate over
boundaries, a centrifugal movement outward to borders, the conflict between
Israel and Palestine has morphed into—or reverted to—a religious war, a centripetal thrust into the vortex of sacrifice. At the center of this vortex are a
rock and a story.

The Rock

The great feature of the Mosque of Omar is the prodigious rock in the centre of its ro-
tunda. It was upon this rock that Abraham came so near offering up his son Isaac—this,
at least, is authentic—it is very much more to be relied on than most of the traditions,
at any rate. On this rock, also, the angel stood and threatened Jerusalem, and David
persuaded him to spare the city. Mahomet was well acquainted with this stone. From it
he ascended to heaven. The stone tried to follow him, and if the angel Gabriel had not
happened by the merest good luck to be there to seize it, it would have done it. Very
few people have a grip like Gabriel—the prints of his monstrous fingers, two inches
deep, are to be seen in that rock to-day . . . along with [Mahomet's] foot-prints . . . I

should judge that he wore about eighteens. But what I was going to say, when I spoke
of the rock being suspended, was, that in the floor of the cavern under it they showed
us a slab which they said covered a hole which was a thing of extraordinary interest
to all Mohammedans, because that hole leads down to perdition, and every soul that
is transferred from thence to Heaven must pass through this orifice. Mahomet stands
there and lifts them out by the hair. All Mohammedans shave their heads, but they are
careful to leave a lock of hair for the Prophet to take hold of. Our guide observed that a
good Mohammedan would consider himself doomed to stay with the damned forever
if he were to lose his scalp-lock and die before it grew again.

MARK TWAIN, *Innocents Abroad*[2]

The rock is the fundament of the world in the three monotheistic traditions—
and it takes a large dose of humor to pry proprietary fingers from this site.
The designation *har ha-bayit*, Mountain of the House, or Temple Mount, the
site where Abraham nearly sacrificed his son—"this, at least, is authentic"!!!—
dates from the rabbinic period, the first centuries of the Common Era, when
all but a few physical traces of the (so-called) Second Temple had been eradicated.[3] The area was renamed Aelia Capitolina by the Romans after Hadrian
restored the site, at first as tribute and then, after the Bar Kokhba revolt of
132–36, as triumphant appropriation replete with pagan temples and statues
of the emperor.[4]

During the Byzantine period under Constantine and his successors, Jerusalem, now devoid of its Jewish inhabitants, was renamed Aelia;[5] the Temple
Mount lay in ruins and was virtually effaced from official memory—as reflected in the famous Madaba mosaic map from the sixth century, which features the Church of the Holy Sepulchre but not the Temple Mount.[6]

Shortly after the Muslim conquest of Jerusalem in the seventh century,
however, a shrine—the Qubbat Al-Sakhrah (Dome of the Rock)—and the
Al Aqsa mosque were constructed on the site explicitly identified with Solomon's Temple and its successors (Masjid Al Aqsa, also called Masjid Bayt
al-Maqdis, resonates with the Hebrew term for the Temple, *beit ha-mikdash*).
The Mount itself has been referred to in Muslim sources since the seventh
century as Al Haram al Sharif or The Noble Sanctuary.[7]

As the pendulum swings between acts of homage and acts of conquest,
the early Muslim tributes to the destroyed Temples give way to the Crusaders'
bloody conquest of the area in 1099, which will result in tens of thousands of
Muslim and many Jewish casualties. The Dome of the Rock and Al Aqsa will
undergo only minor physical changes, most saliently some internal additions
and, presumably, the replacement of the crescent on the roof with a cross
(or at least that is the way it is represented in the illustrated manuscripts and
maps of the time)—but they will be renamed and broadcast in Christendom

as Templum Domini and Palatium Salomonis, respectively—attesting to the power of visual iconography and verbal representation.[8]

Less than a hundred years after the Crusader conquest, a letter attributed to Maimonides testifies to the selective permission granted to prominent Jews during this period to visit their ruined shrine: "I entered the Great and Holy House and I prayed in it on Thursday, the sixth day of Marheshvan" (corresponding to October 14, 1165).[9] There is lively discussion among scholars as to what Maimonides would have meant by "the Great and Holy House," given the ancient Jewish prohibition against "unclean persons" unknowingly trespassing on the site of the Holy of Holies. What would have been a contentious issue for the Rambam's interlocutors and followers in the twelfth century is no less urgent in twenty-first-century Jerusalem.

Twenty-some years after Maimonides's putative visit, in 1187, Saladin conquered Jerusalem and reinstated Muslim rule; he replaced the cross finial on the Dome of the Rock with the Islamic crescent, and some version of that emblem has remained to this day, not only in the physical site, but in most representations of the site.

It is clear even from the most cursory sketch that, on the whole, Jews fared better under the various Muslim rulers than they did under Christian rule. Jews began to return to Jerusalem in the twelfth–thirteenth centuries under the Ayyubids, followed by the Mamluks and the Turks—though access to the Temple Mount was restricted.[10] Even the Jewish iconography of the Sacred Center represented the Dome of the Rock with its mosque and finial crescent, as *mekom ha-mikdash* (Place of the Temple) throughout the medieval and early modern period and as late as the 1920s, creating a fused, layered, or (relatively) peaceful coexistence of symbolic languages.[11]

Additionally—reflecting centrifugal impulses that had evolved during the Babylonian exile—there was, possibly as early as Second Temple times, and continuing through the Byzantine and early Muslim periods, another physical site in Jerusalem that competed with or complemented the Temple Mount. Buttressed by a talmudic text reflecting a practice that had expanded in the first centuries after the destruction of the Second Temple, the Mount of Olives—located on a mountain ridge directly facing the Temple Mount—was designated as the site to which the *shekhina*, the female presence or emanation of the Divine, had migrated.[12] As powerful as the dialogue with Islam would become in its focus on the Temple Mount, another, subtler, dialogue with Christianity would evolve between the two mountains. The Mount of Olives and the adjacent mountain ridge would come to function as portal to a more pluralistic approach to the locus and emanation of holiness and would continue to animate the messianic as well as the poetic imagination. It is likely that Maimonides's own pilgrimage would have begun on the Mount of Olives and proceeded as far as the Wailing Wall.

Even if Jews have a less plastic imagination than Christians for the details of eschatology, a rich Jewish mythology grew up around the cemetery on the Mount of Olives, where privileged souls have been buried over the centuries and where the Resurrection is scheduled to be launched. Stories and local folk practices from many diasporic communities testify to the belief that a grave there (or proof of purchase of such a plot *in absentia*) will expedite the process; when the Messiah arrives and a cosmic traffic jam ensues as the dispersed dead make their way through underground tunnels to the Holy Land, these privileged souls will already have reserved places. The Jews of Samarkand, Uzbekistan, for example, prepared to meet their Redeemer by buying one grave in the local cemetery and another plot on the Mount of Olives. It was, by all accounts, a "valid legal transaction, with a bill of purchase placed in the hands of the deceased and buried with him or her."[13] The same impulse animates the eponymous character in S. Y. Agnon's story "Tehila," who periodically renews her "contract" with the burial society on the Mount of Olives until it is time, at the age of 104, to claim her plot (in both senses of the term).[14]

It may not be self-evident that having a "second" sacred center allows for a more expansive and inclusive imagination of the locus of holiness.[15] On the other hand, that centripetal fantasies of proximity to and exclusive control over the Temple Mount breed only tragedy based on sacrificial impulses can be corroborated by a glance at the daily news headlines at almost any time over the past two millennia. Each successive clerical regime, when empowered and radicalized, has spawned its own culture of vengeance centered on the Temple Mount. When tolerance and coexistence give way to Holy War, there is room only for the Self in its most engorged form. Today, long after the swords of the Crusaders have rusted into artifacts and the blood of their victims irrigated the poetry of martyrdom, it is the turn of the Jews and the Muslims.

Actually, pilgrimage to an *absent temple* was hardly what the biblical redactors had in mind when they legislated the three holidays centered on the Temple of Solomon (Ex. 23:17; Deut. 16:17)—and, indeed, as we have already noted, later rabbinic injunction explicitly forbids ascent to the Temple Mount for risk of entering the space of the Holy of Holies in a ritually impure state. As we can see even in the ambiguity surrounding Maimonides's "ascent" to the "House of God" in the twelfth century, most Jews over the centuries found substitutes for cults that had been suspended after the Temple was destroyed in 70 CE; only a handful of the Karaite "mourners of Zion" persisted in visiting the ruined shrine in sackcloth and ashes on the anniversary of the destruction of both Temples.[16]

Yet these words are being written during a time of ongoing violence sparked by religious Jewish zealots ready to kill and die for their exclusive claims to proximity to and sovereignty over those thirty-seven acres of real estate.[17] The delicate status quo—in which the Waqf[18] has authority over the mosques on the Haram al Sharif, Moslems are allowed to pray at the Dome of the Rock/Al Aqsa after rigid security checks, and Jews are generally barred from such access except as occasional tourists or by special permission—was reconfirmed after Israel conquered East Jerusalem, but is periodically challenged by Jewish messianists.

For the past few decades, beginning with Ariel Sharon's provocative visit to the Temple Mount in September 2000—which sparked the violent "Second Intifada"—tensions have tended to mount in late fall, around the time of the pilgrimage holiday of Sukkoth, when a handful of Jews flout the status quo and attempt to "fulfill" the commandment of pilgrimage to the Temple. A timeline of the events of the summer and fall of 2014 would probably begin on June 12, with the abduction and murder of three Jewish boys from a bus stop in the West Bank; continue with the kidnapping and immolation of an Arab youth from East Jerusalem; followed by rocket fire from Gaza and the devastating Gaza war that left some two thousand Gazans and seventy Israelis dead—and culminate in the Temple Mount "pilgrimage," October 13–14, when Israeli police locked a group of Muslims inside Al Aqsa Mosque based on reports of munitions stockpiled there, as well as rocks and fireworks that were tossed at the police from inside the mosque. Actually, from the YouTube videos posted soon after, it appears as if both sides were well rehearsed and fairly self-controlled; along with a lot of noise and minor injuries, the incident seems to have passed more as theater than as warfare.[19] This is, of course, not merely an exercise in theater—though sometimes it's so well choreographed that it is hard to tell the difference. And that could change in an instant—and it did, a few weeks later, when one of the most strident of the Jewish "Faithful of the Temple Mount" was seriously wounded by a Palestinian gunman who was himself—presumably—shot and killed by Israeli troops, which then precipitated a number of terrorist incidents including the shooting of US-born right-wing activist Yehuda Glick on October 29, the killing of his presumed attacker, and finally, on November 19, the killing of four Jews praying in a synagogue and a Druze police officer in West Jerusalem.[20]

Apocalyptic fantasies have animated the Jewish imagination since early in the Zionist project—but what makes the present moment so dangerous is that the most extreme among today's so-called pilgrims, including those who ascended the Temple Mount in October 2014, are intent on not just praying at the site but eradicating the existing shrines in order to realize their messianic fantasies of building the "Third" Temple.[21] In March 2019, as tensions escalated, the headline of Nir Hasson's column in *Haaretz* was: "Muslim religious trust is caught between a rock and a hard place."[22] Never was such a truism more true.

The Story

Meanwhile, hiding in plain sight, is the secret of the story that animates the rock—a laconic narrative of preempted ritual slaughter (see fig. 1).[23] Genesis 22,

FIGURE 1. Rembrandt van Rijn, *The Sacrifice of Abraham* (1655). Image courtesy of Rijksmuseum, Amsterdam, https://www.rijksmuseum.nl/en/collection/RP-P-OB-63.

which recounts the binding and near-sacrifice of Isaac, is itself full of holes that have generated generations of interpretations, from the "exiled" rabbinic voices in Genesis Rabbah to an exiled Erich Auerbach in Istanbul.[24] The explosive power of this mountain, and the animating myths of competing monotheisms, can be defused, I submit, only by close rereadings of constitutive biblical texts such as Genesis 22. My own *literal* reading is meant to elucidate the *literary* tropes and patterns that have been overlooked or so transformed by centuries of appropriation as to become invisible.[25]

The akeda, the "binding" and *near*-sacrifice of Abraham's sons—Isaac in one version, Ishmael in the other—anticipates or is superseded by the *actual* sacrifice of Jesus a few steps away in the third version. It should be noted that the site of the "binding" of the son in the Koran is Mecca and not the Haram al Sharif, and most Muslim commentators assume that it is Ishmael who is the chosen sacrifice.[26] But the implicit dialogue continues: Mohammed is believed to have tethered his magical winged animal Al Buraq to the Herodian retaining wall—subsequently referred to in Islam as "Al Buraq"—after his nighttime journey from Mecca to Jerusalem and before ascending to heaven from the rock on the Haram al Sharif.[27] The arabesque of Jewish-Muslim religious imagination would designate the rock with Mohammed's "footprint," over which the Dome of the Rock was erected in the late seventh century, as the very place of Isaac's "binding," the foundation of Solomon's Temple, and farther back still to *even hashtiya* or the fundament from which the world was created. Over time, as Mark Twain attested, in his inimitable way, the sons and the sites became conflated and the rock and the story congealed in the popular monotheistic imagination.[28]

My own attempt to wrest the Temple Mount from the grim hold of today's Jewish messianists (who, along with their Evangelical Christian supporters and fanatic Muslim counterparts, are doing their brutal best to hasten the apocalypse) through an act of interpretation—a close, *literal*, reading meant to expose not only the literary tropes but also the comic underpinnings of the constitutive text—may seem trivial if not perverse. But in cultures where texts matter as much as matter itself, I offer it as antidote to the toxic exegetical structures that have been built on these textual foundations and that groan under the weight of redemptive expectations.

Literary Archaeology at the Temple Mount:
Excavating the Comic Version of the "Sacrifice" of Isaac

It is important to emphasize at the outset the most important principle that is common to the many definitions of comedy, from Aristotle to the present: that no one dies in the theater of the comic imagination. As Umberto

Eco demonstrated in *The Name of the Rose*, the secret of comedy is the key to unlocking and disempowering the hard hearts and proprietary minds of the official guardians of Scripture (and classical texts anointed with scriptural status); in Eco's novel, it meant recovering the lost manuscript of book 2 of Aristotle's *Poetics*, the treatise on comedy.[29]

It is crucial to bear in mind that the physical and textual sites—the rock and the story—that animate the Hebrew imagination are not only interwoven but far more elastic and artificially contrived than one would surmise from their representations in contemporary theological or political discourse. What can cleanse the place of its toxins is recovering its *textuality*: restoring the comedy at the heart of the "Binding of Isaac" will save us from incendiary clerical claims in modern Israel as radically as the discovery of Aristotle's lost manuscript on comedy, through a detoxification of its poisonous safeguards, might have saved Christendom from the cruelties of competing religious orders under Pope John XXII in fourteenth-century Italy.

This entails going back to the "beginning," to that rather undefined space that would coalesce over the course of the Hebrew Bible into one spot. In the introduction, we saw how the site of revelation and sacrifice moves: from the imprecise injunction to Abraham in Gen. 22 to "go forth to the *land of Moriah* and offer [Isaac] up as a burnt offering on *one of the mountains* which I shall say to you," through a number of extemporaneous altars and dramatic encounters at the Burning Bush and Mount Sinai, to a movable ark accompanying a people in the wilderness, and, finally, to one fixed shrine in Jerusalem. In later biblical texts, with the addition of geography and power to the mix, the akeda itself will move from a literary, mythical trope to a precise geographical topos. The locus of the original crucible—"one of the mountains" in the "land of Moriah," traditionally connected to a town called Shalem (Gen. 33:18)[30]—acquires specificity and *gravitas* as it travels through the books of Samuel and Kings, becoming the center of David's passion and Solomon's concrete deeds until it is reconfigured as a specific and immutable site where the "house of the Lord" was built on "Mount Moriah" (II Chr. 3:1).

We have also explored the ambivalence that persists over confining the divine presence in one physical space and underscored the elusive textual fact that although the ruined Temple continues to designate the holiest place in Judaism, it was from its inception not the "house" of the Lord but the site where the human voice could name, invoke, or imagine the Deity. As the shrines and hills consolidated, however, and as history and myth congealed, all the holiness and all the squabbling stories and stones, like the squabbling brothers, became concentrated in that spot.

The argument that the *symbolic* status of the site—a wandering signifier—was constructed at the same time as the material edifices atop an immutable mountain necessitates a suspension of exegetical traditions that have led to exclusive claims. The "topocentric" need for what Mircea Eliade would have called the *axis mundi* will of course continue to compete with the insight that more spacious, inclusive, and self-conscious linguistic flexibilities are hidden in plain view in six chapters in Genesis, culminating with the "Binding (or Sacrifice) of Isaac." That is what makes the task so urgent.

"Literary Archaeology at the Temple Mount" will entail, then, a *literal* reading of a much-interpreted and much-appropriated text.[31] Given how imprecise the reconstruction of ancient history is, archaeologists tend to find what they're looking for even when scientific procedures are rigorous; current archaeology of the area around the Temple Mount is, unfortunately, governed by those who discard evidence in which they are not ideologically invested. Although physical remains of the reign of David are virtually nonexistent, Elad, the right-wing Israeli group in charge of the excavation and reconstruction of the so-called City of David, creates what is presented as an authentic evocation of the past through visual and textual means, architectural "reconstructions" and "archaic" landscapes—while eradicating or occluding virtually all traces of Islam or Arabs, past or present.[32]

Unlike physical archaeology, and the political and journalistic debates swirling around ruins and vacated sites, *literary* archaeology has the advantage of keeping your hands clean, even while you are paging through a text that is thousands of years old. The biblical passage can, like later appropriations in midrash and in other monotheistic traditions, be twisted or squeezed to yield various versions and meanings; its pages can be poisoned to keep careful readers away. But in the case of the Bible, the "original" text is always there to be rediscovered.[33]

My literal reading of the story itself in the Masoretic text is meant to underline certain structural and rhetorical quirks that determine the genre and, I believe, contain the secret of the akeda.

Genesis 22 begins very theatrically: "And it happened after these things that God tested Abraham." This is a wink behind Abe's back to the audience, who is given some assurance that the old man will pass the test. In what follows, we may be forgiven if we forget the stage wink as we become caught up in the unfolding tragedy. J. William Whedbee, in *The Bible and the Comic Vision*, follows Northrop Frye in calling the U-shaped plot pattern the telltale curve of the comic—"with action sinking into deep and often potentially tragic complications, and then suddenly turning upward into a happy ending."[34] Disaster averted at the last minute through divine intervention is the Hebrew version of *deus ex machina*.

The structural element seemingly needs no elaboration. We all "know" that Genesis 22 ends with Isaac's release; yet readers and "reenactors" repeatedly repress that knowledge so that Isaac can continue to animate the tragic imagination. From the description of Isaac's "death" and "resurrection" in the Midrash[35] through nearly all modern Israeli versions, some of which we will consider presently—and through all its appropriations in Christian iconography—the akeda is apprehended as an accomplished sacrifice.[36] In fact, the occlusion of the "happy ending" in Genesis 22 is fundamental to the evolution of the genre of tragedy as sacrifice; safeguarding the place of the sacrificed son, the *pharmakos*—Isaac or Jesus—is the very "idea of the tragic," as Terry Eagleton argues in *Sweet Violence*.[37] The tradition of reading this passage tragically is so deep-seated that unearthing the *comic* structure in the place of ultimate sacrifice becomes nothing less than subversive.

But the most subversive aspect of the comic structure of the akeda relates to the artificial, theatrical quality of any comedy, which, as we have seen, is subtly marked in the "stage directions" at the beginning of this biblical narrative. As often in classical drama, the comedy becomes fully apparent only at the end, when God or the gods appear, as it were, "from a machine." Comedy performs the world not as it is, but as it should be. Scott Shershow defines those forms of resolution that are endemic to the comic spirit:

> Watching the fortunate resolution to which we always knew the characters were inevitably bound, we feel what the classical critics demand: that this "nevertheless could happen." But the playwright may also draw our attention to the ropes and pulleys of the *deus ex machina* and, indulging us with a beneficent vision of fate, may at the same time suggest "this is not the way it would happen." [The conventional resolution of the comic plot] expresses an ambiguous optimism. The happy ending magnifies the world with its infinite sense of the possible, and diminishes it with its ironic sense of the impossible.[38]

Underscoring even further the comic structure of the akeda in dialogue with an alternative, tragic, denouement is the inner-biblical evidence of the enacted sacrifice as the earlier layer that was probably redacted by editors who thus structurally converted the narrative from tragedy to comedy.[39]

The other signal of the comic in this narrative cycle is *rhetorical* or linguistic: repetition and wordplay that create literary patterns in the Bible.[40] What we discover as we walk slowly through these verses with an open mind uncluttered by two millennia of interpretation and appropriation is that in this most serious of texts, the comic muscle is flexed in its every permutation.[41]

The first version of the word צחק (*z-ḥ-k*), "to laugh," in the six chapters that surround the story of the akeda appears in Genesis 17:17, the "annunciation and nomination" chapter, when God tells Abraham that his wife Sarah will bear a child: "And Abraham flung himself on his face *and he laughed* [*va-yitzḥak*], saying to himself, 'To a hundred-year-old will a child be born; will ninety-year-old Sarah give birth?'" (All italicized emphases in these verses are my own.)

Is Old Abe laughing happily? Incredulously? Is he wondering, as some commentators have ventured to suggest, whether God is "playing a joke"?[42] Stalling for time or trying to digest the news, perhaps, Abraham lobbies for his other son, Ishmael, as heir to the dynasty, but that's more or less ignored here, to be taken up later. God tells Abraham: "you'll call [your son] *Yitzhak*" (17:19)—the name means, literally, "he will laugh"—and goes on to reinforce the promised connection between one's name and one's fate: "My covenant I will establish with *Yitzhak*" (17:21).

In the tradition of irreverent Jewish shtick, one could suggest that after observing Abraham's histrionic, *embodied* laughter—"he flung himself on his face and he laughed . . . to himself"—God thought, "now *that's* a good name!" Whedbee puts it a bit more elegantly and ominously: "God permanently embeds laughter into the line of Israel's ancestors; Isaac will bear in his very being the sounds of laughter. Thus 'God will have the last laugh.'"[43]

In the commentary to his translation of Genesis, Robert Alter notes that "in chapter 17 and subsequent chapters, the narrative will ring the changes on this Hebrew verb [*z-ḥ-k*], the meanings of which include joyous laughter, bitter laughter, mockery, and sexual dalliance."[44] In short, all the elements of the comic genre. Actually, some version of the word *z-ḥ-k* appears *twenty times* in this narrative cycle. Everyone laughs—Abraham, Sarah, Ishmael—everyone, that is, except him whose very name means "*he will laugh*." (Again, however, it is important to note that what we translate as future tense is, in biblical Hebrew, the imperfect tense—here, appropriately enough, an indication of laughter that is not yet achieved.)

The next chapter replicates Abraham's response—this time even more fully embodied. Sarah, who is listening at the tent entrance, hears the annunciation given again to her husband by three mysterious "men"—and she repeats Abraham's earlier response: "And Sarah *laughed inwardly*, saying, 'After being shriveled, shall I have pleasure, and my husband is old?'" Her laughter is the expression of incredulity tinged with sexual titillation, which, as we shall see, will later be associated with both Ishmael and Isaac. At this point, the "men" disappear and the Lord speaks directly to Abraham and then to Sarah:

And the Lord said to Abraham, ?למה זה צחקה שרה "Why is it that Sarah laughed,
saying, 'Shall I really give birth, old as I am?' Is anything beyond the Lord?
In due time I will return to you, at this very season, and Sarah shall have a
son." And Sarah dissembled, saying, לא צחקתי "*I did not laugh*"; for she was
afraid. And He said . . . לא כי צחקת "*Yes, you did laugh.*" (Gen. 18:12–15, emphases mine)[45]

There is much to say about this exchange, which is indeed a replication and
intensification of the earlier encounter between God and Abraham.[46] Since,
unlike Abraham, Sarah doesn't fling herself down, doubled up with laughter,
but *keeps it to herself*, and since God, as we know from His encounters with
Adam and Cain, can read people's minds but sometimes pretends a kind of
parity with His human interlocutors, in this case eliciting Sarah's denial—a
battle of wits ensues.

This passage seems to border on farce. Indeed, Whedbee says it is "farce
befitting domestic comedy";[47] yet something very consequential is at stake.
The transaction manifested hilariously in Sarah's incredulous laughter and
God's putdown actually points to a disparity that will remain fundamental
to the Jewish conception of the comic: despite the miracles that are regularly
performed throughout the Five Books of Moses, especially in Genesis and
Exodus, a healthy Jewish suspicion about any supernatural intervention that
disrupts the normal processes of nature is rooted in this passage. God may be
all-powerful, but parturition on the part of a ninety-year-old woman raises
the same skepticism as Immaculate Conception will over a thousand years
later. I see this as the beginning of the Jewish version of the Divine Comedy
as it is passed down from Genesis to Philip Roth.[48] We will return to this. But
now back to that first story.

As the Genesis narrative proceeds, the laughter intensifies, becomes darker—
and then fades altogether. In the middle of chapter 18, the sequence is inter-
rupted by the episodes of Sodom and Gomorra and Abraham and Sarah in
Gerar pretending to be sister and brother in the court of King Abimelech. Our
thread resumes in chapter 21, which is the crescendo of Isaac's comedy. Some
form of the root *z-ḥ-k* appears nine times in this chapter: six times as Isaac's
name, twice as Sarah's joyful laughter, and once as a sign of discord, taunting,
scoffing, or even homosexual dalliance between Isaac and Ishmael. This incident between the brothers underscores that in the story of dynasty and covenant, even laughter is a serious business. When Sarah catches Ishmael מצחק
(*metzaḥek*)—laughing or scoffing at Isaac—there are dire consequences. Robert
Alter suggests that "Sarah sees Ishmael as '*Isaac-ing* it . . . presuming to play the
role of Isaac, child of laughter, presuming [that is] to be the legitimate heir.'"[49]

In Genesis 21:16, laughter turns briefly to tears as Hagar and Ishmael are banished—and then rescued by a supernatural force—foreshadowing what will transpire with Isaac in the next chapter, a dress rehearsal of the "U-shaped plot" that leads to the denouement.

Finally, we come to the moment toward which the entire narrative has been building: Genesis 22, the story of the *akeda* or *binding*, when tragedy meets and is defeated by comedy. This chapter opens dramatically, as I have already indicated, with a very self-conscious voiceover: *Va-yehi ahar ha-devarim ha-eleh* . . . (And it happened after these things . . .). The conjunctive suggests continuity and familiarity, an ongoing story enacted in intimate space: *ve-ha-elohim nisa et Avraham* (And God tested Abraham).[50] Anticipating in some ways the opening of the Job story, we have here a kind of *divine tribunal*, a theatrical setup with the Director speaking to the audience. Abraham and Isaac don't know what the outcome will be—but, presumably, *we* do. Remember that in comedy no less than in tragedy it is crucial to ascertain where the center of consciousness is located. This sets up the ironic dramatic situation, as irony is always based on the power of knowledge. Nonetheless, as we've seen, there is an underlying feeling of dread. Northrop Frye writes that "an extraordinary number of comic stories, both in drama and fiction, seem to approach a potentially tragic crisis near the end, a feature that [he calls] the 'point of ritual death.'" Whedbee calls this "comic agony."[51]

The agony builds slowly in 22:1: After a long list of epithets and deferrals, Isaac is finally named: "*Take, pray, your son, your only one, whom you love, Isaac*, and go forth to the land of Moriah and offer him up as a burnt offering on one of the mountains which I shall say to you." Isaac appears again by name in verses 2, 3, and 6, and then, finally, in verse 7, he speaks—for what will be the only time in this entire narrative sequence: "And Isaac said to Abraham his father, 'Father!' and he said, 'Here I am, my son.' And he said, 'Here is the fire and the wood but where is the sheep for the offering?'" His father answers, "God will see to the sheep for the offering, my son"—effectively silencing his son for the duration. In verse 9, Isaac is mentioned by name for the last time; in the rest of the chapter, verses 11–19, there are several indirect references to him but no explicit mention of the name itself or its many mutations. The chapter ends with a curious reference that, along with other lacunae in the text, spawned centuries of commentary and elaboration: Abraham returns—alone?—to "his lads" and then on to Beersheba.[52]

One could say that this is the beginning of Isaac's ghostly afterlife; unlike the Cheshire Cat's, however, Isaac's smile goes first. The comic resonances associated with his name reappear once more, several chapters later, when Isaac, in an exact replay of the scene between his mother and father and King Abimelech, is described "playing with" or "fondling" his wife Rebecca, whom he is trying to pass off to the Philistine king as his "sister": *ve-hineh yitzḥak metzaḥek et rivka ishto* (Gen. 26:8).[53] (Here, the clearly erotic overtones also reinforce such connotations in reference to Ishmael's behavior with Isaac in Gen. 21.)

Now, after twenty instances of wordplay on his name, and a brief interval of sexual dalliance, Isaac's laughter disappears altogether—as if his near-death experience on the sacrificial altar effaced whatever good humor he had. PTSD, a far more potent reflex than humor, would animate centuries of poetic reflections on the akeda, which we will glance at later.

But one can conclude from the convoluted historical and textual genealogy of the biblical narrative—the many stories, poems, and commentaries that, in response to historical persecutions or the temptations of Christ on the Cross, actually invoked "Isaac's ashes"—that the very essence of Yitzhak, embedded in his name, is betrayed in the test that Abraham, and all his descendants, actually *failed*: what was at stake was belief in a God who *would* want child sacrifice, or for that matter, any human sacrifice. No, the story states simply, God—the tarrying *deus ex machina*—would actually prefer the comic version of human history and human-divine relations.[54]

Along with the comic impulse comes the value of substitution. The ram substituted for Isaac, the animal for the child—the foundation upon which, one could argue (after René Girard), the entire sacrificial system is based in Western traditions[55] is grounded in this Genesis narrative. And to this foundation the very pillars of diasporic culture were affixed: the rabbinic imagination that conjured the replicable synagogue for the one-and-only Temple, prayer and text-study for sacrifice, also construed har ha-moriah (Mount Moriah) as "har ha-*temura*" (mountain of substitution). Shalom Spiegel foregrounded this in his postwar essay, arguing that "the Akedah [story] came into being with no purpose other than to ... provide the basis for the practice of making *proxy* offerings" (emphasis in original).[56] And there, of course, lies the internal contradiction in the rabbinic tradition, which values substitution but continues to countenance the accomplished sacrifice as the only adequate response to the challenges of history and theological competition.[57]

There is one other element that authorizes the Jewish Comedy, especially in the Diaspora: the messianic faith that posits the inevitability of salvation but also its *deferral*:

אני מאמין באמונה שלמה בביאת המשיח ואף על פי שיתמהמה אם כל זה אחכה לו בכל יום שיבוא

"I believe with perfect faith in the coming of the Messiah, and *even though* he tarries"—like God on Mount Moriah?—"I will wait for him every day."[58] This credo, the twelfth of Maimonides's thirteen principles of faith, is perhaps the most significant of the hard-won diasporic lessons of deferred gratification.

That tarrying God and that proxy offering remain the core principles of both the ethics and the poetics of Judaism, making life not only possible but also capacious and inclusive.

Modern Subversions: The House Is Never Ready

The comedy I am endorsing, then, depends on belief in the possibility of a better world but replaces the always-already-tarrying deus ex machina with human intervention and mediation, plus a heavy dose of patience. It is comedy grounded in faith but driven by human agency. This version has been most powerfully articulated in the bloody twentieth century in the writings of Franz Kafka and the ethics of Jacques Derrida.

In June 1921, Kafka shared with his diary and a few friends his doubts about the viability in his own universe of Kierkegaard's Abraham, the "Knight of Faith." The reasons are purely "domestic":

> I would conceive of another Abraham for myself—he certainly would have never gotten to be a patriarch or even an old-clothes dealer—who was prepared to satisfy the demand for a sacrifice immediately . . . but was unable to bring it off because he could not get away, being indispensable; the household needed him, there was perpetually something or other to put in order, the house was never ready . . .[59]

Kafka's Abraham is the ultimate comic Jewish figure with a hidden soteriological promise; his would-be old clothes dealer, purveyor of "alte sachen," may, as legend has it, turn out to be the messiah himself.[60] In any event, this Abraham cannot obey the call-from-without because he is too embedded and *obligated in this world*.

John Caputo describes "obligation" as replacing more traditional ethics, implicitly going back to the story of Abraham and Isaac and forward to Derrida—this time with a possible way out. "For Derrida . . . ethics ought to be sacrificed in the name of obligation," Caputo writes. "Obligation calls, but its call is finite, a strictly earthbound communication, transpiring here below, not in transcendental space (if there is such a thing) but rather wherever we are, in the middle of the fix we find ourselves in . . . Obligation is . . . the feeling of being bound (*ligare, ob-ligare, re-ligare*)."[61]

Since in Hebrew the word *akeda* literally means *binding*, the interpretative act that returns the story to its original action and language emphasizes intervention and obligation, the feeling of "being bound," preempting sacrifice.[62]

Kafka's dispute with Kierkegaard actually yields *four* Abrahams: the "real" one and three alternatives—the busy one, the childless one, and the unworthy one. But what is common to all the "other" Abrahams, as Robert Arnold Darrow claims, is that they all "remain firmly in the world. For various reasons, they are unable or unwilling to abandon rationality and enter into the religious level of existence." Kafka insists that "the only reality is the confrontation between the world and the individual."[63] This reality, one could add, is the very essence of Kafka's comedy—and the context for Gilles Deleuze and Felix Guattari's understanding of the function of laughter in Kafka: "Two guidelines only are needed to follow Kafka: he is an author who laughs, deeply joyful, with a joie de vivre, in spite of and with his clownish declarations, which he uses as a trap or as a circus. From end to end he is a political author, a prophet of the future world . . . Never has there been an author more comic and joyful in the aspect of desire; never an author more political and social in the aspect of the spoken. Everything is laughter . . . Everything is political."[64] Here the comic politics of desire and obligation comes up against the tragic politics of sacrifice and closure. As *tragedy*, the akeda knows only one thing, which Jacques Derrida poses as a rhetorical question: "Is it [the akeda as sacrifice] not inscribed in the structure of our existence to the extent of no longer constituting an event . . . *the sacrifice of others to avoid being sacrificed oneself*[?]"[65]

What Derrida seems to be getting at, based on *his* reading of Kierkegaard's warnings, and what comic appropriations of the akeda such as Kafka's insist on, is that this "event," Abraham's "act," or his willingness to act, is not meant to be emulated by mortals who struggle to perform in accordance with human ethical codes. "Kierkegaard," Derrida tells us, "insists [that] the sacrifice of Isaac is an abomination . . . The ethical point of view must remain valid: [even if he didn't carry out the deed,] Abraham is a murderer."[66]

The problem is that this "event," enshrined as *memory*, is what nails us to the tragic-sacrificial mindset and the suspension of the "ethical point of view." "Memory serves tragedy," writes Carey Perloff. "In the Sophoclean universe, to hold the memory of an injustice in one's ongoing consciousness is a heroic act. In today's world, it can be a form of psychosis."[67] Indeed, the "sacrifice" of Isaac moves, over vast stretches of time and space, from a remembered "event" to an existential posture. Psychotic memory abolishes the wedge that distance and deferral provided. "[The] secret of the sacrifice of Isaac," Derrida insists, is the "space separating or associating the fire of the family hearth and the fire of the sacrificial holocaust."[68] Recall that the "whole-burnt offering" that Abraham was to offer in the form of his son is *'olah* in Hebrew—*holocaustum* in the Latin Vulgate.

Negotiating that space, *between* the family hearth—the Kafka quotidian—and the fire of the sacrifice, is the forgotten secret that connects the Temple Mount to all the alternative spaces of the diasporic imagination.

Here, then, we return to the connection between story and site. It is comedy that inserts a wedge between text and territory and that keeps the divine presence and the sacrificial holocaust at a safe distance from human temptation and the family hearth. In an exchange with Max Brod, Kafka referred to the Greek imagination of the "decisively divine" as being far from the human:

> The whole world of the gods was only a way to keep that which was decisive at a distance from the earthly body, to provide air for human breath . . . In theory, there exists a perfect earthly possibility for happiness, that is, to believe in the decisively divine and *not* to aspire to attain it.[69]

A similar insight seems to have motivated Maimonides some eight hundred years before Kafka, when he composed *The Guide of the Perplexed*. As we shall see in chapter 3, acts of the imagination that produce anthropomorphisms are, to his mind, acceptable as long as they are understood as such, and not as stepping-stones to a topocentric view of the divine presence. And that from a philosopher who, presumably, testified to having "entered the Great and Holy House and . . . prayed in it." House of Prayer and naming, invoking, the Divine? Yes. House where the Jewish God dwells and demands the sacrificial holocaust? Hardly:

> Every mention of approaching and coming near that you find in the books of prophecy referring to a relation between God, may He be exalted, and a created being has this last meaning. For God, may He be exalted, is not a body, as shall be demonstrated to you in this Treatise . . . *There is no nearness and proximity, and no remoteness, no union and no separation, no contact and no succession* [between the human and the Divine]. (Emphasis mine)[70]

The only human exception to this principle, as we shall see in chapter 3, is Moses, who approaches the "place on the mountain upon which the light, I mean the glory of God, has descended."[71] One may deduce from this that it is only Moses—the one prophet who is never in danger of misusing language—who can approach spatially, and even then it is clearly *only Mount Sinai, and not any other sacred center (i.e., the Temple Mount)* that can be considered consecrated space in which such encounter is possible:

> You must, however, hold fast to the doctrinal principle [lit., root] that there is no difference whether an individual is at the center of the earth, or, supposing

that this were possible, in the highest part of the ninth heavenly sphere. For he is not farther off from God in the one case [lit., here] and no nearer to Him in the other [lit., there].[72]

The Akeda as Israeli Tragedy

Nearly every generation is challenged to learn these lessons anew. Along with an elastic relationship with the center of holiness comes an equally fraught engagement with the meaning of Jewish death. There persists, in the Bible itself and throughout the chronicled history of the Jews, beginning with Josephus, a dichotomy between the topos of war-and-peace and the theodicy of catastrophe-and-(deferred)-salvation. Early modern Hebrew responses to *hurban*, or catastrophe, including the poetry of Shaul Tchernichovsky and Haim Nahman Bialik, interrogated and even dismantled the martyrological tropes that had prevailed from medieval times.[73] Bialik's short poem "'Al ha-shehita" (On the Slaughter), written after the Kishinev pogrom of 1903—but before he had traveled to the town itself to collect testimonies and to write his magisterial *poema*, "Be-'ir ha-harega" (In the City of the Slaughter)—is an akeda registered as protest against whatever power rules the universe:

> *On the Slaughter*
> Heaven, beg mercy for me! If there is
> a God in you, and a pathway through
> you to this God—which I have not
> discovered—then pray for me! . . .
>
> . . . You, executioner! Here's my neck—go
> to it, slaughter me!
>
> . . .
>
> . . . Let the blood seep
> down to the depths of darkness, and
> eat away there, in the dark, and breach
> all the rotting foundations of the earth. (1903)[74]

The word "slaughter" (*shehita*) is the term used to describe Abraham's intended act on Mount Moriah; it denotes both the sacrificial act and, in post-biblical Hebrew, the sacramental act of kosher butchering. This poem can be considered the first example of what would become the modern Hebrew akeda as protest poem.

Even if the topos of war and peace has ancient antecedents that would seem more appropriate as models for the modern state of Israel, the theodicy of sacrifice and (deferred) salvation has maintained a far more powerful hold on the Hebrew imagination. Whether delivered in a posture of acceptance or of defiance, the assumption in nearly all Israeli iterations of the akeda is that Isaac is a designated sacrifice and that an implacable authority sends him to his death. Sometimes that authority is an inscrutable supernatural agent; sometimes it is the State. The most canonic of such poems is Haim Gouri's "Heritage" (Yerusha), first published in 1960:

> The ram came last of all. And Abraham
> did not know that it came to answer the
> boy's question—first of his strength
> when his day was on the wane.

> The old man raised his head. Seeing
> that it was no dream and that the angel
> stood there—the knife slipped from his
> hand.

> The boy, released from his bonds, saw
> his father's back.

> Isaac, as the story goes, was not
> sacrificed. He lived for many years, saw
> what pleasure had to offer, until his
> eyesight dimmed.

> But he bequeathed that hour to his
> offspring. They are born with a knife in
> their hearts.[75]

"As the story goes," Isaac "was not sacrificed." But his "offspring . . . are born with a knife in their hearts." That is, the *misreading* of the story is its heritage: the very key to understanding Jewish suffering in its ancient, medieval, and modern incarnations.

There has been much scholarship on the subject of the akeda in Israeli literature and art,[76] and I wish to examine here only a few of the most powerful voices of the more recent generations as they highlight the struggle between comedy and tragedy while elevating the secular authority to the status of divine-and-inscrutable or divine-and-implacable. The playwright Hanoch Levin, who was Israel's most prominent satirist and a major voice in the protest culture that evolved after 1967, wrote *Bathtub Queen*, a satire on current political figures and policies, in 1970. Performed by the Cameri theater, it caused great controversy, like most of his political satires, and had to be taken down after eighteen performances. The "akeda" appears in the middle of the text as both a familiar trope and a disrupting force. Isaac and Abraham prove themselves faithful readers of the canonic text, in both its tragic and its comic iterations:

ABRAHAM: Isaac, my son, do you know what I am going to do to you now?

ISAAC: Yes, father, you are going to slaughter me.

ABRAHAM: God commanded me.

ISAAC: I have no complaints against you, father. If you need to slaughter, go ahead, slaughter.

ABRAHAM: I have to slaughter, I'm afraid there's no choice.

ISAAC: I understand. You don't have to make it hard for yourself. Simply get up and draw the knife at me.

ABRAHAM: I am only doing it as God's messenger.

ISAAC: Sure, as a messenger, father. So get up, as a messenger, and draw the knife, as a messenger, at your son, your one and only, whom you love.

ABRAHAM: Very nice, Isaac, make it hard on your poor father, put him in a mood, as if he hasn't got one anyhow.

ISAAC: Who's making it hard, father? Get up quietly, and liquidate, in one fatherly motion, your miserable son.

ABRAHAM: I know, the easiest thing is to blame me. Sure, why not, blame your lonely father.

ISAAC: Why blame? You're only God's messenger, right? And when God tells you to slaughter your son like a dog, you just have to run ahead and slaughter.

ABRAHAM: Great, great, this is just what I deserve at my age. Put all the blame on me, if it makes things comfortable for you. On your old and broken father, who is obliged, at his age, to climb this mountain with you, to bind you to the altar, to slaughter you, and then go tell everything to your mother. Do you really think I have nothing better to do at my age?

ISAAC: I totally understand you, father, I'm really not complaining. They tell you to slaughter me? To sever with your own hands your dynasty, to wash your hands with your own blood? I'm ready. Go ahead, father, slaughter. Come on, slaughter . . . slaughter, merciful and compassionate Daddy, . . . slaughter me, pious Daddy.

ABRAHAM: Kill your father, bandit! Kill him!

ISAAC: Slaughter, exemplary Daddy. Daddy with a warm Jewish heart. Slaughter!

ABRAHAM: Bury your only father alive, you scoundrel!

ISAAC: Cut, Pappe'le, cut and bring the flesh home to Momme'le!

ABRAHAM: Murderer (*He grabs Isaac by the neck*). Lie down!

ISAAC: A voice! A voice! I hear a voice!

ABRAHAM: What voice? No way. Lie down!

ISAAC: A voice from Heaven!

ABRAHAM: Where do you get a voice from Heaven?! Lie down!

ISAAC: I don't know. He said, "Lay not thine hand upon the lad."

ABRAHAM: I heard nothing.

ISAAC: You've been hearing impaired for a long time now. Here, he's repeating it for the second time, "Lay not thine hand upon the lad," didn't you hear?!

ABRAHAM: No.

ISAAC: I swear to you . . . "Lay not thine hand upon the lad."

(*Pause. Abraham loosens his grip*)

Father, I swear to you I heard a voice from Heaven.

ABRAHAM (*after a pause*): Well, if you heard, I guess you must have heard. I am, as you said, a little deaf.

ISAAC: No problem, you know that on my part I was ready, but a voice is a voice. (*Pause*) You saw for yourself that on my part I was fine. (*Pause*) We were both fine. (*Pause*) On our part we were both fine, right, father? (*Pause*) We weren't fine? (*Pause*) It all ended happily, father, why are you sad?

ABRAHAM: I'm thinking of what's going to happen if other fathers have to slaughter their children, what will save them?

ISAAC: There always can be a voice from Heaven.

ABRAHAM: (*In acceptance*) Well, if you say so.[77]

Here, indeed, irony competes with pathos to "re-create" the akeda in the manner of many midrashic and poetic retellings. But despite the biting satire and despite the fact that the execution is stayed at the last moment, true to the comic structure of the biblical story, it is the tragic element that prevails. The outcome for future generations is the same as in Gouri's poem, posed as a question: who/what will save future Isaacs from their fathers' knives?

If Levin's Isaac is a pathetic, compliant son who manages, nonetheless, to speak truth to power, Yitzhak Laor's Isaac is an idiot (*metumtam*). Two versions of his poem "Ha-metumtam ha-ze Yitzhak" (This Idiot Yitzhak) raise the question of the father's sanity or reliability ("remember what your father did to Ishmael your brother," the speaker warns Isaac; better to lock up such a father in jail or in the cellar). At the end of the second version, "Ha-metumtam ha-ze Yitzhak (Girsa me'uḥeret)" (This Idiot Yitzhak, Later Version), the son requests that his father not send him to the army ("she-lo yikḥu oti la-tzava"); his father tries to reassures him, in a "somewhat foreign accent": "I am the ram / I am the angel / I am your father":

אֲנִי הָאַיִל
אֲנִי הַמַּלְאָךְ
אֲנִי אַבָּא שֶׁלְךָ[78]

Here the Israeli army is the stand-in for the divine authority, determining the fate of all these Isaacs—and no father, especially one with a "foreign accent," can prevent the slaughter.

Note that the sacrificial figure, like the sacrificing figure, and like the authors of these akeda poems, is always male. For the most part, the women do not take part in the drama of the akeda, except to weep and wail at home. The exceptions include the poet Raya Harnik, who, after losing her son in the 1982 war in Lebanon, wrote: "I will not offer / My first born for sacrifice ['olah] / Not I . . . not my son / and not / for sacrifice." Ruth Kartun-Blum wrote that "it is through distancing herself from the family archive, from the model of the Binding of Isaac, that Harnik makes a political statement."[79]

But others would follow. In David Grossman's To the End of the Land, published in Hebrew in 2008, the main character, Ora, undertakes a long trek in order not to be home to receive the (inevitable?) news of her son's death in combat. It is possible—as scholars including Michael Gluzman and Iris Milner have argued persuasively—to view Ora's stance as ultimately complicit with the sacrificial mentality of the society in which she lives (Gluzman refers to the portrait of Ora as Grossman's "Stabat Mater").[80] This may be true of the narrative as a whole, and of its afterlife in the public square, but I agree with Yael Feldman that Ora has consciously opted out of the akeda mindset.[81] Sitting in a car driven by Sami, her Palestinian Israeli driver, watching parents bringing their children to the army induction point, Ora engages in an internal dialogue with herself and her country:

> In every car sits a young boy, the first fruits, a spring festival that ends with a human sacrifice. And you? She asks herself sharply. Look at you, how neatly and calmly you bring your son here, your almost-only-son, the boy you love dearly, with Ishmael as your private driver.[82]

But there is another reference to the akeda in this narrative, which could signal the author's understanding of the comic foundation of the biblical story. The novel is founded on a triangular relationship, a kind of ménage à trois, between Ora, her future husband Ilan, and their friend Avram, incubated when all three were hospitalized in Jerusalem during the war of 1967. Several years later, Ora buys a notebook for Avram, a compulsive scribbler—and when he insists that she inspires him, she laughs. "He looked at her warmly and said that now he knew what Sarah's laugh had sounded like, when she was told at the age of ninety that she would give birth to Isaac."[83] This comment, ostensibly unrelated to the narrated action, can be an invitation, along with other references and, of course, Avram's name, to read both the akeda and its comic underpinnings into the novel.

The fact that *To the End of the Land* is a novel written by a male author with a compelling female subject is not, of course, new in the history of the novel. But what makes this unbearably poignant is that the author, also the father of a soldier, was finishing this novel when his son Uri was killed in Lebanon in 2006.

The date is significant also because in Jewish timelines, dates and places are interwoven as chronotopes of war and catastrophe: 587 BCE and 70 CE are indelibly wired into the Jewish brain as the time/place of the destruction of the two Temples.[84] And especially in contemporary Israel, any act interpreted as sacrificial leads invariably to The Place. The topos of the akeda remained a floating signifier for over two thousand years. Even after 1948, because the site of the presumed binding of Isaac was occluded from view and inaccessible to Israelis, because there really *was* space between the family hearth and the sacrificial fire, the Temple Mount remained, in effect, diasporic space. The shrines in Jerusalem that constituted the "official" Israeli landscape included Yad Vashem and Mount Herzl as memorial sites; the Knesset as the site of modern Jewish sovereignty; and the Israel Museum as a shrine to ancient and modern art.[85]

But since the Israeli victory over East Jerusalem in 1967, the reconnection of rock and story has unleashed the most powerful and insidious forces. As messianic fervor has grown, most memorial and sacramental activity has converged on the Wailing Wall, with the Temple Mount above as site of ultimate aspiration. Even nonmessianists reflect a kind of biblical fundamentalism that is also a basic misreading of the text itself. The internal and external landscapes of Israel are dotted with the artwork of Menashe Kadishman, whose versions of the akeda include many paintings and sculptures. But perhaps the most revealing is his statement that, standing

> on Mount Moriah and [looking] towards the Mount of Olives . . . there pass before me scenes from the events of the past—love and sacrifice . . . The Binding of Isaac occurs in our time, in every place we send our children to wars, but its emblem remains one: Jerusalem—the place where it really happened.[86]

The place where *it really* happened?! Reminiscent of Mark Twain's tongue-in-cheek reference to the rock on which Isaac was nearly sacrificed—"this, at least, is authentic"—such sober literalism, coming from a prominent artist, underscores the unexamined assumptions behind so much of contemporary Israeli culture. "It" signifies a sacrifice that, as we have just seen, *never happened*—in history or in text. But the place where "it happened" is also the presumed site of the original—and therefore potentially the ultimate—encounter between the sons of Isaac and the sons of Ishmael.[87]

A. B. Yehoshua had touched this subject in a number of his fictions, but he took it beyond the secular-military context and Israeli death on the battlefield into the very heart of darkness in his novel *Mr. Mani*. I have written about this elsewhere[88] and wish to emphasize here only the climax of the novel, where Joseph Mani, who lives in Jerusalem in the middle of the nineteenth century, is, according to one version of the story, slaughtered "on the steps leading to the Dome of the Rock, [where] he had his throat slit."[89]

Although this sacrificial character lives in a time when there would have been access for Jews to the Wailing Wall but no claims to sovereignty, the novel was written during the early months of the First Intifada. In interviews after its appearance, Yehoshua claimed that he had killed off his character in order to "annul the sacrifice of Isaac by its fulfillment."[90] He also admits to conflating the stories of Isaac and Ishmael in order, as it were, to make two murderous stories go away. But his claim flies in the face of every reenacted and "fulfilled" akeda since postbiblical times. It is important to emphasize that while claiming to finally put an end to the akeda mania, Yehoshua, like most of his predecessors and contemporaries, actually reproduces the most fatal and profound misreading of the biblical narrative.

Given even this cursory glance at modern Hebrew iterations, the exceptions, or near-exceptions, to the tragic appropriation of Genesis 22 remain the most instructive. And they are particularly poignant when they are located in Jerusalem and in proximity to the Place Itself, understood since rabbinic times as both physical and metaphysical site of holiness.[91] The one narrative in modern Hebrew literature where we can find the recovery of the comic force of the biblical story is in some ways also the most surprising: in chapter 5, I will argue that the "unbinding of Isaac" courses as a quiet, comic-quotidian current through S. Y. Agnon's magnum opus, *Tmol shilshom* (Only Yesterday). Isaac (Yitzhak) Kumer becomes the son of Kafka's Abraham, who, like his "father," can't answer the call from without because his house needs constant attention. Finally, however, as we will see, this current will be buried under the weight of the tragic tradition inscribed in his name.[92]

Agnon wrote this novel in Jerusalem during World War II and published it immediately thereafter—but, crucially, before the establishment of the State of Israel and well before the war of 1967. The Holocaust and, later, post-'67 Jerusalem would generate new Hebrew versions of the akeda. The poet who inhabited both "places," and for whom the akeda as sacrificial death would seem to offer the most natural topos, is Dan Pagis. Having survived the shoah in camps in Transnistria, he came to Palestine after the war and became a poet and scholar of medieval Hebrew literature. Pagis's first poems were published in 1959, but his collection, *Gilgul* (Metamorphosis), published in 1970, established him as a major poetic presence in Israel and a spokesperson for the humanity of the self, and the enemy, in the face of collective parochialism and inherited martyrological reflexes. Pagis's laconic poems, crafted in an ironic voice, engaged the topical and the whimsical with resonances of biblical and medieval Hebrew. Yet there is not a single akeda poem in his entire published oeuvre, and so far as I know, none in his unpublished manuscripts. He remains a lone voice insisting on the parity of war-and-peace anchored in the biblical paradigm not of Abraham-and-Isaac but of Cain-and-Abel. The enmity of these squabbling brothers eventuates in the death of the latter but potentially, given the level playing field depicted here, it could have ended in the death of the former: indeed, Cain "dreams that he is Abel."[93] Pagis's other Cain and Abel poem, "Written in Pencil in the Sealed Railway-Car," has become so canonic in Israeli public culture that it is engraved in stone below the monument featuring a Nazi boxcar at Yad Vashem. The speaker is Eve, the mother of these brothers—the mother, as the story goes, of all humankind:

> here in this carload
> i am eve
> with abel my son
> if you see my other son
> cain son of man
> tell him that i[94]

Eve's words to her son Cain (Cain son of man also translates as "Cain son of Adam") remain open-ended: "tell him that I . . ." But official Israeli culture cannot stand a vacuum and therefore "completes" Eve's statement by declaiming the poem in cyclical fashion on ceremonial occasions such as Holocaust Remembrance Day ("tell him that I [am] here in this carload . . .").[95] Yet when one reads the poem as written, one can conclude that rather than ventriloquize a female voice that "distances [herself] from the family archive," as Harnik does, Pagis engages the other characters in that family archive, the murderous brother and the murdered brother.

Throughout his life, Pagis remained on the margins, maintaining a moral compass that, against all odds, insisted on the parity and humanity—for better or for worse—of the adversarial parties. Ultimately, however, it is the quintessential poet of Jerusalem, Yehuda Amichai, who, in his last poems, will return to the biblical topos of the akeda and retrieve the missing component: compassion, sister to comedy. I will consider these poems at some length in chapter 7.

What is clear from even our cursory glance at this vast library is that for most of Israel's history, the traditional reading of the akeda has prevailed. As it has for centuries, the story continues to animate the Hebrew imagination as a topos of martyrdom, especially as the Hebrew project came closer to the place where "It happened." What is common to all these versions, whether in acceptance of or in protest against the Powers That Be—those powers that send our sons to their death—is the tragic version of the akeda as an accomplished sacrifice, the Israeli iteration of what Salo Baron called the "lachrymose conception of Jewish history."[96]

The Akeda as American Comedy

So along with Israel's loss of a sense of boundaries, and of ethical space between Jews and their Sacred Center, has come the crucial endangerment of that well-heeled Jewish sense of humor. The place where the Comedy of Isaac flourished for a time, after leaving Kafka's Prague, was North America. I mentioned earlier that Philip Roth articulated the most powerful version of the Divine Comedy in modern Jewish garb. The faith at the center of his short story "The Conversion of the Jews" is a child's naïve presumption of divine power along with a benign version of human history. In the narrative, published in Roth's debut collection of short stories, it expresses itself as what might be called the "Judeo-Christian" version of divine intervention. When the Hebrew school teacher, Mr. Binder, tries to inculcate a sense of the absurdity of Immaculate Conception into his pre–bar mitzvah pupils, Ozzie Freedman objects: "If God could create the heaven and the earth in six days, and He could *pick* the six days He wanted right out of nowhere, why couldn't He let a woman have a baby without having intercourse?" It is virtually the same question the naïve reader might have addressed to ninety-nine-year-old Sarah as she suppressed her incredulous laughter behind the tent flap. Threatening to jump off the roof of his school, to which he's been chased by his incensed teacher, Ozzie commands all the onlookers who have gathered below—his schoolmates, his teacher, the janitor with the sign of Auschwitz on his arm, his mother, the firemen who have come to save him—to repeat the following doxology: "Tell me you believe God can do Anything." Then: "Tell me you believe God can make a child without intercourse." And finally, the catechism: "You should never hit anybody about God."[97]

In this little story, which inaugurated in comic mode what I call the "urban congregation" in mid-twentieth-century America, Jewish skepticism about divine intervention in human affairs is bested by naïve Jewish faith in a benign creator—and naïve Christian faith in Immaculate Conception.[98]

Among the American Jewish writers who would reflect Kafka's humbling of Kierkegaard's elevation of Abraham as Knight of Faith, and his implicit rejection of Kierkegaard's Abraham as an affront to common (as to comic) sense, is Woody Allen, in a story that appeared in 1974. After bantering back and forth with the Lord, his Abraham adverts to the authority of His voice:

> And so he took Isaac to a certain place and prepared to sacrifice him but at the last minute the Lord stayed Abraham's hand and said, "How could thou doest such a thing?" And Abraham said, "But thou said . . ."
>
> "Never mind what I said," the Lord spake. "Doth thou listen to every crazy idea that comes thy way?" And Abraham grew ashamed. "Er—not really . . . no . . ."
>
> "I jokingly suggest thou sacrifice Isaac and thou immediately runs out to do it."
>
> And Abraham fell to his knees, "See, I never know when you're kidding."
>
> And the Lord thundered, "No sense of humor, I can't believe it."
>
> "But doth this not prove I love thee, that I was willing to donate mine only son on thy whim?"
>
> And the Lord said, "It proves that some men will follow any order no matter how asinine as long as it comes from a resonant, well modulated voice."
>
> And with that, the Lord bid Abraham get some rest and check with him tomorrow.[99]

Bob Dylan's "Highway 61," recorded in 1965,[100] conveys a similar healthy American skepticism about any supernatural authority not answerable to pragmatic norms. Such midcentury encounters were fertilized by a comic tradition that had been imported from Eastern Europe in the first decades of the twentieth century, when Sholem Aleichem landed on American shores and ratified what would become Borscht Belt comedy—though at least fifteen years had to elapse after the end of World War II before the comic muscle could be revived again.[101]

The Story and the Rock, Again

But even in America, by the turn of the next century, the urban congregation had begun to disperse into isolated communities and the comic muscle had begun to atrophy. And in Israel, we are brought back, again and again, to the beginning, to the story that animates the rock. The akeda continues to excite the Jewish imagination, usually in the tragic form of an accomplished sacrifice. From earliest postbiblical times, as recorded in the Talmud, and throughout the medieval and early modern periods, historical circumstance and, perhaps, a perverse need to complete the story, in ongoing dialogue with

Christianity's version, generated a procession of fathers who "sacrificed" their sons.[102] Again, Shalom Spiegel's warning—which was sounded in the immediate aftermath of the Holocaust—of the temptations and dangers emanating from a *misreading* of the biblical text largely fell on deaf ears.

I am aware that, while claiming to unearth the foundational layer of the story that has animated so much of Western monotheism in order to expose the ethical mandate as well as the generic structure at its core, I am questioning the way the story has been read for two millennia. But my motive is based on the evidence that even if it is the so-called fundamentalists, the jihadists and the messianists, who do the mischief and grab the headlines, the more accommodative forms of religious imagination are equally fundamental and indigenous to the three monotheistic religions. The invitations by Spiegel, Kafka, and Derrida—and their American counterparts—to read the Hebrew Bible against the grain of prevailing exegesis and tragic history continue to resonate in unexpected places. My own "fundamentalist" reading of Genesis 17–22 is meant to widen that spacious, ongoing, *comic negotiation* between the material world and the Divine—with faith in, but without need of, Salvation Now.

"You are as majestic as Jerusalem": The Song and the City

Jerusalem achieves its fullest articulation in the Song of Songs. (See fig. 2.)[1] There are different versions and notions of urban space in the Bible, but when the generic term *ha-'ir*, the city, is used, it generally refers to Jerusalem (see Mic. 6:9; Zeph. 3:1)[2]—never more palpably than in Shir ha-shirim. Indeed, it can even seem to the uninitiated reader that, from Genesis on, the entire biblical corpus has been preparing for this encounter with the city in its fullness.[3] The Song is replete with architectural, botanical, zoological, and social metonymies of the city and its environs that both represent and interact with the human body: "Shelaḥa'ikh pardes rimonim 'im pri megadim" (Your branches [arms] are an orchard / of pomegranate trees heavy with fruit); "Ani ḥoma ve-shadai ke-migdalot" (I am a wall / and my breasts are [as] towers, Song of Songs 4:13, 8:10).

I invoke the "uninitiated reader" while cognizant that few interlocutors who have even cursory knowledge of postbiblical Jewish or Christian exegesis or later poetic iterations would approach this text as a tabula rasa.[4] But there is heuristic value in adopting a self-consciously naïve reading of the Song, which projects a powerful metaphor: not of the city as woman, such as we find in Lamentations, in Micha, etc., but of the woman as city. When the poet-prophet of Lamentations turns to a destroyed Jerusalem in the second-person feminine singular and asks the primordial question, "To what shall I compare thee that I may comfort thee?" (*ma ashveh lakh va-anaḥamekh*, Lam. 2:13), he is not only implicitly acknowledging the original rhetorical act that has already personified the city as woman, but also launching millennia of poetic hyperboles and the sociopsychological comforts that will attend them.[5] But in contrast to the feminization of Jerusalem, in which her houses and thoroughfares, her shrines and shops, her flora and her inhabitants, human and bestial,

FIGURE 2. Baruch ben Shemariah of Brest-Litovsk, *Song of Solomon* (1794). Old Testament, Bible. Image courtesy of Beinecke Rare Book and Manuscript Library, Yale University, 1168747.

are signs of an essence that precedes and transcends physical boundaries, the primary referent or tenor in Shir ha-shirim is human and physical. Because this is not a poem of lamentation for or a love poem to the city of Jerusalem but a song of love and yearning between a young woman and a young man *in* Jerusalem, there is intimacy but no ownership, connection but no exclusivity.

Ilana Pardes's lovely volume on the Song is subtitled "A Biography."[6] One could add that it is a biography with a difference—a biography of a text that features not only a speaker who exhibits at the very outset "a craving to be kissed,"[7] but also, by extension, generations of readers and lovers. Indeed, perhaps more than any other biblical text, Song of Songs resonates with the voices of all who have embraced, interpreted, and reconfigured this poem.

Pardes's book, like mine, was composed in Jerusalem. The sense of belonging that makes this text part of one's personal biography stems from the fact that, again, there is no appeal or address in the Song to Jerusalem as metaphor, as an other, an oppositional figure. Walking the streets and crossing the parks of Jerusalem in springtime today, one sees the same budding pomegranates and the same henna blossoms that the Shulamite would have caressed with eyes made dewy with love (or spring allergies). And the soundscape of Jerusalem is filled with modern Israeli renditions of songs derived from that infinite well of inspiration. Most significantly for the exegetical edifices that were built upon this secular ground, holiness in the Song itself resides within and not beyond the human sphere. The structures and rhetoric of the divine are not so much missing in the Song of Songs as transmuted. Calling attention to both the act of signifying and the primacy of the human body, the Shulamite entreats her lover to "bind me as a seal upon your heart, / a sign upon your arm" (8:6). Robert Alter notes that this phrase is "a daring adaptation of religious imagery, for it is reminiscent of the injunction in Deuteronomy 11:18 to bind God's words on heart and hand and as a frontlet between the eyes."[8] Taking this logic a step further, I would argue that this verse can be read not so much as an adaptation but as a repudiation of, or alternative to, the rhetorical landscape of holiness—and this is even more true of the physical landscape. Consider, for example, the comparison of the female beloved to a "dove in the clefts of the rock" (*yonati be-hagvei ha-sel'a*, 2:14) as a transposition of the image of Moses encountering the divine presence from the fissure of the rock (*be-nikrat ha-tzur*, Ex. 33:22); in this case, the words are different, but the image is nearly identical. This implicit dialogue with older passages in the Hebrew Bible could argue for the relative lateness of the text, though, as we shall see presently, there is renewed scholarly debate over the dating of many of the verses in the Song. In any event, what is reinforced by all such research is the lively internal dynamic within the canonic corpus.[9]

Another sign of this presumed dialogue appears as reference to the architecture of holiness: the "tower of David" is evoked by the male speaker to describe the "splendor" of his beloved's neck (Song 4:4). Seemingly a reference to an extant edifice that would be identifiable by any modern walker in the urban space now known as the City of David, this "tower" is, as Ariel Bloch elucidates, a poetic invention not mentioned elsewhere in the Bible.[10]

Rhetorically, the sanctity of place and of text is implicit in the very first line, as David's son Solomon is singled out as the proprietor or author of the

Song. "Shir ha-shirim asher li-shlomo" appears as the "title page" of the translation by Ariel Bloch and Chana Bloch: "The Song of Songs, which is Solomon's." Solomon as King, along with his palaces and material possessions, is
evoked throughout the poem. As Chana Bloch writes, "whenever the poet al-
ludes to queens and concubines, horses and chariots, the cedars of Lebanon,
gold, ivory, and spices"—and even Pharaoh, with whom he traded—"the reader
is imaginatively invited into King Solomon's court." There are also references to folklore associated with Solomonic extravagance from extrabiblical
sources (3:7–11).[11]

And yet the Temple and other sacred Real Estate are conspicuously missing from this text, as is any mention of the Deity.

This curious omission of any explicit reference to physical sites of holiness, and specifically to the Temple, in the city identified as Jerusalem under
the reign of King Solomon—who, as we saw, is credited repeatedly in the Hebrew Bible with building the "House to the Name of God" on Mount Moriah[12]—is apparent in any "naïve" reading of the Song. It becomes even more
egregious as we consider the many other representational details—the flora
and fauna, the architecture and populace—of "Solomon's" Jerusalem in this
text. The presumed history of the composition of Shir ha-shirim makes such
an omission curiouser and curiouser.

The story of what became the first of the "megilloth" or scrolls that compose one section in the "Ketuvim" (Writings) division of the Hebrew Bible[13]
begins in its composition and reception and continues in its forms and ep-
ochs of transmission. Wild speculation floated by Chaim Rabin and others
locates sources and composition of the Song as far back as ancient Tamil love
poetry, based on the dominant presence in both traditions of a woman's autonomous voice. David Shulman retorts that "Rabin's theory posits a wildly
improbable scenario that has Israelite mariners stuck in south India because
of the monsoon and thus encountering Tamil love poetry. There's a gap of
close to a thousand years between the Tamil poems and Shir Ha-shirim."[14]

Although the dating is far from settled, most scholars now trace the canonic, final form of the Hebrew text to around the fourth–third century BCE,
citing wide-ranging linguistic, syntactic, thematic, and artistic influences and
conventions, from intrabiblical and Aramaic references to resonances of surrounding Hellenistic, Egyptian, and possibly also Persian cultures—as well
as intratextual references to and possible polemics with older passages in
the Hebrew Bible.[15] Such dating would confirm that composition was coter-
minous with the still-functioning "Second" Temple, making its omission in
the Song even more noteworthy—and generating centuries of hermeneutic
acrobatics.

The Song's perceived contemporaneity whenever Hebrew is revived as a poetic language and/or vernacular may also have something to do with its late composition. In her study of biblical syntax, Chana Kronfeld, citing Talmy Givón, argues that the "'Song of Songs marks the "endpoint of the change" within biblical Hebrew itself [from aspect to tense]' . . . and is therefore the 'most progressive dialect-level evident in the Old Testament.'"[16]

And yet. Even such seemingly settled debates among scholars continue to be upended by new interpretations. In the following pages, I can only gesture toward the mountain of scholarship that has attended this text over hundreds of years, toward its appropriations in Jewish (and Christian) liturgical, exegetical, and literary spaces, while focusing on a few forks in the road. The present moment is one of those forks; as with the akeda, my primary concern is to pry open proprietary spaces to allow for a more fundamental encounter with Shir ha-shirim in the context of contemporary Jerusalem.

Kissing the Bride through a Veil: Composition, Translation, Transmission

Appropriations of this text over the centuries have taken the form of exegetical, liturgical, and poetic renderings, along with translations into myriad languages. In addition to the process of its composition and the acrobatics attending its inclusion in the Hebrew Bible, which I will consider briefly below, I will glance at the oldest extant translations, the Aramaic oral versions referred to as the "Targum," dating from early antiquity, as well as some of the Song's many iterations in the Jewish world. My own reading is being offered in English while my primary referent is the Hebrew Bible and its presence in the culture and politics of modern Jerusalem. The insights, research, and translations of many contemporary scholars, including Chana Bloch, Ariel Bloch, Marcia Falk, Yair Zakovitch, Robert Alter, and Daniel Boyarin; pathbreaking interpretations by generations of feminist scholars including Phyliss Trible, Carol Meyers, Athalya Brenner, Fiona C. Black, and Carole Fontaine; and readings within the purview of modern Hebrew literature by Chana Kronfeld and Ilana Pardes reflect an ongoing two-way dialogue between an American-inflected "diasporic" approach and a Jerusalem-based encounter with this text. Some of the freedoms enhanced by that double lens are implicit in Robert Alter's endorsement of the English translation by Chana and Ariel Bloch:

[O]lder English renderings, beginning with the King James Version, do have their splendid moments, but they also often fudge the frank sensuality of the original, trading tresses for demure veils . . . [Even] in the proliferation in our own age of new English versions of the Song ... translators have had difficulties negotiating between the extremes of clunky sexual explicitness and the pastels of greeting-card poetry ... The problem of conveying the Hebrew poet's candid yet beautifully tactful imagination of love is compounded by the sensuous concreteness and the harmonious compactness of the poet's language ... Chana and Ariel Bloch's translation, a rare conjunction of refined poetic resourcefulness and philological precision, brings us closer to the magical freshness of this ancient Hebrew love poetry than has any other English version.[17]

Veiled tresses, indeed. The origin of this particular act of camouflage is in a linguistic confusion vis-à-vis the original Hebrew, in verses such as "How beautiful you are, my love, / my friend! The doves of your eyes / looking out / from the thicket of your hair" (4:1). "Tresses," "thicket," or "locks" of hair (*tzamatekh*, 4:3, 6:7) are rendered in many translations as "veils."[18] If, as the folk adage has it, reading in translation is like kissing the bride through a veil,[19] the efforts to cover the unabashed nakedness of the Hebrew text in order to render it less provocative would yield multiple and elaborate imaginative feats. But this unabashed nakedness is also bound up with the metaphorical and grammatical status of the Hebrew language itself as female.[20]

A fresh look at the original reveals, from the very outset, what Alter calls the "frank sensuality," the seemingly unselfconscious sensuousness of the body depicted in nature, in the city streets, and at home, both conforming to and stretching literary conventions. Scholarship on the sources of those conventions has been rich and varied. As Pardes writes, J. G. Wetzstein, the nineteenth-century diplomat and would-be scholar "who served as the Prussian consul in Damascus," would view "the Song as a collection of wedding songs sung in the context of celebrations of entirely earthly bonds. Relying on the orientalist presupposition that the East had remained unchanged since antiquity," he described contemporary Syrian weddings and drew the line connecting the *wasf*, performed at Arabic weddings, and some of the images in the Song.[21] Generations of later scholars have elaborated on the possibility that, indeed, some version of the *wasf* prevails in the Hebrew text.[22] Derived from an ancient Arabic poetic form covering a broad range of descriptive practices, often with fluid references to human and animal species, the *wasf* is generally associated with detailed descriptions of the male or female body. Such images of the young lovers in various settings provided fodder for endless reframing, of the body parts themselves, of the very nature of the relationship between the two young speakers, between each of them and their environment—and of the cross-cultural pollination that the text reveals and perpetuates.

Beneath the conventions and poetic tropes is, after all, a passionate love story. Chana Bloch writes that "for centuries, exegetes have considered [the] relationship [between the two protagonists] as chaste, ignoring the plain sense of the Hebrew word dodim, which occurs six times in the Song . . . [and] is almost always translated as 'love,' though it refers specifically to sexual love." She elaborates on the various references throughout the poem to acts or elements associated with explicit erotic encounters, all of which "strengthen . . . our conviction that the sexual relationship between the two lovers is not just yearned for—as has often been assumed—but actually consummated."[23] This flies in the face of much commentary, past and present, and frees my hypothetical "naïve reader" for an unencumbered encounter with the text.

Alter expands on this insight in comparing different translations into English over the centuries: the King James Version completed in 1611, the Revised Standard Version begun in the late nineteenth century and completed in 1952, and many in the twentieth century, culminating, in his view, in the Blochs' translation of 1995. He focuses on verses 1:12–14, spoken by the woman and referring to her lover as "my king":

עַד־שֶׁהַמֶּלֶךְ בִּמְסִבּוֹ
נִרְדִּי נָתַן רֵיחוֹ:

צְרוֹר הַמֹּר דּוֹדִי לִי
בֵּין שָׁדַי יָלִין:
אֶשְׁכֹּל הַכֹּפֶר דּוֹדִי לִי
בְּכַרְמֵי עֵין גֶּדִי.

> My king lay down beside me
> and my fragrance
> wakened the night.
> All night between my breasts
> my love is a cluster of myrrh,
> a sheaf of henna blossoms
> in the vineyards of Ein Gedi.

Alter explains the translation of 1:13 as based on the Hebrew word *yalin* which, "as Ariel Bloch rightly observes in his Commentary, means 'to spend the night.'"[24] The Blochs' version, bound by scholarship but freed from convention—and inspired by Chana Bloch's poetic genius—exposes the explicit sexual nature of the lovers' relationship. We will return to these verses later and glance at some of the radical ways in which they have been incorporated into modernist Hebrew poetry and prose; without their veil, many of these passages lay bare surprising erotic possibilities to be picked up centuries later.

The sexual resonances echo within specific physical spaces, which, as Pardes points out, often become "dreamscape[s]."[25] The image of the lover as a "cluster of myrrh, / a sheaf of henna blossoms / in the vineyards of Ein Gedi" is not the only geographical flight in this text. While the verbal exchanges are explicitly located in or emanate from Jerusalem, the Song also contains references to verdant and at times wild landscapes outside of the city. In fact, as any attentive reader notes, the poetic reach extends far beyond the city, beyond even Ein Gedi, to the flora of the Sharon valley, the "clefts of the rock / . . . the shadow of the cliff" (2:14), Mount Gilead (4:1), and the mountains of and beyond northern Israel: Amana, Senir, Hermon, and Lebanon (4:8). Such rhetorical open-endedness, conveying what Ariel Bloch calls "inaccessibility and danger,"[26] is nonetheless articulated in a city ringed by mountains and devoid of any horizon; a boundless horizon composed of leaps of the poetic imagination is, then, one of the most significant dimensions of the freedoms exercised in this text.

But what is perhaps most striking about the poem in its "nakedness" is the intimate, daring inscription of body on landscape and of landscape on body. Emanating from Jerusalem but reaching far beyond the city, this two-directional metaphoric impulse may have inaugurated the centrifugal thrust in Hebrew poetry to counteract the centripetal forces that terminate in the suffocating embrace of the sacred center.

"His thighs like marble pillars on pedestals of gold": Song of Songs as Poetry Workshop

"Kiss me, make me drunk with your kisses," is the opening of the poem that will proceed by monologue, dialogue, and choral attestation (1:2).[27] My own attempt to, once again, reclaim the Song after over two thousand years of appropriation, translation, and exegetical diversion is as enticing as it is daunting. And it is performed, again, while standing in present-day Jerusalem, whose edifices, parks, and thoroughfares are constructed to foreground the (presumed) ancient landscape and architecture, but whose young lovers still find bowers and pavilions, vineyards and chambers in which to enact their private games of hide-and-seek, while the "watchmen" and the "brothers" still congregate to restrain them, releasing both the power and the danger preserved within the formaldehyde of memory.

The most important element of the biblical text is the central status of humanly crafted metaphor, or more commonly, simile, in the exchange between the two major speakers and between them and other inhabitants of the city. But it is this very pinnacle of the human imagination that has often been occluded or superseded by interpretive acrobatics. Once some of the overgrowth has

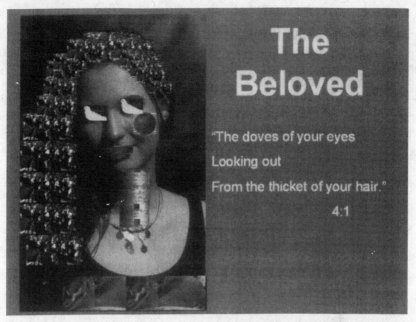

FIGURE 3. Christine L. Godwin, "simile face" of the Shulamite from Song of Songs (2006). "How beautiful you are, my love . . . The doves of your eyes looking out from the thicket of your hair . . . Thy hair is like a flock of goats flowing down Mount Gilead . . . Like the Tower of David is thy neck." Reproduced with permission of the artist.

been cleared away, the reader can begin to reclaim what Alter calls the "candid yet beautifully tactful imagination of love."[28] The images articulated by each of the lovers in their attempts to capture the attributes of the other are, indeed, beautifully tactful at times—but at others so tactile, and so hyperbolic, as to appear almost ludicrous, the free-spirited figurative corollary of erotic play.

Whether originally meant tongue-in-cheek or as a sincere effort at scaling the heights of poetic possibility to match the heights of human love, the Hebrew text in its most "naked" form often evokes a smile if not a chuckle. The neck as a tower, the eyes as doves, the breasts as gazelles, the belly as a mound of wheat (4:4, 4:1, 4:5, 7:3): this reader cannot help but think in those instances of the kind of competition or jousting that would have been appropriate in Cyrano de Bergerac's workshop striving for poetic equivalences for the extremes of infatuation. The playful, hyperbolic, or even grotesque imagery has not escaped the attention of readers and scholars.[29] To demonstrate the ludicrous possibilities in any literal representation of these tropes, figure 3 shows a whimsical pictorial rendition of several verses from the Song, created in 2006 by Christine Godwin (then Devore), who was a student in my course

Imagining Jerusalem at Duke University. Ariel Bloch calls attention to the Hebrew verb *d-m-h* that signifies an act of human imagination: In the verse "my lover [m.] resembles a gazelle or a wild stag" (2:9), the poet/lover presents a "formal self-conscious statement of comparison," in which the seemingly redundant "use of 'or' in the Hebrew [calls] attention to the very act of comparing."[30] The lovers, Alter tells us, do not stop at inventing such images, but go on to act them out, as the "artifice of poetry . . . enters inside the frames of dramatic action." When the Shulamite instructs her lover to "be . . . a buck" (*dmeh lekha dodi li-tzvi*, 2:16), she expects him, as it were, to "act out the poetic simile" and "gambol" all night "on the landscape of her body."[31]

Such redundancy and hyperbole could also support the theory that more than one authorial hand—possibly even a school of poets—contributed to the Masoretic text.[32] Consider the metaphoric excesses in the following verses:

> His arm a golden scepter with gems of topaz,
> his loins the ivory of thrones
> inlaid with sapphire
> his thighs like marble pillars
> on pedestals of gold.
> Tall as Mount Lebanon, a man like a cedar! (5:14–15)

Thighs like marble pillars? Tall as Mount Lebanon?!! Such examples proliferate throughout this text, which, unlike the Book of Esther, is not generally read as parody. But its extravagant rhetoric demands an accounting. Contributing to the abundance, or even abandon, is the gendering of the two voices. What is evident is, if not a battle of the sexes, then certainly a play between female and male voices and the images with which each chooses to depict the other. Among the most innovative readings of the Song in the past half century are those that have looked not only at gender-specific images but also at what might be called gender crossings in the various depictions of the male and female bodies. An early iteration of what would become a whole field of feminist biblical scholarship is Phyllis Trible's announcement that she proposed to "examine interactions between the Hebrew Scriptures and the Women's Liberation Movement" and that the "hermeneutical challenge is to translate biblical faith without sexism."[33] While some of the images that have been scrutinized are clearly gender specific, some are not. Carol Meyers explored the female body as depicted in the Song through architectural, military, and even "faunal" images that are "counter to stereotypical gender conceptions," conveying "might, strength, aggression, even danger." The prominence of the mother's house and the absence of the usual "androcentric setting" of the biblical world only emphasizes the originality of such imagery.[34] While some of this may derive from conventions of pastoral, courtly love in the ambient cultures, the text that emerges is not just a string of hyperbolic images but a drama with several voices and venues: the female voice, the male voice, the chorus of "daughters of Jerusalem," the brothers, the watchmen, each with their own gendered discourse, along with stunning border crossings.

Clearly, however, the female voice predominates. Franz Rosenzweig identified an intense subjectivity in the Song: "Comparatively speaking, the word 'I' occurs this frequently in no other book in the Bible ... Like a single sustained organ note, it runs under the whole melodic-harmonic texture of mezzo-sopranos and sopranos."[35] Zali Gurevitch reconstructs what he identifies as the move from "dilug" (leap or skip) to "dialogue"—the yearning for the other, the "leap" that evolves into the dialogue between the lovers; he brings his own poetic sensibilities and an inclusive embrace of all the layers of tradition as he traces the Song through over two thousand years of its journey.[36]

Perhaps the most innovative recent interpretation, and the one most resonant with my own project, is that of Israeli Bible scholar Yair Zakovitch. Building on his earlier research, which identified different genres of songs or poems that constitute more of an anthology than a coherent rendering of a primary female and a primary male voice,[37] Zakovitch's recent study of the Song gives a precise roadmap of the tropes and poetic structures that recur throughout the text. His most radical argument—and the focus of his debates with fellow Bible scholars—regards the dating of the Song, its placement in the biblical canon, and its specific poetic properties. He upends centuries of biblical and talmudic scholarship by arguing that although Shir ha-shirim most likely acquired its final form around the third century BCE, and although its canonic status continued to be debated well into the early centuries of the Common Era, various sections not only were composed much earlier but may in turn have influenced other texts, including sections from Proverbs and a number of the prophetic books. His suggestion, for example, that Proverbs 31, which describes the demure "Woman of Valor," might well be a response to the eroticism of Song of Songs, depends on a radical reading of both the texts themselves and the dynamic process of placement of different books in the long course of Bible formation:

We submit ... that Sages who read the Song of Songs according to its literal straightforward sense—the *peshat*—as love poetry between a man and a woman, placed it following Proverbs but preceding Ecclesiastes, while others, who supported the allegorical reading, placed it after Ecclesiastes. The author of "Woman of Valor," who wrote his composition as a polemical retort to the poems in Song of Songs—as an antidote, of sorts, to be taken before reading the book of love poetry—positioned it as the connecting link—the cement—between the two books, between the conclusion of Proverbs ("the words of Lemuel") and the beginning of Song of Songs.[38]

This challenges the fairly broad consensus that prevailed not only on the late date of the Song, but on its polemic position regarding earlier, mainly prophetic, texts. What remains fairly certain, again, is that no matter which "came first," these texts were "talking to each other" for centuries while the canon was being constructed.

Zakovitch's primary contribution to my own project lies in his identification of poetic tropes spoken mainly in the female voice and of riddle forms expressed in different voices that eventually come to be resolved in the voice of the Shulamite. We will return to this, but something even more radical is at stake: a brief reprise of the imagery of 5:14–15, which we just looked at as an example of hyperbole and even humor, will give a taste of the power of Zakovitch's analysis as a basis for other daring exegetical leaps. His translation of the text differs slightly from that of Chana Bloch:

> "His legs are marble pillars set upon pedestals of gold . . ." The ornamentation with stones here and in the continuation calls to mind a description of a statue and not of a living person, as though her lover were as beautiful as the statue of a god in a temple.[39]

Clearly, Zakovitch's rather casual reference here is to a pagan temple replete with icons, but this seems not to concern him, as he goes on to suggest other references in the same passage to the "stones on the priest's breastplate," which would, of course, allude to the priestly garments worn in the *beit ha-mikdash*. He then argues that the female speaker "return[s] in v. 16 to her beloved's head, to his mouth, finishing her words with a reminder that the object she describes is no statue but something living, her lover."[40]

So even in this intriguing explication of such imagery, Zakovitch elides references to pagan temples and *The* Temple. If we accept his interpretation, the implications are significant for our own project, suggesting not only the sublimated presence of The Temple and of other houses of worship in this "secular" text, but also their presumed coexistence in the centuries of the Song's composition.

Other evidence of the capaciousness of this text can be found in what Alter describes as the "commingling" or "interweaving" of "different realms, different senses" that constitute many of the tropes, the juxtaposition or even synaesthetic fusion of sight, sound, taste, and smell—with touch "implied" as both sense and gesture, signaling the consummation of love.[41] One recurrent but elastic image he traces is that of the pomegranate. It first appears as metaphor—"the curve of your cheek / a pomegranate in the thick of your hair"

(4:3)—then reappears in 7:13 as a flowering part of the "actual landscape," and is finally transformed into fermented wine (8:2).[42] What is significant for us is that the pomegranate, like other images, including, perhaps, the stones Zakovitch associates with the priest's breastplate, acquires what Alter calls "metonymic as well as metaphoric" status.[43] But here the referent is entirely secular, reflecting the quotidian life of the city. It is a fruit that represents the perennial flora and the wine-making economy of Jerusalem itself while providing vehicles for the rhetoric of love. "In more explicit erotic literature," Alter writes, "the body in the act of love often seems to displace the rest of the world. In the Song, by contrast, the world is constantly embraced in the very process of imagining the body."[44] Although, as we have seen, other sites are referenced, the "world" evoked here is the City, its inhabitants and its properties. Could this be read as a subtle way of authenticating poetry and love in Jerusalem while effectively erasing the edifices that would support the religious cult?

Again, we can reinforce this by reference to contemporary perceptions of Jerusalem—and, again, it is the pomegranate that is the ubiquitous reminder of the persistence of the ancient flora and fauna. "When I look at the pomegranate trees in my garden I do not think about silver pomegranates on priestly garments," writes Athalya Brenner. "Neither do I think about other cultic applications, or about place names. It is the SoS pomegranates, six times used in the SoS in metaphors for skin colour and wine-drinking, which come immediately to mind, together with the verses they are part of."[45]

"The Song of Songs is the Holy of Holies!": The Poetic Imagination in Formaldehyde

The reading that an unencumbered reader can perform was of course not lost on the rabbis who were struggling to construct the boundaries of the biblical canon:

> Rabbi Shimon ben Azzai said, "I have a received tradition from the mouths of seventy-two elders, on the day they inducted Rabbi Elazar ben Azaria into his seat [as head] at the Academy, that the Song of Songs and Ecclesiastes render the hands impure." Rabbi Akiva said, "Mercy forbid! No one in Israel ever disputed that The Song of Songs renders the hands impure, since nothing in the entire world is worthy [and no human time has value] but for that day on which The Song of Songs was given to Israel; for all the Scriptures are holy, but the Song of Songs is the Holy of Holies!" (Mishna Yadayim 3:5)[46]

It is striking that, in this much-cited passage, Rabbi Akiva draws an implicit analogy between text and place and, for that matter, between temporal and physical manifestations of the world, as locus of holiness. But what is even more striking is that he would claim such status ("Holy of Holies") for a text situated in Solomon's Jerusalem with, again, no mention of the edifices and practices that signify holiness—namely, the Temple and the Priests—and no mention of God.

The challenge of parsing Rabbi Akiva's statement is ongoing and can be found in a number of contemporary scholarly arguments. David Stern suggests that the term "Holy of Holies" could refer in the context of Akiva's remarks to the sanctity of the text and the status of its interpreters as its guardians, that just as the High Priest alone was authorized to enter the Holy of Holies in the Temple, the Song of Songs is itself "a mysterium, a sanctum on account of its esoteric character that only the mystical initiate can enter through study."[47] This would be a fairly explicit endorsement of the diffuse text culture that had already begun to replace centralized cultic practices of sacrifice on the Temple Mount, as well as an attempt to establish exegetical controls within that culture. Rachel Elior goes further to claim that there is an explicit textual connection between Shir ha-shirim and the site itself, an actual reference in the Song to the Temple and its rituals, in the catalogue of spices and oils enumerated throughout, especially in 4:13–14—myrrh, aloe, henna, spikenard, saffron, cinnamon, and frankincense—that would justify Akiva's claim. "The only context in which 'holy of holies' pertains explicitly to the text of Song of Songs appears to be in the listing of fragrant plants from which the sacred incense was prepared," she writes: the incense that was "offered on the golden altar within the curtain, inside the Holy of Holies."[48]

But even if cultic remnants of the Temple service survived, they were, like the sacred architecture of Jerusalem, clearly transmuted in the Song into the "secular" space of human love.[49] As Chana Bloch tells us, "when Rabbi Akiva warned, 'whoever warbles the Song of Songs at banqueting houses, treating it like an ordinary song, has no portion in the World to Come,' the emphatic prohibition [made] it perfectly clear just what people were doing, and where" (!!).[50] We latter-day readers, who may have reclaimed a more "naked" reading of the text, can appreciate both its radical nature in its own time and its insidious presence through the ages.[51]

Whatever original sources may have informed the Song itself, the exegetical and then the mystical traditions would combine them, preserve them in the parabolic orchard, and elevate them to the status of the Holy of Holies, inaugurated by the statement attributed to Rabbi Akiva. We cannot but gesture toward the ingenious exegetical acts that have attended the history of this text, transmuting it (back, these exegetes would claim) into the language of divine-human encounter.

Yet whether or not it defiles the hands that touch it, this text, like (as)
the Shulamite in her nakedness, will remain subversive of every proprietary
reading. Descendants of Rabbi Akiva (d. 135 CE), self-appointed guardians of
a certain kind of memory, will labor long and hard to preserve it in the formaldehyde that I call the "allegory of suspicion" until such (messianic) time as
it would be deemed safe to reclaim the ground beneath the images. As Chana
Bloch argues, "the theologians prevailed: for twenty centuries, the Song was
almost universally read as a religious or historical allegory"—first by Rabbi
Akiva himself, who "taught that the Song was about the love of God and the
people of Israel," then elaborated by Rashi, Ibn Ezra, and others, and for their
part, by the Church Fathers, who saw the text as illuminating the relations
between "Christ and his bride, the Church."[52]

Unlike the story of the Garden of Eden, which foregrounds what Chana
Bloch calls the "consequences" of the loss of innocence, the Song "looks at the
same border-crossing and sees only the joy of discovery."[53] Bloch contends
that the main reason that the rabbis and the Church Fathers resorted to allegory was that the "very fact of sexuality had become problematic," thereby
impelling them to spiritualize the carnal aspects of the text.[54] In an early iteration of this insight, Phyllis Trible juxtaposed the two texts, suggesting that
"perhaps the Paradise described in Genesis 2 and destroyed in Genesis 3 has
been regained, expanded, and improved upon in the Song of Songs." She asks,
rhetorically, whether "one mark of sin in Eden" has "been overcome here in
another garden with the recovery of mutuality in love? . . . Male dominance
is totally alien to Canticles . . . Can it be that grace is present? In many ways
[therefore] . . . Song of Songs is a midrash on Genesis 2–3 . . . The first couple
lose their oneness through disobedience . . . The second couple affirm their
oneness through eroticism." She concludes by implying that because God is
missing from the second garden, we need them both, and that "depatriarchalizing is not an operation which the exegete performs on the text. It is a hermeneutic operating within Scripture itself. We expose it; we do not impose
it . . . Therein we shall be explorers who embrace both old and new in the
pilgrimage of faith."[55] But in our own "pilgrimage of faith," there is, I submit,
another, equally compelling force operative, especially on the rabbis and suc-
ceeding generations of interpreters: the status of Jerusalem "herself."

I would go so far as to argue, from the evidence offered above, that the first
act of "translation" in the Song of Songs took place in the text itself: the transposition of "Solomon's" Jerusalem into secular space. The absent, effaced, or
occluded Temple that haunts every verse of the Song would, in turn, generate
some of the most daring acts of the exilic imagination living in eschatological suspense: the "restoration" of the divine-human encounter and of sacred

spaces in the city, now remembered and reimagined as suspended in her desolation. That is what would transpire in the following two millennia in tomes of exegesis and liturgical appropriation that make up the Jewish bookshelf.

Michael Fishbane, in his erudite commentary to the Song of Songs for the Jewish Publication Society, does not define his point of departure as I have, though he starts by acknowledging the poetry articulated by two lovers and their attendant choruses that constitutes the biblical text—with its antecedents and parallels in other ancient cultures. He then traces the paths that the Song took through centuries and continents, beginning with its almost immediate incorporation into other forms of discourse—intimating, as did the first commentators and allegorists, that "these songs of human desire [might] mean just what they say . . . or might conceal some hints of sacred history and worship, and not be as secular as they seem." He defines his task as representing many of the Jewish "readers past and present [who] have pondered this matter and taken different positions."[56] Fishbane painstakingly lays out the entire rabbinic apparatus that composes the "PARDES" or "orchard of interpretation": *peshat* or the "text's plain sense," *derash* or "meanings developed through midrashic exegesis," *remez*, a level of reading "founded on philosophical interests and concerns," and *sod*, the approach that is "mystical in aim and method."[57] He then makes it clear that what characterizes this "orchard" is the transformation of eroticized bodies into a love affair between Israel and her God. To his meticulous explication of the many retellings, transformations, and appropriations of the biblical text—exegetical, liturgical, poetic, narratological, philosophical, and mystical—in Jewish literature, Fishbane adds an "Excursus" that traces the paths the Song took through many avenues of global Jewish culture over some twenty-three centuries.

Perhaps the most interesting and revealing of such appropriations is actually one of the earliest: the Targum or Aramaic "translation" of the biblical text that was meant to make it accessible through oral preaching to unlettered congregants. Based on ancient oral practices and compiled, presumably, in the seventh or eighth century CE, the Targum survived in its own right for millennia and set precedents for myriad translations throughout the Jewish Diaspora, from "Judeo-Arabic, Judeo-Persian [to] Yiddish" and all the languages of Europe.[58] What is common to all these translations is that they are themselves unacknowledged acts of exegesis. The Artscroll edition, familiar to a certain swath of contemporary synagogue-going English readers, is advertised on its website as "the first English translation faithful to the allegory that is the Song's authentic meaning . . . The beautiful love song between G-d and Israel that Rabbi Akiva calls 'Holy of Holies.'"[59] As Fishbane acknowledges, the Targum already incorporated the interpretive act that read the Song as a dialogue between God (the male voice) and Israel (the female voice) and interpolated sacred architecture into the secular space of the original text:

> *I have come into my garden, my sister and bride; I have gathered my myrrh . . .*
> *Eat lovers* (5:1). TARGUM: The Holy One, blessed be He, said to His people, the House of Israel, I have come into My Temple, which you have built for Me, My Sister, Assembly of Israel, who is likened to a chaste bride . . . I have received the incense of your spices . . . Now come, priests, lovers of My precepts, and eat . . . of the offerings.[60]

Among the more recent commentators on the Song, R. Joseph B. Soloveitchik (1903–93) is cited by Fishbane as one who reflected traditional Jewish understanding inflected by modern Western thought, especially that of Kierkegaard and neo-Kantian philosophy.[61] But in one of his most influential texts, he articulates the more common midrashic appropriation of the Song:

> The epithet "kodesh ha-kodashim" [the Holy of Holies], which appears in Mishnah Yadayim 3:5 with regard to Shir ha-shirim . . . refers to the Divine symbolism inherent in it. However, this description also expresses a Halakhic principle: *this scroll may not be interpreted literally* (*ki-pshuta*). Throughout the Torah we are permitted to interpret verses according to their literal or their midrashic *meaning*. "Pshuto shel mikra" [the literal text] is a value . . . With regard to Shir ha-shirim, the literal meaning was excluded from the category "Torah" to be replaced by the allegorical text ("midrash shel ha-ktuvim"). [In this case] *the symbolic method is the only method. Anyone who explains this scroll on the basis of the literal words (pshutam shel ha-ktuvim) with regard to sensual love, desecrates its holiness and denies the Oral Torah.* (Emphases mine)[62]

Again, the compensatory element that the exegetical project had to provide was the introduction not only of the divine voice and presence, but also of Solomon's Temple. One striking example of the ingenious narrative acrobatics necessary for such acts is the rendition of 1:16–17, which the JPS translates as "And you, my beloved [m.], are handsome, / Beautiful indeed! / Our couch is a bower; / Cedars are the beams of our house, / Cypresses the rafters." This verse yields, as Fishbane elucidates, to the following "derash":

> This "couch" is the Temple. Its sanctuary was the locus for God's indwelling . . . and thus a font of earthly bounty . . . Indeed the Ark (with its staves) was deemed a virtual marital bed for God's fructifying presence . . . The Temple thus marks the spatial and spiritual nexus of God's conjunction with Israel; it symbolizes their covenant marriage.[63]

Another passage from Shir ha-shirim Rabbah inserts the Temple as one of the three places where Shir ha-shirim was, presumably, first recited.[64] In addition to "restoring" sacred architecture to the Song's Jerusalem, minds intent on reconstructing the topography of holiness were also presented with other challenges. Like landscape architects with exclusive claims to a meaningful relation with the land, rabbinic exegetes would clear the area of the seductive breasts of the Shulamite while preserving the flora and fauna in a virtual zoological garden. Chapter 4:5, for example, is spoken by the young male lover, who self-consciously constructs an elaborate conceit that compares his beloved's body parts to a local gazelle and her offspring, using the particle "as" to establish the poetic simile: "your breasts are as two fawns, / twins of a gazelle, grazing in a field of lilies." In the midrash on Song of Songs, these two breasts are first redefined so that they become a source of maternal nourishment rather than female temptation—and through that association they can become gender-fluid and morph into Moses and Aaron: "as the breasts fill with nourishing milk, so Moses and Aaron fill Israel with Torah" (Shir ha-shirim Rabbah 4:5).[65]

In the other encounter with breasts that we considered above, the rabbis, experienced codebreakers that they were, must nonetheless have toiled long over the verse "all night between my breasts / my love is a cluster of myrrh" (1:13) to reveal the ethereal love between "knesset yisrael" (the community of Israel) and her divine beloved, or to identify the phrase with Abraham in his ultimate test as father.[66]

The figure of "ha-shulamith," "the Shulamite," whose generic name could signal "resident of Jerusalem,"[67] and who would haunt the Hebrew imagination for thousands of years, was, then, first captured in the intoxicating similes and metaphors of her Song and subsequently embalmed in a series of parabolic cubicles that converted each of her body parts and erotic encounters into something else.[68]

The critical engagement with and transformation of the poetry in the Song extends from the Talmud into the Zohar to Hassidism and beyond,[69] and it is safe to say that the various iterations of the midrashic and mystical imagination, with their even more stringent correlates in Christian literature, have colonized approaches to texts that keep them safely within the boundaries of a controllable discourse.

It may be necessary to reiterate here that it is not merely the exercise of the human imagination that I am attempting to foreground, but the theological and existential distinction between two forms of the imagination: the metaphorical and the parabolic.[70] The imaginative ingenuity revealed in the rabbinic, the Zoharic, and other tendentious appropriations of the Song has been amply recognized.[71] But the imposition of the parable presupposes a Sacred Being, active in history, to replace the human act of imagination in the Song.

My own reading resonates with those that valorize this text as exhibiting the extraordinarily ordinary human capacity for metaphor and simile in celebration of human love as the highest expression of the sacred.

Some of the more interesting current investigations of the poetic qualities of Song of Songs in midrash are being conducted by Tamar Kadari. Looking at rabbinic exegesis of the Song as amenable to literary interpretation, Kadari claims that the sages themselves "regarded the Song of Songs as a poem and were attuned to its poetic qualities." She proceeds to analyze a number of passages mainly from Shir ha-shirim Rabbah in literary terms—more specifically, in structuralist terms defined by Jonathan Culler: she considers the "number of speakers," the "identity of the poetic speaker and to whom he [sic] is addressing his [sic] song, and the situation of utterance: what event is described in the Song . . . according to the rabbis and what is the atmosphere that dominates therein."[72] Among the debates Kadari brings to demonstrate the "poetic" sensitivity of the rabbinic interlocutors are, then, the questions of who is speaking and to whom. What is problematic in this account of the ingenuity of the dialectical rabbinic imagination, in addition to the seemingly unselfconscious attribution of a singular male voice,[73] is the lack of an exploration of the very license at the heart of the project—the denial, as a matter of course, of the primary speech act in the poem: the poetic human dialogue between two lovers, female and male, in a "secular" city.

One of the more ingenious turns cited by Kadari, in which the rabbis converted an explicitly earthbound text into a dialogue between God and His human interlocutor, is in the name of Rabbi Nathan:

> Rabbi Nathan interprets the opening verse of the book as an explicit attribution of authorship: "The Song of Songs, which is Solomon's" [שיר השירים אשר לשלמה].
> He interprets the name Shelomo as it sounds, but with a change in spelling: שלומו, as if it were a possessive noun: "His peace" or "He to whom peace pertains." Peace belongs to God: He is referred to as "He who makes peace." . . .
> By means of this simple exegetical move, Rabbi Nathan removes the Song of Songs from its declared author, King Solomon, and turns it into a work written by God.[74]

What Kadari refers to as a "simple exegetical move" actually indicates the radical act of rewriting involved in the rabbinic appropriation of this, as of other, problematic texts. Additional wordplays on that first line of attribution, which could signal both a mischievous cast of mind and the enormity of what is at stake, include the statement attributed to Rabban Gamaliel: "The ministering angel said it. 'The Song of Songs'—the song of the ministers (shir ha-sarim), the song that was said by the supernal ministers."[75] Such word games, implicitly acknowledging the genius of the human imagination while explicitly clipping its wings, also anticipate the freedom that will characterize Hebrew poetics in medieval Spain and in modern Israel—when, provisionally at least, the burden of exegesis will give way to the liberated mind and body. But it may be that in addition to the explicit sexual and corporeal references and the absence of any mention of holy real estate, it was precisely the literary quality of the Song that both appealed to and threatened the commentators. David Stern quotes from the Amoraic collection *Avot de-Rabbi Natan* (700–900 CE), in which the Song of Songs, along with Proverbs and Ecclesiastes, was deemed to be "hidden (*genuzim hayu*), i.e., removed from public circulation, for since they were held to be stories (*meshalot*) and not part of the Holy Writings, [the religious authorities] arose and hid them."[76] What such texts suggest is that the scriptural status of the Song was doubly problematic: as "stories" or "fictions" and as "inappropriately erotic or hedonistic."[77]

The threat of—and to—the free exercise of the imagination varies as the times demand. The ambiguous status of what Kadari calls "simple exegetical moves" that characterize rabbinic discourse will reverberate through all the diasporas and all the pathways of engagement with constitutive Jewish texts. What may be the greatest achievement of this practice, however, and the most relevant to our present concerns, is its hermetic quality. But to appreciate this requires some fine tuning in the definition of the midrashic enterprise, and here Daniel Boyarin's insights provide a clue to one of the central concerns of this chapter—namely, the relation between text and place. Arguing convincingly for a cardinal difference between allegoresis and midrash, Boyarin claims that whereas allegory, practiced by Origen and his followers, posits a world with an "outer shell and inner meaning," with an "ontological structure . . . founded in a Platonic universe," the Midrash links not "texts with their meanings, but . . . texts with texts—not signifiers and signified but signifiers with signifiers." By these lights, the Song of Songs becomes "a figurative poem interpreting the text of the love between Israel and God at the moment of their nuptials"—which Boyarin locates in the dramas of the Exodus from Egypt and the giving of the Torah.[78] This could account not only for the difference between the practices of Jewish and Christian exegetes (with allowances for overlaps that Boyarin explores), but also what I am calling the protective hermetic space in which the Midrash preserved Solomon's Jerusalem; the places that appear erased in the biblical text, become, then, present through the other texts with which the Song is in dialogue.

The contemporary theoretical debate on allegory, from Walter Benjamin to the present, is rich and ongoing and is, for the most part, beyond the scope of this chapter. I can only put a stake in the ground to signal its relevance for our focus on modern Hebrew iterations and specifically on Jerusalem. Following forms of Christian exegesis, we can discern parallels between Paul de Man's defense of allegorical forms and Julia Kristeva's embrace of Song of Songs as allegory; as I wrote elsewhere, Kristeva

> conflates [this] text with the editorial context that introduced the book into the canon in the first centuries of the common era. She celebrates what I view as the ultimate danger of allegory: not only that human love will be occluded and dwarfed by love for the divine but also that love allegorized will become the "intersection of corporeal passion and idealization, its incarnation (the spirit becoming flesh, the word-flesh)."[79]

This becomes particularly acute in times of cultural redefinition. Jon Whitman, in tracing the history of allegory, asserts that "the turn to allegorical interpretation repeatedly marks civilizations trying to keep—or in danger of losing—their intellectual and spiritual equilibrium." One point of inflection in Christian hermeneutics was Martin Luther's insistence in the sixteenth century that "the complaint in a psalm is 'literally' (ad litteram) a complaint of Christ."[80] This comes close to the various translational practices we have looked at vis-à-vis the Song, beginning with the Targum, in which the interpretation is already incorporated into the translation.

"The flock of your people, exiled and scattered, . . . haven't forgotten your folds . . . they strain to climb and clutch the fronds of your palms":[81] Jerusalem as Woman—from Midrash to Piyyut

Every attempt to unveil the Shulamite entails its own temptations and dangers. Kronfeld offers one of the most radical readings of the origin of the midrashic turn vis-à-vis the Song in the rabbinic academies: "The rabbis could invert [the text] . . . because that [act meant] . . . just returning it to the already established conventional metaphorical system of Zion as woman"—the metaphorical system that, as we saw, began in the prophetic discourse.[82]

Even a cursory glance at the prophetic discourse reveals a variety of rhetorical moves along with their built-in protections, which would be augmented in the Talmud. Although within Lamentations itself, the initial act of personifying the city as woman is already taken for granted, the scroll attributed to the prophet Jeremiah showcases new exercises for the poetic muscle. In the introduction to his translation of Lamentations, Robert Alter points to the many poetic qualities peculiar to the text.[83] The image of Zion or Jerusalem as female persona in the prophetic address that, as we saw, inaugurates the discourse of memory and consolation ("to what shall I compare thee?,"

Lam. 2:13) makes explicit the existential value of such acts of projection.[84] The license exercised here would prevail over hundreds of years of poetic invocation in times of both strife and celebration.

What is significant is the self-consciousness built into prophetic tropes. Somewhat mischievously, Kronfeld posits the radical theological absurdity inherent in a literal rendering of the poetry of prophecy: the intricately personified Jerusalem is described in the first line of Lamentations as follows:

אֵיכָה יָשְׁבָה בָדָד הָעִיר רַבָּתִי עָם הָיְתָה כְּאַלְמָנָה

> How she sits alone,
> the city once great with people.
> She has become like a widow. (Lam. 1:1)

Here, Kronfeld argues, are "logical entailments of the metaphorical system," which undermine the very foundation of biblical religion: if Zion is a widow, and God is her husband, then "Gott ist tot"![85] But, as the rabbis themselves implicitly acknowledged, it is precisely those "logical entailments of the metaphorical system," the tiny particle "like" or "as," that establish the mediation of the simile and save us from such anthropomorphic—and blasphemous— literalizations, safeguarding not only theological doctrine but also human imagination:

> She is become as a widow. Reb Judah said in Rab's name: As a widow, yet not a widow in fact: as a woman whose husband had gone overseas, but intends on returning to her. (Tractate Sanhedrin 104a)[86]

There remains a tension in such rhetorical flights that would continue to inform prayer, exegesis, and poetry over the centuries—particularly when these three come together. While Eikha Rabbah and Shir ha-shirim Rabbah would take Lamentations and the Song of Songs into the many avenues of Jewish exile, the most dramatic site of an implicit struggle between the freedoms of the imagination, the shackles of ritual context, and the dominance of exegetical discourse is the liturgical poem or *piyyut*. Originating in Palestine as early as the fifth century, the classical *piyyutim* were not, strictly speaking, diasporic in origin or orientation—though of course the absence of the Temple and its attendant rituals was constitutive of the genre. But as this tradition migrated, the pathos of exile became its major impetus—and the comforts were proffered in compensatory tropes that expressed the freedoms of the Jewish imagination. The piyyut spread throughout the Byzantine world to Egypt, Babylonia, Italy, to Spain in the tenth to twelfth centuries, to Ashkenaz (Germany), France, North Africa, Yemen, Turkey, Aleppo, and the entire Jewish Diaspora into the modern period.[87]

It became customary, at least as early as the eleventh century, to chant the Song of Songs during Passover and on other ritual occasions, and often elaborate piyyutim, interspersed with verbatim verses from the Song (usually in different font), appeared in the holiday prayerbooks or *maḥzorim*. One of the most popular examples is a piyyut for the morning Passover prayer from the tenth–eleventh century by R. Meshullam ben Kalonymus, who hailed from Italy and was one of the founders of the Ashkenazi piyyut. His alphabetical acrostic is formed by the repetition of sequential letters of the alphabet in each of the four lines of each verse; at the end of the verse is a snippet from the Song that rhymes with the second or third word of the verse and is somehow related to it. Figure 4 is one rather striking example. The verse— לִי יִשְׁקוֹד לְדׇרְשִׁי / מִכַּף מְשַׂדַּי וְחוֹרְשִׁי / לְהַרְבִּיצֵנִי בִּנְוֵה מִדְרָשִׁי—loosely translated as "He will be quick to deliver me from those who pursue me and restore me to my sanctuary," concludes with שְׂמֹאלוֹ תַּחַת לְרֹאשִׁי (His left hand beneath my head, Song 2:6).[88] The speaker is entreating God to deliver him from his oppressors, those who "plow him under" (*ḥorshai*), and to allow him to be free in the "field" or "bower" of his "midrash" (*neveh midrashi*). The commentary in Rashi script in the margins explains that "his left [arm] under my head signifies God's protection from any adversity that befalls me" (*be-khol tzara she-ʿoveret ʿalai*).[89]

While the agricultural nuance is clear from even this superficial rendering, the deeper meaning is not. There are at least two possibilities for parsing this verse, reflected by different contemporary scholars of piyyut. Almog Behar suggests that the particular intertext from the Song ("his left arm beneath my head") "is often inflected in the mystical traditions that seek for union of the human and the Divine; here the paytan expresses such desire not within the context of collective deliverance from Galut, but as privileged oneness within the confines of the beit midrash [study house], without the threat of external oppression." Ariel Zinder argues, on the other hand, that the most likely reference in "neveh midrashi" is to the redemptive return to the Holy Land and the restored Temple.[90] These conflicting interpretations reflect the inherent and ongoing tension between the exercise and celebration of diasporic liberties and the promise of redemption and restoration.

The different nuances in interpretation also reveal the subtleties of the poetic imagination as well as the particular locus of their delivery. Fishbane notes that "congregants hearing cantorial recitation [of this and other *piyyutim*] would simultaneously hear the Song framed by its rabbinic interpretations."[91] And that is precisely my point: whatever was understood by the paytan himself, by his targeted audience, or by later interpreters, the juxtaposition of text and interpretation maintains a foundational tension. Unlike the Targum that claims to convey the exact meaning of the text in a ritual context,

יוצר ליום שני של פסח

גדרש על הקב"ה שנקר' תפוח בעצי היער:יתלנוֹ כנבור מתרונן מיין כן הקב"ה שנ' ויקן כשן
הקב"ה כציבול ונדמה כאילו חגר כלי זיין להלחם בוגרים: והריק ל' ויֹרק את מכיכיו וכל זאת
התורה שכתוב בה לחֹך הכהנים איך ינכסו יין על המזבח:הביאני אל ביתהיין לבית המקדש
יתֹני ביום רֹאמון : או הביאני לבית תורה נהֹר סֹיֹ: כפות משיחכם בושֹשות חרפוני טוֹחי

כְּפוֹת מְשִׁיחֲכֶם בּוֹשֵׁשׁוֹת ׳ חֶרְפוּנִי טוֹחֵי עֲשֵׁשׁוֹת ׳
כְּלַפִּיד אֵשׁ בַּחֲשֵׁשׁוֹת ׳   סַמְכוּנִי בָּאֲשִׁשׁוֹת:

לְ יֵ יִשְׁקוֹד לְדָרְשִׁי ׳ מִכַּף מְשַׁדְּדִי וְחוֹרְשִׁי ׳
לַהֲרְבִּיצֵנִי בִּנְוֵה מִדְרָשִׁי ׳   שְׁמֹאלוֹ תַּחַת לְרֹאשִׁי:

לִסְבּוֹל עֹל גָּלוּתְכֶם ׳ בְּלִי לִדְחוֹק גְּאֻלַּתְכֶם :
לְהָחִישׁ יֶשַׁע בְּעִתְּכֶם ׳   הִשְׁבַּעְתִּי אֶתְכֶם:

מֵ רִים רֹאשִׁי וּכְבוֹדִי ׳ לֶקַח טוֹב דְּהֶזְבִּידִי :
מַלְאָכָיו צַו לְדוֹדִי ׳   קוֹל דּוֹדִי:

מִגֵּר בְּאַף מַעֲצִיבִי ׳ נַחֲלַנִי חֶמְדַּת צְבִי ׳
מִדְמֶה לְעוֹפֶר נִצִּיבִי ׳   דּוֹמֶה דוֹדִי לְצְבִי:

נֵ עֵר מֵצַר לִי ׳ עֲנָנִי בְּצַר לִי ׳
נִינִי חַסוּ בְּצִלִּי ׳   עָנָה דוֹדִי וְאָמַר לִי:

נְגִידִים לִי דִּבֵּר ׳ שִׁבְעָה קוֹלוֹת כְּמִדְבָּר ׳
נִטְפֵי מוֹר הֶעֱבַר ׳   כִּי הִנֵּה הַסְּתָיו עָבָר:

סָ כַּת שׁוֹעֵי וַיִּרֶץ ׳ שָׁלַח גּוֹדְרֵי פֶרֶץ ׳
סוֹנִים חֻבַּל כְּמָרֶץ ׳   הַנִּצָּנִים נִרְאוּ בָאָרֶץ:

סוּגָה עָֽעוֹ מוּגֵיהָ ׳ מוּף כַּדֹרוֹנֶג לְמוּגְגֵיהָ
סוֹעֲרָה מֵאֲנָחָה לַהֲפִיגֵיהָ ׳   הַתְּאֵנָה חָנְטָה פַגֶּיהָ:

עֲ זִים שָׁת כְּסֶלַע ׳ וְרָאשֵׁי תַנִּינִים לְקַלֵּעַ ׳
עֲלוֹת פְּדוּיֶה לְצֶלַע :   יוֹנָתִי בְּחַגְוֵי הַסֶּלַע:

עוז

without signaling the controls it has incorporated—and even if the piyyut has internalized the rabbinic conversion of the human love song into a paean to human-divine love—the power of the "naked text" and the freedoms of the poetic imagination are available to the literate reader or congregant alongside the exegetical-liturgical inflections meant to constrain its meaning.

One of the most fertile sites for examining the tensions inherent in this phenomenon is the poetry of the greatest of the paytanim, Yehuda Halevi (1075–c. 1141), specifically the corpus that became known as "shirei Tzion" or "poems to Zion." Infused with the growing urgency of Halevi's decision to "ascend" to the Land of Israel, these poems demonstrate that whenever the possibility arises of the return from exile and of the substantiation of biblical tropes, diasporic freedoms are endangered by passion for the hypostasized products of the imagination. I have argued at length elsewhere that the breathtaking metaphors and similes floated by Halevi while still in Andalusia became more intense and sacramental the closer he came to actually arriving in the Holy Land and to consummating his pilgrimage to the moribund, or somnolent, yet ever-enticing Zion-Woman.[92] But in this context, it should be noted that his erotic-thanatopic fantasies, animated by verses from Song of Songs, of actually mounting the hills of Jerusalem and perishing in "her" embrace—"The flock of your people, exiled and scattered, / from mountain to valley, haven't forgotten your folds, / they cling to your fringes and strain / *to climb and clutch the fronds of your palms*" (italicized words are from Song of Songs 7:9)[93]—are complemented by his repeated evocation of the Temple in the empty space that marks its ruin. That is, his own poetry becomes a compensatory projection that both grounds the imagination and reconstitutes the Temple in textual space.

Acknowledging, somewhat begrudgingly, the existence of synagogues as substitutes for the Temple, Halevi implicitly invokes the poetic and ethical privileges and freedoms that go with such mimetic edifices, while demonstrating their endangered status—without of course, acknowledging the threat to his own poetic freedom: "Are synagogues our only sanctuaries?" he asks wistfully; "How can we forget the holy mountain?"[94] In his dreamscapes, Halevi invokes the rebuilt Temple and presages his own pilgrimage, culminating in the enactment of his Levite obligations:

> I dreamed that I was in God's Temple
> watching every lovely, holy rite:
> the whole-burnt sacrifice, the meal and wine,
> the thick smoke twisting upward,
> Levites singing, me among them, blissful,
> as they did their service . . .[95]

At the conclusion of a piyyut for Passover, Halevi incorporates the verse from Song of Songs that begins "Shuvi shuvi ha-shulamith . . ." (literally, "return, return, Shulamite," Song 7:1). The Blochs translate this clause rather liberally as "Again, O Shulamite, / dance again . . ." But Halevi's version imagines the Shulamite as actually returning to a Jerusalem with its Temple restored:

> Have you thirsted to behold the splendor of God,
> and serve Him eternally?
> Return, return, O Shulamite,
> —to your Father's Shrine, as in your youth![96]

In our time, as we shall see, S. Y. Agnon's Nobel acceptance speech will resonate with similar fantasies of return to a restored Temple, though more as poetic privilege granted by his Levite lineage than as sacrificial-messianic impulse. But, as with his latter-day counterpart, Halevi's own abiding ambivalence about the locus of holiness and his nostalgia for his diasporic place of origin and the poetic and ethical privileges that adhere to it may be not only what held him back for so long but also what keep bringing modern readers back to his poetry.

The Song made its way through ritual and poetic landscapes over hundreds of years, and I have highlighted only a few of its inflections both at a distance from and in proximity to sacred space. In the next chapter, I will consider how Halevi's near-contemporary, the philosopher Maimonides (1135–1204), responded to poetic tropes in general and to the exercise of poetic privilege in relation to spatial challenges: first the anthropomorphic language in the Bible and then sacred temptations in the Holy Land. The Rambam's concern for the theological dangers involved in the presumption of proximity to the sacred—and his ambivalent attitude toward the poets whose imagery flirts with such images—will inform my entire project.

What becomes clear even from this short survey of the Song's myriad appearances over the centuries is that one threat to moral and poetic balance comes from an excessive suspicion about the products of the imagination while the other threat comes from an ecstatic passion for those same products. The sacramental, like the allegorical, move is the annihilation of the free-spirited metaphoric one. The simile acts as a kind of buffer in this ongoing seesaw: because it holds the two parts in an explicitly artificial relationship, it would seem to furnish the easiest transition to the midrashic question "le-ma ha-davar domeh?" (to what can this be compared?). One similitude that I considered in Song of Songs—the Shulamite's breasts likened to two fawns—reached in the young lover-poet's feverish mind to "har ha-mor" (the mountain of myrrh) and "giv'at ha-levona" (the hill of frankincense).[97]

These acts place human eros center stage and invoke the cosmos as a great warehouse of vehicles for its representation. But those who reverse the order are placing the Idea—theological geography—center stage as touchstone for the human universe. Then "har ha-mor" and "giv'at ha-levona" all too easily become contested hills—first on a hermeneutic and then on a political map.

"You are as majestic as Jerusalem": Return of the Poetic Imagination in the Age of Return

The allegorical lenses, such as they are, are removed in times of theological and existential upheaval that permit linguistic risk-taking and poetic invention—although such lenses may be recruited again to serve messianic or utopian impulses. Ilana Pardes reminds us that, in 1778, Johann Gottfried Herder re-appropriated the Song as an "earthly dialogue between two human lovers." This marked "a moment of radical departure from traditional allegorical readings of the text and had tremendous impact on the modern perception of the Song—first in European circles and later in Zionist ones." But, she continues, even as the Zionist project was nurtured by a preoccupation with biblical as opposed to talmudic discourse, and even if the focus on the Song was initiated by Ben Gurion's setting "the Song of Songs on a pedestal as one of the key texts of the new secular literalism" in Israeli culture which was intent on removing "the allegorical layers that had been piled upon it," this very culture would in time create its own allegorical substitutes.[98] Pardes traces the resonances of the Song in modern Zionist discourse, which is on its face more tolerant of naked bodies, unabashed sexual desire, and a liberated poetic imagination. Yet when the Zionists generated a unique parabolic system of their own, substituting love between the Jewish community and the Land of Israel for the love between God and Knesset Yisrael, they confirmed that "it is the exegetical imagination [itself that is] so riveting":

> If the exegetes of Song of Songs Rabbah were somewhat oblivious to the literal dimension of the text, the Zionists were only semi-aware of the allegories that they themselves were spinning around the ancient love poem and of their own contribution to the forging of a new mode of consecration. What is more, in the end of the day, even the Zionists ... cannot quite face the intensities of earthly eros and love.[99]

If we accept Daniel Boyarin's argument about the midrashic correlation of signifiers to signifiers, how does the modern Zionist appropriation of the Song relate to this practice? What Pardes identifies as a modern Zionist infatuation with allegory, and the widespread resistance to "fac[ing] the intensities of earthly eros and love" without exegetical camouflage, may actually, I believe, signal a process more reminiscent of the evolution of Christian allegoresis, moving beyond the internal dialogue among texts to the land-text dialectic.

Sometimes it is not unselfconscious impulses or slippage between the poetic and the allegorical but a more capacious embrace of the possibilities inherent in both the Song and the rich culture that evolved around it that accounts for complementary rather than competing sensibilities. Both Franz Rosenzweig and Zali Gurevitch, each in their own idiom, view the divine as channeled through the human love story, so that the "naked" poetic and the allegorical language come to complement rather than either contradicting or superseding the other.[100]

It is the human love story that has incited the poetic imagination throughout the Bible-reading universe in all its languages and iterations.[101] But "ha-shulamith" remains tied intrinsically to the Hebrew imagination; the dark-haired "Shulamite" clearly personifies her race as she faces the blond "Margarete" in Paul Celan's iconic poem "Todesfuge."[102] And there are more radical appropriations. It turns out that the Hebrew poetry of the late nineteenth and early twentieth centuries also includes some voices that remained under the radar for a while, not only resisting the allegorical turns, ancient and modern, but actually liberating elements of the imagination that had hardly been reclaimed since the composition of the Song. A number of scholars have explored the imagery of Song of Songs as it permeates the work of early modernist poets, male and female. Training a breathtakingly new lens on an ancient text in its modernist inflections, Chana Kronfeld also exposes unprobed possibilities in the original. Those writers who remained "on the margins of modernism," like David Fogel, Esther Raab, and Dahlia Ravikovitch, not only "reinvented Hebrew for their own time and place," but also "offer[ed] in their love poems a rather dramatic example of both the Hebrew stylistic crisis and its resolutions," liberating, in the process, forces that had lain dormant in the Song itself.[103]

Kronfeld argues for this double achievement in Fogel's eleven "maiden poems" series ("Shirei ha-na'ara"). Activating the "entire metaphorical system embedded in the Song of Songs," which elides erotic love and kinship— "the woman is a sister-bride (*ahoti kala*); the male lover is (homonymously and figuratively) an uncle (*dod*); and alternatively the man is like a brother unto the woman, a brother 'that sucked the breasts of (my) mother'"—Fogel realizes these potentialities in the most radical ways.[104] In his afterword to the Blochs' translation of the Song, Robert Alter calls attention to such sibling images and claims that "fraternal incest serves as a surprisingly beautiful metaphor"[105]—but Kronfeld takes this even further, as it provides license for modern Hebrew poets like Fogel, Raab, and Ravikovitch to create their own transgressive images.

Juxtaposing the prophetic trope of Land as Woman and the unfettered tropes in Song of Songs, Kronfeld claims that Fogel (1891–1944) abandoned the prophetic model for poetry and, essentially, adopted the Song of Songs in its pre-allegorical reading, writing a series of poems from the "female lover's point of view"[106]—a move that would contribute to his marginalization among mainstream Hebrew writers affiliated with the Zionist project.

The liberated poetic and critical forces have also generated an intriguing kind of literalism in our time, which acknowledges the erotic while literalizing the poetic. This is represented in Ariel Hirschfeld's graphic reading of the Song as a fairly accurate description of the body in a state of erotic arousal. Implicitly taking Kronfeld's argument one step further, in reference not only to contemporary Hebrew poetry but also to the original text, Hirschfeld focuses on verses 5:2–6, which he reads as presenting various images of the woman in an orgasmic state, especially the "sweet flowing myrrh" (5:5). What is most striking about this analysis, which allegedly takes its inspiration from Roland Barthes's "discours amoureux,"[107] is that it quite explicitly deprives the poetic language of its status: "Simply put, the metaphor in the lovers' discourse is the truth," Hirschfeld writes.[108] While such readings claim to liberate the imagination from the shackles of millennia of commentary, Hirschfeld's actually imposes its own kind of shackle, lessening both the power of the language of innuendo and the multivalence of metaphor and simile. Gurevitch makes a similar point while maintaining the magical, defamiliarizing, effects of poetic language.[109] But the greatest threat in our time comes from a different kind of literalism.

Song of Songs after 1967: Facing the Temple Mount

In the introduction to his commentary on the Song of Songs, as we have seen, Michael Fishbane describes and implicitly endorses the process that, through "sober reinterpretation," "recast" the human love song with its "erotic energy" into something more "spiritual."[110] This process would continue over two millennia. I argued above that the Song was kept in the formaldehyde of the "allegory of suspicion" until such time as it would be deemed safe to reclaim the ground and the body beneath the images. But what ground and what body? Are we to assume that when the exiles "return," they will finally be empowered to read the text, once again, as a love poem between a nubile young woman and a young man with the most fertile and unfettered imaginations in a Jerusalem uncluttered by holy sites? It should be clear by now that I identify with readers like Athalya Brenner; attesting to the power that the Song exercised on her as a ubiquitous cultural force in the Israel of her childhood, she went on to become a feminist Bible scholar who deems it "improbable" that a hidden intent was inherent in the original text, that "the SoS text is anything else but what it declares itself to be by its contents: songs of love and love-making between heterosexual humans."[111] And yet we have already seen that the allegorical imagination would take hold even of the so-called liberated writers of the modern Hebrew renaissance.

But the factor that is at least as important as Zionism's predilection for its own allegorical performances is the political status of the city in which the Song resonates—or what might be called the "politics of poetry." Again: in the Yishuv of the first half of the twentieth century, before the establishment of the State, the sacred center was accessible but under Ottoman and then British sovereignty—and a kind of diasporic imagination, based on mediated distances and mimetic practices, could still prevail; this intensified after 1948 under Jordanian control, when physical access was no longer possible. It may also have saved the writers and their readers from the "apocalyptic thorn" that Gershom Scholem warned against in his much-quoted letter to Franz Rosenzweig in 1926.[112]

So while early Zionist writers and poets were infatuated with the re-newed exercise of Hebrew linguistic and cultural muscles—with the license and ability to engage texts like Song of Songs without need of translation or other forms of mediation, and to encounter a Hebrew whose putatively late date of composition or compilation made it more accessible than that of other biblical texts—there also remained crucial continuities with lessons and constraints acquired in "exile." The liberating force of metaphor and the freedoms granted by distance from the sacred would be tested when Israel captured East Jerusalem in the war of 1967.

We have already seen that in the half century of Israeli control over what came to be called the "Holy Basin," messianic urgency has been reignited, obscuring these hard-won lessons and practices. As the Jewish citizens of Is-rael have become increasingly God-intoxicated, as exclusive claims of owner-ship increase the probability of catastrophe, fundamental treasures have been lost: the biblical vocalization of the naked human love song and the diasporic wisdom that privileges the imagination as buffer against the fatal results of proximity to the sacred.

I have been arguing that the particular palimpsest of Bible-plus-midrash was needed to preserve the love song both in its day and as a poetic text to ac-company the Jews in their diasporic spaces, promoting a culture of interpre-tation to replace the cultic practices of proximity. How, then, is our latter-day license to be understood: as a reclaiming of the *nimshal*, that is, a reified version of the rabbinic imagination—a return not to the Shulamite's breasts, but to the holy ark? By these lights, a return to the lovers' "couch" would be a return to (read: restoration of) the Temple in Jerusalem.

The implications of this claim go beyond hermeneutics or the status of the free or fettered exercise of the imagination within a community of faith. Since the floodgates were opened by the military victory in 1967 and the subsequent "unification" of the entire city,[113] young priests have been practicing sacrificing goats on Passover, red heifers are being bred, and Levites are weaving the garments for the High Priest to wear on Yom Kippur in the "Third Temple."[114] In so doing, they are not only denying the legitimacy of other sacred structures and claims of other religions on the Temple Mount/Haram al Sharif, but also obliterating millennia of imaginative and mediated Jewish encounters with that place. They are literalizing and territorializing not the Song itself, but the rabbinic and mystical transmutations of that text; they are denying, that is, both that the Song ever existed in its "naked" poetic form and that talmudic acrobatics have legitimacy as a self-conscious mental exercise in their own right at a distance from the sacred center, and as both preservative and buffer against the idolatry of proximity.

As a counterargument to that form of idolatry, and a gesture to the unfettered religious imagination, I would endorse Robert Alter's reading of a "kind of divinity" into the Song itself: "In a poem that never mentions God's name, love provides access to a kind of divinity; the physicality of love in the Song is an implicit metaphysics of love."[115] The authors of the Song may indeed have gestured toward the "metaphysics of love," but it would take over two thousand years to begin to realize this promise. S. Y. Agnon and Yehuda Amichai, two modern Hebrew writers born elsewhere, were each to take their stand in Jerusalem and reshape the traditional texts and their political-cultural resonances for generations to come. I will argue that it was in the breach between the human self and the sacred center that Agnon knew his place to be; yet he could hardly actualize it for himself or his characters.[116] Amichai and his poetic selves lived in that breach.

One of the last verses of Shir ha-shirim has a curious circumlocution that returns us to the Shulamite's breasts:

אֲנִי חוֹמָה וְשָׁדַי כַּמִּגְדָּלוֹת אָז הָיִיתִי בְעֵינָיו כְּמוֹצְאֵת שָׁלוֹם. (Song 8:10)

Literally, the verse means: "I am a wall / and my breasts are [as] towers; then I was in his eyes as one who finds shalom." In parsing this enigmatic verse, Carol Meyers emphasizes the military image projected onto the female body;[117] Yair Zakovitch suggests, more poetically, that it resolves the enigmatic exchange between the Shulamite and her brothers.[118] But when Chana Bloch rendered this verse "I am a wall / and my breasts are towers. / But for my lover I am a city of peace," she may have been superimposing the spirit of Yehuda Amichai, whom she also translated, on the biblical text. In one of Amichai's last poems, "two lovers talking to each other in Jerusalem" explicate, "with the excitement of tour guides," the "archaeological layers" of their bodies and souls, their thighs and eyes, the "mosaic" of their "spirit" from far away and long ago. At the end of the catalogue, they announce, as a kind of obvious conclusion: "*we* are holy places" (*anaḥnu mekomot kedoshim*; emphasis mine).[119]

"Apples of gold in ornaments of silver": Maimonides's Guide to the Poetic Imagination

The Guide of the Perplexed (1185–91), Dalalāt al-Hairin or Moreh ha-nevokhim,[1] the monumental treatise by Moses ben Maimon (known by his Hebrew acronym as the Rambam), or Maimonides, has as one of its primary goals to help the intelligent, philosophically trained reader navigate through the figures of speech that inform biblical language—in particular, that of the prophets—to find the truth enfolded in such figures. The medieval philosopher's defense of biblical discourse would elevate rationality while leaving space for poetic impulses. A tour de force in what might be called the "poetics of theology," it can also serve, in rather surprising ways, as a guide through the labyrinth of modern temptations that he could hardly have anticipated. The convergence of poetic and hermeneutic energies in the wide gravitational force field that radiated from medieval Andalus and presented certain challenges for Maimonides's contemporaries and immediate successors are, mutatis mutandis, replicated in Israeli poetics and politics, particularly in the second half of the twentieth century and the early decades of the twenty-first.

In the dedicatory epistle to his disciple, Joseph ben Yehuda, who had moved from Morocco to Alexandria, Maimonides explains that he wrote it because "you were perplexed and . . . your absence moved me to compose this Treatise."[2] As Joel Kraemer writes, "by making Joseph the formal addressee, Maimonides signaled who his target audience was—intellectuals learned in the law and initiated into the arcana of philosophy and science who were perplexed by Scripture's contradictions of reason."[3] Even in modern Hebrew, navokh means perplexed or abashed. Every reader who approaches this text with an open mind, and at least minimal training in philosophy and/or Hebrew/Arabic hermeneutics and poetics, feels personally addressed in this treatise.

The conundrum at the center of Maimonides's *Guide* is simply stated: by its very nature, figurative language, especially as it relates to the Divine, violates the basic injunction against anthropomorphic representation and therefore constitutes a mendacious form of speech bordering on idolatry. Since God is categorically lacking in any attribute associated with material bodies or physical entities, the assignation of corporeality, even in acts of representation, remains suspect. And yet it is impossible for ordinary mortals to "apprehend" the invisible or to "approach" the incorporeal. As Menachem Lorberbaum writes, the Rambam is concerned not just with the "what" but with the "how": how can human beings express what cannot, what must not, be articulated?[4]

Poetic creativity, speaking in "similitudes," is, then, deemed both necessary *and suspect* in the world Maimonides is addressing—and both the necessity and the danger will again become consequential in our time. Even though Maimonides is addressing his fellow Jews in exile in the twelfth century, by focusing on the metaphoric imagination and its function in prophetic language, by taking explicit and implicit stands in theory and in practice vis-à-vis the spatialization of the Jewish imagination, he actually foreshadows the challenges that will become politically and theologically consequential eight hundred years later, in the Age of Return (שיבת ציון)—and more particularly, after the capture of and proprietary claims to sacred sites on the Temple Mount and throughout the West Bank. We have already begun to explore how the presumed reintegration of land and language, of territory and text, in post-1967 Israel would come to compete with and all but supplant millennia-old diasporic strategies of approaching the Divine through distance and simulacra. In his own twelfth-century idiom, the Rambam is instructing those who have the patience to follow him as to the idolatrous and potentially lethal consequences of return to a "material" encounter with the Divine.

Nothing demonstrates this point more than the extension of the definition of idolatry in the *Guide* to worship of the Divine as manifest *in space*.[5] I submit that the risk of literalization of figures of speech is at least as consequential for the modern thinker, writer, or politician in proximity to the physical sites of holiness as it was for the medieval philosopher.

It will be necessary, as we proceed, both to connect and to distinguish between the ways that God is perceived as sacred and the ways that space, time, or objects can be sacred. As we shall see, objects can be vessels or veils for the sacred, even if God per se cannot be contained in a bodily envelope. In safeguarding the rational constraints on imaginative flights of fancy while protecting the very license to engage the imagination, Maimonides is, I believe, warning against the real danger: that of falling in love with the object of one's desire, even when—especially when—that object is Zion or the physical habitations or emanations of God "Himself."[6] At risk is a hard-won understanding of both the liberating function of figures of speech and their constraints in Jewish thought. The literalized, spatialized image may be the most insidious form of idol worship because it is so deeply couched in the recesses of the Hebrew imagination.

I am not claiming Maimonides either as a proto-Zionist or as a proto-*post*-Zionist, but as one who articulated in his own idiom the dangers as well as the temptations of a physical approach to the sacred. Anachronistic readings of classical Hebrew texts may have been sanctioned in the first place by the talmudic rejection of chronological fidelity.[7] Nevertheless, I am aware that uncritical, ideologically driven anachronism can turn a scholarly endeavor into a procrustean bed in which to fit our politically convenient readings of long dead authors. The most egregious example is the appropriation of Yehuda Halevi as, by turns, hailing, resisting, or remaining extraneous to the Zionist project *avant la lettre*.[8] *The Guide of the Perplexed* invites such readings by presenting itself self-consciously as a vessel to be unlocked by the keys vested in the secret sharer in each generation (and, presumably, specific to the exigencies of the generation), thereby safeguarding the secret while countenancing privileged points of entry. James Arthur Diamond calls attention to the Maimonidean distinction that originates in Proverbs between *ishim* or "people," those who are *called* by God, and *bnei adam* or "sons of man," the multitude who can hear the words that speak in "their" language but cannot plumb their depths.[9]

If the first of the *ishim* or interlocutors was Joseph ben Judah, the pupil explicitly designated by Maimonides in direct address in the *Guide* itself, he was soon joined by Samuel Ibn Tibbon and Judah al Harizi, the two contemporaries who translated the *Guide* into Hebrew, and by Maimonides's son Abraham. There ensues a long procession of self-appointed addressees—and Kraemer goes so far as to insist that Maimonides's use of "you" turns every reader into an addressee.[10] In our time, as I will elaborate later, I would single out Leo Strauss and Shlomo Pines, who collaborated on the monumental two-volume English translation of the *Guide* published in 1963.

What is common to all the self-selected readers over the ages is the presumption of a carefully guarded secret that the interlocutor can unlock and divulge selectively to his (*sic!*) learned contemporaries. But perhaps the first of the "secret sharers" was Maimonides himself, who by more than innuendo designated himself the heir to Hebrew prophecy; more specifically, as Kraemer writes, he "saw himself as Moses *redivivus*, a redeemer and savior of his people."[11] This self-coronation is ratified by the popular accolade, ממשה עד משה לא קם כמשה (from Moses to Moses there has never been one like Moses).[12]

Moses ben Maimon was not only constrained by rational philosophical principles and procedures; his faith in redemption punctuates his writings and, in certain respects, provided inspiration for such early kabbalists
as Abraham Abulafia (1240–c. 1291). But even if he identified with the first
Moses, the greatest of all prophets and lawgivers, and even as he—possibly
in response to popular sentiment couched in family tradition—went so far
as to calculate the messianic advent down to the day,[13] a few strictures in his
thought and action qualify the man universally revered and referred to as
"the Great Eagle"[14] to serve as dialogic partner with modern Hebrew writers,
thinkers, and actors. His careful attention to figures of speech, his complex
approach to sacrificial Judaism, and his ambivalence or even diffidence about
the settlement of the Holy Land and spatialization of the sacred in active anticipation of the advent of the Messiah can act as both inspiration for and
constraint upon contemporary poetics and politics.

Similes, Parables, Metaphors

And by the ministry of the prophets have I used similitudes . . .

וביד הנביאים אדמה . . .

HOSEA 12:11

The Guide of the Perplexed sets out methodically to monitor the necessary
but dangerous properties of representational speech, particularly the anthropomorphic and anthropopathic language attributed to the Divine. In Maimonides's view, the biblical world, replete with figurative language, is protected from idolatrous temptations in the first instance by the dominant
presence of Moses, who was the only one to "face" God and speak to Him
"mouth to mouth" (Num. 12:8; *Guide* I:37, p. 86; *Guide* III:51, p. 628; and see
below). Furthermore, he claims, Moses was the only prophet who did not
speak through "similitude" or "parable": "the imaginative faculty did not enter into his prophecy" (שלא התנבא במשל כשאר הנביאים, II:36, p. 373; see also II:45,
p. 403).[15] The "imaginative faculty" is the broad English rendering of the word
mashal in Ibn Tibbon's (and Kapach's) Hebrew translation of this passage,
which also signals its ubiquity in exegetical discourse throughout the Jewish
Diaspora. As we have seen, this term, with its origin in talmudic discourse,
means, loosely, a compressed story whose apprehension is controlled by the
nimshal or official interpretation. But in Maimonides's text, "mashal" gestures
toward all iterations of the imaginative faculty—signaling, interchangeably,
"parable," "figure of speech," or similitude.

Besides Moses, the other prophets, who liberally employ figures of speech, are disciplined by the divine encounters that engender the prophetic word and by their own highly developed rational faculties. As vessel of God's word, then, the prophet comprehends the ungarbed and unembodied nature of divinity while using imagery (the "imaginative faculty") to convey what is incomprehensible to the uninitiated. Prophecy is "an overflow overflowing from God, may He be cherished and honored, through the intermediation of the Active Intellect, toward the rational faculty in the first place and thereafter toward the imaginative faculty" (*Guide* II:36, p. 369).

Anybody with the requisite faculties and training is conditioned to avoid the temptations of literalizing or hypostasizing figurative language by not attributing autonomous value to it. The perfected qualities of the prophet are thus meant to be replicated, up to a point, by disciplined reader responses. The figures that pervade prophetic rhetoric have only one purpose, according to Maimonides, who proceeds by means of his own intricate metaphors and parables as well as through exegesis and elaboration of biblical and rabbinic rhetoric: as human speech, similitudes, parables, riddles, and images appear to have relatively little worth in themselves; rather, they constitute a silver "*filigree*" or "*ornament*" (משכיות) through which the initiate can glimpse the golden apple within—the truth of the Law (introduction to *Guide*, I, pp. 10–11; italics in the quotation refer to a biblical or talmudic prooftext).[16] This image, itself rather enigmatic, is from Proverbs 25:11, which tradition attributes to the authorship of King Solomon: "A word fitly spoken is like apples of gold in ornaments of silver" (תפוחי זהב במשכיות כסף דבר דבור על אפניו).[17] Even if the silver ornament is of less value than the gold that it both conceals and reveals, figures of speech not only are not worthless—since in the world of affairs silver is prized for its own value—but are the pinnacle of human achievement.

From this we might infer that poetry and the sister arts are prized in the marketplace for their evocative power, if not ostensibly for their truth value. Leo Strauss, in his introduction to Shlomo Pines's translation of the *Guide*, argues that there is generally more poetic freedom in the biblical texts than in their postbiblical incarnation as prooftexts in the Talmud; in his reading, Maimonides sets up a "tacit confrontation" between "the talmudic view according to which the outer [façon] of the similes is 'nothing' and . . . Solomon's view according to which it is 'silver,' i.e., politically useful."[18] That is, Strauss argues, Maimonides is implicitly siding with the biblical view in not only performing and explaining but also valorizing poetic speech. (And, it should go without saying, both the gold *and* the silver in the original proverb are metaphors!)

Three of the rhetorical dimensions explored in the *Guide* speak directly to our concerns: the status of the imaginative faculty; the function and differentiation of figures of speech; and the interrogated poetics of spatiality.

The Imaginative Faculty: Poets and "Preachers"

Like Plato, Maimonides condemns precisely that writing which can be considered the most "poetic"—that which is not indentured to the unchanging truth or the disciplined passions. Those "poets and preachers" or masters of the rhetorical flourish (in Ibn Tibbon's Hebrew translation, from 1204, they are rendered as המשוררים והמליצים) may not be mindful of the false affect, movement, and corporeality they attribute to God, even when their prooftexts are biblical.[19] They then claim the license to "take [their images] according to their external meaning, to derive from them inferences and secondary conclusions, and to found upon them various kinds of discourses" (*Guide* I:59, p. 141). These poets, or would-be poets—[20] מי שיחשב שהוא עושה שיר—who do not seem to acknowledge that it is in *silence* that God is best apprehended and celebrated (לך דומיה תהלה, Ps. 65; *Guide* I:59, p. 139) suffer from an overflow of the imaginative faculty without prior development of the rational faculty (*Guide* II:37; see also III:51). This is so dangerous as to amount in some cases to "an absolute denial of faith" that should make wise men "laugh"—or "weep" (*Guide* I:59, p. 141).[21]

Yet, having made such a strong denunciation, Maimonides refuses to cite specific examples, claiming that he is "unwilling to set out the deficiencies of those who make these utterances" (*Guide* I:59, p. 141). The implicit acknowledgment of the incompatibilities between the poetic and the philosophical impulse never amounts, then, to an explicit condemnation of any specific poetic project, though Maimonides comes close to it in his consideration of the religious poetry that enters the prayer canon. Intimating, perhaps, that such writers may be erasing the line between the literal and the figurative, he never goes further, possibly because those authors, the *paytanim*, are his esteemed predecessors and contemporaries, and many of them, like Yehuda Halevi, are philosophers in their own right.[22]

Norman Roth surveys the debate among modern scholars over the degree and intent of Maimonides's condemnation of poetry and the poets; I will only allude here to some of the major voices in this debate. Isadore Twersky was the most vehement in claiming that poetry "aroused Maimonides's ire [and that he] indiscriminately lambasted their authors . . . with a mixture of Platonic disdain and Voltairean irony."[23] After reviewing the relevant passages, primarily in Arabic, Roth concludes that Maimonides's position was far more ambiguous. Like Plato, again, Maimonides indeed objected mainly to love poetry, for its arousal of lust; in regard to Hebrew, his objection was that it defiles the holy tongue. But the medieval philosopher, who did quote Yehuda Halevi at least once in a letter,[24] who was at least as influenced by Aristotle as by Plato,[25] was himself a sometime poet, and, most important for our discussion, demonstrates in the *Guide* through the extensive use and analysis of figures of speech, especially of similes and parables, the exquisite power of figurative language—used "under caution."

What is crucial here is that while Maimonides is explicitly endorsing figurative language in the Bible as necessary to prophetic communication, given the limitations of human comprehension of invisible truth, he is implicitly devaluing postbiblical, exilic poetry as dangerous—not intrinsically, but because it escapes the bounds of prophetic discipline. He seems to assume that regardless of their native capacity, diasporic writers cannot exercise the self-discipline of the prophets—since they cannot, by definition, have been visited by God. As we have already seen, such visitation is the first of the two authorizing criteria for the use of poetic language.

Maimonides appears, then, to ratify the poetic language of the receiver, but not the maker, in Diaspora. That is, it would seem to be all right to *read* the poetry of prophetic discourse in *galut*, with the proper discipline and constraints, even to incorporate it in a selective and controlled manner into the liturgy—but to *compose* it without the natural constraints that devolved on the prophets is to enter into a very dangerous realm. Indeed, Maimonides refers to prophets who are in exile as being deprived of "vision" from the Lord, since "prophecy was taken away during the time of the Exile [and] . . . the instrument has ceased to function."[26] He holds as an article of faith that prophecy will be "restored to us in its habitual form, as has been promised in the days of the Messiah, may he be revealed soon" (*Guide* II:36, p. 373). And yet there are other indications throughout the *Guide* that this latter-day Moses embraced the possibility that certain diasporic souls may be worthy vessels of prophecy: "Many texts . . . maintain this fundamental principle that God turns whom He wills it, into a prophet—but only someone perfect and superior to the utmost degree" (*Guide* II:32, p. 362).[27] And as an occasional poet himself, he frequently demonstrates the ambiguities and internal contradictions in his own position.

Alive or Dead: The "Life" of Figures of Speech

In a discussion of the philosophical and cultural ambience that constitutes the background to Maimonides's theory of poetic forms, Mordechai Z. Cohen draws a distinction between the "hermeneutic" and the more "poetic" models of metaphor, and acknowledges the medieval Jewish exegete's natural embrace of the former as applied to Hebrew scripture.[28] But Cohen shows that in regard to the linguistic categories that are being interrogated in the *Guide*, Maimonides combines the two. The Arabic term *isti'āra* (lit., borrowing) is the translation of the Greek μεταφορά (*metaphora*); its Hebrew equivalent is השאלה (*hashalah*) or השם המושאל (*ha-shem ha-mushal*), "the borrowed name." *Isti'āra*, Cohen explains, is a "poetic borrowing intended to conjure up an imaginary scene . . . Instead of determining the metaphorical sense of these BH [Biblical Hebrew] terms, Maimonides observes that Scripture imaginatively 'lends them' (i.e., attributes the limbs they denote) to God."[29]

What is being borrowed and *for how long* may be the two central questions in Maimonides's interrogation of this form, as well as our own conduit into the dilemmas of the modern Hebrew writer in Jerusalem.

Without trying to reproduce Cohen's elaborate analysis, I want to focus on his discussion of the one-time, temporary or temporal—i.e., "vital"—metaphor as opposed to those images that have become so commonplace as to have lost their originality along with (what might be called) their toxicity. In the case of the latter, the very quality that has been borrowed, the *tenor* in I. A. Richards's system, supersedes or colonizes the *vehicle*. In the first forty-nine chapters, which form what Cohen calls the long "lexicographic" unit in the *Guide*,[30] Maimonides considers the process by which metaphorical constructions involving bodily parts, functions, and properties have, for all intents and purposes, been voided of their figurative power. The word "wing" (כָּנָף), for example, is presented as having migrated denotatively from the appendage of a living airborne creature to the "extremities and corners of garments" to "the farthest ends and extremities of the habitable parts of the earth" (as in "that it may take hold of the wings [i.e., ends] of the earth," Job 38:13; *Guide* I:43, pp. 93–94). Such "use became so frequent in the [Hebrew] language and so widespread," Maimonides concludes, "that it has become, as it were, *the first meaning*" (emphasis mine; the Arabic signifies "*conventional meaning*," *Guide* I:30, p. 64).[31] These locutions, which do not call attention to themselves anymore as acts of the imagination, have, for all intents and purposes, taken on the ontological status of the signified; they reflect the "semantic" or "semantic-substitution" theory of metaphor, stretching from Aristotle into the twentieth century.[32]

Myriad examples make it clear that particularly in regard to anthropomorphisms, such common constructs are less in danger of idolatrous trespass than are the live, "vital," or one-time metaphors: if, as Cohen argues, God's *eyes* are invoked frequently to signify providence, the frequency "indicates that it can be applied to God without activating the literal sense, which would conjure up an image of His eyes."[33] Cohen continues that Maimonides appears to have "manipulated" the categories of his Muslim predecessors and his own earlier writing "in order to devise a distinctive approach to the problem of biblical anthropomorphism . . . [Being] uncomfortable with the prospect of imagining God in human form . . . by ignoring the special poetic charm of the anthropomorphic biblical locution, [he] reveals his preference for theological and philosophical propriety over literary sensitivity."[34]

That may indeed be the conclusion that Maimonides would want us—the uninitiated, the vulnerable, the still-"perplexed"—to reach; however, what might be called his obsessive preoccupation with figures of speech and his acrobatic efforts to detoxify them suggest the very opposite—at least they do to this reader. Far from "ignoring the special poetic charm of the anthropomorphic biblical locution," as Cohen claims, the Rambam seems, based on the inconsistencies and internal conflicts in his own writing, to be engaged in a near-desperate attempt to control the consequences of its charm—and, more important, its power.[35] The more acceptable epistemological and theological status of what would today be called "dead metaphor"—i.e., as Cohen explains it, "one used so often that it is not perceived as such and functions as a literal expression"[36]—seems to provide at least a partial solution to this seeming contradiction.

Paul Ricoeur describes the necessary tension that defines metaphor. "In the case of . . . dead metaphor, the tension with the body of our knowledge disappears . . . In living metaphor, on the other hand, this tension is essential." Myth, he acknowledges, following Cassirer, "represents a level of consciousness where tension with the body of our knowledge has not yet appeared."[37]

In any discussion of the legitimacy of figurative language in the context of the religious imagination, each position is determined by the status accorded the free exercise of human creativity. The ongoing debate about whether writers of the Hebrew Bible used figurative language self-consciously, or whether that self-consciousness was introduced into the later books under Greek or Persian or other influences, is beyond the purview of this chapter, except that I must note once again the prevalence of clearly self-conscious metaphoric constructs in such texts as Lamentations and, of course, in the sui generis Song of Songs.[38] Recent research by scholars of ancient and medieval thought and literature, including Kalman Bland and Daniel Boyarin, suggests a much more complex approach to anthropomorphic language, as well as to acts of representation in general, than the more common concept of aniconism would reveal. Bland argues that "Greek philosophers and Israelite prophets [may have] preferred to speak or write their minds rather than paint or sculpt their ideas. They nevertheless found visual images irresistible and visual metaphors indispensable ... Moses Maimonides spoke for them all when he 'likened prophecy to dream images generated by imagination and seen by the mind's metaphorical eye.'"[39]

Obviously, medieval theories of language, of mythopoesis, and of the poetic imagination—informed by the rich interweave of Jewish and Arabic praxis and philosophy inflected by Greek models—and the intricate and dynamic scholarly discourse around them can be acknowledged here only in the most cursory fashion.[40] But debates on what constitutes tradition or trespass are very much alive in contemporary cultural theory. In our own time, Paul de Man's broadside against metaphor dominated literary studies for decades. And coming from another quarter is the current proliferation of interest in and valorization of myth and mysticism or of esoteric readings of classical texts. At the risk of simplification, I am suggesting for our purposes a distinction between those who regard the image—simile, metaphor, conceit—as a degraded form of myth or of the naïve, literal, animated view of the world that is organic with its language and those who regard metaphor as the highest exercise of the freedom of imagination.

Cohen acknowledges that Maimonides privileges dead over live metaphors. And no less significantly, the twelfth-century rationalist explicitly endorses the preferred talmudic literary form, the parable or *mashal* (משל), over the more elusive and insubordinate metaphorical construction *hashalah* (השאלה)—as demonstrated in his own parable of the palace, which I will discuss below. The Rambam even allows for a certain exegetical freedom regarding the various parts of the *mashal* as long as the overriding meaning can be parsed. In his earlier *Mishneh Torah*, written in Hebrew and thus devoid of some of the nuances and challenges of Arabic poetics, he wrote: "The matters communicated to the prophet in a prophetic vision are communicated to him in symbolic form [i.e., by way of parable—*derekh mashal*—דרך משל]. And immediately the interpretation [or solution] (פתרון—*pitron*) of the *mashal* is impressed upon his mind in a vision so that he grasps what it symbolizes (lit., is)."[41] The examples he brings, among others, are of Jacob's ladder and Jeremiah's steaming pot and almond tree. In the dedicatory epistle to the *Guide*, Maimonides makes this quite explicit:

> When, therefore, you find that in ... this Treatise I have explained the meaning of a parable [*mashal*] and have drawn your attention to the general proposition signified by it, you should not inquire into all the details occurring in the parable, nor should you wish to find significations corresponding to them ... Your purpose, rather, should always be to know, regarding most parables, the

whole that was intended to be known . . . [In a given instance] my remarking that [a given story] is a parable will be like someone's removing a screen from between the eye and a visible thing. (Epistle Dedicatory, *Guide*, I, p. 14)

Similes are, for purposes of this discussion, grouped together with parables as amenable to a clear one-to-one correspondence and therefore more controllable by the rational exegete.[42]

Metaphoric constructs that are original, one-time flights of fancy are, therefore, far more dangerous. But what exactly is the danger? It is of *literalization*. The untutored mind is apt to think that God speaks, sees, and has all the functions and therefore limitations of the human being. But the danger, I believe, goes beyond that: it is the worship of things, including *space itself*, that Maimonides is really warning us against.

Parable of the Palace: Interrogating the Poetics of Spatiality

Opening his treatise with a series of glosses on physical nouns such as "place" (the highly charged word *makom*)[43] or "throne" and verbs, gerunds, or verbal nouns designating motion in space—"to descend [descending]," to "ascend [ascending]," "to sit, to arise, to approach [sitting, arising, approaching]" (I:8–13, pp. 33–39; see also I:18, pp. 43–45; I:26, pp. 56–57)—Maimonides goes so far into the logic of his argument as to make a claim against *space itself* as the locus of the divine-human encounter. As a kind of intermediary form, the gerund or, in Hebrew, the action noun is a substantive that suggests motion. Since it is in history or action rather than in corporeal attributes that God should be known, there is a preference for this form over the static noun. The union between the self and God is a

> union in knowledge and drawing near through apprehension, not in [lit., of] space . . . Every mention of approaching and coming near that you find in the books of prophecy referring to a relation between God, may He be exalted, and a created being has this last meaning. For God, may He be exalted, is not a body, as shall be demonstrated to you in this Treatise. And, accordingly, He, may He be exalted, does not draw near to or approach a thing, *nor does anything draw near to or approach Him, may He be exalted, inasmuch as the abolition of corporeality entails that space be abolished* [lit., "Inasmuch as in virtue of the abolition of corporeality space is abolished"]; so that there is no nearness and proximity, and no remoteness, no union and no separation, no contact and no succession. (*Guide* I:18, p. 44, emphasis mine)

That Jews live in time, not in space, that the divine word is located in the portable scroll or text, and that the divine presence fills the entire universe—and is not limited to one mountain or one edifice—seems to need periodic reaffirmation. The only exception to the prohibition on "nearness and proximity" is the biblical Moses, who approaches the "place on the mountain upon which the light, I mean the glory of God, has descended" (*Guide* I:18, pp. 44–45). One may deduce from this that it is only Moses—the one prophet who is never in danger of misusing language—who can approach spatially, and even then it is clearly only Mount Sinai, and not any other sacred center (i.e., the Temple Mount), that can be considered consecrated space in which such an encounter is possible.[44]

What follows throughout the treatise is a fairly methodical effort to expose all spatial imagery, all forms of motion, indeed all materiality, as a function of the limited human perception of what is incorporeal and inhabits neither space nor time. So Maimonides's parable of the palace at the end of the *Guide* takes the reader by surprise:

> The ruler is in his palace [Heb. *ha-melekh be-armono*], and all his subjects are partly within the city and partly outside the city. Of those who are within the city, some have turned their backs upon the ruler's habitation or courtyard [Heb. *ḥatzar ha-melekh*]; their faces being turned another way. Others seek to reach the ruler's habitation, turn toward it, and desire to enter it and to stand before him, but up to now they have not yet seen the wall of the habitation. Some of those who seek to reach it have come up to the habitation and walk around it searching for its gate. Some of them have entered the gate and walk about in the antechambers [Heb. *ba-prozdorim*]. Some of them have entered the inner court of the habitation [Heb. *reḥavat he-ḥatzer*] and have come to be with the king, in one and the same place with him, namely, in the ruler's habitation. But their having come into the inner part of the habitation does not mean that they see the ruler or speak to him. For after their coming into the inner part of the habitation, it is indispensable that they should make another effort; then they will be in the presence of the ruler, see him from afar or from nearby, or hear the ruler's speech or speak to him. (*Guide* III:51, pp. 618–19)[45]

The supplicants' orientations and degrees of proximity to the ruler become the subject of the extended interpretation of this passage, which precedes Kafka's Castle by eight centuries. Coming near the end of the *Guide*, it is defined explicitly as a *mashal* or parable. Granted, as we have seen, the *mashal* is more acceptable in Maimonides's eyes than the "vital" metaphor; since it doesn't exist autonomously without its interpretation, its *nimshal* or *pitron*, it is amenable to hermeneutic control. And since, as we have also seen, the parable or *mashal* supposedly means only one thing, the "parts" need not be interpreted. Nevertheless, I submit that there is within this parable, even when adjusted for overriding exegesis, a revelation of an ongoing internal struggle that can never be fully resolved.

Most significant is the key word that signifies place or placement in the parable. From the above passage, the reader may have already discerned a difference between the English and the Hebrew translations; these reflect different interpretations of the Arabic *dār*, commonly understood as *house*, but according to Joseph David Kapach, who edited and commented on the more recent Hebrew edition, this rendering is based on an early mistranslation; Shlomo Pines replicates this in his English rendition. The Hebrew word *ḥatzer*, on the other hand, signifies a courtyard or anteroom, which would then yield to the *prozdorim* or antechambers. Needless to say, this is a significant issue of interpretation as well as translation.

Maimonides's parsing of his own *mashal* makes it absolutely clear that those at the highest level of rational development are inside the palace. If the journey to truth has been rendered through a sustained spatial conceit, we might assume, given our knowledge of his aniconism, that it is those with their faces *turned another way* who would be valorized. Yet within the universe of the parable, those who have achieved the "rank of the prophets" are imagined as having a kind of physical proximity to the ruler (*Guide* III:51, p. 620). The Rambam's ethnic Great Chain of Being, offensive to modern eyes,[46] is very revealing:

> Those who are outside the city are all human individuals who have no doctrinal belief, neither one based on speculation nor one that accepts the authority of tradition: such individuals as the furthermost Turks found in the remote North, the Negroes found in the remote South, and those who resemble them from among them that are with us in these climes. The status of those is like that of irrational animals . . . Those who are within the city, but have turned their backs upon the ruler's habitation, are people who have . . . adopted incorrect opinions. [And so it goes, until we arrive at the one] who has achieved demonstration, to the extent that that is possible, of everything that may be demonstrated; and who has ascertained in divine matters, to the extent that that is possible, everything that may be ascertained; and who has come close to certainty in those matters in which one can only come close to it—has come to be with the ruler in the inner part of the habitation [Heb. *he-ḥatzer*]. (*Guide* III:51, pp. 618–19; Heb. p. 404)

The most palpable, physical object, the resplendent palace or courtyard of the ruler, like the magnificent silver filigree that encases the golden apple—and the parabolic form itself—appears simultaneously, then, as both affirmation of and injunction against the material world and the poetic imagination that represents it.

The complex moves between a discussion of figurative language and a consideration of spatiality and materiality demonstrate how logically inter-connected they are. It is no accident that these passages influenced the work and practice of later mystics such as Abraham Abulafia. And Maimonides implicitly recognizes the danger to which his older contemporary, the poet Yehuda Halevi, arguably, succumbed: the love of the object of his own imagining and the impulse driving him toward physical union with it. In the *Kuzari*, Halevi's philosophical treatise on the comparative merits of Judaism, Christianity, Islam, and philosophy, written shortly before the poet undertook his ill-fated pilgrimage to the Holy Land, the Rabbi who is Judaism's proponent explains to his interlocutor that the "Sabbath begins in China eighteen hours later than in Palestine, since the latter lies in the center of the world."[47] Compare the following passage from the *Guide*, which we glanced at in chapter 1:

> You must, however, hold fast to the doctrinal principle [lit., root] that there is no difference whether an individual is at the center of the earth, or, supposing that this were possible, in the highest part of the ninth heavenly sphere. For he is not farther off from God in the one case [lit., here] and no nearer to Him in the other [lit., there]. (*Guide* I:18, pp. 44–45)

אין הפרש בין היות האיש במרכז הארץ או בעליון שבגלגל התשיעי (אלו היה אפשר)—
שהוא לא ירחק מן ה׳ הנה ולא יקרב לו שם. (תה.אבן תיבון, א׳ ,עמ׳ 92)[48]

Perhaps even more provocative with respect to Maimonides's "doctrinal principle" is Yehuda Halevi's poem "The Palace of God" (הֵיכַל אֲדֹנָי וּמִקְדָּשׁ הֲדֹמוֹ), where the poet graphically evokes the divine palace and the Temple as the physical orientation of the scattered flock of Israel:

> The palace of God and the Temple, His footstool—
> gone is its glory, its people are scattered.
> Yet from afar they all send their greetings,
> bowing toward it, each man from his place.
>
> . . . The remnant of Zion residing in Spain
> here among Arabs, there among Christians—
> trembling, ready to leap toward the Temple . . .
> dream of themselves returning to Zion . . .[49]

"This poem," claims Raymond Scheindlin, "transfers to the national level the anxiety of direction that Halevi developed so subtly" in earlier poetry ("Where Can I Find You, Lord?"). "But here, there is no ambiguity about where God is to be found . . . : far away; in the Land of Israel, where the Temple lies in ruins, and in heaven, aloof from His people's prayers."[50] Evidently written before Halevi had even conceived the idea of an actual pilgrimage to the Land of Israel, this poem does not reflect either the intensity preceding, or the early stages of, the journey that would bring the poet physically closer to the holy sites in the Land of Israel—and to his own death. It does, however, reflect what Scheindlin calls the "anxiety of direction" and what I am calling, after Jonathan Z. Smith, a "locative" view of sacred space[51]—the very danger that Maimonides is strenuously resisting even as he recruits the image for its parabolic power. The real distinction between the two is that Yehuda Halevi's palace is a real (or remembered) place toward which centuries of Jews have oriented themselves; Maimonides's palace, in this context, anyway, is a parable guarded by strict exegetical principles.

I have argued elsewhere that as he approaches the Holy Land, Halevi's metaphors intensify in degree and range, and in anticipation of reaching his destination, which has already been inscribed in centuries of "dead metaphors" as a desolate woman awaiting a redemptive kiss, the images are animated and approximate ecstatic or sacramental realization.[52] That is, I believe, the very danger that Maimonides is warning against, even as he acknowledges its attraction.

Nonetheless, the distinction remains untidy. The philosopher's own pilgrimage to the Holy Land and to Jerusalem, as well as references elsewhere in his work to the Temple, the commandments attendant upon it, now and in time to come, illuminates the struggle between his reverence for, and his deep apprehension about, a locative view of holiness. That struggle is enhanced by various documents and different interpretations among scholars. As we have already seen, in a private letter and in the *Epistle to Yemen*, Maimonides describes his brief visit to Jerusalem, where he reports to have prayed in the "Great and Holy House."[53] If, as some believe, this refers to the site of the Temple,[54] it is contrary to several strictures in place at the time: the Jewish practice of viewing the Temple Mount from the Mount of Olives; the restrictions on Jewish pilgrimage to and habitation in Jerusalem imposed by the Crusaders before Saladin relaxed such controls (twenty-two years after Maimonides's visit); and, most important, the traditional interdiction that the philosopher himself elaborates elsewhere against entering the ruins of what may have been the Holy of Holies. Further, by leaving Jerusalem after only a few days and the Holy Land after less than a year, he seems to violate his own directive in various legal rulings that a Jew who visits the Holy Land should settle there.

But most important for our discussion is not the Rambam's behavior so much as the passages in the *Commentary on the Mishnah* and the *Mishneh Torah* that contain specific commandments and practices related to the Temple, which is regarded as preserving the aura of holiness even in its devastation, "because the sacredness of the Temple and Jerusalem is on account of the Divine Presence [השכינה, ha-shekhinah], and the Divine Presence is never annulled" (*Mishneh Torah, hilkhot beit ha-behira* 6:16). There is even an extant diagram, presumably in Maimonides's own hand, in the *Commentary on the Mishnah*, with the Holy of Holies clearly demarcated.[55] The incompatibility between the philosopher's affirmation of a specific, physical locus of holiness, even one as diaphanous as the *shekhinah* or "Divine Presence,"[56] and his resistance to anthropomorphizing or delimiting the physical parameters of the Divine, iterated in the *Mishneh Torah* and elaborated in *Moreh ha-nevokhim*, is never fully resolved;[57] it becomes most blatant in the messianic projections that punctuate his writing.

Sacrifice and Survival

Maimonides's complex approach to sacrificial Judaism touches on many of these problems. It bears repeating in the context of our discussion of his aniconic approach to language that the Rambam professed belief in the messianic promise that would entail restoration of the Temple service. But even such articles of faith are expressed in a distanced, historically conditioned exploration of elements of the sacrificial cult, his justification for the commandments relating to Temple sacrifices, in the *Guide* (III:46–47, pp. 581–97). Nahmanides would criticize what Kraemer calls "Maimonides' anthropological approach to sacrifices, which rendered them obsolete. He [Nahmanides] rather viewed them positively as theurgic actions and supreme symbols."[58]

The question that Maimonides might have posed to Nahmanides is the same one I will imagine him posing to Agnon in the next chapter, in our anachronistically hypothetical dialogue—and it is at the heart of my entire project: what do we do with the cult of sacrifice when, after living for so many centuries in the *bimkom*—that is, in the re-place-ment, substitutional, or mimetic world of symbols—the "symbol" is brought "home"? Agnon prepared us for his own complicated response in multiple puns on the word *makom* or place in his iconic story "Tehila." Set in the alleyways and interior spaces in the Old City, this narrative of pre-'48 Jerusalem focuses its gaze on the Wailing Wall and its throngs of displaced persons, those who have arrived in the Holy City but have not yet found secure lodgings:

From Jaffa Gate as far as the Western Wall, men and women from all the communities of Jerusalem moved in a steady stream, together with those newcomers whom The Place had restored to their place, although they had not yet found their place.

‏. . . שהביאם המקום למקומם ועדיין לא מצאו את מקומם. . . .‏[59]

Moving between a world-embracing sense of the Divine (*ha-makom*, or Place Itself) and a sanctification of a specific place—without succumbing to idolatrous claims—will become Agnon's task in the twentieth century as it was Maimonides's in the twelfth.

One trenchant response to this quandary can be found in the Rambam's discussion of sacrifice in the context of overcoming the temptations of idolatry:

> They say: How can *Jeremiah* say of God that He has given us no injunctions *concerning burnt-offerings and sacrifices*, seeing that the greater part of the commandments are concerned with these things? However, the purpose of the dictum is as I have explained to you. For he says that the first intention consists only in your apprehending Me and not worshipping someone other than Me: *And I will be your God, and you shall be My people.* Those laws concerning sacrifices and repairing to the temple were given only for the sake of the realization of this fundamental principle. It is for the sake of that principle that I transferred these modes of worship to My name, so that the trace of *idolatry* be effaced and the fundamental principle of My unity be established. (*Guide* III:32, p. 530)

Again, note the "transfer" of modes of worship to "My name, so that the trace of idolatry be effaced." The implication is, I submit, that worshipping the Divine as confined in space—even if that space is the site of the Holy of Holies—is a form of idolatry.

I suggest we continue to approach this somewhat circuitously by looking briefly at the Rambam's explicit guidelines to his fellow Jews, articulated in the *Epistle on Forced Conversion* (*Iggeret ha-shmad*, c. 1160–65), and elaborated in the *Epistle to Yemen* (*Iggeret teiman*, 1172), where he urges them to choose survival, with its compromises, even and including external conversion, over martyrdom.[60] Although the two dimensions of sacrifice seem quite different, I believe that Maimonides's humane approach to both emanates from the same profound conviction, which can be extrapolated from the following directive from the *Guide*: "It behooves you to compare a rite in which for reasons of divine worship a man burns his child with one in which he burns a young pigeon" (*Guide* III:47, p. 593).

As we have already seen, the animal substituted for the child, the foundation upon which the entire sacrificial system is based,[61] is grounded in the

Genesis narrative of the binding of Isaac. One can add that where humans are concerned, even the cultic reflex would privilege survival over martyrdom. But the conditions of religious coercion in the early Middle Ages gave rise to martyrological responses in Europe as in the Middle East and reprised some of the talmudic debates about self-sacrifice.

Kraemer calls Maimonides's attempt to "release Jews from their martyrdom obsession and esteem for sacrificial victims" a response to "the Masada complex."[62] To our ears this may sound like a page borrowed anachronistically from modern Israeli military history, but it should be borne in mind that Josephus's version of the mass suicide and homicide on the part of the Jews at Masada, which had been written late in the first century CE but was occluded from view for centuries, became newly available to medieval Jewish readers through the tenth-century retelling in the *Book of Josippon*, and was reinforced a century later by the martyrological responses to the Crusades in the Rhineland.[63]

For the most part, the question of whether Maimonides himself converted to Islam in order to accommodate to the dictates of the increasingly oppressive Almohad regime in Fez, where he was living at the time, has been resolved,[64] but such an act would not be inconsistent with the behavior of many of his fellow Jews and with his own admonition to those living under oppressive religious regimes in the *Epistle on Forced Conversion*.

The privileging of survival through dissembling over martyrdom for the sanctification of God's Name is, I submit, fundamentally consistent with the epistemological, political, and ethical implications of poetic camouflage as elaborated in the *Guide*—and is particularly instructional for our own generation.[65] I will go so far as to claim that there is a loose analogy between Maimonides's cautious embrace of biblical poetry with its dangerous ambiguities and his equally cautious embrace of the doubleness, subterfuge, or camouflage that living in Diaspora may entail for a Jew under Muslim or Christian aegis.[66] Like the golden apple, Truth—the truth of self or of God—lies beneath the veneer of self-fashioning, as of poetic fashioning, even if truth is at times hard to discern under successful acts of accommodation or apparent duplicity. As Kalman Bland observes,

> this "dissembling" is a highly developed theme in Islamic thinking: *taqqiyah* or *takkiyah* is the term for the permission Shi'ites or Sunnis have in adopting the outward form of their host society, something like the Marrano experience for Jews. Can a Shi'ite living in a Sunni society pretend to be a Sunni? One could go so far as to say that Maimonides lived his poetics in the flesh . . . That's even more decisive proof of his poetic or critical stance toward language than his apophatic theology and his related doctrine of negative attributes.[67]

Eretz Yisrael

There is another stricture in Maimonides's thought and action that qualifies him as both dialogical partner with and constraint upon modern Hebrew temptations: his complex relation to the Holy Land. The discussion of the status of the Land of Israel is of course intimately connected with the question of Jerusalem, the Temple, the messianic promise, and the sacrificial cult. What concerns me here is what I consider to be the most subtle dimension of that question, which manifests itself as Maimonides's impatience with all physical or spatial apprehensions of the godhead. Let me attempt, then, to summarize briefly the areas of relative agreement from the vast research that has been done on both the status of cultic sacrifice and the status of the Land in Maimonides's thought, as it relates to our central concerns. What Kraemer calls Maimonides's "anthropological" approach to the sacrificial cult is matched by what has been called his "normative" approach to the holiness of the Land of Israel.[68] Both of these recognize contingency, history, and human agency as crucial to the practice and assignation of holiness.

Although he identified with the mission of the prophet and believed in the imminence of a new prophetic age presaging the coming of the Messiah and the ingathering of the exiles, Maimonides fell short of either identifying the prophet with the Messiah or heralding the messianic age with a call to return to Eretz Yisrael. His own attitude to the holiness of the Land is divided between a "normative" or "anthropological" approach to the Land that would be sanctified by human deeds, and a regard for Jerusalem and the Temple Mount as the site of immanence, from which, as we saw, the *shekhinah* or divine presence has never departed.[69]

The "anthropological" approach to the sacrificial cult is grounded in a kind of evolutionary apprehension of Jewish practice meant to distinguish it from the idolatrous cultures surrounding it (as in the example of the child and the pigeon).[70] It bears repeating that even as he spent a year or so in the Holy Land, staying mainly in Acre but visiting Jerusalem briefly, presumably rending his clothes and performing the appropriate rites of mourning for the destroyed holy sites, Maimonides seems to have avoided participating in either the rhetoric or the practice of "hastening" the coming of Messiah through (re)settling the Promised Land. The symbolic valence of his pilgrimage to the ruined shrine, and the difference between pilgrimage and settlement,[71] distinguish his brief visit from the aborted attempt of his older contemporary, the poet-philosopher Yehuda Halevi, or the more successful migration of his successors, the approximately three hundred rabbis from France and England who first went to Alexandria and then to Fostat, to meet with Maimonides's son Abraham.[72]

Modern Inflections

Maimonides's project in the *Guide* can be summarized as four-pronged: *biblical exegesis* predicated on *philosophical enlightenment* in preparation for *prophetic reception* in a time of rising *messianic expectations*. Each of these dimensions has elicited entire libraries of scholarly exegesis.[73] My own reading of the *Guide* informs my inquiry into the poetics of return to the Holy Land in the late modern age of rising messianic expectations. Granted, there is little in Maimonides's time that anticipates the secularized messianism that became Zionism, because, *inter alia*, of the highly ambivalent approach in classical Zionism to Jerusalem and the holy sites;[74] additionally, once the State was established, physical distance from those sites between 1948 and 1967 kept eschatological forces at bay. But the terms of reference that are interrogated in the *Guide* become highly relevant in the post-'67 era that has witnessed a resurgence of religious messianism and mysticism and a return to the locative dimensions of the human-divine encounter.

The nonvigilant exercise of the monotheistic imagination, against which Maimonides warns, would become dominant in the political sphere in the late twentieth and early twenty-first centuries; religious attitudes whose literalism borders on idolatry translate into proprietary, exclusive political claims to sacred space in modern no less than in ancient Israel. Sacrifice in its many dimensions again becomes a compelling template for collective action.[75] At the end of his magisterial legal code, the *Mishneh Torah*, Maimonides makes it quite clear that the messianic age is meant to usher in not a change in the natural order, but a period of calm for the children of Israel who have lived for—at that time—over a millennium under foreign rule. But he was equally adamant that renewed Jewish sovereignty was not meant as an excuse for conquest or subjugation of others:

> The sages and prophets did not long for the days of the Messiah that Israel might exercise dominion over the world, or rule over the gentiles, or be exalted by the nations . . . Their aspiration was that Israel be free to devote itself to the law and its wisdom, with no one to oppress or disturb it, and thus be worthy of life in the world hereafter.[76]

So it is the two strictures emanating from Maimonides's system of belief and practice—his complex approach to sacrificial Judaism and his complex messages regarding the spatialization of holiness, especially in Jerusalem—along with his elaboration of biblical poetics in the *Guide* that make him an ideal interlocutor for the Hebrew writer in the Age of Return.[77]

Leo Strauss's reading of Maimonides's *Guide* acknowledges the dangers and ambivalences but produces a trap of its own. Esoteric, like allegorical, readings are meant to safeguard dangerous meanings that have been encased in riddles, parables, and images. Based on the medieval philosopher's exhortation to his addressee that his elucidation of terms is meant to provide a "key permitting one to enter places the gates to which were locked," Strauss's view is that the entire *Guide* is an "enchanted . . . and enchanting forest"; his own esoteric reading is, then, a kind of key to the key to the forest.[78]

Strauss is, of course, responding also to the challenges of his own time. The Second World War was already underway in 1941 when he published the "Literary Character of the Guide for the Perplexed," which would inform his introduction to the two-volume English edition published over twenty years later. "Persecution and the Art of Writing" appeared in 1952, during the first years of the Cold War and the onset of McCarthyism in America. In that text, Strauss explored a kind of "writing between the lines" as response to persecution: "for the influence of persecution on literature is precisely that it compels all writers who hold heterodox views to develop a peculiar technique of writing." He imagines "a historian living in a totalitarian country" who would "have to state the liberal view before attacking it," thereby conveying what he is ostensibly rejecting. Such writing is "addressed, not to all readers, but to trustworthy and intelligent readers only," who outwit "the most intelligent censor." Writers who composed their work under varying levels of persecution or orthodox hegemony may be understood "exoterically" by most readers while a few choice readers can appreciate the "esoteric teaching of the author." A long string of writers from fifth-century BCE Athens through nineteenth-century Germany—including Maimonides—"witnessed or suffered, during at least part of their lifetimes, a kind of persecution" that limited free inquiry. Maimonides (like Plato in his time) is, then, Strauss argues, responding not so much to direct control as to the gulf that separates the "wise" from the "vulgar." They produced "exoteric" books with a "popular teaching" in the "foreground" and a "philosophic teaching . . . indicated only between the lines." The works of such writers "are very beautiful even from without. And yet their visible beauty is sheer ugliness, compared with the beauty of those hidden treasures which disclose themselves only after very long, never easy, but always pleasant work." With a nod to the difference between the time of composition, in which "public opinion was . . . ruled by the belief in the revealed character of the Torah or the existence of an eternal and unchangeable law," and the present moment of interpretation in which "public opinion is ruled by historical consciousness," Strauss nonetheless emphasizes the importance of bringing Maimonides's "secret teaching . . . to light" for this generation—and designates himself the most current in the long line of what I am calling Maimonides's "secret sharers." Such an interpreter should "imitate Maimonides" himself: "an adequate interpretation of the *Guide* would . . . have to take the form of an esoteric interpretation of an esoteric interpretation of an esoteric teaching." Therefore, "the interpretation of the *Guide* cannot be given in ordinary language, but only in parabolic and enigmatic speech"—something "wholly impossible for the modern historian." The secret teaching is accessible to us in two different versions, then: in the original biblical version, and in the derivative version of the *Guide*.[79]

There are of course other ways of reading the *Guide* and of approaching Maimonides with less danger of anachronistic projections and more tentative arrogation of the privileged position of reader-interlocutor. Sarah Stroumsa makes a solid argument that challenges the Straussian approach, especially as regards the predominance of Platonic philosophy, by "reading Maimonides in his historical context" and demonstrating the effects particularly of the Almohads—the dominant Islamic sect during Maimonides's formative years in Fez.[80]

Nevertheless, like Strauss in his time, I am clearly responding to the political challenges of my own time and place. Without presuming to wade any further into these deep philosophical waters, and certainly without designating myself a secret sharer, except as every reader is explicitly invited to do, I wish to conclude by training the lens on our own time and place.

Let us focus, then, once more on the contemporary significance of the silver ornament or filigree, the "visible beauty," as it conceals and only partly reveals the golden apple, the "hidden treasure." Leaving the apple itself, as it were, to the philosophers—Maimonides himself and his self-appointed successors in changing contexts—I wish to highlight here the value of the poetic image as self-conscious act of camouflage, comparison, and distancing from the object "itself." Despite all the obvious differences in culture and temperament, but largely because of historical developments of the past fifty years, I believe that the challenges of the present study are more consistent with Maimonides's fundamental passions than may be apparent at first.

My theory of Jewish aesthetics focuses on metaphor as a distinguishing and essential component of the Jewish imagination in Diaspora. Maimonides's position as expressed in *The Guide of the Perplexed* is, on its face, a serious challenge to this theory. While I have argued at some length elsewhere that it is in Exile that the verbal mimetic arts realize their fullest potential as strategies of creative distancing from the physical sources of the sacred,[81] we have seen that according to the *Guide* it is precisely in Exile that they could prove most dangerous because of the absence of the very constraint that binds the language of prophecy: access to the divine word mediated through dreams or visions.

Still, the temptations of exile are, for most of Israel's long history, limited to acts of representation and imagination that prove far less consequential than those performed within the gravitational pull of the sacred center, ancient, medieval, or modern. Maimonides's declared motivation is theological and philosophical. As clairvoyant as he may have been, he could not have anticipated the ways in which archaic religious impulses would undermine political *and poetic* wisdom eight hundred years after his death—wisdom garnered from thousands of years of diasporic negotiations. Michael Marmur connects A. J. Heschel with Shlomo Pines, who translated the *Guide* into English, in arguing that for Maimonides, "the only positive knowledge of God of which man is capable is knowledge of the attributes of action, and this leads and ought to lead to a sort of political activity which is the highest perfection of man. The practical way of life, the *bios praktikos*, is superior to the theoretical."[82] These claims are based not only on the fact that Maimonides was passionately involved in the medical and political life of his communities, but also on a careful reading of the *Guide* and other Maimonidean texts. As we have seen, *action*, *time*, or *history*, the medium in which Jewish aesthetics and theology thrive, is the antidote to *space* with its attendant anthropomorphisms, sacrificial and messianic temptations. And the philosopher's concern to preserve the nonmaterial concept of the deity from the temptations of idolatry—without denying the critical function of the imaginative faculty in perceiving the world—is consistent with what I am defining as the contemporary repercussions of a reconnection with the physical sites of holiness.

The primary challenge behind Maimonides's query in twelfth-century Fostat is not, I submit, how one sweetens the time in Exile, or even how one affirms the sojourn that is Exile by acts of the imagination while awaiting the endlessly deferred redemption. Nor is he responding to any real movement of return to the Holy Land outside of the challenge of a few remnants of the "Mourners of Zion"[83] and his older contemporary, the Andalusian Hebrew poet-philosopher Yehuda Halevi. Rather, he is explicitly concerned with how one comes close to comprehending the truth through study, prayer, intellectual discipline, and action, while avoiding the perils of proximity.

What I am suggesting is that the return to the physical sources of the sacred presents a more acute challenge for the modern Hebrew imagination than even that which Maimonides faced: after so many years of handling the object, one hardly notices when one takes the ornament for the thing it is meant to cover; one is no longer able to separate the signifier from the signified—or, if you will, sacred space from the sacred ineffable that cannot be housed in space. That is the challenge to which the two writers of modern Jerusalem, S. Y. Agnon and Yehuda Amichai, responded in a lifetime of work.

PART TWO

Agnon's Dilemma

4

"What may this be likened to?":
Agnon and the Poetics of Space

Who were my mentors in poetry and literature? That is a matter of opinion. Some see in my books the influences of authors whose names, in my ignorance, I have not even heard, while others see the influences of poets whose names I have heard but whose writings I have not read. And what is my opinion? From whom did I receive nurture? Not every man remembers the name of the cow which supplied him with each drop of milk he has drunk. But in order not to leave you totally in the dark, I will try to clarify from whom I received whatever I have received.

First and foremost, there are the Sacred Scriptures, from which I learned how to combine letters. Then there are the Mishna and the Talmud and the Midrashim and Rashi's commentary on the Torah. After these come the *Poskim*—the later explicators of Talmudic Law—and our sacred poets and the medieval sages, led by our Master Rabbi Moses, son of Maimon, known as Maimonides, of blessed memory.

s. y. agnon, Nobel Prize acceptance speech, 1966[1]

In his short speech accepting the Nobel Prize in Sweden in 1966, S. Y. Agnon capped his nearly sixty years of creativity by highlighting the "Jewish Book-case" that authorized his fictions. While keeping him safely within the precincts of the Hebrew conversation, such a list leaves open just a crack the question of "outside" influences, those anonymous "bovine" agents who may have provided him with some nourishment (whether or not he had "heard of" or "read" Kafka, for example, has provided a topic of lively scholarly debate for decades).[2] What is remarkable about Agnon's official proclamation of affinity or influence is that the only ones singled out by name from among the chorus of classical Hebrew "poets" and "sages" are Rashi (Rabbi Shlomo Yitzhaki, France, 1040–1105) and Maimonides (Rabbi Moses, son of Maimon, or "the Rambam," Spain, Morocco, Egypt, 1135–1204).

In this chapter I will focus on the poetic principles and figures that recur in two of Agnon's canonic stories ("The Tale of the Scribe" and "Agunot") and illuminate much of his prose. From that perch, I will attempt to construct a hypothetical dialogue between the Rambam, the "Great Eagle" of the twelfth century, and the Israeli Nobel laureate of the twentieth. The philosopher and the writer separated by eight centuries are meant to serve here as bookends of medieval and modern responses to space: the poetics of space and the temptations of proximity to the sacred.

Although there are explicit references to the Rambam throughout Agnon's oeuvre, they more often than not reflect missed encounters. In an autobiographical fragment, the writer reports a visit in Leipzig to his publisher, Shlomo Zalman Schocken, where he refers to his father's large "treatise on the Rambam" that burned, along with Agnon's own writings, in the fire in Bad Homburg in 1924.[3] And in the posthumously published novel *Ba-ḥanuto shel mar Lublin* (In Mr. Lublin's Store), the narrator states his intention to study the Rambam's writings on the anniversary of the philosopher's death, as is his wont. But this narrative actually recounts his missed engagement with the texts he intended to study, as he minds Mr. Lublin's store in Leipzig, where there are no such books. What he is left with, then, is but "zikhron shmo bilvad," only the trace memory of his name.[4] I, too, shall work in the traces, arguing for implicit engagement on several levels.

Having outlined Maimonides's strictures on representation of and approach to the sacred in the previous chapter, I will now focus on Agnon's use and interrogation of figures of speech, specifically the parabolic form known as *mashal*, its neighbor the simile, and its foil, the metaphor. These form the rhetorical foundations for Agnon's struggle with the sites and topoi of holiness, culminating in Jerusalem and filtered through the Book of Jerusalem, namely, the Song of Songs.

No modern Hebrew writer is more beholden to the poetic license exercised by the composer(s) of Song of Songs and by the medieval *paytanim* than S. Y. Agnon. But he is also connected to the talmudic discourse that warns of the dangerous "power of the imagination," and to its elaborations in the Rambam's work. This term, *ko'aḥ ha-medameh*, which designates the "imaginative faculty" in the *Guide*, is cognate to terms that appear in many of Agnon's self-reflexive fictions, all derived from the root *d-m-h* (דמה), to compare or to liken. In the discursive space shared by Maimonides and Agnon, the imaginative faculty faces its ultimate test as a means to theological apprehension; the paradox (and what saves it) is that the idolatrous potential of language is mitigated by its very status as a noncorporeal mediating force between the self and the ineffable Other.

But language also describes and designates elements that have shape and take up space, the vessels and sites of holiness. As such, it gestures toward, while being protected from, the dangers of anthropomorphic desire, even as the perils of representational speech intensify in proximity to the divine. As we shall see in this and the following chapter, the aesthetic dimensions of return to the sacred can be defined in much of Agnon's fiction as a struggle between the temptations of proximity and the instruments of mediation. In the story "The Tale of the Scribe," the sacred object is the Torah scroll; in "Agunot," it is the ark meant to house the Torah scroll. In *Tmol shilshom* (Only Yesterday), Agnon's magnum opus, it is the *kotel* (the Wailing Wall), the Temple Mount, and the presumptive site of the "Holy of Holies."

Almost inevitably, the attempts of Agnon's artists to touch or to mingle with the sacred object will be subject to the same annihilating force that consumed Nadav and Avihu, guilty of drawing "too close to the presence of the Lord" (Lev. 10:1, 16:1), and that killed poor Uzzah (II Sam. 6:6; see also Num. 4: 15).[5] The etymological connection between the word for drawing too close (*be-korvatam*) and for "sacrifice" (*korban*) stresses the perils of proximity.

Of all the characters we will consider in Agnon's narratives, it is the man of average stature at the center of *Tmol shilshom*, Isaac (Yitzhak) Kumer, the lowly artisan and housepainter, who emerges from the encounter with the Holy of Holies unscathed—and that is, I will argue, because he approaches the sacred through the mediation of his profane craft and without the pretense of mingling with the sacred. But in the end, he dies a hideous death— perhaps because he is too closely affiliated, through his name, with that other text, the *akeda*. The postbiblical, sacrificial misappropriations of this text continue to fuel the lethal power that emanates from the Sacred Center and consumes all within its radius.[6]

Once again, I am extending a plumb line between the modern and the ancient texts, performing a kind of "literary archaeology" meant to recruit alternate readings to inoculate us against the lethal effects of a "literal" return to the place itself. The two stories I will explore in this chapter, among the most familiar and most critically explored of Agnon's fictions, are being recruited for revisionist readings that will connect us to the classical texts we considered in part 1.

"The Tale of the Scribe" (1972; first version, 1917) concerns a pious scribe whose life's work culminates in the creation of a Torah scroll in his wife's memory. We will begin our discussion at the critical moment when the scribe has completed the week of mourning and is about to commence this task.

"Aggadat ha-sofer": A False Poetics

At the end of the seven days of mourning, Raphael the Scribe arose, put on his shoes, went to the marketplace, and obtained sheets of parchment, bundles of quills, a string of gallnuts for ink, and soft gut-thread for sewing together the sheets of parchment, and set his heart to the writing of a Torah scroll in memory of the soul of his wife whom God had taken away.

What may this be likened to? To a great gardener who raised beautiful plants in his
garden, and all the officials who were to see the king would first come to his garden and
buy beautiful flowers to take with them. Once the gardener's wife was to see the king,
and the gardener said, "All others who visit the king take flowers from my garden. Now
that my own wife is to visit the king, it is only proper that I go down to my garden and
pick flowers for her."

The comparison is clear [והנמשל מובן]. Raphael was a great gardener. He planted beautiful Torah scrolls in the world. And whoever was invited to appear before the King—
the King over kings of kings, the Holy One, blessed be He—took a Torah scroll with
him. And now that Miriam's time had come to appear before the King—the Holy One,
blessed be He—*Raphael immediately **went down to his garden***—*that is, to his pure and
holy table*—*and **picked roses***—that is, the letters of the Torah scroll he wrote—and made
a beautiful bouquet—that is, the Torah scroll he had prepared. Thus the work began.

S. Y. AGNON, "Tale of the Scribe" (emphases mine)[7]

Actually, the comparison is not at all clear. The narrative distance implicitly created from the "pious" folk tale, the irony that suffuses the mechanical
equivalences of simplistic allegorical procedure ("Raphael immediately went
down to his garden—*that is*, to his pure and holy table—and picked roses—
that is, the letters of the Torah scroll," etc.), invite us to tread cautiously and
warily in that archaic space. (The words I have marked in *italics* in this story
and the next establish the midrashic discourse of equivalences; the words
marked in **bold** are intertexts from the Song of Songs, which I will address
presently.)

Generations of readers have considered the classical discourse and the
folk elements in the opening paragraph and in this story as a whole, both for
their continuities with and their discontinuities from "tradition."[8] And more
recent scholarship has considered the quotations from the Song of Songs in
Agnon's prose in terms of classical resonances—but also with an eye to contemporary appropriations in the modern Hebrew culture in which the author lived most of his adult life.[9] In approaching both the intertexts and the
governing midrashic discourse through Maimonides, I am invoking the philosopher who employed his own figures of speech rather liberally and at the
same time instructed his readers to exercise extreme caution around figurative language. Such conjunctions are meant to suggest that what we have here
is anything but a self-evident set of equivalences—and that the midrashic
discourse of equivalences may actually be undermined by intertexts from the
Song of Songs.

I would go so far as to argue that the above quotation from one of Agnon's
most beloved fictions is an example of a *false poetics* meant to throw the

reader, trained in midrashic procedures and traditional (or even modern, Straussian) apprehension of the Rambam, off track.[10]

We are invited to approach this passage, which appears toward the end of "Tale of the Scribe," somewhat ironically because we have already learned, from even a superficial reading up to this point, that Raphael, in his monomaniacal devotion to his holy vocation as scribe of memorial Torah scrolls, has neglected the call of both conjugal duty and human eros. His wife Miriam, bride of his youth and epitome of Jewish piety and housewifery, dies lovesick and childless, while he devotes himself to the production of holy objects— often meant as talismans for childless women! Miriam is not the "gardener's" wife; she is Raphael's own flesh and blood wife. His "pure and holy table" has been desecrated by his very pursuit of purity and neglect of his own domestic table—and bed. His sin, I submit, is cognate with that of medieval poet Yehuda Halevi as he drew closer to Jerusalem, the object of his desire, leaving behind in Andalusia his table, his bed, and his poetic range through sacred and secular realms—giving in to the ecstatic anticipation of mingling with the dust of the ruined shrine. It is the sin of sacramentalizing the products of the artistic imagination and fetishizing the cultic artifact—even (especially) if it is the Torah or the Land of Israel itself.[11] In Maimonidean terms, as I understand them, the danger lies in reifying the symbolic universe by spatializing the sacred.

David Stern locates Agnon within a "parabolic" universe of classical discourse. He looks at the parabolic question ("to what can this be compared?") within the formal structure of a number of stories as Agnon's way to "invoke the stable universe of meaning that characterized traditional Judaism and its world," while showing that the narrative itself, like the parabolic structure, actually undermines that stability.[12] Other scholars, including Ariel Hirschfeld, Ilana Pardes, Michal Arbel, and Galili Shachar, following and complicating the work of their predecessors, begin to see the parabolic structure as the element of folk culture that forms one of the axes of Agnon's narrative universe but is anything but stable. And yet, as we have seen in our discussion of the *Guide*, the parable may still be the safest exercise of the "power of the imagination," as it is subject to the trained mind's exegetical control. (Next would be the simile, which holds tenor and vehicle in their naked and tenuous state. The metaphor, again, is the most elusive of the figures of the imagination.) Using this observation as my point of departure, I would counter that it is precisely the *instability* of meaning that Agnon is gesturing toward, and that the explicitly parabolic structure is often a diversion from or foil for the real workings of the imagination.

"Lefi Sha'a": Parsing Agnon

Every scholar who dares to offer a new interpretation of an Agnon narrative encounters a daunting library of critical books and essays that painstakingly annotate and document the classical sources underpinning this writer's fiction and that base specific decodings of the mysteries in a given story on such detective work.[13] Among the most astute of an older generation devoted to uncovering the subtexts was Shmuel Werses, and among the most inventive but also the most humble in offering definitive interpretations based on such discoveries was Dov Sadan. To this have been added—especially in the wake of Dan Laor's exhaustive biography of Agnon—layers of autobiographical excavation.[14]

If specific subtexts and parabolic structures that contain their own controlling hermeneutics are two of the elements that define Agnon's poetics, much of the scholarship on his work consists of acrobatic attempts either to decipher and thereby resolve what is presented as a riddle, a puzzle, or a mystery, or to offer tentative and therefore more open-ended resolutions. Dov Sadan admonished his fellow detectives to add "lefi sha'a" (for now) to whatever interpretations of Agnon they tender.[15] Avraham Holtz lets even more air into the critical echo chamber by invoking Richard Eastman's definition of the "open parable" in the context of Agnon's more elusive narratives. "Through a designed instability," argues Eastman, an "open parable" offers a "single ethical motif with variations of indefinite number and strength." In order to keep the reader from "closing the parable," the author's rhetoric "must be constructed with certain opaque irreducible details [so] as to block the verification of any one hypothesis."[16] Contrasting Kafka's *Trial* or Beckett's *Endgame* with a closed parable like that of the Good Samaritan in the New Testament or Dickens's *A Christmas Carol*, Eastman in this short evocative essay offers a capacious hermeneutics to counter the exhaustive efforts of all the detectives, no matter how ingenious and scrupulous their labor toward a hermetic interpretation may be. It is important to underscore in our context both the "single ethical motif" and the impossibility of verifying "any one hypothesis" that Eastman insists on. Holtz applies this approach to *Sefer ha-ma'asim* (The Book of Deeds), Agnon's most Kafkaesque, enigmatic story cycle.

My argument is even more radical. Although I agree that seductively enigmatic allusions appear in many of Agnon's fictions as so many breadcrumbs for the Hansels and Gretels among the scholarly community to spend years tracking down and deciphering, I am claiming that the exegetical practice is itself called into question in fundamental ways. In a number of narratives, and not only in the more mysterious tales in *Sefer ha-ma'asim*, the parable in its allegorical guise is invoked because it is, ostensibly, the easiest verbal structure to control and the least given to the dangers of a runaway imagination. But often it also serves to divert attention away from the more insidious or radical poetic project that is unfolding under the radar.

Returning, then, to "Tale of the Scribe" and the allegory at its heart: the parabolic procedure seems to accomplish a closure of meaning—but that is both a diversion from and a camouflage of the real work of the narrative. This can be seen through the seemingly innocuous but actually subversive voice of the narrator: by casting the story itself as a link in the midrashic chain, through a series of parables that run through the narrative, the narrator obscures the story's polysemic potential. By elevating Raphael above his embedded human life to theological status, the narrator appears to exonerate the character's sinful behavior—which is, precisely, his monastic, unmediated devotion to his sacred task. In Hebrew the word for spiritual devotion, *devekut*, invoked several times in connection with Raphael's piety in finishing the Torah scroll in memory of his wife, rendered in English as "devout ecstasy" and "wondrous fervor" (E 178, H 140, 141), signifies clinging, and has the same root as the modern word for "glue." But its primary connotation is the devotion of a man to his wife. In the Book of Genesis, Adam is admonished to "leave his father and his mother and *cling* to his wife" (Gen. 2:24). And as Daniel Boyarin so persuasively argued, the sexual relations between husband and wife were actually sanctified in the talmudic discourse that dwelt on the smallest carnal details.[17] It is this cardinal injunction, the primordial value of two *clinging humans*, that Raphael the Scribe has violated—for which no act of piety can atone.

Indeed, much of Agnon's literary career is devoted to constructing and deconstructing this injunction, adumbrated in his very first story, "Agunot."

"Agunot": A Story That Signs and Seals

It is said: A thread of grace is spun and drawn out of the deeds of Israel, and the Holy One, blessed be He, Himself, in His glory, sits and weaves—strand on strand—a tallit all grace and all mercy, for the Congregation of Israel to deck herself in. Radiant in the light of her beauty she glows, even in these, the lands of her Exile, as she did in her youth in her Father's house, in the Temple of her Sovereign and the city of sovereignty, Jerusalem. And when He, of ineffable Name, sees her, that she has neither been sullied nor stained even here, in the realm of her oppressors, He—as it were—leans toward her and says, **"Behold thou art fair, my beloved, behold thou art fair."** And this is the

secret of the power and the glory and the exaltation and the tenderness in love
which fills the heart of every man in Israel. *But* there are times—alas!—when
some hindrance creeps up, and snaps a thread in the loom. Then the tallit is
damaged: evil spirits hover about it, enter into it and tear it to shreds. At once
a sense of shame assails all Israel, and they know they are naked. Their days
of rest are wrested from them, their feasts are fasts, their lot is dust instead of
luster. At that hour the Congregation of Israel strays abroad in her anguish,
crying, **"Strike me, wound me, take away my veils from me!" Her beloved
has slipped away, and she, seeking him,** cries, **"If ye find my beloved, what
shall ye tell him? That I am afflicted with love."** And this affliction of love
leads to darkest melancholy, which persists—Mercy shield us!—until, from
the heavens above, He breathes down upon us strength of spirit, to repent, and
to muster deeds that are pride to their doers and again draw forth that thread
of grace and love before the Lord.

   And this is the theme of the tale recounted here, a great tale and terrible,
from the Holy Land, of one renowned for his riches—Sire Ahiezer by name—
who set his heart on going up from the Diaspora to the holy city Jerusalem—
may she be rebuilt and established—to work great wonders of restoration in
the midst of her ruins, and in this way *to restore at least a corner of the anteroom which will be transformed into our mansion of glory on the day when the
Holy One, blessed be He, restores His presence to Zion—may it be soon, in our
day!* (Emphases mine; once again, the words I have put in italics designate
exegetical instructions and the words in bold are familiar lines from Song of
Songs)[18]

"It is said." "מובא בכתובים" literally means, "as it is written . . ." Although this
passage, which introduces Agnon's debut Hebrew story, is composed of many
biblical intertexts from Genesis, the Song of Songs, Ecclesiastes, etc., and
although its language is midrashic or aggadic,[19] this "quotation" is uniden-
tifiable. In his essay on this story, Gershon Shaked offered both specific intertexts from classical Hebrew literature and, for the introductory passage
as a whole, the concept of "pseudo-midrash"—an authorizing fiction posing as a classical source. "Agunot" was not only the earliest story that Agnon
published in Hebrew, shortly after his arrival in Palestine in 1908, but also
the story from which the young Shmuel Yosef Czaczkes constructed his new
identity. More than a *nom de plume*, "Agnon" became the name by which he
was known from that moment forward. As Shaked writes: "Agnon so identified himself with the name of his story that what we have here is an extension
of the fictional into the real, the fictional narrative becoming a kind of . . .
interpretation . . . [of] the existential and poetic experience of the author,
an interpretation which has forced him to displace the chief element in his
identifying sign."[20] The story also anticipates themes, images, characters, and

literary procedures that will permeate and define this author's entire literary project.

Agnon identifies his opening passage not as a parable (*mashal*) but rather as a "theme" or statement of authorial intention: "*And this is the theme of the tale recounted here*"—or more literally: "and it is this thing that the author of the following tale intended" (ולדבר זה נתכוון המחבר בסיפור המעשה שלהלן).[21] Words and things are interchangeable in biblical as in modern Hebrew; by making his intentions explicit and reified, Agnon seems to establish an additional authorizing source, on a par with that of the sages: the voice of the third-person omniscient narrator. Whereas intention is integral to the parabolic structure—it is in fact the controlling mechanism that allows the midrashic imagination to take leaps of fancy—the authorizing fiction in "Agunot" functions in a more modern, i.e., open-ended, fashion than the traditional *mashal* that invites a systematic exposition of correspondences. After invoking the general or cumulative authority embedded in the anonymous "it is written," the narrator-as-author takes explicit responsibility for the story, adding his own authority to the collective voice. The series of anthropomorphic ascriptions in this passage—God as weaving, wooing, watching, and waiting—may actually be more potent, then, because they are governed not by a traditional exegetical exposition but by the more complex intentionality of the implied author.

This passage, while it could qualify as a "pseudo-midrash," functions a bit differently from what I called in connection with "Aggadat ha-sofer" a "false poetics" meant to throw the reader off-course. Here it creates, rather, a parable-*like* structure, inviting the reader into a narrative space that is itself both representational and exegetical. It should also be noted that here the author offers the exegetical key even before the story itself unfolds, a cunning device meant to inoculate the reader, perhaps, against the real sting of this narrative and of many narratives to come: the sting of thwarted love, lost souls, and wandering rabbis or beggars seeking to repair what has been torn asunder. By preemptively defining this "affliction of love" as "lead[ing] to darkest melancholy," which will eventually be dispersed when "from the heavens above, He breathes down upon us strength of spirit, to repent, and to muster deeds that are pride to their doers and again draw forth that thread of grace and love before the Lord," Agnon places his prose safely within classical exegetical literature[22]—while actually undermining its very premises.

The narrative is fairly simple and adumbrates the plot structure in many of Agnon's subsequent stories. Written in Jerusalem in the early years of the *yishuv*, still under the authority of the Ottoman Empire, it is placed in a historically nonspecific—i.e., both unredeemed and nonpolitical—time. It

opens with the grand redemptive scheme of Sire Ahiezer ("Sire" is Baruch
Hochman's rendering of the archaic Hebrew honorifics, עשיר מופלג, קצין), who
"goes up" from the Diaspora (golah, גולה) to Jerusalem: his intention is to
marry off his beloved daughter Dinah to a renowned scholar who will, in
turn, draw young students to a reconstituted beit midrash in Jerusalem, thus
enacting "great wonders of restoration in the midst of her ruins" and preparing a "corner" of the "anteroom" of the "mansion" for the "restored" divine presence ("ke-she-yaḥzor ha-kadosh barukh hu shekhinato le-tzion").

The first part of the narrative is full of hope and activity, while messianic
desire is tempered by diasporic constraints. The synagogue-study house that
Ahiezer builds is referred to as a "mikdash me'at" (מקדש מעט) or miniature
temple (the diasporic designation of the synagogue, translated here as a "hall
for prayer," E 37, H 107), anteroom of the mansion, i.e., the Temple, that will
eventually accommodate the "divine presence"; it is lavishly decorated and
missing only an ark of the covenant. Ben Uri is the name of the artist retained
to create such an ark in time for Dinah's nuptials and to consecrate the beit
midrash. His biblical namesake, Bezalel Ben Uri, is the craftsman who designed the tabernacle that would house the (replacement!) Tablets for the
Children of Israel in their wanderings in the desert before entering the Land
of Israel (Ex. 31, 35:30).

If Ben Uri, the modern craftsman, and Raphael, the modern scribe, who
are both housed not in a tent in the desert but in a modern Hebrew narrative,
understood their surrogate status, they might have followed the siren call of
their hearts and performed a task far more divine than the fashioning of another holy icon. In "Agunot," as in "Aggadat ha-sofer," the devekut or devotion
of the craftsman to his holy craft will blind him—rather than bind him—to
the human love that stands before him.

Still, at first everything seems aligned to bring two lovers together, and the
siren call is Ben Uri's voice, resonating in Dinah's heart: "his hands wrought
the ark, his lips uttered song all the day." Dinah is "drawn to the singer as
though—God save us—a spell had been cast." "But" (as in the opening paragraph of the story, the onset of entropy is often signaled in an Agnon narrative by the Hebrew word aval) "as Ben Uri, who was at first drawn to Dinah,
pursued his work, he cleaved [nitdabek] more and more to it, until both his
eyes and heart passed into the ark" (E 38, H 107). The inevitable collapse is,
thus, caused by a surfeit of piety, and as in "Tale of the Scribe," the cleav-
ing is to an object of piety rather than to the human beloved. All memory
and thought of Dinah erased from his mind and heart, Ben Uri eventually
"stopped singing altogether . . . Rapt, Ben Uri wrought, possessed by a joy he
had never known before. In no kingdom, in no province, in the course of no

labor had he exulted as he exulted here, in the place where the *shekhinah was revealed and then reviled*, in the multitude of our transgressions." And, when he finished the ark, he himself had become an "empty vessel" (E 39, H 108, emphasis mine).

Jerusalem, where Ben Uri works, and the destroyed Temple in its midst, are invoked here as "the place where the *shekhinah* was revealed and then reviled." But even in the space of ultimate redemption, the master craftsman is engaged in the quintessential diasporic act of substitution: building an ark for the "mikdash me'at," the prayer hall that is a miniaturized version of and *replacement* for the Temple, the Beit ha-mikdash. We can already see here the pull of the sacred center as well as the constraints that two millennia of "galut" have inscribed on the Jewish soul.

Satisfied with his finished product, but emptied out emotionally, Ben Uri goes down to the garden, where he falls into a deep slumber. Dinah, hungering for her beloved, goes to his workshop and there "Satan" appears to her and tells her that it was the ark itself that silenced Ben Uri's voice and put out the flame of his love. She, in turn, reaches out and pushes the ark through the window onto the garden below. Ben Uri still sleeps in that same garden, oblivious to another voice: the narrator's erotically charged (but midrashically camouflaged) rhetoric that compares the fallen ark to a woman. We will return to this passage, in which, I believe, the narrator is providing us with both the lock and the key to a more subversive reading.

But perhaps the most powerful, because somewhat buried, subtext in this tale is that primordial example of the tragic consequences of clinging to the holy object: the story of Uzzah. The insinuation that the ark may have fallen on Ben Uri and killed him in the garden invites the connection with Uzzah, though in the case of "Agunot," the peril of proximity is manifest in the sacrifice of human love to the construction of holy vessels. Here, then, in Agnon's "signature story," is the motif that will run throughout his life's work, as time after time the male protagonist abrogates Adam's primary commandment to "cling" to his beloved (Gen. 2:24). One of the only exceptions to this, as we shall see, is Isaac (Yitzhak) Kumer, the unsung hero of Agnon's magnum opus.

"Agunot" then proceeds to its inevitable conclusion: the ark is carted away and then disappears, as does any trace of Ben Uri. Confusion and sadness reign. Forced to marry the scholar, R. Ezekiel, whom her father has imported from Europe, Dinah confesses to the rabbi on her wedding day that it was she who pushed the ark. Ignoring the warnings of his own heart, the rabbi nevertheless decides to go ahead and consecrate the marriage of these two star-crossed lovers (the groom, Ezekiel, had himself been betrothed back in Europe to his beloved Friedele). The marriage, though, is never consummated.

Dinah's abiding love is expressed in her song, which is interpreted as the voice of Ben Uri's spirit, a dybbuk-like presence that will reappear in many of Agnon's stories. In a parallel pose, Friedele is reported as sitting in the "Go-lah," singing her forlorn love song for her distant beloved, even as she too is betrothed to another.[23] As the love stories are dismantled, so, eventually, are the *beit midrash* and Sire Ahiezer's redemptive schemes.

Since from the beginning, this narrative was outlined as one of perfection, decay, and redemption, so the failure of the human plot will also signal the deferral of that Other Plot. Dinah and her mismatched husband are divorced, and she leaves Jerusalem with her father. Finally, the rabbi who presided over their nuptials despite his own misgivings, and then presided over their divorce, has a dream followed by a series of visions disclosed to him by "Providence" ("heruhu min shamayim"). The dream teaches him that "he would suffer exile" (a loaded term suggesting both a physical and a spiritual, existential state). This is followed by a vision of "the Shekhinah in the guise of a lovely woman, garbed in black . . . nodding mournfully at him."[24] Fasting and inquiring as to the "signification of his dream," he beholds

> with the eyes of spirit the souls of those bereaved of their beloved in their lifetime groping dismally in the world for their mates. He peered hard and saw Ben Uri. Ben Uri said to him, "Wherefore hast thou driven me out, that I should not cleave to my portion of the Kingdom?" "Is it thy voice I hear, Ben Uri, my son?" the rabbi cried, and he lifted his voice and he wept.

Awaking from the "sleep" that has given him instruction, the rabbi *calls* to his wife while *kissing* the mezuzah (!), takes up his staff and goes out into exile "לתקן עגונות," to repair the world by "redeem[ing] the forsaken in love" (E 47, H 196, emphasis mine)[25]—in effect, as many critics have pointed out, forsaking his own wife. This is the first of many instances in which a saintly figure or penitent undertakes such a task in an Agnon story. I agree again with most readers that it is this act that defines both Agnon's self-nomination and his entire project, which enlarges the term ʿaginut to include not only the narrow legalistic definition of a wife who has been abandoned (though that too) but all star-crossed lovers or, indeed, all forms of disharmony.[26]

The final paragraphs describe the rabbi and also, possibly, Ben Uri as two phantoms reappearing in many sites in the "world of confusion," even in the Holy Land. But whether the itinerant figure is in fact "the rabbi," "God alone knows for a fact" (E 47, H 196). This coda, which literally means "God has the solutions" (לאלקים פתרונים), is taken from Joseph's prelude to his interpretation of the dreams of Pharaoh's chief butler and baker (Gen. 40:8) and can serve as the motto of Agnon's entire oeuvre, anticipated in this, his very first story.

Struggling against the hubris that infects every critic, I will now offer not a *pitaron*, or solution, to any of the riddles or conundrums, which *only God knows*, but rather a response to the challenge that is meant to protect its fundamental enigma. I will do so by focusing on the resonance of inter-texts and exegetical procedures relating to Song of Songs in both "Tale of the Scribe" and "Agunot" as the key to Agnon—and to his implicit dialogue with Maimonides.

Song of Songs: Unbinding the Allegory

Along with those figures of speech explicitly subject to parabolic controls or exegetical procedures, the biblical intertexts in Agnon's stories open various interpretive strategies. Of the two biblical texts we are following—the *akeda* and the Song of Songs—the first circles around the Sacred Center and at-tendant sacrificial temptations, which we will explore in the next chapter; the second maintains the tension between theocentric and anthropocentric eros. In many of Agnon's narratives, including the two we are considering here, in-texts from Song of Songs appear on the surface as an invitation to allegori-cal or parabolic interpretation, but then, like the Song itself in its "nakedness," they bubble up from under the surface in provocative ways.

In the course of "The Tale of the Scribe," Solomon's Song is explicitly sum-moned through different rhetorical discourses. We already looked at the pas-sage that I called a "false poetics," which describes Raphael's scribal devotion as he creates a scroll in his wife's memory. But the midrash-inflected biblical references that place the reader in a talmudic frame of mind from the very beginning, conflating the Song with its interpretive layers, also cover over some of the story's internal conflicts, which are, then, hidden in plain sight. Raphael is introduced as the scribe dedicated to writing memorial scrolls. "*What may this be likened to?*" asks the narrator (משל למה הדבר דומה). "To a man who travels far from his own city, to a place where he is not known, and the watchmen who guard that city find him . . ." (E 167, H 131). Already implicit in the parabolic structure is an allusion that will become salient later in the story. The Hebrew for the action of the watchman here (מצאוהו השומרים הסובבים בעיר) reflects the consternation of the female speaker in the Song who tells her girlfriends that she can't find her lover: "Then the watchmen found me as they went about the city. 'Have you seen him? Have you seen the one I love?'" (Song 3:3, p. 67).

But the "watchmen" who act in this passage as benign tourist guides or crossing guards will appear later in the Song itself in a more nefarious role. In chapter 5:7, the "watchmen of the walls" treat the Shulamite brutally: they "beat me . . . bruised me . . . tore the shawl from my shoulders" (Song 5:7, p. 85). In Agnon's story, although Raphael is introduced as a scribe of memorial scrolls, and the exegesis ("what may this be likened to?") takes us to a far-away city and eventually to the next world, in order to return dialectically to the subject of the memorial scroll, the allusion to the watchmen has already set up the story rhetorically and thematically as one of elusive love but also, potentially, of cruelty.

The next allusions to the Song in this story are ceremonial, as the text read on Passover,[27] and then poetically performative, as the occasion on which the "birds of heaven" return from their migrations to the Land of Israel, in order to hear the Song read in the synagogue and the classroom, and to "sing their own song" by the window of the pious scribe (E 173, H 136). The Song will appear later in its conventional form as midrashic intertext in the passage we considered above, in which the now-bereaved husband sets out to write a memorial scroll for his own wife. But there, as I have already suggested, the thwarted love of Miriam for her pious husband is expressed *beneath* the parabolic camouflage of the garden and the gardener: "it is only proper that I go down to my garden and pick flowers" (E 176, H 139). The Hebrew for what is here translated as "flowers" is שושנים and the overt intertext is, again, Song of Songs, 6:2.[28]

Shir ha-shirim appears more nakedly in other passages in the narrative—and the cumulative effect of all of these references, I submit, is actually to *undermine* the midrashic status of the Song. The most salient expression of this subversive practice comes toward the end, just as Raphael has completed the scroll in memory of his wife—though it circles back to the beginning, as the first encounter between the young Raphael and Miriam, who is still a girl, is recounted by the narrator.

It is the evening of Simhat Torah, when the end—and the beginning anew—of the annual lectionary cycle is celebrated and congregants dance with the Torah scrolls in the synagogue. At the point when Torah scholars are invited to join the procession, "the distinguished young man, Raphael, is honored with the honor of the Torah, and with the singing of a beautiful melody." Raphael comes forward, accepts the scroll, and leads the procession, quieting the other congregants with his mesmerizing melody, or *nigun*.

> At that moment a young girl [holding the customary flag and candle] pushed her way through the legs of the dancers, leaped toward Raphael, sank her red lips into the white mantle of the Torah scroll in Raphael's arm, and **kept on kissing the scroll** and caressing it with her hands. Just then the flag fell out of her hand, and the burning candle dropped on Raphael's clothing. (E 181, H 143, emphasis mine)

What ensues is that Raphael's father brings an "action" against the girl's father—but the "rabbi, indulging himself in the pleasure of a wise remark, said to the girl's father, 'God willing, for their wedding day you will have a new garment made for him'" (E 181, H 143–44). Unlike the rabbi in "Agunot," this rabbi clearly understands the erotic yet innocent gesture of the young girl, which is cloaked in the language of Song of Songs (though camouflaged somewhat by this English translation). The Hebrew that is rendered here as "kept on kissing the scroll" appears in the original as "ve-nishka et ha-sefer mi-neshikot piha"—literally, "and she kissed the scroll with the kisses of her mouth." This is a clear reference to the opening line of the Song: "yishakeini mi-neshikot pihu," "may he kiss me with the kisses of his mouth." There could be a subtle reference here to a tannaitic midrash that represents the Song as a love poem not between God and Israel but between God and the Torah; in Shir ha-shirim Rabbah, the verse "his head is finest gold, his locks are curled and black as a raven" (Song 5:11) is parsed: "His head [rosho] is the Torah . . . finest gold: this refers to the words of the Torah . . . His locks are curled: this refers to the ruled lines [in the scroll]. And black as a raven: this refers to the letters."[29] So the transference of the girl's erotic attraction from Raphael to the Torah follows one exegetical path and, in a way, anticipates Raphael's own unselfconscious transference from earthly to "divine" passion.[30]

The story concludes as the memory of that first day blends in Raphael's feverish mind with their wedding day; Miriam's bridal gown, now envisioned by the despondent scribe as a curtain for the ark that will house the scroll he has written in her memory, hovers as a phantasmagoric projection. The house is filled with dancing Torah scrolls, and the setting sun is God's own tallit spread over the universe (a transparent intertextual allusion to the opening of "Agunot"). Spilling the little sack of holy soil from which he had taken a handful to throw into Miriam's grave, Raphael stood "as a man who stands on sacred ground." A "tongue of flame" leapt up from the oil lamp and Raphael "sank down with his scroll," covered by his "wife's wedding dress" (E 183, H 144–45).

We might pause at the dramatic end of this story to ask whether the "sacred ground" (admat kodesh) on which Raphael is standing is the soil of human love, or the ground of his sacred craft. The soil itself is, of course, both symbol and synecdoche of the Land of Israel. So he is "literally" and figuratively "stand[ing] on sacred ground." Has the scribe finally realized—too late—that his real sacred duty was to consecrate his wife and their love, or is he under the delusion until the end that the consummation of his being is in the completion of the holy scrolls, no matter what the human cost? As in "Agunot," the interweaving of the figurative and the literal creates the mystery. Le-elokim pitronim. God knows.

Most contemporary critics and exegetes, including Alan Mintz, Anne Golomb Hoffman, Ilana Pardes, and Ariel Hirschfeld, have noted the ironic distance between Raphael's pose as pious scribe and his sin as neglectful husband, while documenting the many resonances of the parables on the Song that the story invokes.[31] That is, the ironies have been noted, but the status of the midrashic procedure itself is not called into question. What I wish to emphasize is how, here as elsewhere in Agnon's fiction, the midrashic pretense actually conceals the power of these narratives much as Song of Songs Rabbah conceals the power of the Song itself—how the very *devekut* or *clinging* to the artifact of piety precludes the most basic form of human cherishing.

Another curiosity that appears toward the end of "Tale of the Scribe" is the redundancy of a simile that is, logically, negated in the moment when vehicle and tenor are united. Having completed the Torah scroll in memory of his wife, except for inserting the name of the Lord in a certain passage, Raphael must purify himself, as is his wont. The bathhouse is under repair, so he goes to the river, breaks the ice, and immerses himself, then returns home and writes "the Name with the joy of wondrous fervor. At that moment Raphael attained the merit of discovering the divine secret that before a man is able to rise to the height of joyous fervor he has to be *like* a man who stands in icy water on a snowy day" (E 178–79, H 141, emphasis mine). Clearly the simile is superfluous: if, when in the river, "he is like a man who stands in icy water," he has finally blended with his own image.[32] Thus, as in the image of Raphael standing on "sacred ground," and indeed in his entire life's work as a scribe—and like Ben Uri's devotion to the holy ark—the figurative enterprise, which is the insertion of the human imagination into the space *between* the self and the sacred, has been made superfluous, and ultimately obliterated, by religious zeal.

Which brings us back to "Agunot." As in "The Tale of the Scribe," it pays to take a brief second look at the intertextual references from Song of Songs as they appear in the opening section, which I have emphasized in bold:

> **"Behold thou art fair, my beloved, behold thou art fair"** . . . At that hour the Congregation of Israel strays abroad in her anguish, crying, **"Strike me, wound me, take away my veils from me!" Her beloved has slipped away, and she, seeking him**, cries, **"If ye find my beloved, what shall ye tell him? That I am afflicted with love."** ("Agunot," E 35–36, H 405, emphases mine)

Baruch Hochman chose to enclose such intertexts in quotation marks in his translation, though they do not appear so demarcated in the original, since they would easily resonate with most Hebrew readers—a resonance that would come automatically layered with rabbinic commentaries and controls on the erotic language. Still, even while echoes of rabbinic voices in the various

midrashim on the Song accord these words allegorical valence, we have already seen that the ultimate authorizing force is that of the narrator; by subtly
taking the reader back to a more "naked" reading of Song of Songs, these lines
spoken in the narrator's voice can be seen as setting the stage for the missed
erotic opportunities that will follow.

This process comes to a climax when, as we saw, Ben Uri, asleep (or dead?)
in the garden beside (or under?) his fallen ark, remains oblivious to Dinah
and to the narrative voice that articulates both the verse and its exegetical
restraint: the fallen ark, earlier animated by Satan, is now

> compared . . . to a woman who extends her palms in prayer, while her breasts—
> the Tables of the Covenant—are lifted with her heart, beseeching her Father in
> heaven: "Master of the Universe, this soul which Thou hast breathed into him
> Thou hast taken from him, so that now he is cast before Thee, like a body with-
> out its soul, and Dinah, this unspotted soul, has gone forth into exile . . . God!
> Till when shall the souls that dwell in Thy kingdom suffer the death of this life
> in bereavement [te'agena ha-neshamot she-be-'olamkha] . . ." (E 40, H 109)

The soul in this midrashic construct is clearly Dinah, and the now-emptied
body is that of Ben Uri. The narrator is providing us here with both the lock
(the Tables [tablets] of the Covenant) and the key (the ark "deconstructed" as
an innocent woman in her corporeal piety *and* desire) to the heart of the matter,
while also equipping us with different interpretive possibilities for the narrative
as a whole. The multiple levels contained in this passage include the narrator's
first act of comparison, the simile of the ark as a woman; then the controlling mechanism of rabbinic allegory, taken directly from midrashim on Song of
Songs, where, in an ancient moment, the Shulamite's breasts were "disappeared"
by being transmogrified first into Moses and Aaron and then into the Tables of
the Law (Song of Songs Rabbah 4:5);[33] and, finally, the definition of the author's
own literary project—and very identity—as scribe of bereaved souls ("te'agena
ha-neshamot she-be-'olamkha"). But closer focus on the rabbinic language reveals actual *inversions* in the midrashic procedure; Gershon Shaked calls attention to the fact that "instead of the woman being compared to the Ark of the
Law, the Ark is compared to the woman."[34] He calls this an "inverted metaphor"
and cites similar inversions throughout the text. I see this as a signal of an even
more radical upending of midrashic authority and privileging of the poetic act.
I would go so far as to claim that Agnon is performing a Pygmalion-like reversal of the dead image, bringing to life the woman calcified for so long in stony
tablets and petrified for the duration of this story in the Ark of the Covenant.

Still, as Pardes argues, no matter what one does with this story, for Agnon
and for the Zionist imagination in its many iterations, "the intensities of

earthly eros and love" were hard to accept on their own terms. It was, rather, the "exegetical imagination [itself that was] so riveting" to them.[35] She elaborates on this in the conclusion to her more recent "Biography" of the Song by reference to another, very short story by Agnon, in which Solomon himself is the main protagonist. Entitled "And Solomon's Wisdom Excelled" ("Vaterev ḥokhmat Shlomo," 1950), this tale is, Pardes claims, "a peculiar cross between midrashic commentary and fiction." In a possibly serious, possibly mischievous reference to the tension between the naked text and the layers of interpretation, the narrator tells us that Solomon hid many additional verses he had written because they had been misunderstood:

> There was one circle in Jerusalem . . . of good for nothing sages, who would take the holy words out of context and twist the plain meanings. Of these people Solomon observed: "Little foxes that spoil the vineyards" [Song 2:15]. To which vineyard does he refer? To none other than the vineyards of the Lord of hosts, of the House of Israel. What did this circle of sages say? "Look at Solomon! The people of Israel are building the Temple and he busies himself writing love songs!"[36]

Seeking to conceal his songs from the misprision of his readers, Solomon in this tale flees and buries his verses in Baʿal Hammon (Song 8:110). But, Pardes notes, the verses spring from the ground and entice the young maidens:

> verses of the ghostly Song that were supposedly forgotten . . . crop up in every line of Agnon's tale, coloring every . . . episode in Solomon's life . . . [While playing with the many layers of interpretation and appropriation, Agnon] challenges literalizers of the text for ignoring the ways in which the Song never ceases to generate allegorical readings. Even if we are inclined to read the Song literally, that is not entirely a viable option for a text that is replete with metaphors and sexual double entendres that call for a reading between the vines [!!].[37]

Indeed, even as we continue to read the verdant reality back into the vines, we've had occasion to see how what Pardes calls the "intensities of earthly eros and love" have caused discomfort in many readers, ancient, medieval, and modern—who have then gone on to spin their own allegorical screens. That might explain in part why, as I observed in chapter 2, what often gets overlooked in discussions of the resonances of this text is that Song of Songs is the most poetically self-conscious of any biblical text. As Chana Bloch puts it, quoting Robert Alter, the poet is "flaunting the effect of figurative comparison"; she goes on to say that the author of Song of Songs is "deliberately calling attention to the workings of simile and metaphor, and by extension, the workings of the imagination."[38]

Again, the "workings of the imagination" often border on delightful absurdities as the young, exuberant apprentices in love and in lyric hone their similes and metaphors. The simile, recall, is more amenable to control; it is the parable's "neighbor" because, as in the distinction between the *mashal* and the *nimshal*, the very act of comparison remains transparent and the distinction between the realms is maintained. When the Shulamite says she is "dark as the tents of Kedar, lavish as Solomon's tapestries" (1:5), every reader knows the difference between a dark-skinned maiden and a tent or a tapestry, even while looking for the quality that connects them. The metaphor is the parable's "foil" because it is evocative but not transparent and because it imagines the actual transformation of the given world.

Inevitably, then, any "literal" reading of the Song is also a "literary" reading, privileging the quest for the perfect image to match those "intensities of earthly eros and love." In advocating for a *naked* reading of the Song as it bubbles up in Agnon's fiction, I am arguing for those very acts of imagination that shape these intensities in both the biblical poem and Agnon's prose, those acts of imagination that actually celebrate human proximities by privileging distance between the religious object and the human subject: namely, the as-if nature of similes and metaphors.

Agnon's short narrative "And Solomon's Wisdom Excelled" foregrounds the other reason why readers in every generation are uncomfortable with a "naked" reading of Song of Songs: recall, again, that the most "subversive" element in the biblical text is the absence of any mention of the apparatus of holiness, specifically of the Temple that is associated in Jewish imagination with King Solomon—constituting the primary challenge to the rabbis, who had to work overtime to "restore" the holy artifacts to Jerusalem and the Temple to its King. Whether, as Agnon's Solomonic figure seems to insist, the Song is "really" about the Temple and its holy vessels is, then, the challenge for every reader in every generation, but never more so than in ours.

The space between the self and the holy is the space of human imagination—and of human love. This is the key I am offering to a new reading of both Agnon and Song of Songs. As we will see in the next chapter, Agnon's most prosaic protagonist, Isaac (Yitzhak) Kumer, becomes the unlikely vessel of this connection between human love and the creative imagination.

The Song: From Medieval Andalus to Twentieth-Century Jerusalem

This is also where the dialogue between Agnon and the Rambam on figural language, and the centrality of Song of Songs to that dialogue, is consummated. First let me summarize, briefly, the ways in which the Song enters into the discourse of the Great Eagle himself. Among the many biblical prooftexts in the *Guide*, there are in fact relatively few references to that most poetic of texts, so it is all the more remarkable that such references appear at the end of the treatise as what may be an implicit attempt to rechannel the passion of both *eros* and *poesis* by associating them with the only "safe" conduit: Moses—and his siblings.

"Let him kiss me with the kisses of his mouth . . ." The very opening line of the dialogue between the Shulamite and her lover, this liberated and unmasked encounter between two loving beings that produced the most far-flung of Hebrew poetic acts, is vouchsafed by the sages to Moses, his brother Aaron, and their sister Miriam. Only these three are said, Maimonides reminds us, to have "died by a kiss . . . The apprehension that is achieved in a state of intense and passionate love for Him . . . [is called] *a kiss*, in accordance with its dictum, *Let him kiss me with the kisses of his mouth*" (*Guide* III:51, p. 628). Moreover, this ultimate proximity to the Divine is enacted in the rabbis' and in Maimonides's vision not in the passion of youth but in the wisdom of old age. Michael Fishbane claims that this is the kiss of—which is—death.[39] Kalman Bland softens this reference and affirms Maimonides's appreciation for the external senses, though touch is the lesser of the senses: "In *Guide* 3:50 the kiss of God, alluded to in the biblical Song of Songs, is construed to mean that Moses, Aaron, and Miriam died pleasantly in a 'state of intense and passionate love' due to the perfection of their intellectual grasp of God."[40]

What is interesting about this image, as we have seen, is that in its *original* context, it is not a metaphor or even a simile but an indirect, third-person, erotic invitation by the female speaker to her lover: "Let him kiss me with the kisses of his mouth." It is only the rabbinic appropriation of the Song as a parable of love between God and Israel that anthropomorphizes an anthropocentric image and necessitates the kind of exegetical acrobatics that conclude the *Guide*.

Most worthy of notice in our own Age of Return is that the extraordinary conclusion to the magisterial medieval text is not only a midrashic cooptation of the Song along the lines followed by generations of biblical exegetes and sanctioned by Maimonides's consistent embrace of parabolic form, but also, implicitly, a warning against the unmediated approach to holiness through all its personifications. The "kiss" is vouchsafed to only three mortals: Moses and his two siblings. The warning extends, most urgently for twelfth-century Andalusia, to the figure of Jerusalem herself: the peril of the sacralization or reification of the poetic imagination through union (first metaphorical, then actual) is presented as the ultimate form of blasphemy. "*The whole earth is full of His glory*," quotes Maimonides from Isaiah 6:3, "all this being intended firmly to establish the notion that I have mentioned to you, that we are always before Him, may He be exalted, and walk about to and fro while His Indwelling is with us" (*Guide* III:52, p. 628).

So the mortal danger that was enacted in poet-pilgrim Yehuda Halevi's fateful voyage to Zion may be implicitly alluded to by the philosopher who was five years old when the poet died. Maimonides's own struggle with the invitation to approach the Divine through the delicate mediation of simile or parable is salient throughout the *Guide*—never more than in his discussion of the kiss that launches the Song and concludes his treatise. Remember, again, that it is not the use of figurative language per se that is at stake so much as the temptation to enact a direct human-divine encounter by *hypostatizing or literalizing* the figures of speech through *removing* the mediating level, i.e., the silver filigree itself, ostensibly to uncover the golden apple within.[41]

The danger that the rabbinic process tends to conceal (or, rather, addresses-by-not-addressing) is precisely what the Rambam addresses explicitly, though with the medieval philosopher's caution: even while controlling for a literal reading of the Song as love poem, with all its images of naked bodies and carnal desire, he acknowledges the power of the poetic imagination.

Embedded in the eight hundred years that separate the philosopher Moses ben Maimon in Cordoba, Fez, and Fostat from the writer Shmuel Yosef Halevi Czaczkes in Buczacz, then S. Y. Agnon in Jerusalem, are many twists and turns in the Hebrew imagination—the greater privileging of poetic autonomy being perhaps the most salient as it comes to fruition in the twentieth century. But as I read them together, I have discerned enough multidimensionality in the Rambam's invocation and interrogation of human metaphors and exegetical procedures, and enough complexities in Agnon's practice, to establish a virtual dialogue. Most relevant for our time and place are the medieval philosopher's repeated warnings against the temptation to literalize and spatialize the poetic imagination. And although, as we saw, his own pilgrimage to the Holy Land was short, in the context of contemporary messianic currents, it may have fueled the urgency with which he addressed the question of proximity to the sacred in the *Guide*.

Maimonides's Final Pilgrimage in Agnon's Prose: From Parable to Metaphor

Eight hundred years later, in his own sojourns to and eventual settlement in the Holy City—that is, within the very force field of the sacred and with the accelerating temptations of physical proximity and propriety—Agnon was, I believe, privileging the same distancing mechanisms of the imagination.

Brushing against the grain of generations of Agnon scholarship and "updating" the Rambam's lessons for our age, I have offered a radical reading that espouses the ethical foundations of eros and desire, expressed in similes and metaphors, over the controlling and literalizing mechanisms of the parable. Again, we might apply the interpretation of the open-ended allegory that was offered by Eastman and Holtz, and that earlier in the twentieth century Walter Benjamin suggested as a strategy for reading Kafka:

> Kafka's writings are by their nature parables. But it is their misery and their beauty that they had to become *more metaphor than parables*. They do not modestly lie at the feet of the doctrine, as the Haggadah lies at the feet of the Halakah. *Though apparently reduced to submission, they unexpectedly raise a mighty paw against it.* (Emphasis mine)[42]

As long as the exercise of the parabolic imagination remained far from the sources of the sacred, or from the practicality of physical proximity and political hegemony, the "couch" of the two young lovers in the Song could signify the Temple where the "spiritual union with God" transpires. Indeed, as we saw, and as Fishbane elucidates, the "Ark (with its staves) was deemed a virtual marital bed for God's fructifying presence" (Song of Songs Rabbah 1:16.3).[43] In the rabbis' own freewheeling and inconsequential rhetoric, human eros and flights of poetic fancy could be contained and transcended through midrashic acrobatics. But the dangers of literalizing and grounding those images that had solidified into physical sites over generations of exegesis came home to roost as Agnon was struggling with his own fictional, ethical, and political project.

The parabolic practice of Israel's Nobel laureate often seems, indeed, to conform to Benjamin's defense of allegory as an attempt to reintroduce temporality into the presumed absolutism of the romantic (or, in Jewish terms, the mystical, kabbalistic) symbol. Similarly, Agnon's narrative gaze both incorporates and defers nostalgia for the lost edenic past and a glimpse at the messianic future. Certainly not every *mashal* in his fiction is a "false" parable. But there is an unresolved conflict between parable and symbol—between the form known as "mashal" and what I've called its neighbor the simile and its foil, the metaphor—that remains at the heart of Maimonides's and, mutatis mutandis, Agnon's poetics. Maimonides, I submit, was caught in a paradox of sorts, presuming an inability to grasp the incorporeal and yet finding in hermeneutic practice grounded in philosophical reasoning a traditional language capable of grasping and communicating revelation. Agnon replicates this paradox in a time and place that are even more consequential.

My argument, then, is that Agnon often sets up the parable as something of a straw man, not in the name of literalism, but rather in the name of *literariness.* Ultimately, his fictions can be read as privileging the metaphoric imagination above those exegetical acts that would reify the holy and endorse the physical proximity to holiness. As we saw in two of his most canonical stories, "Agunot" and "Aggadat ha-sofer," the space of human love is also the space of the human imagination. But as we will see in the next chapter even more dramatically, the two competing systems—the controlled literalism of the exegetical-rabbinic imagination and the open-endedness of the erotic-poetic imagination—are never fully reconciled in his fictions, certainly not in the heart of Jerusalem.

"Every day I have regretted not having stood in the breach": Agnon in Jerusalem

Maimonides' observations on the holiness of Jerusalem are the most salient, as a result both of their phrasing and of the idea of holiness in them . . . In most cases, Maimonides attributes holiness to God, and the holiness ascribed to various objects (such as Torah scrolls, mezuzot, phylacteries, the holy language) stems from this singular and specific source and is teleological. The sanctity of Jerusalem, however, was created in a particular manner by the divine presence; holiness results from the presence of the *Shekhinah*. God's presence renders space sacred . . . On reading the description of Tu bi-shevat or the prayer for dew in S. Y. Agnon's *Korot Betenu* . . . , one understands the importance of literary formulation and of historical memory preserved and strengthened by literary description which affords a vicarious experience in the absence of a direct and immediate one. *Maimonides' remarks helped to restore the Temple to active historical consciousness.* It is also possible to say that remarks like these served as a *shield against any spiritualizing exegesis which is liable to find Jerusalem in Lithuania or New York or in the Jewish soul. The divine presence is immovable, the parameters of its sanctity unchangeable, and it is impossible to find a substitute for it.*

I S A D O R E   T W E R S K Y, "Maimonides and Eretz Yisrael," 285–86 (emphasis mine)[1]

The above quotation is from Isadore Twersky's essay exploring Maimonides's attitudes toward (and sojourn in) the Holy Land. A meditation not only on the Rambam, but also on late twentieth-century repercussions of issues addressed in the twelfth century, Twersky's essay presupposes a scale of holiness based on proximity to Jerusalem, the immanent and immutable sacred center. The derivative nature of any sacramental object provides a "vicarious experience" of holiness. Diasporic culture, which is by definition vicarious, premised on substitution, mimesis, and mutability, is here implicitly dismissed as "Lithuania . . . New York . . . the Jewish soul" itself. In this reading, all derivative objects and acts are meant to be disarmed in Jerusalem, where the "divine presence is immovable, the parameters of its sanctity unchangeable, and it is impossible to find a substitute for it."

Perceiving the viability, and necessity, in present-day Jerusalem of diasporic wisdom and practice gained in "exile," I would dispute the implacability of Twersky's premises. And, given my own readings of the *Guide* offered in chapter 3, I would also argue that Twersky's essay elides some of the fundamental and unresolved conflicts that characterized the Rambam's life and work.

It is revealing that it is Agnon whom Twersky pairs with the Great Eagle, as the modern writer who understands the surrogate nature of literary description vis-à-vis Jerusalem. The story he cites is from a cycle called *Korot Bateinu*—"our roofbeams"—which are the words that close the first chapter of Song of Songs ("Our roofbeams are cedar, our rafters fur," Song 1:17). We already saw how central the Song is to Agnon's imaginative universe, but in the story cited by Twersky, which was probably written just a year or so before the author's death and published posthumously,[2] the narrator camouflages the original biblical reference by exploiting the double entendre that renders the same phrase—*korot bateinu*—as "chronicles of our homes."[3] The homes referred to here are the abandoned and then destroyed dwellings of the Jews of Buczacz and Galicia generally; implicitly, then, the roofbeams in Jerusalem echoed in the phrase from Song of Songs are displaced by the roofbeams of Buczacz, which, in turn, were themselves demolished.

It is worth taking a closer look at the particular passage Twersky cites, where he acknowledges that memory is preserved through "vicarious experience" represented by "various objects" and invoked by "literary description." He is insisting that what is meant to be superseded in Jerusalem is precisely those diasporic metonymies or synecdoches of the Holy Land. But Twersky ignores the fact that in the Agnon story he cites, such "objects" include the ceremonial citron or *etrog* grown in Eretz Yisrael that, in a lean year, had been cut *into pieces*, distributed among many Polish Jewish communities, and then finally transformed—that is, literally *preserved*—as jam.[4] The "literary formulation" Twersky inadvertently cites is, then, the verbal preserve of the confected preserve of the symbol or metonymy of Eretz Yisrael. Such a "vicarious experience" is clearly two or three removes from the Sacred Center. Yet such diasporic practices will, it turns out, not be relinquished—even in Jerusalem itself.[5]

In enlisting Agnon to corroborate and update his claim that the Rambam "helped restore the Temple to active historical consciousness," Twersky overlooks the profound conflict that such a process entailed for both writers. In the *Guide* as in his own life, as we have seen, the Rambam struggled with the internal contradictions inherent in precepts and language that govern proximity to and substitution for sacred space. Eight centuries later, these struggles will reappear in the fictions of Israel's Nobel laureate.

In the hypothetical dialogue I constructed in the previous chapter between Maimonides and Agnon, the iterations of holiness do, indeed, inhere in "various objects" such as the Torah scroll and the Ark of the Covenant, along with advisories about ascribing holiness to physical space. It is these very objects that underscore, for Agnon's first readers and even more urgently

for those of us encountering these texts decades later, the *value of surrogacy*
and the *dangers of fetishizing such objects and privileging them over the sanctity of . . . human love*. Exegetical-rhetorical figures such as the "mashal" (parable), moreover, have the potential for generating consequential acts of literalization in the age of return to sacred space. The liberating force of simile or
metaphor, the free exercise of the human imagination, has never been more
consequential than it is today.

Nothing illustrates Agnon's vexing ambivalence more than *Tmol shilshom*
(Only Yesterday), the novel that explores the holiness in Jerusalem herself
and penetrates even to the very center of holiness: the ongoing site of conten-
tion in modern Jerusalem, the Holy of Holies. In this chapter, I will examine the artistic and ethical strategies that nearly save the protagonist from
his own tragic-sacrificial destiny. Finally, I will briefly consider the profound
challenges that newly acquired access to, and sovereignty over, the sites of
holiness presented to the aging writer in his last years.

The Belated Levite and the Surrogacy of Prose

As a result of the historic catastrophe in which Titus of Rome destroyed Jerusalem and
Israel was exiled from its land, I was born in one of the cities of the Exile. But always I
regarded myself as one who was born in Jerusalem. In a dream, in a vision of the night,
I saw myself standing with my brother-Levites in the Holy Temple, singing with them
the songs of David, King of Israel, melodies such as no ear has heard since the day our
city was destroyed and its people went into exile. I suspect that the angels in charge of
the Shrine of Music, fearful lest I sing in wakefulness what I had sung in dream, made
me forget by day what I had sung at night; for if my brethren, the sons of my people,
were to hear, they would be unable to bear their grief over the happiness they have lost.
To console me for having prevented me from singing with my mouth, they enable me
to compose songs in writing.

                    s . y . a g n o n , Nobel Prize acceptance speech, 1966[6]

In the preceding chapter, we looked at one section of Agnon's Nobel acceptance speech, in which he named his sources and influences. Another section
of the speech defined his lineage and his vocation. Although it may have reso-
nated exotically in the august concert hall in Stockholm and provided future
generations of readers with quaint readings within the line of "tradition,"[7]
what Agnon's Nobel acceptance speech insists upon is consistent with the
particular practice of Jewish culture in exile. The status of prose is presented
here and elsewhere as surrogate for the Real Word, i.e., the psalms sung by the
writer's Levite ancestors on the steps leading to the Real Place, i.e., the Temple.[8] (What is at work here might be called the "Levite envy" of belatedness,

reminiscent of the nostalgia and projected visions of Yehuda Ha-Levi [lit., Yehuda The Levite]). This is of a piece, ostensibly, with Twersky's reading of the Rambam and with Agnon's persistently entropic stance, beginning, as we saw, with his first Hebrew story, "Agunot": namely, that events unravel from, or are predicated on, an edenic place or point of origin which is the *telos* of the poetic as of the religious project. In the meantime, then, rhetoric itself evolves as a default mode for an originary source.

As he declared in his Nobel acceptance speech, Agnon regards himself as practicing what every Hebrew writer has done since the closing of the biblical canon and the destruction of the "second" Temple in Jerusalem: establishing surrogacy or mimesis as a placeholder in the "meantime" between dispersal and redemption. The desire and the danger are that much greater, then, when they are enacted within the gravitational force field of the Sacred Center, which, Twersky imperiously insists, brooks no substitutes.

The fullest iteration of the temptations generated by Jerusalem itself, and of the rhetorical and thematic resources available to a descendant of the Levites, is the novel that remains Agnon's greatest achievement. *Tmol shilshom* (Only Yesterday) was written during the Second World War and published in the war's immediate aftermath, but before the establishment of the State of Israel. It focuses on the period corresponding to Agnon's first years in Palestine, or the *yishuv*—approximately 1908–11. Seventy-plus years and thousands of pages of exegesis later, this 607-page novel remains the site of the most enigmatic struggle between conflicting forces and conflicting interpretations, with repercussions that go beyond the poetic to the theological and, in the most profound sense, the political.

We have already seen that the opaque intertextuality of any page of Agnon's prose creates puzzles that keep his fictions alive and unresolved. Deciphering or decoding Agnon is, indeed, a lifelong and intergenerational pursuit, as purposeful—or fanciful—as any midrashic enterprise. Some critics remain convinced that if we just try harder—more money, more time, more research assistants—we will uncover the hidden truth;[9] others assume that every generation adds its own bricks and mortar to what must remain forever incomplete, a sort of Gaudi-like tribute to the endless quest for Agnon's secret.[10]

In endorsing the latter position, that the secret is not a riddle to be solved but an enigma to be honored, I am also suggesting that every layer of critical prose is not only mortar for the edifice, but also a mirror of the mason's face. Beyond identifying and either "solving" or respecting the specific riddles or enigmas in this text, it is an enigmatic *approach* that I am endorsing, such as that articulated by T. W. Adorno:

Aesthetics cannot hope to grasp works of art if it treats them as hermeneutical objects. What at present needs to be grasped is their unintelligibility . . .
Achieving an adequate interpretive understanding of a work of art means de-
mystifying certain enigmatic dimensions without trying to shed light on its
constitutive enigma . . . To solve a riddle in art is to identify the reason why it
is insoluble—which is the gaze art works direct at the viewer.[11]

In the following pages, I will read the novel through the lens of two biblical
intertexts: Genesis 22 and Numbers 22–24. If, as I argued in chapter 1, the biblical narrative in Genesis that we refer to as the akeda has the structural and
rhetorical properties of comedy, reviving the comic mode in the holiest site
in Jerusalem immediately after the shoah is a feat that only Agnon could have
pulled off. But, I daresay, this feat lay buried for decades after the publication
of the novel under the weight of other readings. And the presence in the novel
of the chapter indexed in the cyclical synagogual reading as Parashat Balak
has escaped attention altogether.[12] By casting light on these two intertexts, I
am attempting to illuminate an impulse that Agnon himself hid deep within
his narrative and that, when exposed, can serve to restore the human dimension: a respect for the quotidian and mediated distance from the sacred. Such a
reading augments the sense of mystery and enigma, while revealing the comic
layer that, as we have already seen, is the well-kept secret of the akeda.

Tmol Shilshom and the Sacrifice of Isaac: Reading Backward

The title of Agnon's magnum opus, *Tmol shilshom*, a biblical phrase translated by
Barbara Harshav as *Only Yesterday*,[13] actually means *habitually, as in days of yore*,
or *yesteryear*. In many ways, this novel applies the habitual, mimetic approaches
to Jerusalem that have been practiced worldwide for over two thousand years—
put to the ultimate test in the presence of sacrificial temptations at the Sacred
Center. That those temptations will prevail in a novel at war with itself will become clear at the end. I will, therefore, begin my exploration of this novel from
its hideous conclusion, as it is only when read backward, or "backshadowing," in
Michael André Bernstein's felicitous phrase,[14] that many of the loose threads of a
meandering narrative are bound into a coherent, tragic-sacrificial whole:

They *bound Isaac with ropes* [*kashru et Yitzhak be-havalim*] and put him in
a room . . . *by himself* [*yehidi*] . . . In the end, the muscles of his body and the
muscles of his face became paralyzed. Finally, his pained soul passed away and
he returned his spirit to the *God of spirits for whom there is no laughter and
no frivolity* [*hishiv ruho le-elohei ha-ruhot she-ein le-fanav lo tzhok ve-lo kalut
rosh*]. (E 640, H 605, translation slightly emended, emphases mine)

As demonstrated in the words I have emphasized, the denouement is satu-rated with the rhetoric of Genesis 22; the narrator's description of *Isaac* sitting *alone* in his room, *bound* with ropes, resonates for every Hebrew reader with the language of the akeda. The reference to a pitiless God with no sense of humor, Who, one might say, hasn't read His own scriptures properly, is some-thing to which we will return.

Additional references in this passage come from Lamentations, as Isaac in his death throes recites the verses describing Jerusalem lamenting her own fate: "Isaac sat alone in the dark room and lamented from the Book of Lam-entations, 'She weeps in the night and her tears are on her cheeks'" (*Yitzhak mekonen be-kol eikha . . . bakho tivke ba-layla ve-dim'ata 'al lihyeha*, E 640, H 605, translation emended). So Isaac's "sacrifice" and Jerusalem's destruc-tion become the determinant images in a retrospective reading.

The conclusion of *Tmol shilshom* is as satisfying as the climax of a Wag-nerian opera or a Cecil B. DeMille movie. Isaac's death from rabies will be followed by claps of thunder and torrents of rain falling on the parched earth, making it the necessary sacrifice, as the heavens provide cosmic evidence of divine wrath expended and placated.

Indeed, resonances of the rhetoric of Genesis 22 and of Lamentations ren-der the denouement so dramatic that it threatens to reduce the novel to the bare contours of a plot revealed only at the end. Arguably the most canonical of modern Hebrew fictions, *Tmol shilshom* remains, despite much decipher-ing and decoding, also the most mysterious. It is, briefly, the story of a man and of a dog. Not a man and *his* dog.[15] Rather, it is the tale, rendered in re-alistic prose, of Isaac (Yitzhak) Kumer, a man of average stature, a dreamer who proves useless in his father's shop in Galicia and is dispatched to the land of his dreams. Linking his fate to the grand narrative of Israel's national rebirth during the period that would come to be referred to as the Second Aliyah, Isaac fails almost immediately at his ambition to become a pioneer in the Land of Israel, as he fails at his love for the bohemian Sonia in the cof-feehouses of Jaffa. But he reinvents himself in the alleyways of Old Jerusalem, gaining some professional stature as a house and sign painter and a measure of personal happiness in his requited and, eventually, consummated love for the pious Shifra. Isaac's chance meeting with a stray dog at the moment of his greatest contentment and hard-won equilibrium, and his frivolous and mendacious painting of the words "crazy dog" (*kelev meshuga'*) on the ca-nine's back, mark a shift in the novel's center of gravity—both in the focus of consciousness, from human to animal, and in the texture of the prose, from realism to something I will call, for the moment, "magical realism." The narrator's interest moves to the mind of the accursed dog, "Balak,"[16] whose

peregrinations through Jerusalem's ultra-Orthodox neighborhoods in search
of food and kindness—or, failing that, some comprehension of his outcast
state, the code to which he knows to be inscribed on his back—lead directly
to his last, fatal encounter with the painter who branded him. Looking not
so much for vengeance as for *truth incarnate*, Balak sinks his now-rabid teeth
into Isaac's flesh and brings about his ghastly death.

Ostensibly, when read backward through the topos of the akeda, the
melodramatic fate of this latter-day Isaac seems to satisfy its hyperbolic beginning: Isaac Kumer the *naif*, whose inflated dream of Zion carried the seeds
of its own destruction, is bitten by a mad dog and sacrificed on the altar of
the most primitive version of Jewish theodicy, the "fulfilled" akeda. Nothing unusual there: as we saw in chapter 1, most postbiblical retellings of the
akeda—Jewish and Christian—preclude all substitutes or last-minute interventions so that the only constant is a misreading of the text that construes
the actual sacrifice of Isaac. Even the animal that appears in this novel is not a
replacement for but *the very instrument of* Isaac's death—endowed, moreover,
with the consciousness of his own deed. What is, nevertheless, highly unusual
for a modern theodicy is both the hideous detail and the level of authorial
assent implied in the redemptive effects of that death. As we shall see, the
sometimes-intrusive narrator does briefly express dismay at such undeserved
punishment, which, after all, like every version of the akeda, is based on a
misreading.[17]

And yet many early readers who belonged to the century about which,
and in which, *Tmol shilshom* was written seemed inclined to dismiss the
structural and rhetorical echoes of the akeda, preferring to read the novel
as an epic of the Zionist pioneering project. The ancient Jewish passion play
was hardly the foundation on which modern Hebrew nationalism was being
constructed in the years leading to the establishment of the State of Israel,
though, as we saw in chapter 1, that would soon change as dead soldiers on
the battlefield would be recruited as so many Isaacs on the altar.

Today's readings are of course also inflected by today's opportunities
and threats. In the century—or millennium—inaugurated by an escalation
of hostilities in the Holy Land, a surge of messianic fundamentalism, and a
hardening of sovereign claims to holy sites, the dominant image in our mirror
may be the terror of (or desire for) impending apocalypse. Out of sympathy
or despair, then, some readers may be tempted to revert to the most intracta-
ble of Jewish myths, effectively declaring the bankruptcy of other paradigms
of Jewish history, Jewish imagination, and the locus of Jewish sanctity.

In the following pages, I will argue against such apocalyptic determinism
by suggesting that although the "completed" akeda may function here, as it

has in the religious imagination for over two thousand years, as the explicit governing mythos, a careful reading of this novel, like a careful reading of the akeda itself, uncovers the comedy that governs both texts, rhetorically and structurally. And, as we saw in chapter 1, whenever the constitutive story of the akeda is reimagined on the human stage, it promises to enter the realm of the ethical, the universal, where it would break the bonds of its own silent acquiescence to an inscrutable, peremptory, and morally perverse command—and where it could also conjure the divine source of laughter and comedy. From retellings in midrashic narratives that supply the human exchanges missing in the received text, through the fictions of Søren Kierkegaard, Franz Kafka, and Hanoch Levin, something is inevitably released that undermines the traditional apprehension of the text.[18]

Recall that when Kafka imagines Abraham for himself, it is an Abraham who, though

> prepared to satisfy the demand for a sacrifice immediately . . . certainly would have never gotten to be a patriarch or even an old-clothes dealer . . . unable to bring it off because he could not get away, being indispensable; the household needed him, there was perpetually something or other to put in order, the house was never ready.[19]

The human comedy, embedded in the quotidian, becomes, then, the most humane response to any outrageous suprahuman demand.

So when Agnon's noisy conclusion to his 607-page novel reinstates the tragic *telos* in all its terrible grandeur, it seems to be declaring the House Ready through putting an end to what might be called the "ethics of imagination," overriding the fiction with a peremptory myth that ties all the loose ends together. We shall see that whatever agency was ascribed to Isaac as he slowly gained stature throughout the course of his narrative, whatever digressions he was permitted into the byways and alleyways of a private life, whatever dignity he reached as diminished but still recognizable embodiment of a modern hero connected to his fate by his deeds, by some eventual recognition of the consequences of those deeds, and by a healthy dose of contingency and the mediation of his humble imagination, and whatever access he had to the human comedy are drowned out in the thunder of an absurd apocalypse.

Most of the contemporary critical debates on what is surely Agnon's bleakest and most powerful fiction have revolved around generic questions prompted by the horrendous ending as well as by internal inconsistencies or contradictions in the texture of the novel. Defined by one reader as a *rav-roman*, masternovel or polygeneric novel,[20] it appears to be trying on and discarding fictional discourses like so many ill-fitting clothes, and then, finally

satisfied with the fit of the akeda, it binds Isaac to an ending that corrobo-
rates the most mythic reading and accords some symbolic unity to its parts.
Although there are those who still value the novel for its social or even "documentary" quality,[21] the most interesting discussions of the novel have reclaimed it for its tragic vision. Dan Miron's monumental exploration of *Tmol
shilshom* both rescues Isaac as the *homme moyen sensuel* with affinities to
Emma Bovary and Anna Karenina and places him and Balak in the space first
visited by Faust and Mephistopheles (in the guise of a dog).[22]

There is a certain slippage in the critical discussion between the paradigms
of tragedy and theodicy, which is also a slippage between fiction and myth. Arnold (Avraham) Band was one of the first to call attention to the akeda as topos
in the novel, reflecting the author's response to the catastrophe in Europe that
was concluded as he was concluding his novel; Band entitled his essay "Crime
and Punishment," implying the kind of affinity between a man's deeds and his
fate that belongs to the tragic imagination, filtered through Dostoevsky's polyphonic prism.[23] Even in Miron's riveting analysis, the akeda is not presented as
mythic alternative to the tragic paradigm of sacrificial death; rather, it is invoked
somewhat casually as the default mode of the Hebrew tragic imagination.[24]
Such slippage occludes the crucial distinctions between the two with respect
to the most vigorously debated issues: the guilt or responsibility and stature of
the hero, and the presumption of meaningful, if inscrutable, design. "Abraham
[and, by extension, Isaac?] is . . . at no instant the tragic hero, but something
quite different, either a murderer or a man of faith," argues Kierkegaard.[25]

And yet, whether Isaac Kumer is punished for his "sins," or whether he is
the innocent scapegoat projected as an ironic, anachronistic, sacrifice in a pitiless cosmos that has just countenanced the death of his brothers and sisters in
Galicia and the rest of Europe, whether his fate is redemptive, absurd, or grotesque, his death is seen as superseding all the other claims of the novel. And
that is—so it might be imagined—Agnon's last word, conveying, depending on
your point of view, either the mystery or the absurdity of Jewish theodicy.

Rather than reading the text backward, I submit an open-ended exegetical
approach that focuses on the House and its inhabitants, who are, in fact, in
need of constant attention. By construing even the akeda more imaginatively,
through what Bernstein calls "sideshadowing,"[26] we can indeed uncover an
entirely different narrative arc in *Tmol shilshom*.

Reading Forward: Following the Balak Trail

Like the five chapters that, as we saw, surround Genesis 22 with comic possibilities,[27] the "Balak trail" leads us to another buried biblical subtext, with its own

disruptive potential. I suggest reading *Tmol shilshom* also through Numbers 22–24, not so much for its explicit theme as for its texture, its implicit invitation to a more indeterminate, unresolvable fount of mystery, meaning, and authority. This narrative, in which a non-Israelite prophet, Balaam, has been recruited by King Balak of Moab to curse the children of Israel, continues by means of supernatural visions, a sentient donkey, an angel, and Balaam's eventual conversion of the curse into a blessing. It is not in specific parallels between Agnon's dog Balak and his royal namesake, but in the rhetorical and structural elements of the biblical story in which this character appears—and the threads it supplies to other biblical passages—that an alternative reading of the entire novel lies. Availing ourselves of the dog's name as an invitation to read the ancient narrative into the modern one provides another comic shadow-text. It licenses a different approach to the intrusion of the supernatural in a realistic narrative, a different apprehension of the human-animal encounter, a different understanding of symbolic mediation in the representation of reality—and, most significantly for our project, a different view of the locus of holiness.

There is a way in which the Balak trail can actually lead us back to the first, "pristine," readings of *Tmol shilshom*. Advertised for its social panorama of the Second Aliyah, the narrative, which appeared in two volumes in 1945–46, was awarded the Menahem Ussishkin Prize for the author's "accurate representation [*realiut*] of their world." Agnon's admiring contemporaries had to repress or marginalize the two main discrepancies between the text and their appraisal of it: the appearance of a sentient dog in a realistic novel, and the ending that finishes off the hero with a death so horribly redemptive that all attempts to naturalize it are doomed to failure.[28] There was even an attempt to "naturalize" the hideous fate of Isaac Kumer: the horrible details of death by rabies, depending as they do on a medical report widely circulated in the Yishuv at the time, could, it was argued, be read as a "realistic" representation of the "average" death of an "average" Zionist idealist.[29]

The reading that I am suggesting allows us to recover some of this original faith in the material world represented by the realism of the human comedy, without sacrificing the mystery introduced by both the canine Balak's consciousness and his hideous final act. It privileges and affirms the natural world while remaining both available to and skeptical about the supernatural. To the naïve hopefulness of Agnon's contemporary readers and our own generation's apocalyptic determinism, this approach adds a more tentative epistemological dimension. And the two impulses released, respectively, through the revisionist reading of the akeda and the traces of "Parashat Balak" are powerful contenders for a Jewish aesthetic and moral stance in the world after 1945—and especially after 1967.

Once we acknowledge it, we can see that the introduction of a sentient dog as Isaac's counterpart in this novel, like the introduction of a talking ass as Balaam's counterpart in Numbers 22, does not displace an otherwise fairly consistent realistic discourse, but it does destabilize it and licenses *undecidability* as an alternative hermeneutic principle. What emerges is a more fluid, enigmatic, and humanistic reading than the one that privileges sacrificial death and apocalyptic thunderbolts. With these subtexts in mind, I am equating Parashat Balak with what Robert Alter would call "novelistic thinking"— and *akedat yitzhak* with the myth or theodicy that displaces or supersedes the fictive. Alter identifies "the general norm of historical and psychological realism that, despite the occasional intervention of divine agency or miraculous event, governs classical Hebrew narrative."[30] Such subliminal themes and imagery in the novel both serve the postmodern stance of uncertainty, skepticism, and humility and provide a reading of Agnon that can counter the exclusivist eschatological stance vis-à-vis Jerusalem herself.

The Dialectical Imagination

Even at the end of the novel, the ostensibly resolved conflict between natural and supernatural authority leaves remainders, recalcitrant traces of discarded forms that could prove to be the reader's most important resource. And this, in turn, is bound to the almost unnoticed but persistent development of Isaac's own imagination, the "still small voice" beneath, behind, or after the storm.

What will evolve as the protagonist's small voice and the reader's complex response begins as a barely perceived prelude to, derivative and remainder of, an epic battle. We saw that in a first, "backshadowing" reading, the mythic topos of the akeda appears as the final resolution of a rhythm that has governed the novel, an ongoing oscillation between promise and collapse as perfect worlds are constructed and deconstructed. Both Zionism and anxious messianism have produced a dialectic of expectation and disappointment that yields, in the end, to the peremptory authority of the akeda. What informs this narrative from its opening sentence is a search for coherence and harmony in every domain—ideological, metaphysical, and aesthetic. The first passage syncretizes memories and visions of perfection from ancient and modern sources:

> Like all our brethren of the Second Aliya, the bearers of our salvation, Isaac Kumer left his country and his homeland and his city and ascended to the Land of Israel to build it from its destruction and to be rebuilt by it. From the day our comrade Isaac knew his mind, not a day went by that he didn't

think about it. A blessed dwelling place was his image of the whole Land of Israel and its inhabitants blessed by God. Its villages hidden in the shade of vineyards and olive groves, the fields enveloped in grains and the orchard trees crowned with fruit, the valleys yielding flowers and the forest trees swaying; the whole firmament is sky blue and all the houses are filled with rejoicing. By day they plow and sow and plant and reap and gather and pick, threshing wheat and pressing wine, and at eventide they sit every man under his vine and under his fig tree, his wife and his sons and daughters sitting with him, happy at their work and rejoicing in their sitting, and they reminisce about the days of yore Outside the Land like people who in happy times recall days of woe, and enjoy the good twice over. *A man of imagination was Isaac, what his heart desired, his imagination would conjure up for him.* (E 3, H 7, emphasis mine)

One way of reading this is as a seamless interweaving, or what Amos Oz calls a "naïve synthesis," of Zionist-utopian and scriptural-messianic rhetoric—from the Bible to the Bilu. He explains: "The opening paragraph of *Only Yesterday* is a mosaic of biblical verses inlaid with echoes of poems by the Hebrew poets of Hibat Zion (the Lovers of Zion in Russia in the 1880s) and of Bialik's poem 'To a Bird,' with a slight whiff of the mid-nineteenth-century Hebrew novelist Abraham Mapu, propaganda clichés of early Zionism, and slogans of BILU, the idealistic founders of the First Aliya."[31] The snake enters this garden, inevitably, just a few pages later, when Isaac Kumer has actually made the pilgrimage from his hometown in Galicia to the shores of Jaffa. No sooner does he disembark than he is attacked by sunstroke, bedbugs, deception, and disillusion:

An hour or two ago, he was drinking the air of other lands, and now he is drinking the air of the Land of Israel. No sooner had he collected his thoughts than the porters were standing around him and demanding money from him. He took out his purse and gave them. They demanded more. He gave them. They demanded more. Finally, they wanted *baksheesh*. When he got rid of the Arabs, a Jew came and took Isaac's belongings . . . [He found himself in a hostel where] the food was thin and the bedbugs were fat, the bugs sucked his blood by night as their owner sucked his blood by day. (E 39–40, H 40–41)

The imagination of perfection is predicated on distance; it is in this sense that Isaac is originally presented as "a man of imagination" (*ba'al dimyonot*).[32] The temptation to draw near, to step off the train or the ship onto dry land is, inevitably, to yield to the idyll's counterpart—to the dystopia that is the waking side of the dream.

This seesaw between utopia and dystopia, so central to Agnon's semikabbalistic aesthetic of repair and disrepair, perfection and dissolution—adumbrated, as we saw, in his earliest story "Agunot"[33]—is only one of a series of binary moves that dominate the rhythm of this text. We become so habituated to this rhythm that we automatically look for the dialectical "other" in every taxonomic field, whether geographical (Galicia and the Land of Israel [*hutza la-aretz, eretz hefetz*], Jaffa and Jerusalem), erotic (Sonia and Shifra), zoological (Isaac and Balak), ideological (secular Zionist and ultra-Orthodox), or aesthetic (wholeness and fragmentation).

Even within the vertigo produced by this seesaw, we recognize that there is plenty of "reality" in this novel, as Agnon's contemporaries were quick to appreciate. The narrative even appears in places like a precise snapshot of Jewish society in Palestine at the beginning of the twentieth century, under the sign, respectively, of the Zionist dream (Jaffa) and rigid Jewish pietism (Jerusalem).[34] The other level of historical consciousness, the other reality that informs the novel—the Nazi nightmare of the 1940s, the years during which the novel was being completed—weaves its way insidiously through these landscapes like the dark, brooding presence of clouds that never release their water.

But the dialectical structure dictates that even with all this detail, it is not so much history's nightmare—the time during which this novel was written or even the time about which it was written—as the *deconstructed dream* that is, inevitably, its own foil. The prose, no matter how referential, is almost entirely bound by its own discursive principles. Not one but *two* dreams or utopian visions—the Zionist and the messianic—intersect, overlap, and compete as models of artistic and social perfection.[35] The nightmare is, then, not so much the intrusion of "history" into the edenic picture, as the dialectically inevitable, self-inflicted, mutilation of the picture. Before Isaac is "done in" by the author through the agency of Balak, he is "done in" by the narrator, through the agency of satire.

But, like the rhetoric of the akeda, the seesaw dynamic itself with its inexorably dystopic, satiric version of the dream masks what is, I believe, the more fundamental form of historical consciousness in *Tmol shilshom*: the judgment of human time, the present tense, the materiality of the surface, weighed against any vision of perfection or redemption. In the noise and cacophony, the thunder and lightning of the epic, melodramatic, or satiric sections of the novel, this voice is so quiet and tentative that it can easily be overlooked; so understated that it can be heard only by putting one's ear nearly to the ground; so diminutive that, like the size of Isaac's imagination, it appears invisible or insignificant beside the works and words of his betters. I hope to show that Isaac's most significant voyage is not between the dream and the awakening but the slow and tentative venture into the recesses of his own soul, the discovery and acceptance of his own agency as *ba'al dimyonot*. His is a hesitant and ultimately only partial journey out of the forms of discourse—utopian or magical—in which he is caught. The pendulum's swing has not entirely succeeded in camouflaging the slow but steady emergence of a subtle and nondialectical undervoice, the appearance of the smallest space between the portrait of human redemption or social perfection and its default mode, between utopia and dystopia, dream and reality.[36]

Ba'al Dimyonot: The Birth of the Fictive Mind

In holding a magnifying glass to that space, or turning up the volume on that undervoice, I am, admittedly, reading against the grain of prevailing critical opinion. Even in the discussions of *Tmol shilshom* as a novel of social realism, Isaac is rarely accorded the dignity and singularity of his character. Seen as emblem or victim of his historical moment, as passive, superficial, or even boring receptacle of full-blown ideologies—Zionist or ultra-Orthodox—he is hardly granted a significant place in his own story.[37] Even readers preoccupied by the challenge of a sentient dog and his connection with Isaac's hideous fate hardly hear Isaac's voice.

But when trying to "redeem" Isaac in the interstices of his own story, we will not have recourse to the usual tricks of the trade, to the magic that would rescue the character from his penury, his mediocrity, or his melancholy. There is no magic in *Tmol shilshom*, unless you include sentient dogs (!), and no miracles, unless you include the rain falling on drought-seared Jerusalem at the end. That is, there *is* a miracle of sorts at the end, but no magic. The text relentlessly eliminates all of its supernatural temptations. As Isaac walks through Jaffa, "the Lord of Imagination [*ba'al ha-dimyonot*] walks about with him."[38] But what that means, as Isaac will learn, painfully and repeatedly, is that he must become lord of his *own* imagination, because

> miracles don't happen to every person, especially not to a fellow like Isaac, who isn't worth it to the Lord to perform a miracle for him even in a natural way . . . His heart became the home of thoughts for honest and naive people, like Reb Yudel Hasid his ancestor [protagonist of Agnon's *Hakhnasat kalah* (The Bridal Canopy)] and his three nubile daughters, who, when they were over their heads in troubles, the Lord summoned up for them a cave and they found a treasure. Isaac raised his head slightly and peeped into the cave and said, But here there is no treasure. (E 64, H 64, translation slightly emended)

The universe in which Isaac lives, then, is disenchanted—and even if he ultimately consecrates the soil by his own death, it is hardly worth the price. The topos of the akeda will save neither the character nor the novel. Rather, as solutions to life and to literature are sought with utopian-messianic urgency, and ultimately absorbed into the governing myth, each character—Kumer in his turn, Balak in his (and the reader in hers)—also moves through more compromised forms of novelistic inquiry, negotiation, and hesitation.

The relation between magic, with its forms of enchantment or divination, and "truth," as sought, veiled, and revealed in the phenomenal world, is at the heart of the biblical subtexts I am invoking as the hermeneutic key to the novel. To reread *Tmol shilshom* under the sign of Parashat Balak and through the comic license of the akeda is to pay close attention to the realism in all three texts. In the Hebrew Scriptures, symbolic negotiations between the real and the sacred often take place in a universe lived in the promise of revelation yet bound by the phenomenological. As I have already indicated, Balak's kingship over Moab is represented in one of the more naturalistic passages in the narrative of Israel's sojourn in the wilderness; it almost has the quality of historical fiction. Even the exchange between human beings and the Deity is limited to privileged vessels and nighttime encounters. Magic is ultimately displaced in this context by the pagan soothsayer Balaam, whose more truthful divination of the universe comes through his direct encounter with the God of Abraham (who in turn, and with transparent stagecraft, manipulates all the characters, human, superhuman, and animal, to serve the divine purpose). "For," as Balaam proclaims once his eyes have been opened, "there is no divining in Jacob, / and no magic in Israel; / Now it is said to Yaakov, / to Israel, what God intends" (Num. 23:23–24). Martin Buber interprets "now" (*ka-et*) as "in time," that is, in the real world, not through magic.[39]

The mystery of Balaam's story is in the surface realism that has not, apparently, been ruffled. The appearance of a supernatural agent (or "messenger," as he appears in most contemporary translations)[40] with a sword, blocking Balaam's way, is so intrusive in an otherwise realistic story that it is revealed only to the ass—and the reader. But fantasy is heightened when the ass opens her mouth: the appearance of a *talking* ass is so disruptive of the texture of the narrative that some scholars assume it to be an interpolation from folkloristic sources.[41] Nevertheless, even after the animal begins speaking—at which Balaam registers no particular surprise—and, finally, even after the blinders have been removed from the diviner's eyes so that he can see what the ass saw, none of the others in his entourage seem to have noticed anything out of the ordinary, neither talking animal nor divine messenger.

The biblical text supports what theorists from Jean-Paul Sartre through Tzvetan Todorov and Rosemary Jackson have defined as the "fantastic": that liminal site where cosmic and social truths are challenged through the enigmatic presence of the unreal. What remains crucial to this genre is the response of the reader; as Todorov writes:

> In a world which is indeed our world, the one we know . . . there occurs an event which cannot be explained by the laws of this same familiar world . . . The fantastic is that hesitation experienced by a person who knows only the laws of nature, confronting an apparently supernatural event . . . The reader must adopt a certain attitude with regard to the text: he will reject allegorical as well as "poetic" interpretations.[42]

The invitation to read the "crazy dog" Balak through Parashat Balak is, I submit, what allows for an Agnonistic hesitation not only between the real and the marvelous but also between the reality of the twentieth century—and realism as its language of representation—and a worldview that is archaic but still accessible. The biblical story of Balak and Balaam combines elements of realism, sorcery or magic, human imagination, and divination as well as divine providence, authorizing what would appear many centuries later as an audaciously enigmatic form of modernism. Not quite magical realism, the fantastic is also manifest in *Tmol shilshom* in its most distilled form, since it is "experienced" only by the narrator and the reader. Nothing, that is, challenges the premises of realism from the point of view of the residents of this novel—so that a kind of hesitation remains regarding the ontological status of the sentient dog. There is just enough uncertainty about the appearance of the supernatural to create an uneasy mix of realism and enchantment: is the sentient dog, like the she-ass with X-ray vision, "real," then—or only a projection of the (character's? narrator's? reader's?) imagination? This is the central epistemological question of Parashat Balak—in its ancient and its modern forms.

As for the dog Balak, most readers view him as somehow a commentary, allegory, or projection, if not the alter ego, of Isaac. Dan Miron's reading of the entire novel through the model of Goethe's *Faust*, and of Balak through the Mephistophelean canine, views the latter as even more integral to the structure of the novel than the former.[43] Others, like Nitza Ben-Dov, mischievously suggest that the whole dog section may be Agnon's sly way of diverting the attention of his critics: "Maybe Balak is nothing but a piece of meat that Agnon threw to his critics so they could cook it to fit their palate and their worldview."[44] As stated in the previous chapter, I tend to agree with her and her predecessors, Dov Sadan in Agnon's generation and Avraham Holtz in ours, that all the symbolic constructs are open-ended, all interpretations tentative—"lefi sha'a"—and at times reflect the interpreter's own struggle as well as elusive textual possibilities.

The struggle between "truth" and its veiled forms of representation is the core of the biblical drama and drives my reading of *Tmol shilshom*, which privileges texture over plot, and journey over *telos*. The crucial difference between the biblical and the modern text lies, of course, in the ultimate resolution of uncertainty at the narrative level. In both the novel *Tmol shilshom* and the biblical Parashat Balak, the animal is the purveyor of truth—first in its metaphoric and then in its material manifestation—and the appearance of animals as both figures of speech and speechifying figures is the most salient poetic interruption of the surface realism. Agnon's Balak is prefigured in emblem and metaphor, from his first appearance as a canine figure on Sonia's bedspread. The biblical story too begins with a prefiguration of the animal as image and as character: "Moav" says to the "elders of Midyan: look now, this assembly will lick up everything around us *like an ox* licks up the greenthings of the field!" (Num. 22:4).[45] Later, after the she-ass appears in her personified state, Balaam takes up his "parable" and describes the people of Israel "*like the horns of the wild-ox . . . like a king of beasts, like a lion*" (Num. 23:24, emphasis mine). But in the biblical world where divine revelation is always the most likely resolution to any ontological conundrum, the she-ass also *knows* the truth—and, eventually, so does Balaam. In the world from which revelation has been withdrawn and knowledge is always speculative, the animal, like all mortals, is still searching—even though (especially because) the truth is inscribed on his back—and the reader is still hesitating . . .

There's more. If we look again at our two biblical subtexts together, at Genesis 22 in light of Numbers 22–24, the resonances of *akedat yitzhak* in Parashat Balak become so salient as to suggest that the second could even be read as a comic rewrite of the first—or, more radically, as a vindication through "history" of the *akeda as comedy*. Factor in the alacrity with which Balaam, like Abraham, rises the morning after his nighttime encounter with a heavenly voice, the presence of donkeys in both narratives (although only one is a chatterbox), the presence of two servants who see nothing, hear nothing, and say nothing, the appearance of angels or divine messengers who save the main character—and of course, the curse that becomes a blessing, akin to the existential threat that becomes an act of rescue. Robert Alter taught us to identify "high comedy" as a version of "the Bible's polemic monotheism" in such narratives. Here is his gloss on the Balaam/Balak story:

Balaam goes riding off on his ass to answer Balak's invitation [and needs to be jolted three times. Finally], in his wrath, Balaam hardly seems to notice the [ass's] miraculous gift of speech but responds as though he were accustomed

to having daily domestic wrangles with his asses . . . Meanwhile, of course, the
unseen angel has been standing by, sword in hand.[46]

So close to some inclusive version of Jewish theodicy is Balaam's voice that
in a talmudic discussion of the "canon" and authorial responsibility, Moses is
said to have written "his own" book and "Parashat Balaam" (*sic*) (Baba batra
14b–15a).[47] Parashat Balak/Balaam read as the "fantastic real," like the *akeda*
read as aborted tragedy, permits us rare, if tentative, glimpses into worlds beyond the phenomenological, without ever losing our foothold in this world.

Finally, as we peel back the layers of references, looking in occluded
spaces for the novel's real work, we find more evidence for the shifting place
of "imagination" or "fiction" as the site of both creative play and ethical action
in and vis-à-vis Jerusalem.

Ha-Domeh La-Domeh: Surrogates and Substitutes in Jerusalem

Jerusalem, as both template of perfection and mise-en-scène for the imperfect human drama, is the primary site of negotiations with the sacred and the
symbolic. As the storyteller most associated with Jerusalem, Agnon may have
been more tempted than any other modern Hebrew writer by the promise of
proximity to sacred space, and by perfection and wholeness as its aesthetic
correlates. Whereas he explored the seductions and dangers of such proximity over a lifetime of writing, they become explicit in this narrative as warring
sacramental, psychological, and aesthetic forces.

We saw that the "lesson" learned in Isaac's first encounters with the land of
his dreams is that wholeness exists only at a distance and that proximity, the
view from up close, inevitably involves an act of dissection or dismantling.
Soon after disembarking, while talking with his new "comrades," would-be
ḥalutzim (pioneers) who could not find work in the agrarian villages, Isaac
"learned what he hadn't learned all the years, for all the years he had seen the
new Land of Israel as one body [*ke-ḥativa aḥat*], and that night he learned
that she too divided herself into many sections [*she-af hi 'asta et 'atzma
ḥativot ḥativot*]" (E 54, H 55, translation altered).[48]

The symbolic language in this novel evolves slowly in the laboratory of
Isaac's imagination. It can be traced through those moments that are not dialectical, when perfect harmony is not a naïve flight of fancy deconstructed
upon landing. Only in fleeting moments of proximity to the religious and
psychological matrices of his being—as when he recites the kaddish for his
mother at the *Wailing Wall*—will Isaac achieve the unity or wholeness that is

otherwise just out of reach. After he has recited the kaddish, the prayer for the
dead, stones and worshippers congeal in his vision into oneness before God
(*hativa ahat lifnei ha-makom*)—the oneness with Place that is the ultimate
form of place-ment (E 369, H 351).[49] This is a messianic foreshadowing that
can be glimpsed only as it fades. Isaac's more pragmatic lesson is that it is
through fracture, veiling, or other forms of mediated encounter that proximity to place is enacted in a broken world.[50]

This insight is reinforced by narrative practices in and vis-à-vis Jerusalem
that are compatible with the aesthetic as well as the spiritual project of the Jew
(who is always) in exile: acknowledging *symbolic* distance from the fulfillment of the project leaves room for human activity, for human flaws and the
imperfections that can be (always only provisionally) addressed by humble
and self-deprecating acts of creativity. Jerusalem is encountered in an instant
of perfection when Sabbath grace covers the dissensions, the poverty and enmity, and divine providence (*hashgaha*) countenances even the unworthy:
"Anger vanished from their faces and every speech is soft and good, and from
every house and every courtyard shine many candles, and the whole city is
like a palace adorned with candles and lights" (E 271, H 262).

Again, this model of perfection, of wholeness, of perfection as wholeness,
like all the others, lapses into satire or, worse, despair, in those impatient to
realize heaven in the quotidian, whether such impatients are messianists or
Zionists. But then we realize that there is an alternative, and it is embedded
in the narrative fabric itself: even the panoramic view of Jerusalem in the twi-
light of Sabbath eve, the glimpse we just had of the world to come, adorned
with candles and lights, is a view of holiness as a series of figurative, signifying, gestures: "the whole city is *like* a palace adorned with candles and lights."
This passage continues, exposing symbol-making or substitution as the very
scaffolding of religious practice:

> Here a lamp is lit and there a lantern . . . Here a bowl of olive oil and there pure
> white candles. Here two candles *for* [*ke-neged*] remember the Sabbath day and
> keep the Sabbath day, and two tablets of the Covenant, and there ten candles
> *for* the Ten Commandments. Here seven candles *for* the seven days, and there
> twelve candles *for* the twelve Tribes of Israel. (E 271, H 262, emphases mine)

All these candlelighters are engaged in some form of substitution for the main
thing, the thing signified: the Temple sacrifice, the tablets of the Covenant,
the seven days, the twelve tribes—*that which is always at a mediated distance
from us (ke-neged), even in the Old City of Jerusalem*. Like the ram that substitutes for Isaac, signifying distance as well as surrogacy, the Mishnaic term *ke-
neged*, "as opposed to," signals the textual comparative basis for an argument

while denoting spatial relations, facing the other side. In Masekhet Berakhot 3:17, the term is used for positioning oneself toward (*ke-neged*) the sacred center, even in the Holy Land, even in Jerusalem, and even while standing where the Temple stood, so that all of Israel, no matter where they may be, are praying "le-makom eḥad" (to one place).[51] These symbols, with the clear recognition of their surrogate status, are what save us from idolatry in the human imagination as in cultic practice.

That is, beneath the discursive structure of the deconstructed whole is another paradigm for encountering and representing the world, especially in Jerusalem: access to holy space through the distance preserved in acts of proxy, mediation, or substitution. And finally, as we uncover the barely registered changes in Isaac himself as he becomes lord of his own imagination in the phenomenological world he learns to celebrate and to decorate, we realize that after a long journey through different imaginative realms and before his terrible end, he will come to embody one of Agnon's greatest acts of substitution.

Isaac's own imagination evolves as a slow exploration of the symbolic universe. In the first place, his father sends him to the Holy Land to see for himself that the Zionist vision of the Land of Israel is a "fiction the Zionists made up" ("she-kol ʿinyan eretz yisrael davar badui hu," E 5, H 9). The Hebrew word *badui* clearly signals a literary or imaginative act. But, it turns out, it is not just the Zionist fiction—which is, after all, for Herzl's followers, the fiction to end all fictions ("*ein* zo aggada")—but also Agnon's own fictions that must be tested, especially *Hakhnasat kalah* (*The Bridal Canopy*) and *Bilvav yamim* (*In the Heart of the Seas*), whose protagonists are under a divine protectorate. Isaac has to be reminded often that, even if he is a descendant of R. Yudel Hasid (protagonist of *The Bridal Canopy*), he is not living in an enchanted world, and he has to work much harder than his predecessors and even to engage in subterfuge—not only to survive himself but to help others survive. This too is defined as a leap of the imagination in what we come to understand as an evolving aesthetic and moral faculty. Isaac's kindnesses are coded as acts of "fiction." When he furnishes food for the indigent and ill, the families of his ailing patron, the painter Samson Bloykoff, and later of Reb Fayish, the paralyzed father of his beloved Shifra, Isaac invents stories to deceive the wives and daughters of these men into thinking that he received the food as a favor or as recompense for his labor. This work is accomplished through "similitudes" or similes of similes (*ha-domeh la-domeh*, E 338, H 322). What is crucial here is that this act of imagination produces a form of similitude that has nothing of resemblance in it but only substitution. Paul Ricoeur argues that the "pact between substitution and resemblance" in metaphor is axiomatic in the long history of rhetoric;[52] in this narrative there are, however, moments of dissociation. R. Fayish, the ritual slaughterer, is the one who supplies real fish and meat; when he falls ill, Isaac can provide only ersatz: bread and eggs—and even those require acts of inventiveness. But if his "pocket is small, his imagination is big. Every day he makes up something, just so Shifra and her mother won't lack food" ("Yitzhak eyno yage'a mi-livdot kol yom devarim hadashim," E 338, H 322). His imagination has gone from a myopic view at a distance to a microscopic focus on the quotidian, the domestic (putting his house in order)—until the distance between lens and object is filled with fictions of compassion and kindness.

The remaining fictions belong, then, to the realm of the human: mortal, vulnerable, and flawed. Isaac's soul finds equilibrium when he reaches a level of consciousness that can support his life without magical thinking, and a level of happiness that needs little or no rhetorical projection—while he himself seems to acknowledge the power of the symbol or simulacrum. He sits in the home of a woodcarver in Jerusalem who engraves miniature friezes of the "place of the Temple" and other holy shrines on olive wood; as he revels in the presence of children and family warmth for the first time since leaving his hometown, his delight in his surroundings merges with his longing for his own siblings. He asks himself, "Am I really in Jerusalem? And in his mind's eye emerge a host of visions he had conjured when he was in Diaspora. And two loves, the love of Jerusalem in the vision and the love of Jerusalem in reality, *come and mate and give birth to a new love, which has some of the former and some of the latter*" (E 557–58, H 527, translation slightly altered, emphasis mine).

The town he left behind is not only the source of such dreams but also, like all such Polish towns and, for that matter, every settlement outside of Zion, the simulacrum of Jerusalem—and, in the endless recycling of the nostalgic mind and diasporic practice, the souvenir replicas of Jerusalem, of its holy places, made *in Jerusalem*, find their way back to the town, like the etrog from the Land of Israel, cut into many pieces and preserved as jam.

Finally, then, the original language of longing that was composed of what Oz calls the "naïve synthesis" of verses and quotations, of formulaic scriptural and political hyperbole, has given way to the conjugation of vision and reality in the rhetoric of consummated love. For Isaac does eventually achieve fulfillment: a lucrative job, a comfortable family environment in which to live and work, and finally, the hand of Shifra, the pious Jerusalemite he has allowed himself to love. It is only *then* that he gets bitten by the (now-rabid) dog, Balak.

Isaac could engage in such mating or matchmaking of what is near and far, such amalgamation of incompatible realms because, like the woodcarver who creates simulacra of the sacred center, he is a craftsman—not a *real* painter, like Samson Bloykoff, but a house painter, a decorator, a "*smearer*" (*lakhlekhan*).[53] He is not one of Agnon's great artists or artisans, like Ben Uri ("Agunot") or Raphael ("Tale of the Scribe"), who, as we saw, are so absorbed in their art that they take leave of the human sphere and the human love available to them in order to merge with their creation; he is not one of the great *metaknim* or repairmen, like Hananiah in *Bilvav yamim*, or the rabbi in "Agunot." Isaac is the perfectly (or perfect*ably*) average man—the perfect subject for the novel Agnon would write—if "only" he could live at peace within the precincts of the modern novel.[54]

And that is just the point. Agnon *has* written that novel, but it is so deeply embedded in the "other novel" as to be all but invisible. Isaac's craft is the exact reflection in the material, visual world of the work of his soul—as the language of equanimity is its rhetorical reflection. Isaac's approach to the sphere of holiness is always mediated—by his own humility and by the very nature of his vocation, just as his approach to the inner sanctum of true artistic activity is mediated by his distance from other, "truer," painters.

A "state of equanimity" (*midat ha-hishtavut*), the perfect balance or "mating" of expectation and reality, desire and the world, borrowed from the Hassidic lexicon,[55] will become, in the course of Isaac's narrative, the dam holding back the waters of literalism. Here it is *not substitution* but *resemblance* that constitutes the metaphoric act. It is, Ricoeur reminds us, the explicit display of the "moment of resemblance that operates implicitly in metaphor. The poet, as we read in the *Poetics*, is one who 'perceives similarity.' "[56] Even the *pretense* of a simile, so seemingly superfluous in those rare moments of religious revelation or emotional bliss, will be enough to signify the crucial act of signification. "Milk and honey Isaac did not find in Jerusalem, but he did attain a state of equanimity [*midat ha-hishtavut*]" (E 230, H 223). Thus concludes chapter 5 of book 2. The milk and honey of impossible utopian dreams and alien discourse will be replaced by something more humble in the opening of the next chapter: Isaac, who has become a respected craftsman in Jerusalem, walks with a heavy gait, "*like a craftsman* whose pace is weighed down by his tools" (E 230–31, H 223, emphasis mine).

But, the reader protests, he *is* a craftsman weighed down by his tools! What appears, then, as a "pseudo-simile," in which signified and signifier are identical, a perfect state of equanimity as alignment between the world represented and the language of representation, is also a critical placeholder for the very human act of symbol-making.[57] *It is precisely such small interventions of the imagination that will save Isaac from unmediated proximity to the holiest site in Jerusalem.*

Isaac's first entry, by wagon, into Jerusalem is heralded portentously by a "still, small voice" (*kol demama daka*)[58] blowing through the mountains and filling his heart with sadness; the voice blends with the wordless melody (*niggun*) of the carter and produces the equilibrium that is represented through the same kind of pseudo-simile: "Isaac looked before him and his heart began pounding, *as a man's heart pounds when he approaches the place of his desire*" (E 195–96, H 189–90, emphasis mine). Then his consciousness moves into the visual field, in what could be considered his own unselfconscious *ars poetica*, magnificent in its understatement and abstract form:

> Because he was somewhat consoled by the voice of the old man [the carter] sitting and singing melodies of prayer, he removed the gloom from his heart. Before him, the wall of Jerusalem suddenly appeared, woven into a red fire, plaited with gold, surrounded by gray clouds blended with blue clouds, which incise and engrave it with shapes of spun gold, choice silver, burnished brass, and purple tin. Isaac rose up and wanted to say something. But his tongue was hushed in his mouth as in a mute song. He sat down as if carried away by a sitting dance. (E 196, H 190)

The wall of Jerusalem and the surrounding clouds are a great tapestry of colorful threads "incising and engraving" (*hortzin ve-hortin*) shapes that only hint at figuration. Alluding to the colors and textures of the Temple vestments, they remain undefined, color with only an intimation of form; and the Mishnaic Hebrew in which these verbs appear already indicates their linguistic status as proxies for the Temple that has been destroyed.

A Smearer in Jerusalem: Inside the Holy of Holies

As belated sojourner in Jerusalem, Isaac will always paint canvases that are color without form and sing a muted song. And, as painter of walls, he will preserve his distance from iconographic temptations. We come to understand that the Holy City is best approached through a veil. Samson Bloykoff, the truest artist of Isaac's acquaintance, draws a "curtain" or "partition" between himself and the world as he sits in Jerusalem and paints his last pictures, which are a "reflection of a reflection" (*bavua shel bavua*) of the visible world (E 253, H 244). When Isaac approaches the site of holiness, it is, again, with formless color and muted speech. This time he is realizing his vision: painting what he saw in his first glimpse of the holy city, using the materials of his trade—his colors and brushes. Isaac's reputation as housepainter has reached the foreign consuls and gone as far as the Turkish Pasha himself, who invites the Jewish craftsman to repair "their" house of worship on "our" Temple Mount. "Isaac may have been the *only one* to enter the Holy of Holies and to practice his craft in the place of our Temple," the narrator tells us. "*Too bad* our comrade Isaac isn't much of a storyteller and can't tell what his eyes saw there" (E 227–28, H 219–20, emphases mine).

Too bad? Indeed, this slight passage, like the earlier entry to Jerusalem camouflaged in a noisy, satiric chapter, underscores the ethics of the unarticulated, the nonliteral, the mediated, a truth brought back to the sites of holiness from two thousand years of negotiating distance: neither shape nor word can give form to the experience of proximity to holiness without endangering the life or the sanity of the pilgrim. Resonances of the akeda are salient in the passage just quoted, which the Hebrew ear will discern: "ha-faḥa . . . shalaḥ lahem *et ḥavereinu, et Yitzḥak,* ve-efshar she-yitzḥak *yaḥid* haya be-davar ze."[59] Recall that, according to tradition, *akedat yitzhak* took place on the very site of the Temple Mount. As we have already noted, this reference, to Isaac as the "only one," will recur at the end of his story. Given the strictures placed on presumptions of physical proximity as spelled out in Maimonides's *Guide*, the model that Isaac offers is one of abstraction, muteness, and mediation.

But even after this passage—which could be the crescendo of the novel, if it were not hidden, so to speak, in plain sight—the problem, articulated repeatedly by the narrator, remains one of sheer interest: how to engage the reader in Isaac, who, living as he does by default or mediation, is reported to be less than fascinating to his friends and neighbors—and by extension, to us. Even as evidence to the contrary piles up, as people like Bloykoff and Moshe Amram, Shifra's grandfather, are drawn to Isaac and as his imagination develops in quiet but riveting ways, we are repeatedly told by the narrator that he is not really a subject of interest. So, as a kind of diversion from what I am claiming to be the real work of the novel, readers and critics are invited to engage in allegorical interpretations of the many evocative names in the novel—such as that of the fiery preacher Rav Gronam yakum purkan (Rabbi Grunam May-Salvation-Arise)—and in hermeneutic disquisitions on such figures as Balak and such *topoi* as the "binding of Isaac."

In such a place, we are tempted by the seductive and magical power of letters. Recall that Isaac is also a *sign painter*, and as such his fate will eventually be sealed. Ostensibly less treacherous than graven images, letters can nonetheless be lethal when subjected to certain iconic readings. It is not as "smearer" but as signer that Isaac paints "crazy dog" on Balak's back and enters into the "kabbalistic" realm where letters have consequences in the real world, consequences that will eventuate in his own death. Words that lose their symbolic status and become literalized actually precipitate the downfall of the two main characters in *Tmol shilshom*, as the encounter between them produces a text that runs wild.[60]

What has been noted by most readers, especially those who pay particular attention to the modernist aspects of *Tmol shilshom*, is the extent to which Balak is dangerous *only* as text. The branded dog, writes Anne Golomb Hoffman, "wanders around Jerusalem in search of a reader, who can decode for it the mysterious inscription on its back."[61] But Balak is a "readerly" text from the beginning, even before his fateful encounter with Isaac. One of the lesser-noted elements of the Balak sections of the novel is that his consciousness is shared (overheard) by only two others: the narrator and the reader. We have already noted that for all intents and purposes, everyone else, including Isaac, regards him as a mangy stray dog. When the center of consciousness moves from Isaac to Balak, the dog appears as a sentient but not a talking animal who therefore does not really disturb the realistic texture of the novel. Again, like the ass in Numbers 22, but unlike an animal in a fable dressed in human clothes and interacting with other characters in human language, Balak remains in all his behaviors fully canine. (The only external concession to his human consciousness is the frequent reference to his bark as a "shout" [E 289, H 278, and passim].)

Indeed, Balak's own fate, like Isaac's, depends entirely on the reception of that inscription. If people really understood the nature of signs, that they are human in origin, or even if they grappled with the imputed power of the word in mystical traditions, they would take care not to confuse signifiers with the Real Thing and would not treat a marked dog as if he were really mad, thus driving him mad and turning a semiotic mark into a self-fulfilling prophecy. His *craziness* is his arbitrarily branded status as social outcast; his rabid *madness* is the outcome of systematic misreading. Misrepresentation, then, is matched by misreading: the sin of Isaac's mislabeling the dog in painting the "sign" on his back is compounded by the literal-mindedness of those who read it.[62]

Writing "dog" on a dog is, as most critics have been quick to note, the ultimate challenge to all forms of signing. Yet in terms of the symbolic procedures I have been tracing, this redundancy appears, at first, to signify the world through an act of equivalence or equilibrium, having the same effect as the "pseudo-simile"—comparing the craftsman Isaac to a craftsman. But what is missing in this one act of Isaac's and later in the dog's response is precisely that self-conscious gesture of restraint embodied in Isaac's own definition of his craft as a surrogate for the "real" artistic project, and in the narrator's rhetorical distance through metaphor or simile. *Kaf ha-dimyon* (the letter indicating *as* or *like*) is a term that also suggests the *scales* of imagination (and justice) as well as the *means* of imagination, the smallest mediation of simile between the self and the lethal repository of hidden truth. The encounter with the dog is the only instance where Isaac undermines his own profound understanding of his vocation and the ethics of his imagination.[63] As a consequence, the dog's quest for the "truth" of his fate, which Isaac sealed with the unmediated conflation of signified and signifier, is what brings him to bite Isaac. He is trying to reach the essence, to find the truth in the thing itself—"I'll bite him and the truth will leak out of his body" (E 628, H 593)—a sacramental act not unlike entering the Holy of Holies without mediation or distance. The communion/crucifixion allusion can be reinforced by reference to the phrase with which the dying artist Bloykoff, after nearly choking, curses his fate: "dam klavim [lit., dog's blood], ha-genihot ha-lalu aynan menihot la-adam le-saper 'im havero"—which is ingeniously translated by Harshav as "'S blood, that wheezing doesn't let a person talk with his friends" (E 225, H 218, emphasis mine).[64]

Like Balak seeking to possess the Truth, attempts abound in this narrative to own exclusive artistic or religious visions. But the competing aesthetic and moral vision affirms that the only access without lethal consequence is through acts of mediation or commensuration.

In what may be the most revealing—because so well-concealed—passage in the novel, the narrator produces a verbal equivalent of painting behind a veil. Just before he dies, Isaac calibrates and reconciles imagination and reality. A few days after his wedding, and only moments before the fatal encounter with Balak, "Isaac stood and didn't see anything, for his soul clung to his wife *like a bridegroom in the wedding week*" (E 623, H 589, 594, emphasis mine). Here the mating of vision and reality, of signifier and signified, is as complete as any human experience need be—only because it has "some of the former and some of the latter"—always separated by the preposition "like" that acts as *kaf ha-dimyon*.[65] As we have seen, this pseudo-simile has appeared several times in the course of Isaac's narrative, but here it serves as his epithalamium—and his epitaph.

A Parcel of Land: The Sequel as Comic Promise

And yet. The apocalyptic vision realized by those literal-minded readers of the dog *in* the novel, and *of* the novel, has its counterpart in the tale of satisfied human desire lived in the promise of final redemption in God's good time. As we saw in the twelfth of Maimonides's thirteen principles, this is messianic Judaism in its deferred mode.[66] It is not sentimental or utopian.

It recognizes the comic inherent in the tragic or mythic vision, even in the akeda itself, under the sign of substitution and mediation. It accords immunity to the "smearer" that does not accrue to the "signer."

Read as aborted tragedy, the biblical akeda is, as we have seen, framed by benevolent intercession: *deus ex machina* appears from the very beginning to announce to the reader what the key actors do not know, that this is (only) a test; and, finally, the substitution of the ram at the end creates a Happy End (well, not so Happy for the ram, but that is another story). As we saw in chapter 1, and as has been pointed out by Shalom Spiegel and elaborated by others, this is the ethical and religious message of the story—if not of its legacy. Recall that Spiegel cites the passage from Pesikta R. 40, in which even the very site of the akeda, Mount Moriah itself, is etymologically altered to read as *Temura*, exchange, substitution.[67]

Having internalized this lesson, on his own terms, "our" Isaac perhaps not surprisingly almost doesn't make it to his own sacrifice. Like Abraham in Kafka's vision, who was too busy putting his house in order to perform the sacrifice, our comrade Isaac was too busy being happy to hear the call. Of course, once he is dragged to the altar and bound with ropes, neither he nor we can overlook the theme of the akeda already embedded in his name. But then let us remember that a subtle negotiation with his biblical prototype, and with the akeda in its comic form, has been going on throughout the narrative: our Isaac is already the "unbound" one—the one who is used to substitutes because, like his namesake whom the ram would replace, all of Isaac Kumer's actions are surrogates for some other, original, plan. His dream of becoming a *halutz* and living in the farming settlements outside Jaffa is exchanged for house- and sign-painting in Jerusalem, his secular behaviors for religious praxis, the pious Sonia for the freewheeling pioneer Shifra. As each utopia yields to its default mode, his presence in the world acquires a different, more material substance and his soul finds equilibrium. Like his craft and his location in physical and emotional space, his very life remains—*until its horrible end*—under the sign of substitution. The Sacrifice of Isaac is an abrupt, intrusive act of closure to a story that, unremarkable as it is, could simply go on and on.

An intimation of the difference between "anxious" messianism in its sentimental-apocalyptic-mythic form and deferred messianism in its novelistic-comic form is given on the last page of *Tmol shilshom*. Perhaps to rescue a work that has been disfigured by its hideous conclusion, the narrator, now appearing as presumed author, gives us a glimpse of redemption; he assures us that *someday*, beginning with rains that saturate the parched earth with a promise of fecundity, a sanguine epilogue will be written about Isaac's friends and family, in a volume to be called "A Parcel of Land":

Finally the rains stopped and the clouds dispersed and the sun shone. And
when we came outside we saw that the earth was smiling with its plants
and its flowers. And from one end of the Land to the other came shepherds
and their flocks . . . and a great rejoicing was in the world . . . All the villages in
Judea and the Galilee, in the plain and in the mountains produced crops and
the whole land was like a Garden of the Lord . . . And every bush and every
blade of grass emitted a good smell, *and needless to say, so did the oranges* . . .
And you our brothers, the elite of our salvation in Kinneret and Merhavia, in
Eyn Ganim and *in Um Juni, which is now Degania*, you went out to your work
in the fields and the gardens, the work our comrade Isaac wasn't blessed with.
Our comrade Isaac wasn't blessed to stand on the ground and plow and sow,
but like his ancestor Reb Yudel Hasid . . . he was blessed to be given an estate
of a grave in the holy earth.

> Completed are the deeds of Isaac
> The deeds of our other comrades
> The men and the women
> Will come in the book *A Parcel of Land* (E 642, H 607, emphases mine)

The reference to Degania, which displaced the Arab farming settlement of
Um Juni[68] during the years corresponding to Isaac Kumer's "life" and following his "death," is a semaphore of the Zionist project that he had come to
join, but from which he defected for old-world Jerusalem. This reference and
the inflated rhetoric of the final paragraph suggest that the promised sequel
will pick up where Isaac's story went astray (around page 2?). But it has also
provided us with a few more clues that return us to Numbers 22–24 and the
Balak trail, which in turn lead to yet another text that reinforces the comic
undertone, or messianism in its comic mode: the Book of Ruth.

In talmudic genealogy, Ruth the Moabite is King Balak's granddaughter
(Sanhedrin 72b)—and, in turn, the progenitor of Messiah son of David. Scattered throughout the Book of Ruth, like the leviathan waiting from the seven
days of creation to swallow Jonah, are phrases that will take on nominative
status in Agnon's narrative. Megillat Ruth contains both the name of the book
that Agnon actually wrote (*tmol shilshom* as adverbial phrase: "just yesterday,"
or "habitually," 2:11) *and* the book he promised to write (*ḥelkat ha-sadeh*, or "a
parcel of land," 2:3, 4:3).

Like the Balak narrative, the Book of Ruth provides a comic, deferred-
messianic counternarrative to the mythic claims of the Hebrew imagination;
in turn, they both provide grounds for a more "novelistic" reading that re-
lieves Agnon's text of some of its mythic pressures. This is reinforced in the
so-called epilogue to the novel, in which Isaac's widow Shifra, who, it is now
revealed, has become pregnant during their honeymoon(!), bears a daughter.

That daughter, in turn, marries the son of Isaac's first love, Sonia, and provides issue and closure if not exactly a happy conclusion to Isaac's unfortunate story. Published posthumously in *Moznaym* in 1971, the epilogue was, of course, never incorporated into the text itself.[69]

Over the course of the narrative, and even at the end, the narrator has resorted to the bombast of urgent utopian-messianic rhetoric and sentimental resolutions—which are as peremptory as the akeda and can be punctured only by the satiric fragrance of hyperbolic oranges. *In such a plot, the Arab village of Um Juni is as effaced as Isaac.* The *other* plot, the comic plot of coexistence, of deferred messianism and life and art at a distance from the promise and the sacred, is never granted official status—and is, therefore, killed off at the end along with Isaac.

From the perspective of the deferred promise, and of Isaac's story before the fatal dog bite, in the mean-time between beginnings and endings, in that narrow space between the picture of perfection and its deconstruction, the narrow space that the literal-minded utopianists and the narrator himself have left Isaac (and the Palestinian inhabitants of Um Juni), there is very little wiggle room. What prevails there is desire, the erotic, the joy in storytelling, in making olive wood *facsimiles of the Temple within sight of the Temple Mount* itself in the home of the woodcarver, and in painting shapeless color on walls and signs that should be read as arbitrary signifiers—in using our imagination to feed the hungry and read to the blind and comfort the sick and find a place for human love.

All of this will remain hidden in plain sight. Literal-mindedness reads the text on Balak's back as well as the text of Genesis 22 as explicit injunction, *killing* instead of *binding* both innocents. Balak at the end of the novel becomes The Real in the Lacanian sense: a traumatic site unmediated and unmitigated by the symbolic or the imaginary order.[70] Giving up substitution in our search for the Real necessitates the Real Sacrifice. The Real is life's terror or trauma without the mediation of comedy or simile. It invites the reading that Hirschfeld and others have suggested: not the bridge of the fantastic but the rift or abyss of the grotesque and the demonic.[71]

Still, a nagging question remains: why such extraordinary intervention in the life of such an ordinary man? Why the last-minute sabotage of a happy ending? The narrator, Isaac's first, rather unsympathetic, and often clueless reader, framed the question for every subsequent reader: "This Isaac who is no worse than any other person, why is he punished so harshly? Is it because he teased a dog? He meant it only as a joke. Moreover, *the end of Isaac Kumer is not inherent in his beginning*" (E 639, H 604, emphasis mine).[72] Why, then, does his creator expend such energy and artifice to "redeem" him from the tedium of a Happy End and to displace the human comedy with a modern theodicy? If the end of Isaac Kumer is *not* inherent in his beginning, are we indeed doomed to reconstruct the story from its end? And the dog—whose mythic or supernatural appearance gives way as he moves through the spaces of the city and the narrative to a "novelistic" interrogation of the cosmos and of human society, as his self-consciousness becomes the fictive instrument for finding things out, potentially a receptacle of either tragic or comic realization—why is he reduced at the end to an instrument of peremptory myth?

Agnon's Balak offered us hesitation as his Isaac offered us equanimity; reading Balak literally cancels the hesitation as well as the human source of the act of signing, and releases the madness. It is then that the symbolic and imaginary orders break down—the order of simulacra or formless color, of wordless encounters with the Holy of Holies, of commensuration as the sign of human invention and human happiness, and of enigma as the sign of the human quest.

Bringing violent closure to Isaac's story is as catastrophic as approaching the sacred without a veil: it shows us only how wanting our vision of redemption is when we efface all the rhetoric and gestures of distance—metaphor, irony, comedy: "Finally, his pained soul passed away and he returned his spirit to the God of spirits *for whom there is no laughter and no frivolity*" ("hishiv ruḥo le-elokei ha-ruḥot she-ein le-fanav lo tzḥok ve-lo kalut rosh," E 640, H 605, translation slightly altered, emphasis mine). It is when the God of Laughter, of the comic principle of substitution, fails that the dog is "read" literally, after passing through the Valley of Hinom (*gay ben hinom*) where children were once actually sacrificed to Moloch. Only then does Isaac lose his symbolic, surrogate, status and become a literal sacrifice; and only then do we lose our own hard-won knowledge of the ethics of distance and mediation.

As we saw in chapter 1, certain scholars have argued that the biblical account includes traces of a superseded layer in which Isaac was indeed sacrificed. Here the author himself leads us to this uncanny place in a rare intervention in the process of deciphering *Tmol shilshom*. In an exchange with Baruch Kurzweil, Agnon first reiterated his antipathy to allegorical interpretations that resolve narrative complexities through literal-minded equivalences, and (whether to reconstruct his own intertextual journey or to put his friend off track by throwing him a "piece of meat" we will never know) he referred him to the Talmud (Sota 3b) for a clue as to the use of dogs in ancient times as messengers of excommunication. Then Agnon added:

As for Balak. I know that the readers and even the good critics would be more comfortable if Balak and Isaac were separated, but I am happy to see them together. And if I could explain the relationship between man and animal I would not refrain from doing so. Certainly not before a man like yourself. I do not see myself as a man to whom the mysteries of life are revealed, but something of life's terror [*miktzat mashehu min ha-havaya ha-mav'ita*] is revealed to me from time to time. And I try as far as possible to accommodate and sweeten it [*le-hatima u-le-hamtika*]. But here I was unable to do anything but to be its scribe. (My translation)[73]

Life's terror (*ha-havaya ha-mav'ita*) is introduced in the narrative just before Isaac's first ecstatic view of Jerusalem that we considered earlier: "The cart is traveling between cliffs and rocks, hills and peaks. Some wear faces of wrath, some of menace [*eima*], and all of them erupt like little volcanoes rolling down onto the crushed earth at their feet, and the crushed earth writhes like a snake twining around the cart and twisting its chains around it" (E 195, H 189). The glimpse of the uncanny can yield, as it does in this passage, to the equanimity of a peaceful reconciliation with the world through a mediated encounter with the holy. Or it can yield to its opposite . . .

Maybe, then, the dog bite is not simply the stagecraft of necessary endings but cosmic nemesis for the murder of desire, for the fatal flaw of literal-mindedness, our own form of idol worship?

Agnon *in* Jerusalem: 1948, 1967 . . .

What I have identified as the comic undercurrent of the akeda in *Tmol shilshom* is, indeed, rare in Hebrew literature generally and in Agnon's fiction in particular. This can be seen by comparing it with a pictorial representation of the akeda in the home of the narrator of his long story "Hadom ve-kiseh" (The Footstool and the Chair), published posthumously. As I mentioned briefly in chapter 1, this rambling and rather surreal narrative follows the narrator and his daughter, who are in the throes of leaving their rented lodgings. Suddenly, an old "akeda" painting commemorating a historical catastrophe is uncovered hanging on one of the walls, though somewhat damaged: *what is missing is the ram*. This small vignette actually creates an ekphrastic representation of the element that has been removed, as we have seen, in most renderings of the akeda: i.e., the "happy end," based on the principle of substitution.[74] This would be put to the ultimate test after 1967, when myth and history intersected once again in the holiest site in Jerusalem.

Timing matters. Isadore Twersky's essay on Maimonides, with which I introduced this chapter, was first published in Hebrew in 1988, eighteen years after Agnon's death and twenty-one years after Israel captured East Jerusalem and the Temple Mount. Twersky's focus on the restored centrality of the Temple in Jerusalem to "active historical consciousness," for which he credits

Maimonides in his time and, by implication, Agnon in ours, reflects the current political climate as well as Twersky's own position. Although Agnon lived long enough after 1967 to sign the manifesto for the "Whole Land of Israel,"[75] which in many ways corroborated his own epistemological and spiritual longings for wholeness and proximity to the sacred center, he evinced in the fictions we have explored (and many we have not), and in his own behavior, how fraught with danger he knew this move would be in the political as well as the theological sphere. And that is why, I submit, he avoided the subject fairly consistently by representing Jerusalem itself as space protected from civic challenges. If we look closely, we discover that Agnon's "nonpolitical" Jerusalem actually resembles the depictions of his hometown of Buczacz in sometimes startling ways.

Consider, again, Isaac's decision to marry the pious Shifra and to live in Meah Shearim. Although most critics see this as a retreat into a benighted world, I am suggesting that he is, rather, establishing profound connections with the town he left behind when he embarked on his Zionist pilgrimage. On the surface, this move appears as an act of penance for having abandoned his father and his siblings to their poverty. But by mapping the one setting onto the other—as we saw Isaac himself doing, rather absentmindedly, when he sat in the woodcarver's house engraving miniature friezes of holy shrines and mused, "am I really in Jerusalem? And in his mind's eye emerge a host of visions he had conjured when he was in Diaspora"—we reveal a palimpsest in which the two places "come and mate and give birth to a new love, which has some of the former and some of the latter" (E 557–58, H 527, translation slightly altered). What emerges, here and in many other narratives, is a reality more profound, and more profoundly homogeneous, than either the Buczacz of Agnon's youth or the Jerusalem of his maturity.

This pattern is repeated many times throughout Agnon's oeuvre, and here I can only signal a few of the landmarks. His hometown, rendered in his fiction sometimes as Buczacz and sometimes as "Shibush,"[76] takes on the dimensions and characteristics of the proverbial small-town "'ayara" or *shtetl* more than the thriving urban center it was (Jews, who numbered around 8,000 on the eve of World War II, composed about 50 percent of the population). But Agnon seemed to deny this when he referred to it consistently as a "city" and described the vast project on Buczacz left unfinished at his death as itself an urban construct. "Ani boneh 'ir"—I am building a city[77]—he stated repeatedly, referring to what became the posthumous collection, *'Ir u-meloah*, and most readers refer to it as such:

> This is the chronicle of the city of Buczacz, which I have written in my pain and anguish, so that our descendants should know that our city was full of Torah, wisdom, love, piety, life, grace, kindness and charity from the time of

its founding until the arrival of the blighted abomination and their befouled
and deranged accomplices who wrought destruction upon it. May God avenge
the blood of His servants and visit vengeance upon His enemies and deliver
Israel from its sorrows.[78]

Agnon's "city," before the advent of the "blighted abomination," is, then, characterized as a fairly homogeneous, Jewish space. I am, admittedly, wading
into turbulent waters by deliberately invoking the problematic term "shtetl,"
which the author himself avoids, and which has itself been interrogated and
complicated by a number of contemporary scholars.[79] But I am using it here to
signify an intimate topos that is experienced as noncosmopolitan, and most
important, as nonpolitical. After exhaustive research on Agnon's hometown,
Omer Bartov claims that "Buczacz was a 'shtetl' for Jews."[80] And Agnon's versions of his hometown rhyme with inherited legends of the creation of the
shtetlach of the Polish Jewish diaspora.[81]

My larger argument here is that Agnon's Jerusalem is in crucial ways a
mirror image of his Polish place of origin. Perhaps the most revealing, and
earliest, indication of this occurs at the end of the 1938–39 novel Oreaḥ nata
la-lun (Guest for the Night), when the narrator peers through the keyhole of
the study house (beit midrash) as he prepares to leave his hometown of Szi-
bucz (Shibush), to which he had returned for what became a prolonged visit.
The lost world, decimated by World War I (and soon to be entirely eradicated
by the coming war), is encompassed within the orb of his eye, and will be
redeemed when the key is brought to Jerusalem—and when the study house,
and, by implication, the town itself, will be restored in his imagination. In
a later story, "Ha-siman," the narrator is sitting in a small synagogue in Jerusalem on the holiday of Shavuoth, having just received the news that his
Galician hometown has been destroyed and all its inhabitants killed or incar-
cerated by the Nazis; he is then "visited" by the eleventh-century Andalusian
poet Solomon Ibn Gabirol, who makes a "sign" for his town by reciting a
poem with the name embodied as an acrostic.[82] In both instances, then, the
town is virtually transported to Jerusalem, which can reflect and contain it.[83]

But implicit recognition of both the doomed longing for lost time and
place, and the danger of relating to Jerusalem as nonpolitical space, would
produce internal, and often insoluble, contradictions in a number of Agnon's
shorter fictions. While, as we have seen, there are historical coordinates even
in Agnon's most fanciful stories, many of his fictions, like "Tehila," which was
written after 1948 and situated in Jerusalem, were actually set in the pre-'48
period, when the Jews had access to the holy sites but no sovereignty over the

Old City.[84] Agnon often seems to go out of his way, engaging in anachronistic acrobatics, to avoid combining sovereignty and the sacred.

Sometimes those acrobatics simply strain credibility, especially in those stories that Agnon was, in all likelihood, editing in his last years, between 1967 and 1970, and that were published by his daughter after his death. One striking example is the unfinished "Lifnim min ha-ḥoma" (Within the Wall). The story unfolds in a historically challenged dreamscape in which the two main characters wander in the Old City of Jerusalem, sometime between 1948 and 1967, in places to which Jews would *not* have had access. The narrator is forced, finally, to admit that the action depicted is hallucinatory, taking place in a dreamscape "where time was as it should be" and the "land was still whole and Jerusalem was not divided."[85]

The overlap between Buczacz and Jerusalem is made nearly explicit in the opening paragraphs of the posthumously published volume 'Ir u-meloah, which expands on the glimpse we got in the epigraph of a state of grace, along with intimations of its default mode:

> My city is situated upon mountains and hills, coming in and out of forests filled with trees and bushes, and the Strypa River flows through the city and alongside the city, and streams bring forth water and feed the reeds and the bushes and the trees, and good springs abound with fresh water, and birds dwell in the trees and twitter from them . . . Below the hills you will find straight places. Some of them were made by heaven and some were made by man. Some are intertwined and some complement each other. For this is one of those instances where the work of heaven and the work of man live side by side in peace and allow each other to complement each other. Most likely these places were created in the early days, when man's heart was whole, without crookedness and without deceit.

In his study of Buczacz, Omer Bartov points out that the allusion in the above quotation is to Psalm 125:

> Those who trust in God are like Mount Zion that cannot be moved but abides forever. As Jerusalem is surrounded by mountains, so God surrounds his people—from this time, and for eternity.

הַבֹּטְחִים בַּיהוָה - כְּהַר-צִיּוֹן לֹא-יִמּוֹט, לְעוֹלָם יֵשֵׁב.

יְרוּשָׁלַם - הָרִים, סָבִיב לָהּ:

וַיהוָה, סָבִיב לְעַמּוֹ - מֵעַתָּה, וְעַד-עוֹלָם.[86]

From all of the above, we can see that even as Agnon referred fairly consistently to the Buczacz of his memory as a "city," both Buczacz/Shibush and

Jerusalem were, in crucial aspects, nonpolitical—and in the most profound sense, nonurban—spaces. What this meant was that the burning political or religio-political issues of the day could be avoided in Jerusalem through the same anachronism that created the illusion of homogeneity in Buczacz/ Shibush.

But this came, I submit, not so much from a place of avoidance as from the implicit acknowledgment of the perils of proximity when place, politics, and messianic religious impulses intersect. It should be clear from the fictions we explored in this chapter and the previous one that whatever the setting, the unmediated mingling of the human and the holy, even if the latter is a sacred object such as a Torah scroll or an ark to house the Torah, is fraught with danger. How much more so, then, in Jerusalem herself. As we saw, in *Tmol shilshom* the political debates took place not in Jerusalem but in the coffeehouses of Tel Aviv/Jaffa, the embryonic metropolis founded around the time that Isaac arrived in Palestine. And even where politics is aired in such spaces, or in the anonymous "State" in *Perakim le-sefer ha-medina* (Chapters for the Book of State), it is satirized and mocked.[87] In Jerusalem, on the other hand, we saw that when the Temple Mount was under Ottoman sovereignty, the Holy of Holies could be safely approached through a veil or at a distance or mediated by nonverbal or noniconic representation. Those stories that Agnon wrote or set in either the Ottoman or the Mandate period did not, then, have to cope with the challenge of political claims intersecting with messianic projections; when "time was as it should be" and the "land was still whole and Jerusalem was not divided" could indeed refer to Jerusalem under the relatively benign control of others, as in Buczacz, "when man's heart was whole, without crookedness and without deceit."

But after 1948, with no access to the Old City, and even more intensely after 1967, with the acquisition of both access and sovereignty, the challenge of averting such claims by representing Jerusalem as a nonpolitical space, thereby circumventing the problematics of sovereignty, became almost insurmountable. Agnon's resolution of the challenge was, I submit, to create a kind of palimpsest in which his hometown of Buczacz was mapped onto Jerusalem in intriguing ways.

In my reading, Agnon avoided political discourse and the attendant dilemmas—at times through fictional devices that indeed strain credibility—by rendering Jerusalem a version of that space where Jews may at times have been a majority but exercised no hegemony, thus eliding the points of inevitable friction between ethnic self and other in the urban marketplace of ideas and civic and commercial encounters.[88] Like the space of the shtetl, then, his Jerusalem is more or less devoid of Others, Christian or Muslim. When they do appear, it is as generic facilitators or intruders: the Pasha as representing benign sovereignty in *Tmol shilshom*, the British as more or less benign rulers, the Arabs as occasional invaders in many stories. Neither Buczacz nor Jerusalem is, then, represented as a political entity but as an internally Jewish space; in becoming mirror images of each other, they avoid the seductions of political sovereignty that would become so consequential in post-'67 Jerusalem.

The political challenges that the aging Agnon faced after 1967 had, then, already been addressed in his earlier work, as well as in some fictions that would see the light of day posthumously. For the writer in Jerusalem it was not, I believe, lack of interest or inability to imagine the political discourse that led him to mock, overlook, or elide the political challenges, but a profound understanding of the consequences of claims to sovereignty in the Holy Land.

Perhaps nothing reveals this as powerfully as Agnon's own contradictory behavior in the short period between the Israeli victory over Jerusalem in 1967 and his death in 1970. Recent scholarship shows that the common assumption that it was Agnon who composed the "Prayer for the State of Israel," with its messianic references to the State as "reshit tzmiḥat geulateinu" (the beginning of our redemption), was based on a misreading of the documents; Yoel Rappel argues that Agnon made only minor changes to the text that was actually composed by Chief Rabbi Herzog.[89] Whatever his role, Agnon would probably have done it more for the privilege of being included as one of Israel's *paytanim*, those poets who grace the prayerbooks of the generations, than as a political statement.[90]

Even more critical are the Hebrew laureate's personal attitude and behavior toward the Wailing Wall. In his biography, Dan Laor reports that Agnon "deliberately refrained from approaching the stones of the Kotel [the Western Wall]" after 1967, which could be understood either as reverence for or ambivalence about proximity to the sacred.[91] Hillel Cohen, who has conducted extensive research on Jerusalem in its many iterations over the course of the twentieth century, points out that Agnon's ambivalence toward political claims to the Temple Mount came as early as the riots of 1929: "The writer S. Y. Agnon, who was close to Rabbi Kook, was *not* one of those who inflamed the situation, although he certainly did not try to calm things down. After the riots erupted, Agnon felt he had made a terrible mistake" in not trying to assuage the nationalist fervor, he writes. In the section of his essay subtitled "Agnon's Remorse," Cohen quotes the writer, from a letter to Reform Rabbi Judah Leon Magnes, as admitting that when the issue of the Kotel [the Wailing Wall] started [*ke-she-hithila parshat ha-kotel*], I stood astonished in the face of the "heroism" that our "heroes" exhibited [scare quotes in the original Hebrew], and I spoke to a few of the leaders and chastised them and asked them, what are you doing? Lay your hands off this [*hanihu yedeikhem mi-ze*] . . . And when I attended the Va'ad Leumi [Jewish National Council] plenum (for the first and last time in my life) and I observed the heroism fever [*shapa'at ha-gevura*] that had infected the heroic speakers, I wanted to yell out: lay your hands off this. But by nature I am the reticent type *and every day I have regretted not having stood in the breach* . . . And may the Lord heal the breach of his people and grant us life and peace. (Emphasis mine)[92]

Isaac Kumer stood briefly in that breach, even if it didn't save him from the tragic end inscribed in his name. The one who would maintain his poetic home in the breach was the other writer of Jerusalem, Yehuda Amichai.

PART THREE

Amichai in the Breach

"He comes out of a swimming pool or the sea . . . and he laughs and blesses": Yehuda Amichai, Poet of the Sacred Quotidian

Whoever puts on a tallis when he was young will never forget:
taking it out of the soft velvet bag, opening the folded shawl,
spreading it out, kissing the length of the neckband (embroidered
or trimmed in gold). Then swinging it in a great swoop overhead
like a sky, a wedding canopy, a parachute. And then winding it
around his head as in hide-and-seek, wrapping
his whole body in it, close and slow, snuggling into it like the cocoon
of a butterfly, then opening would-be wings to fly.
And why is the tallis striped and not checkered black-and-white
like a chessboard? Because squares are finite and hopeless.
Stripes come from infinity and to infinity they go
Like airport runways where angels land and take off.
Whoever has put on a tallis will never forget.
When he comes out of a swimming pool or the sea,
he wraps himself in a large towel, spreads it out again
over his head, and again snuggles into it close and slow,
still shivering a little, and he laughs and blesses.[1]

מִי שֶׁהִתְעַטֵּף בְּטַלִית בִּנְעוּרָיו לֹא יִשְׁכַּח לְעוֹלָם:
הַהוֹצָאָה מִשַּׂקִּית הַקְּטִיפָה הָרַכָּה וּפְתִיחַת הַטַּלִית הַמְקֻפֶּלֶת
פְּרִישָׁה, נְשִׁיקַת הַצַּוָּארוֹן לְאָרְכּוֹ (הַצַּוָּארוֹן לִפְעָמִים רָקוּם
וְלִפְעָמִים מֻזְהָב). אַחַר-כָּךְ, בִּתְנוּפָה גְדוֹלָה מֵעַל הָרֹאשׁ
כְּמוֹ שָׁמַיִם, כְּמוֹ חֻפָּה כְּמוֹ מַצְנֵחַ. אַחַר-כָּךְ לְכָרוֹךְ
אוֹתָהּ סָבִיב הָרֹאשׁ כְּמוֹ בְּמַחֲבוֹאִים, אַחַר-כָּךְ לְהִתְעַטֵּף
בָּהּ כָּל הַגּוּף, צָמוּד וְאַט, וּלְהִתְכַּרְבֵּל כְּמוֹ גֹּלֶם
שֶׁל פַּרְפַּר וְלִפְתֹּחַ כְּמוֹ כְּנָפַיִם וְלָעוּף.
וּמַדּוּעַ הַטַּלִית בְּפַסִּים וְלֹא בְּמִשְׁבְּצוֹת-שָׁחוֹר-לָבָן
כְּמוֹ לוּחַ שַׁחְמָט. כִּי הָרִבּוּעִים הֵם סוֹפִיִּים וּבִלְי תִקְוָה,
הַפַּסִּים בָּאִים מֵאֵין-סוֹף וְיוֹצְאִים לְאֵין-סוֹף
כְּמוֹ מַסְלוּלֵי הַמַּרְאָה בִּשְׂדֵה תְּעוּפָה
לִנְחִיתַת הַמַּלְאָכִים וּלְהַמְרָאָתָם.
מִי שֶׁהִתְעַטֵּף בְּטַלִית לְעוֹלָם לֹא יִשְׁכַּח,
כְּשֶׁהוּא יוֹצֵא מִן הַבְּרֵכָה אוֹ מִן הַיָּם
מִתְעַטֵּף בְּמַגֶּבֶת גְּדוֹלָה וּפוֹרֵשׂ אוֹתָהּ שׁוּב
מֵעַל רֹאשׁוֹ וְשׁוּב מִתְכַּרְבֵּל בָּהּ, צָמוּד צָמוּד
וְרוֹעֵד עוֹד קְצָת וְצוֹחֵק וּמְבָרֵךְ.[2]

The prayer shawl with which the poet wraps himself in his mind's eye is so elastic and ubiquitous that a ritual object becomes a towel, a cocoon, a wedding canopy, the sky itself. The stripes on the *tallis* are a runway to liberate hope and a sense of open horizons. And it is such inclusiveness that provides the ultimate occasion for blessing.

For the exclusive and dialectical—either/or—impulses that prevail in Israeli culture, Yehuda Amichai substitutes the inclusive and the dialogical. His embrace is reminiscent of the metaphysical poets who stretch from seventeenth-century England to nineteenth- and twentieth-century Europe and America—from John Donne to Gerard Manley Hopkins, Emily Dickinson, Rainer Maria Rilke, and Wallace Stevens. But his language is also resonant with that of the "paytanim" or religious Hebrew poets who stretch from the fifth century into the present. He brings his poetry, like theirs, into both liturgical and quotidian spaces as alternatives to the claims of embattled, hermetic monotheism.[3]

In the following two chapters, which conclude this book, I will not attempt to trace the evolution of Amichai's poetics, nor will I delve deeply into aspects of his biography, his reception in Israel and abroad, or his place among his fellow poets within the ongoing disputes, schools, and waves of modern Hebrew literature—except as these issues illuminate his unique presence in and engagement with the poetics of space, and specifically with Jerusalem. All of these subjects have been tackled by a number of astute readers and scholars—most thoroughly and evocatively by Chana Kronfeld in *The Full Severity of Compassion: The Poetry of Yehuda Amichai*.[4]

As I have been arguing throughout, the valorizing of distance and mediation between the self and the sacred is the Diaspora's primary, and most endangered, import into the Israeli imagination. Having traced its complex and conflicted expression in the prose of S. Y. Agnon, I submit that its most capacious realization can be found in the poetry of Yehuda Amichai. Over a lifetime of writing, he managed to bring the Hebrew imagination "home" through a dialogical poetics liberated both from the literalizing or reifying temptations embedded in the idea of return and from the dialectical impulse in the Hebrew imagination reinvented by H. N. Bialik and perpetuated in much of the literature and politics of modern Israel.

In the distilled public discourse in which Amichai matriculated, and which we will explore briefly, "near" banishes "far"; arrival supplants the journey itself; the furniture of Zion negates the detritus of Exile; and, especially after 1967, with renewed access to the Wailing Wall and the Temple Mount, as well as to the shrines that dot the West Bank, holy replaces profane in place as in practice and Jewish claims supersede all other claims to space.

Between 1948 and 1967, and even in the early postwar years, this centripetal process was still buffeted by the centrifugal forces that Jews had carried with them from all their elsewheres. In the ongoing struggle to preserve the chattel of past lives in the narrowing space of the Hebrew imagination, Amichai was in good company: Leah Goldberg, Dan Pagis, Avot Yeshurun, Ronny Somekh, Erez Bitton, Amira Hess, T. Carmi, Harold Schimmel, and other poets inserted their church steeples, their grandfather clocks, their Yiddish or Judeo-Arabic or Ladino phrases, their American cadences, as wedges against inhospitable climes and exclusive claims. This produced a dialogue not only with the collective and personal Jewish past in the countries of origin, but also with the dominant cultures, languages, texts, tastes, and mores in which Jews marinated in Northern, Central, Eastern and Southern Europe, North and South America, North Africa and the Middle East, and it continues to counteract the claustrophobia (or "claustro*philia*") of a people who, after the "ingathering," increasingly defines itself as living alone.[5]

Amichai's poetic oeuvre may be the most sustained articulation of that project, especially in Jerusalem after 1967. While other Hebrew writers defy the exclusive claims of Jerusalem by privileging alternate public spaces—the Kinneret, the kibbutz or moshav, Tel Aviv, the Negev—or by probing the inner spaces of the private soul,[6] Amichai stares directly at Israel's radioactive core. While politicians and religious exegetes attempt to banish longing through territorializing texts and shrinking distance between the self and the teleological Other, Amichai *inserts* distance in Jerusalem in order to aerate, pluralize, and pedestrianize the terrifying space of sacred negotiations.

Through poetic acts that are as daring as they are endearing, Amichai reconfigures the primary places (the Wall and the Temple Mount) and the constitutive texts (the akeda and the Song of Songs) so that a version of diasporic aesthetics and ethics can import a cool wind into the suffocating center of Jerusalem.

But by the time of the poet's death in 2000, preserving that permeable space, standing in the breach, had become far more difficult—and more urgent—than ever before. In the pages that follow, I will explore the poetics of space that both evolves and remains consistent over the decades; in the next chapter, I will focus on Amichai's Jerusalem and transformations in both the existential and the poetic stance of the city's uncrowned poet laureate.

The Dialectical Imagination

To appreciate the radical nature of Amichai's language, consider his prayer shawl in its infinite metamorphoses. Agnon was not alone in indulging the dialectical imagination, which we traced in the preceding chapters, and which, in the opening of his very first story, takes the emblematic form of the *tallit* that is either whole and pure, the emanation of divine perfection, or tattered and threadbare, signifying the fallen human state. Many of the Hebrew writers of the twentieth century reflected in their poetics and their politics some version of this dialectic: in the first place, the tension between sacred and secular as fixed alternatives in a dichotomous universe. Their most influential spokesperson was H. N. Bialik, who, in his poetry, his speeches, and his essays, presented the lexicon of holiness as a quarry to be mined for its secular possibilities. He insisted that this process, founded on mutual exclusion, was endemic to "the Israeli psyche,"[7] itself a battlefield on which a perpetual dualism is enacted. "The whole purpose of Hebrew speech ... the rule of that language over life, is to turn the sacred into the profane," he argued in 1927 before the "battalion of defenders of the language" (*gdud meginei ha-safa*).[8]

It is important to understand that at this early moment, Bialik's references to the "Israeli psyche," and to the "battalion of [its] defenders," though retrograde and rather militaristic in their resonances, relate to the ethnic-historic collective, the language and "people of Israel," and not necessarily to the territorial nation-state. His own anxiety about what the conversion of a literary-clerical lingua franca into a national language would do to the holy tongue is reflected in his poem "There Passed by Me" (Ḥalfa ʿal panai). The "pure doves" of the poet's divinely inspired Hebrew speech are sent out in the morning and return at dusk as filthy crows besmirched by the offal in street bins:

> ... And my language, Lord, made wholly loathsome, a thing gone foul,
> not a word remains that has not been profaned [*nitme'a*] to the root
> not a phrase that filthy lips haven't tortured,
> not a sound that hasn't been dragged to the house of shame [*beit ha-kalon*],
> and at dawn I send my pure doves toward heaven, ·
> and at evening to me they return—crows well-versed in dung and refuse,
> a shriek stuck in their throats, in their beaks the flesh of a carcass ...[9]

The disdain that this poet reveals for the very vernacular that he championed may be understood through the Hebrew root טמא (*tamei*), derived from the religious lexicon; though here translated as "profaned," the word actually signifies "unclean" or "impure." The knight of the revival of Hebrew as literary corpus, and the inspiration for modern spoken Hebrew, would himself remain profoundly ambivalent about what he regarded as the inevitable impoverishment of the richly nuanced, resonant "ceremonial language"[10] of Scripture and

ritual, when reduced to the one-dimensional patois of the street and marketplace. Even as he asserted, in an earlier essay, "Ḥevlei Lashon" (Language
Pangs), that the assets of any language require the "perpetual, cyclical motion of life . . . the power of living speech . . . the total rejuvenation of the language and a renaissance of speech and writing," and in that sense heralded the
changes and phases that modern Hebrew would undergo, in dialogue with
other linguistic shifts that characterized modernism, he still remained ambivalent about such an open-ended process.[11] (The above poem, from 1917, is
one of the few that break—but perhaps also help to explain—Bialik's poetic
silence from 1911 till his death in 1934.)[12]

It is important to recognize that, in this context, the dialectical process is
never meant to culminate in a synthesis or resolution; Bialik's favorite perch
was "on the threshold," between the study house and the natural world, the
sacred and the secular, the collective and the self, the ritual and the unique.[13]
Such fence-sitting, and the deep dialecticism embedded in the "Israeli psyche,"
would persist far beyond Bialik. Indeed, the fear of—and, perhaps, desire
for—the "return of the repressed" has never abated; it can be traced in the
lively debate ignited in the last decades of the twentieth century over the
rediscovery of Gershom Scholem's 1926 letter to Franz Rosenzweig, which
is parsed by most readers as foretelling the inevitable resurgence of the
"apocalyptic thorn" of divine speech that inheres even in secularized modern Hebrew—and that has indeed animated the messianic lexicon of the late
twentieth and early twenty-first centuries.[14] Whatever their political persua-
sion, many of the commentators on this letter seem to agree with Bialik and
with Scholem that the vernacular is a degraded version of the sacred language.
Jacques Derrida is one of the few who apparently celebrate what he calls the
"*profanatory jouissance*" of the quotidian from which the sacred recoils.[15]
Nevertheless, with its sexual, almost lascivious undertones from the psycho-
analytic lexicon, this phrase may reveal even Derrida's ambivalence about the
power of such liberated language. He asks what insights Scholem's prophecy affords into the "Israeli people today";[16] in the decades that have elapsed
since Derrida's essay was transcribed, the question has become only more
poignant.

Amichai's response to this challenge evolved over a lifetime. Into the
reigning paradigm he imports not only the detritus of other places, collaps-
ing "near and far," "sacred and profane," but also a metaphoric process that
liberates the Hebrew "psyche" from its dialectical temptations and impasses.
And to Derrida's question and the burden of the closed cycle of history, he
provides the most compassionate response: the promise of an open future.

The Dialogical Imagination

From the beginning, Amichai's poetry refused to perform the acts of exclusion necessary for those dialectical or dualistic impulses that governed Bialik's world—and much of modern Hebrew culture.[17] In the poetics of space constructed by Amichai, there are, quite simply, no impure precincts. Doves and ravens cavort in the streets, and Arabs and Jews mingle freely, or meet in protected spaces, while elements of *world* are recycled in endless metempsychosis: taking the tallis "out of the soft velvet bag, opening the folded shawl, / spreading it out, kissing the length of the neckband (embroidered or trimmed in gold). Then swinging it in a great swoop overhead / like a sky, a wedding canopy, a parachute." Note that the tallis-towel that enfolds the bather who emerges from the sea imports the sacred into that other, officially secular, space: Tel Aviv, with its coastline and its infinite horizon. The same sea could accommodate Leah Goldberg's hometown church.[18]

Mikhail Bakhtin's theories of "the dialogic imagination" can inform a more spacious reading of Amichai. Although Bakhtin's insights were applied mainly to the novel, they continue to resonate in new places and genres. He described the novel as

> this ever-developing genre . . . [which captures the] indeterminacy [of] . . . the open-ended present . . . The novel has become the leading hero in the drama of literary development in our time precisely because it best of all reflects the tendencies of a new world still in the making . . . Faced with the problem of the novel, genre theory must submit to a radical re-structuring.[19]

Each of the above statements could be applied to Amichai's poetics and helps to define what I regard as his dialogical move, evolving from the earliest to the latest poems. Bakhtin claims that the novel is a relatively new literary form; indeed, a parallel process unfolded in modern Hebrew poetry. Although its antecedents are as old as the Bible, and as we have seen, the ancient poetry inflected by millennia of use continues to serve as a wellspring for modern impulses, something new was created in Israel in the mid-twentieth century for which Yehuda Amichai's voice was constitutive. One of the distinctive characteristics of the novel, as Bakhtin defines it, is its function as "the zone of maximal contact with the present (with contemporary reality) in all its openendedness."[20] Amichai's poetry contains multitudes from the Hebrew and the Jewish past, and yet remains the most open-ended of the poetic voices to have emerged in twentieth-century Jerusalem.

And then there is the wit, the exercise of the comic muscle which Bakhtin emphasized as central to the novel, and which, however endemic it may have

been to Jewish culture in the diaspora, has become endangered in contemporary Israeli society. The comic impulse is one that notices the smallest details
of life as it is lived, in the here and now:

> As a distanced image a subject cannot be comical; to be made comical, it must
> be brought close . . . Laughter demolishes fear and piety before an object,
> before a world, making of it an object of familiar contact and thus clearing
> the ground for an absolutely free investigation of it. Laughter is a vital factor
> in laying down that prerequisite for fearlessness without which it would be
> impossible to approach the world realistically.[21]

To "clear the ground" and view the world up close, memory has to recede.
"Here the role of memory is minimal," writes Bakhtin. "In the comic world
there is nothing for memory and tradition to do."[22] To which Amichai might
reply with his own poem on memory:

> And who will remember? And what do you use to preserve memory?
> How do you preserve anything in this world?
> You preserve it with salt and with sugar, high heat and deep freeze,
> vacuum sealers, dehydrators, mummifiers.
> But the best way to preserve memory is to conserve it inside forgetting,
> so not even a single act of remembering will seep in
> and disturb memory's eternal rest.[23]

Note the details: salt and sugar, high heat and deep freeze, vacuum sealers,
dehydrators, mummifiers. It is the attention to details that keeps one's eye
trained on the here-and-now and keeps memory—with its relentless, ancient,
demands for vengeance and completion—well conserved inside the forgetting that relaxes the comic muscle and allows for forgiveness.

What I am calling the dialogical turn in Amichai's poetics has affinities
to other creative moments in Hebrew culture, and especially to the medieval
piyyut. In the next chapter, I will probe the explicit dialogues that Amichai
carried on with *paytanim* such as Shmuel Ha-nagid (Samuel ibn Naghrillah),
the tenth-century liturgical poet from Andalusia. But here I want to emphasize that even though the wit exercised in those creative acts, and the surprising juxtapositions of medieval and modern voices, may have provided a kind
of license for Amichai's daring flights of imagination, there remains at least
one major difference. As Tova Rosen has shown, Ha-nagid and his contemporaries inhabited both sacred and profane spaces, but unlike them—and,
for that matter, unlike John Donne and other "metaphysicals" in English—
Amichai has a world-embracing reach that is not foreclosed by the *memento
mori* that concludes and authorizes so many of their poems.[24] Death, the great
leveler in the poems of medieval Spain, seventeenth-century England, and

nineteenth-century America, gives way in Amichai's verse to another, human, arbiter of the future.

But still: what of the nonhuman Arbiter of the future? Amichai's "God" is also located in a more modern idiom, somewhere between the American God of Emily Dickinson and the Hebrew God of Zelda Schneerson Mishkovsky.[25] He remains an address for the poetic act that both registers the absence of demarcated sacred space and simulates a worshipful pose in the world at large:

> . . . With the same body
> that stoops to pick up a fallen something from the floor,
> I bow down to God. That is my faith, my religion.[26]

Harmonizing with Emily Dickinson keeping the Sabbath by "staying at Home," and with another modern metaphysical poet, Wallace Stevens, for whom the Sunday "complacencies of the peignoir, and late / Coffee and oranges in a sunny chair, / And the green freedom of a cockatoo / Upon a rug mingle to dissipate / The holy hush of ancient sacrifice,"[27] Amichai sanctifies the everyday. His metaphors are aeronautic without being magical and his world metaphysical without being enchanted. "Because [Amichai] reaches all the way inside the everyday," writes Hebrew novelist David Grossman, "you suddenly feel that each moment, even the most banal, is shot through with light."[28] On either side of the fault line of 1967, this quality will become consequential for Amichai's political as well as his poetic legacy. But while such gestures persist throughout his poetry, so do the markers of God's absent-mindedness—or the absence of divine beneficence in the world. An early example builds on a pun on one of the divine epithets, "O God Full of Mercy," traditionally invoked in the prayer for the dead: "El malei rahamim / Ilmalei ha-el malei rahamim / hayu ha-rahamim ba-olam ve-lo rak bo." "*God Full of Mercy*, / If God were only not so full of mercy / there would be mercy in the world, not just in Him . . ."[29] Amichai's Hebrew God is coeval with—but not exhausted in—the world. This "God" will remain throughout in both the human gestures of reverence and the negative space "He" occupies.

The punning of "ilmalei" ("if" or "if only") and "el malei" (God full of) would seem to be lost in translation, but it has rather been transformed, or replaced, in the radical ways that, as we have seen, characterize most acts of translation and appropriation of canonic texts. The real challenge lies not in the translation but in the reinterpretation of these verses: I am offering them not as parsed by generations of readers in Israel and abroad in binary fashion as a series of secular alternatives or ironic juxtapositions, but rather as a metaphysical reach often *masquerading* as pseudodialectics.

Living on the Hyphen

In approaching such poems as a dialogical challenge to the dialectical mind, I am, then, going against the grain of many readings of Amichai. My approach most resembles that of Chana Kronfeld, who maps out this poet's rhetorical structures and their ethical and political underpinnings in *The Full Severity of Compassion*. In the chapter "Living on the Hyphen: The Necessary Metaphor," she explores the "hyphen" as a trope, a poetic principle, and a "lifeline."[30] Amichai introduces the hyphen explicitly in his poem "Late Marriage": sitting in the rabbinical court waiting with much younger grooms for their marriage certificates, he muses that "the pressure of my life brings my date of birth closer / to the date of my death, as in history books / where the pressure of history has brought / those two numbers together next to the name of a dead king / with only a hyphen between them."[31] As James Wood parses this poem in an essay in the *New Yorker*, suddenly "this figure of the hyphen takes on palpable life, for it is this little temporal bridge which the poet, oldish but renewed by his late marriage, now fiercely cherishes":[32]

> I hold onto that hyphen with all my might
> like a lifeline, I live on it,
> and on my lips the vow not to be alone,
> the voice of the bridegroom and the voice of the bride,
> the sound of the children laughing and shouting
> in the streets of Jerusalem
> and in the cities of Yehuda.[33]

The hyphen, it turns out, is not just a "temporal bridge" between D.o.B. and D.o.D., but the very principle of Amichai's poetic practice—both featuring and keeping separate the binaries of the Hebrew imagination. Kronfeld argues that the two poles at each end of the hyphen are the constitutive artifice of simile that upholds the "narrow between" (*ha-beinayim ha-tzarim*) that is life itself.[34] "Jewish history and world history / grind me between them like two grindstones, sometimes / to a powder," the poet writes in one of his last poems.[35] Functioning not unlike the "kaf ha-dimyon," the (pretense of) simile that we explored as Isaac's almost-imperceptible lifeline in Agnon's *Only Yesterday*, this artifice keeps not only death but also the totalizing, literalizing, imagination at bay. The tenor and the vehicle of each simile remain, then, intact and productive, while the in-between space of the self is not the space of compromise between or synthesis of dialectical extremes so much as the dialogical space of compassion, the messy "in-between-ness" of human life

and the genius of human imagination. As Kronfeld argues, Amichai's metaphor or simile "brings together . . . disparate domains . . . even while it strives
to make the transient, liminal space in between them as existentially meaningful as it can possibly be."[36] I will return to this in the next chapter, in my
consideration of the about-face that takes place in Amichai's late poetic dialogue with the Song of Songs, but here it should be noted that metaphorical
language in general and the unreconciled simile in particular—the simile that
holds fiercely to the two ends of its poles—are the primary agents of what I
am calling Amichai's metaphysical reach.

And there's something else that should be noted in the poem "Late Marriage"; the Hebrew-speaking reader will hear, even in English translation,
the allusions to the verses from Jeremiah that are chanted at every Jewish
wedding: "Yet again there shall be heard . . . in the cities of Judah [be-'arei
yehuda], and in the streets of Jerusalem . . . the voice of joy and the voice of
gladness, the voice of the bridegroom and the voice of the bride" (Jer. 33:10–
11). But only those well versed in the Bible are aware of the elisions in this
blessing: the fuller version of the pronouncement of the prophet, who, sitting
in the "wasted streets of Jerusalem," "voided" of people and animals, gropes
for language to foretell a better future. Only those who, like Yehuda Amichai,
come belatedly to the still-contested "cities of Yehuda [Judah]" and the always-
disputed "streets of Jerusalem" truly know, along with Jeremiah, how endangered are the voices of bride and groom, how easily the laughter, the joy, and
the gladness may become "voided" and "wasted."

Centrifugal Forces: Poetry and War

As the rhetoric of the Holy Land became territorialized in twentieth–twenty-
first-century Hebrew politics and poetry, as its imagery became reified and as
the diffuse and centrifugal gave way to the ingathered and centripetal, Amichai's poetry stood out as offering an altogether different possibility. At times
mimicking but always, I believe, transcending dialectical juxtapositions, Amichai offers a boundless reach, countering what Bialik called the kinus or "ingathering" of people, texts, and poetic practice with a poetics of dialogue and
diffusion. The early poem "Lo ka-brosh" (Not like a Cypress), is a rare example of an ars poetica that explicitly reveals the intricate, limitless embroidery
and seeming abandon at the heart of this poetic project:

> Not like a cypress,
> not all at once, not all of me,
> but like the grass, in thousands of cautious green exits,

> to be hiding like many children
> while one of them seeks.
>
> And not like the single man,
> like Saul, whom the multitude found
> and made king.
>
> But like the rain in many places
> from many clouds, to be absorbed, to be drunk
> by many mouths, to be breathed in
> like the air all year long
> and scattered like blossoming in springtime . . .
>
> And afterward the quiet exit, . . .
> children tired from play,
> a stone as it almost stops rolling
> down the steep hill, in the place
> where the plain of great renunciation begins,
> from which, like prayers that are answered,
> dust rises in many myriads of grains.[37]

Except for a vague reference to "all of me," neither poetry nor the poet—nor even writing itself—is explicitly mentioned here.[38] But in the microscopic attention to details lies the secret of Amichai's poetic power. While distance from the sacred provides protection against the tragic perils of proximity, the view from up close—tending to one's House—provides the comic, domestic, democratic, and dialogical engagement with the mortal here-and-now, "children tired from play, / a stone as it almost stops rolling / down the steep hill." The unidentified, unembodied speaker, like the poetry itself, does not resemble the cypress, the outstanding individual, the king; his appearance is not all at once, not complete or whole, but ubiquitous, quotidian, scattered, diffuse, *necessary*—like grass, rain, the air itself.

There is only one thing that can scramble the exhilaratingly cacophonous coexistence, the "metaphysical" embrace, of competing worlds: war. The sounds and debris of war punctuate Amichai's poetry from the beginning, and can turn any of his landscapes into chaotic minefields of jumbled objects and undiscriminating agents of slaughter, from the Bible to the present:

> Tanks from America, fighter planes from France, Russian
>   jet-doves, armored chariots from England, Sisera's regiments
> who dried the swamps with their corpses, a flying Massada,
>   . . . Muezzins armed with
> three-stage missiles, paper-rips and battle-cries
> of holy wars in all seven kinds

> . . . Elijah's ejection-seat leaping up
> at a time of danger, hurling circumcision knives, thundering
> dynamite fuses from heart to heart . . . mezuzahs filled with
> explosives, don't kiss them or they'll blow up . . .
> fingers of dynamite, prosthetic legs of dynamite,
> eight empty bullet-shells for a Hanukkah menorah,
> explosives of eternal flame, the cross of a crossfire,
> a submachine gun carried in phylactery straps,
> camouflage nets of thin lacy material
> from girlfriends' panties, used women's dresses
> and ripped diapers to clean the cannon mouth . . .[39]

Much of Amichai's own biography and geography appears in the detritus of this passage, along with the public history of the Hebrews, what is referred to in popular Israeli parlance as the trajectory "from the Tanakh to the Palma"ḥ" (from the Bible to the prestate military force).[40] Perhaps the most poignant is the reference to the "prosthetic legs of dynamite," an encoded allusion to Amichai's childhood friend from Würzburg, "little Ruth." As every attentive reader knows, Ruth's prosthetic leg was the result of an accident that profoundly affected Ludwig Pfeuffer; it was, presumably, this prosthesis that later cost her her life during the Nazi period and that would haunt Yehuda Amichai's poetry and prose.[41]

What has been blown up can be glued back together tentatively by the poet, through wordplay and diffuse associative domestication, but the scars remain visible:[42]

> . . . Sea mines
> like the prickly apples used as smelling-salts on Yom Kippur
> in case of fainting, half my childhood in a whole armored truck . . . Dürer's
> praying hands sticking up like a vertical land mine, arms with an attachment
> for a bayonet . . .[43]

Dürer's praying hands? Even if we try to parse the wildly concatenated objects that fly through space, time, textual probabilities, and historical improbabilities, it is hard to account, through any logical process of association, for Dürer's "praying hands," which presumably allude to the pen-and-ink drawing by the fifteenth–sixteenth-century artist Albrecht Dürer whose original is located in a museum in Vienna.[44] This seemingly public reference is inserted as a very private wedge or even warning against public appropriation of what must remain impenetrable. In Amichai's memory poems, ritual objects such as the mother's just-slaughtered chicken,[45] the Shabbat candles, or the father's *tallis* remain personal even as they bear the replicable and portable quality of

all diasporic ritual objects, infusing even Jerusalem itself with a kind of familiar portability. But there comes a moment in nearly every Amichai poem like
the reference to Dürer's "hands" when memory becomes private and inscrutable, forcing the reader into a quietly respectful appreciation for the *enigma*
without trying to resolve the riddle at its heart.[46]

And then there are the many voices: the cacophony of people in the dailiness of their lives. Here, too, like Bakhtin with Dostoevsky, Amichai, through
his speakers, is articulating a "plurality of independent and unmerged voices
and consciousnesses, a genuine polyphony of fully valid voices."[47] "Not like
the single man, like Saul," but like the sounds in the street and the bazaar, in
the classroom and the prayer room, in the bedroom and on the battlefield,
"the voice of the bridegroom and the voice of the bride, / [mingle with] the
sound of the children laughing and shouting / in the streets of Jerusalem /
and in the cities of Yehuda . . ."

Bridges between Worlds

I will focus on Amichai's Jerusalem as human and as poetic space in the next
chapter, but one public image that is imported as private artifact in the dis-
and-re-articulated poema "Travels," from which the above quotations are
taken, is worth mentioning here; it is located in a part of Jerusalem that is
also sufficiently removed from the radioactive center to provide a diasporic
occasion for distance. A kind of accordion effect is achieved in the image of
a stone lion that graces the bridge (fig. 5) in the speaker's recalled childhood
home in Germany—and that is duplicated on the lintel of the poet's Tem-
plar house (fig. 6)[48] on Emek Refaim street in the "German Quarter" of West
Jerusalem:

> The stone lions on the bridges in the city of my childhood
> stood guard with the stone lions of the old house in Jerusalem.[49]

These replicated images of stony protection are connected by greater or lesser
logic or probability but form no accessible narrative. They are remarkable
in that historical accountability—one could say history itself (chronological
order, or what Amichai sardonically calls *be-kivun ha-tkufot* or "in the order
of the eras")[50]—is necessary but absent. As the *major* event that separates
them—the shoah—is elided, the biggest chapter in public history is merci-
fully suspended.[51] Indeed, the stone lions that grace the Ludwigsbrücke (originally called "Lowenbrücke" for the lions in its corners) in Würzburg were
damaged but not destroyed during World War II, even though the bridge
itself was blown up by the retreating Germans in 1945.[52] The gap between

FIGURE 5. Lions on the Ludwig Bridge, Würzburg (2010). Image from Mattes/Wikimedia.

FIGURE 6. Lion at Sandel House, Emek Refaim 9, Jerusalem (2013). Photograph by Shmuel Bar-Am.

the Bavarian and the Jerusalem lions signifies but does not explicitly probe the terrible war that destroyed Amichai's childhood home along with Jewish homes throughout Europe. The shoah that is barely present in "Mas'ot," except for the synecdoche of Little Ruth's prosthetic leg, would have dominated the poem had it been given a foothold, as it were—though it does suffuse Amichai's novel, *Lo me-'akhshav lo mi-kan* (Not of This Time, Not of This Place),[53] a bifurcated narrative that moves between Jerusalem and the protagonist's German hometown.

Amichai's poetry, then, is not overdetermined by events that he did not experience directly. There is, however, another war that Amichai witnessed at a distance and that does enter into his longest *poema* in surprisingly dramatic ways. The poetic jumble we just noted in "The Travels of Benjamin III," in which personal, public, and Jewish history coexist in an often-undifferentiated heap of debris and destruction, was composed in the aftermath of the 1967 war, when Amichai was in America. The implicit antimilitarism in this poem goes against the grain of the triumphalist rhetoric that prevailed in Israel and especially in Jerusalem after that war.[54]

This poetry is carrying on a dialogue not only with the dialectical imagination, but also with its implicit synthesis, the "poetics of the whole" that feeds the apocalyptic/messianic political imagination. The tired lion, resting on his paws as he presides over the lintel in the poet's adult home, also testifies silently to the layered history and ongoing conflict in the poet's adopted city.

When trained on Jerusalem, and specifically on East Jerusalem and the Temple Mount, the inclusive embrace of clashing histories and private lives offers an antidote to the suffocating embrace of arrival and fulfillment, of memory brought full circle, of exclusive claims to sacred real estate and the literalizing of metaphors held in allegorical or symbolic suspension for thousands of years. In the next, and final, chapter, we will examine the iterations of Jerusalem that evolved in Amichai's writing over the decades before the poet's valedictory volume published just before his death.

"Visit my tears and the east wind, which is the true Western Wall": Amichai in Jerusalem

The Wall

It is quite simple. You walk down a street that is no more than a few feet wide and there it is—a large wall—or buttress— . . . grayish and covered with mosses . . .

—Its formal simplicity—its improvised originality—its refusal to make any false promises or foster any illusions. It is a last stop of history, no less than that board in the train station—a blank wall with no open-sesames or hidden crypts . . . It is perhaps the ultimate dam, built to hold back the Jews in their restless proclivity to return to their past. "Halt!" it says. "No Passage Allowed Beyond This Point."

A. B. YEHOSHUA, *Mr. Mani*[1]

. . . [*Bend down into a perfect arabesque.*]
A Crusader influence is evident in the hard jawbones,
in the prominent chin. She touches the earth with both palms
without bending her knees, she touches
the earth that I didn't kiss when I was brought to it
as a child. Come again, ladies and gentlemen, visit
the promised land, visit my tears and the east wind,
which is the true Western Wall. It's made of
huge wind-stones, and the weeping is the wind's, and the papers
whirling in the air are the supplications that I stuck between
the cracks. Visit the land. On a clear day,
if the visibility is good, you can see
the great miracle of my child
holding me in his arms, though he is four
and I am forty-four . . .

YEHUDA AMICHAI, "Travels of the Last Benjamin of Tudela"[2]

To the timeless landscape where History begins and ends, where the Western Wall is the "ultimate dam" serving to thwart personal memories, yearnings, and restlessness, a "blank wall" signifying the end of signification itself,

Yehuda Amichai brings the one-time human body and the unfettered human utterance. Twisted into yoga-like poses that mimic the architecture of successive conquests of Jerusalem—a Crusader column, an arabesque curlicue, a "Gothic arch that reaches / toward the heart and like a reddish Byzantine flame between her legs"[3]—the female body animates the silent stones with her undulations and her supple kisses. The male speaker humanizes the Wailing Wall with his years, his tears, and his fatherhood. The Wall itself is fashioned of wind, and the paper petitions stuck between its cracks, registering every form of human misery and supplication, "whirl in the air" and are caught by a poet's attention that defies the "last stop of history" and the end of poetry. As Ranen Omer-Sherman writes, "though the question of whether the Wall itself constitutes the 'holy' remains respectfully open-ended, the poem addresses the spaces between the stones as sanctified space precisely because they so nakedly reveal the proximity of human beings in duress."[4] And yet, many years later the poet would write, in his poetic valediction: "a city that has a wall, as Jerusalem has, / is like children who have a father, / and neither wall nor father can protect them any longer."[5]

There are Walls and walls. Amichai did not live to see the completion of the wall that snakes through the valleys to the south, east, and north of Jerusalem, cutting the Palestinian sector of the city from its outskirts and from the villages surrounding it.[6] But, in the three decades following the Israeli capture and incorporation of the Old City, the Wailing Wall became the place where Amichai staked his final claim, continuing to insist on the power of history—not collective history but collected history or memory[7]—as tattooed on the one-time, unique human body and reconstituted in every generation, but also periodically hijacked by folly and avarice.

Having been "brought as a child" to Palestine from the northern Bavarian town of Würzburg, Germany, some twelve years before the establishment of the State of Israel, Ludwig Pfeuffer would mature as Yehuda Amichai in the streets and neighborhoods of Jerusalem, the city that would mark his poetry while leaving the lines porous enough to invite access to memories and fantasies incubated elsewhere.

Jerusalem, Jerusalem, Why Jerusalem?

Why is Jerusalem, Yerushalayim, always two, the Heavenly and the earthly?
I want to live in an in-between Jerusalem,
without banging my head up above or gashing my feet down below.
And why is Yerushalayim in the dual form, like hands, *yadayim*,
and feet, *raglayim*?

I want to live in Jerusal, singular;
because I am just I, singular, not an I-im.[8]

לָמָּה יְרוּשָׁלַיִם תָּמִיד שְׁתַּיִם, שֶׁל מַעְלָה וְשֶׁל מַטָּה
וַאֲנִי רוֹצֶה לִחְיוֹת בִּירוּשָׁלַיִם שֶׁל אֶמְצַע
בְּלִי לַחְבֹּט אֶת רֹאשִׁי לְמַעְלָה
וּבְלִי לִפְצֹעַ אֶת רַגְלַי לְמַטָּה.
וְלָמָּה יְרוּשָׁלַיִם בִּלְשׁוֹן זוּגִית כְּמוֹ יָדַיִם וְרַגְלַיִם.
אֲנִי רוֹצֶה לִחְיוֹת רַק בִּירוּשָׁל אַחַת,
כִּי אֲנִי רַק אֲנִי אֶחָד וְלֹא אֲנַיִם.[9]

This poem, barely rendered into English to preserve the grammatical-existential
perplexity in the original, is part of the series with which I began this book
and which sealed Amichai's poetic oeuvre: "Yerushalayim yerushalayim, lama
yerushalayim?" (Jerusalem, Jerusalem, Why Jerusalem?). The question itself,
stated starkly, almost blasphemously, is actually the culmination of this poet's
long series of encounters with, representations and interrogations of, the City.
The cardinal principle of his poetics that we discussed in the previous chapter,
what Amichai himself calls "ha-beinayim ha-tzarim," the narrow in-between, the
hyphen—the irreplaceable self in the present tense—becomes more and more
endangered over the years.

The geographical trajectory of Amichai's life in Jerusalem illustrates this
process. Beginning in the outlying urban areas, Amichai's verses came eventually to focus, like his own habitations—and the intensifying political rhetoric—on the sacred center or the "holy basin." The poet's increasingly imperiled
challenge was to import into that gaze the poetic and ethical stance practiced
in the elsewheres of Jewish history, to combat the dialectics and doubleness
embedded in what Bialik called the Hebrew "psyche" with the humanity of the
hyphen and the indelible, unduplicatable, self. I traced this poetic principle in
the last chapter; here I will explore its iterations in Jerusalem over the second
half of the twentieth century.

The long *poema* "The Travels of the Last Benjamin of Tudela," from which
the epigraph to this chapter is taken, was composed within a few months after the Six Day War but—as already noted—was written from afar, implicitly
validating distance itself as a mediating factor.[10] Even at this relatively early
moment, the speaker insists that the Old City of Jerusalem, the very definition of what is officially Real and Sacred, newly incorporated into Israeli
sovereignty, is best viewed in the space (*revah*) between two people standing
by a window: "Sometimes / I see Jerusalem between two people / who stand
in front of a window, with a space / between them"[11]—a frame that re-creates
profane, "diasporic" distance, as in a stereoscope. *The only form of proximity*

that is validated here is that of the human quotidian: "The farthest distance [the heart] knows is the nearest tree, / the curb of the sidewalk, the face of the belovèd."[12] "Curb of the sidewalk" in Hebrew is *sfat ha-midrakha*, literally "lip of the sidewalk." Note that such physiognomic metaphors, embedded in ordinary spoken Hebrew, are reanimated in Amichai's verses.

When the poet reintroduces longing, at the very end of this long poem, it is not the collective longing of a displaced people for redemption, or for territory, meant to culminate in and be superseded by the act of arrival—but the simple longing of an estranged father for his young son ("the great miracle of my child / holding me in his arms, though he is four / and I am forty-four").[13] As I will elaborate below, what remains consistent throughout Amichai's oeuvre is that every time the first-person plural—even the "dual form" of *Yerushal-ayim* herself—threatens to efface the first-person singular in a suffocating embrace, a small sliver of selfhood inserts itself defiantly—at times inscrutably—preserving its privacy. And the ultimate arbiter of that process is one's progeny.

The longing for one's child can be read also as a validation of longing itself, weighed against the claims of Jerusalem as the site of ultimate homecoming. Since—as we saw in Agnon's fiction—after the establishment of the State of Israel in 1948 and before the 1967 war, Jerusalem remained a kind of diasporic space, with the Wall and the Temple Mount just out of sight and inaccessible, constructing memory palaces was relatively easy. Still, even as he lived and quarried his poetry in the neighborhoods of West Jerusalem, many of Amichai's moves seemed radical to his contemporaries in those years.[14]

In the mid-1960s, the poet could claim direct affinity with one of his medieval predecessors, since he lived for a while on Rehov Binyamin Mi-Tudela, the street in West Jerusalem named after the twelfth-century explorer Benjamin of Tudela and referred to by the popular misnomer "Rehov Metudela"—literally "From-Tudela St." Amichai's play on place and person is enabled by the liminal status of this street, perched on the rim of Emek ha-matzleva (the Valley of the Cross), where legend planted the tree from which the cross was wrought for the crucifixion of Jesus. *Metudela*, both a fellow traveler and a magical street, bears traces of haunting and exotic otherness, a dreamy place that both is and isn't modern Israel. The rocky terraces and springtime cyclamens of the valley below easily accommodate Christian topography and itinerant Jewish liturgy:

> This could have been a song of praise to
> the sweet imaginary God of my childhood.
> It happened on Friday, and black angels

> filled the Valley of the Cross, and their wings
> were black houses and abandoned quarries.
> Sabbath candles bobbed up and down like ships
> at the entrance to a harbor.[15]

Is it the presence of the Monastery of the Cross, with its ancient legends and archaeological layers, reminiscent perhaps of the medieval cathedrals and fortresses of Amichai's hometown, that, like those lions we encountered in both cities, sentinels connecting place to place, allows the "sweet . . . God of my childhood" to emerge from imagin*ary* space into imagin*ative* space? This mysterious valley, with its trees that are meant to support both crucifixion and redemption, also undergoes a weekly transformation into an ecumenical site of worship. At the Jewish bewitching hour when Friday becomes Sabbath eve, its abandoned quarries and the houses on its rim—or the priests in its depths—become black angels, its candles become ships entering a port, swaying to the lilting Hebrew rhetoric of *lekha dodi*, the bridal rhetoric of the Sabbath hymn. And then, almost imperceptibly, all this gives way, as so often in Amichai, to a simple bride of flesh and blood as the most majestic metal gives way to shards of pottery and the lowliest poppy—so that "future archaeologists" will "find and remember" the simple fact of our onetime human existence.[16]

Benjamin of Tudela is not the only medieval traveler whose journey and arrival Amichai conjures—without sacrificing the homes left behind, and without romanticizing the process of acclimation. He imagines Yehuda Ha-Levi en route to the Holy Land:

> . . . His forehead: a sail; his arms: oars
> to carry the soul inside his body to Jerusalem.
>
> But in the white fist of his brain
> he holds the black seeds of his happy childhood.
>
> When he reaches the beloved, bone-dry land—
> he will sow.[17]

What are the chances that, even if this poet's body were to reach Jerusalem, those "black seeds of his happy childhood" would take root in the "beloved, bone-dry land" that he would attempt to sow? About as likely as the failed acclimations of H. N. Bialik, who fell silent after arriving in the Holy Land, and whom Amichai represents as the

> bald knight among olive trees,
> [who] wrote no poems in the land of Israel, for he kissed
> the earth and chased away flies and mosquitoes
> with his writing hand,

and wiped sweat
from his versifying brain and in the khamsin
placed on his forehead a handkerchief from the Diaspora.[18]

In bringing Benjamin of Tudela, Yehuda Ha-Levi, and other explorers and
dreamers "Home," while leaving them in a kind of internal exile, in making
palpable, enigmatic, and enchanted connections between his own homes, Yehuda Amichai made the claustrophobic city porous, the public city private,
the Jewish claims ecumenical, the holy city profane, and the profane holy.
Above all, he preserved the hard-won metaphoric imagination of generations
of Hebrew wanderers from the dangers to body and soul of a poetics of ingathering and a theodicy of redemption.

And the city returned the favor. Aviya Kushner notes that after Amichai
died, on the death notices that appeared throughout the city, "instead of the
usual wife and children listed as mourners, there in black letters were the
mayor of Jerusalem and the city's top officials listed as mourners. The city itself was listed as a mourner. That struck no one as odd."[19] Over the years since
his death, a number of official commemorative sites erected in West Jerusalem have been accompanied by the poet's own words: under a rusting sign on
Emek Refaim denoting "Construction Site of the Yehuda Amichai Quarter" is
a poem that begins: "It's sad / to be the Mayor of Jerusalem" (fig. 7).

Some distance away, at the roundabout connecting Martin Luther King
Street (rather improbably) with Heinrich Graetz Street is the beginning of the
actual Amichai Quarter; inscribed on the official stone plaque is a line from
one of the poems we will consider later: "Yerushalayim 'ir namal 'al sefat
ha-netzaḥ" (Jerusalem is a port city on the shore of eternity).[20] And for many
months in 2013, to commemorate the thirteenth anniversary of his death, another set of semaphores concretized Amichai's abiding presence in the lives
of his fellow Jerusalemites: fragments of his poems hung from lampposts all
along Emek Refaim as a tribute by street artist Arik Caspi (figs. 8, 9).[21] What
is common to all these "street poems" is the defiant physicality of their subjects. The detritus of domesticity—an old newspaper, an overturned book, a
crumpled map of a faraway land, a toothbrush in a cup—serve as memorial
candles in the houses "we" inhabited; the body itself figures as the repository
of all one's ancestors and as the laboratory of the soul. Even when one of the
players is God Himself, He is revealed—and concealed—in the spaces of human intercourse, playing a child's game of "guess Who?"

And below, above, or alongside Amichai's verses, just out of the frame,
are other signals of everyday life in Jerusalem that shared the quotidian space
with Amichai's verses: a yellow bus schedule; a bumper sticker pasted on the

כאן מוקמת שכונת

יהודה עמיחי

3.5.1924-22.9.2000

ראש עיר

עָצוּב הוּא לִהְיוֹת
רֹאשׁ הָעִיר יְרוּשָׁלַיִם.
נוֹרָא הוּא.
אֵיךְ יִהְיֶה אָדָם רֹאשׁ עִיר כָּזֹאת?
מַה יַּעֲשֶׂה בָּהּ?
יִבְנֶה וְיִבְנֶה וְיִבְנֶה.

וּבַלַּיְלָה יְקָרְבוּ אַבְנֵי הֶהָרִים מִסָּבִיב
אֶל הַבָּתִּים,
כְּמוֹ זְאֵבִים הַבָּאִים לְיַלֵּל עַל כְּלָבִים
שֶׁנַּעֲשׂוּ לַעַבְדֵי בְּנֵי הָאָדָם.

FIGURE 7. Street sign on Emek Refaim (2020). "Construction Site of the Yehuda Amichai Quarter." The poem on the rusting sign begins: "It's sad / to be the Mayor of Jerusalem." Photograph by Jan Kuehne.

lamppost in the colors of Peace Now that reads "Teshuva Akhshav" (Repen-tance Now), Jerusalem's homegrown version of a call to the "Born Agains." And so many secrets shared behind closed doors. On the street where Yehuda and Hana Amichai dwelled from 1967 to 1968,[22] in the house presided over by that tired lion, the street appropriately named Emek Refaim (Valley of

FIGURE 8. Arik Caspi street art (2013). "We lived in many houses and left remnants of memory / in every one of them: a newspaper, a book facedown, a / crumpled map / of some faraway land, a forgotten tooth-brush standing sentinel in a cup— / that too is a memorial candle, an eternal light." "Batim batim ve-ahava aḥat," no. 2, *Shirei Yehuda Amichai*, 5:223. "Houses (Plural); Love (Singular)," no. 2, trans. Chana Bloch and Chana Kronfeld, in *The Poetry of Yehuda Amichai*, 463. Reproduced courtesy of the artist.

FIGURE 9. Arik Caspi street art (2013). Left: "Today God was revealed to me in this way: Someone behind me covered my eyes with the palms of his hands: guess Who?" "Hitgalut," *Shirei Yehuda Amichai*, 2:223, my translation. Right: "The body is the workplace of the soul, / the body is the laboratory for experiments, inventions, innovations." "Kenasim, kenasim: ha-milim ha-mamirot ve-ha-dibur ha-shafir," no. 9, *Shirei Yehuda Amichai*, 5:292. "Conferences, Conferences: Malignant Words, Benign Speech," no. 9, trans. Chana Bloch and Chana Kronfeld, in *The Poetry of Yehuda Amichai*, 513. Reproduced courtesy of the artist.

the Ghosts), Amichai's poetry has continued to "live" even decades after his death, animating those ghosts, setting the landlocked city afloat, and always brushing up against the cacophonous dailiness of his townspeople:

> Evening promenade on Valley of the Ghosts Street, German Colony.
> Weariness gives way to the pomp of parading

up and down the street—a ritual, almost. The music I hear
from a house I don't know is inside me now
and words not intended for me are the winds I ride
for the rest of my journey, like a sailboat.[23]

Facing the Temple Mount

From its earliest incarnation, Jerusalem has been what Karen Till would call
a "wounded city."[24] The difference between living in or proximate to an open
wound, and living on the hyphen, or in the "middle," lies in the apprehension
of that space as apocalyptic-traumatic or as therapeutic-inclusive in the religious, political, and poetic imagination. As the poems and the poet himself
came closer to the open wound, and to the very center of holiness, the challenge intensified.

After living on Metudela Street in West Jerusalem, at the edge of Emek
ha-matzlava, the valley where public religions and personal memories could
mingle in quiet cacophony, Amichai and his second wife, Hana, moved to Abu
Tor, the "no man's land" in Israeli-controlled West Jerusalem that buttressed
Jordanian-controlled East Jerusalem. Proximate to the valley still called "Gay
ben hinom" or "gehenna," the gate to Hell, where, according to the Bible, pagan influences prevailed on King Menashe, who set up altars and sacrificed
children to Moloch,[25] it was, in the years leading up to the Six Day War, a liminal neighborhood whose Jewish inhabitants were in constant peril of attack
by Jordanian snipers. "We lived in the Valley of Gehenna in no man's land in
the divided Jerusalem," begins a poem written by Amichai many years later.[26]
To this day, the Valley of Gehenna remains a place for remembering, yearning,
eulogizing, and cursing and provides fertile ground for apocalyptic fantasies.[27]

And yet, in the aftermath of the '67 war, even Amichai would become a
powerful spokesperson for the euphoria of inclusive visions—and the "open
wound" between East and West Jerusalem would become the space of oppor-
tunity and mediated encounters. Although, as we have already seen, "The
Travels of the Last Benjamin of Tudela" was drafted from the American Diaspora, and although the traumas of war and holocaust—ancient and contemporary—are folded into the concatenated detritus of its verses, a reconciled spirit prevails here, and intensifies in the poems written after Amichai's
return to Jerusalem. Although the speaker in the *poema* fashions himself as
successor to the explorer Benjamin who wrote a travelogue of his journey
from Spain to the Holy Land *and back* in the twelfth century, and although
Amichai himself had crossed an ocean in his original "pilgrimage" to the
Land of Israel, it is not the voyage that is foregrounded in the poems written

in the first decades after the war. Rather, Amichai's post-'67 poetry releases the "oceanic feeling" in Jerusalem itself, converting the landlocked city into a buoyant port of entry and egress.

The most liberated of such moments comes in a poem cycle whose location and date are contained in its title, "Jerusalem 1967." It is here that, as we saw earlier, the poet allows himself explicitly to repurpose the messianic vision of Jerusalem as the place from which redemptive waters would flow:[28] "Jerusalem is a port city on the shore of eternity." All visitors and supplicants from all religions arrive here and are welcomed:

> . . . The Temple Mount is a huge ship, a magnificent
> luxury liner. From the portholes of her Western Wall
> cheerful saints look out, travelers, Hasidim on the pier
> wave goodbye, shout hooray, hooray, bon voyage! She is
> always arriving, always sailing away. And the fences and the piers
> and the policemen and the flags and the high masts of churches
> and mosques and the smokestacks of synagogues and the boats
> of psalms of praise and the mountain-waves . . .
>
> And the commerce and the gates and the golden domes:
> Jerusalem is the Venice of God.[29]

In this vision, the most static and immutable of the world's shrines—the place identified in Islam with the footprint of Mohammed and in Jewish folklore with the very fundament of the world and what would be indexed in contemporary Israeli political discourse as the "bedrock of our existence"[30]— becomes a "huge ship," portable and pneumatic. The high masts of churches and mosques and the smokestacks of synagogues fill the air with a cacophony of promise. This inclusive messianic vision, which Ranen Omer-Sherman calls Amichai's "stoic resistance to the euphoria of any form of *proprietorial* love,"[31] is a modern projection of the ecumenical prophecy of Isaiah or Deutero-Isaiah. God, the speaker—as ventriloquized through the prophet— "will bring them [all nations who recognize God's sovereignty] to My holy mountain and make them joyful in My house of prayer . . . for My house shall be called a house of prayer for all peoples" (Is. 56:7).[32] In the inebriating moment of Return some 2,500 years later, the poet can, briefly, ignore the "burnt offerings and . . . sacrifices" that flesh out the biblical passage and therefore avoid what Tikva Frymer-Kensky calls "the tension between Israel's belief in its special identity and its sense that its role as God's people is destined to extend to all other peoples"—a tension that "has never been resolved."[33]

But, as we have seen, Jerusalem, in its most inclusive mode, stretches to embrace not only other peoples and religions but also the other places where

Jews have sojourned—*validating* what A. B. Yehoshua's character *condemned* in the passage with which this chapter opened: their "restless proclivity to return to their past." One of the most salient of such moments in Amichai's oeuvre is the allusion to an undecipherable love story folded into the post-'67 poem that begins "Im eshkaḥekh yerushalayim" (If I forget thee O Jerusalem). Possibly the most public and binding of poetic utterances in the Hebrew canon, these lines from Psalm 137 inaugurated the season of exile that would accompany the Jews from Babylonia to the farthest reaches of Australia. They are uttered on solemn occasions, including under the wedding canopy—when the most private moment is thereby collectivized—and, in some communities, at every *birkat ha-mazon* (prayer after a meal).[34] We have already glanced at the vengeful verses that conclude this psalm and the ways Amichai, in his late poetry, manages to detoxify them by cataloguing them among the games of childhood.[35] In his earlier allusion to Psalm 137, he invokes the solemnity of the pledge but disrupts it with something else:

> If I forget thee, Jerusalem,
> Let my right forget.
> Let my right forget, and my left remember.
> Let my left remember, and your right close
> And your mouth open near the gate.
>
> I shall remember Jerusalem
> And forget the forest—my love will remember,
> Will open her gate, will close my window,
> Will forget my right,
> Will forget my left.
>
> If the west wind does not come
> I'll never forgive the walls,
> Or the sea, or myself . . .
>
> If I forget thee, Jerusalem,
> Let my blood be forgotten.
> I shall touch your forehead,
> Forget my own,
> My voice change
> For the second and last time
> To the most terrible of voices—
> Or silence.[36]

However one parses such references as the "west wind" and the "sea," both possible conveyances for the eastward voyage to the Holy Land (compare the "east wind" that signifies placement in Jerusalem in "Travels"), they only reinforce the impermeability of various allusions and the enigmatic circumstances of an untold love story. We can follow these physical properties to a protected place where the hidden narrative itself can unfold; but the sea and the forest, both public landscapes and safeguards of personal odysseys and intimate rendezvous, must be left behind when entering the rock-rimmed city of Jerusalem, where the lack of horizon and the collective domain of holiness suffocate private space. The only gesture that can secure privacy, then, is the rhetorical barrier that the poet erects.

Safeguarding the private realm in Jerusalem in the precincts of Psalm 137, Amichai has to write against the grain of collective pronouncements that have informed thousands of years of Hebrew memory. The address of the speaker in this psalm is to the *city*, not to any specific sites or selves within what will continue to be conceived for thousands of years as an indivisible whole:

> Should I forget you, Jerusalem, may my right hand wither.
> May my tongue cleave to my palate if I do not recall you,
> If I do not set Jerusalem above my chief joy. (Ps. 137:5–6)[37]

The modern-day lover in Jerusalem who "open[s] her gate" engages, then, in a daring act, liberating the city's garrisoned inhabitants to embrace the outside world; at the same time, *closing the window* ensures privacy for a specific man and woman in this most public of cities and most public of psalms. Such references carve out the small impenetrable spaces of a unique human life, another example of the "Yerushal," the indivisible self, clinging to the "hyphen" between date of birth and date of death, that fiercely safeguarded realm of Amichai's poetic subject—or the tenuous "present continuous" squeezed between the engorged past and the voracious future.[38]

All of this plays off the rhetorical-theological quirk that, as we saw, originated in the very dawn—or early morning—of Hebrew monotheism: the gendering of Jerusalem. Since then, we have known that if we Forgot Thee (fem. sing.), O Jerusalem, we would suffer dire consequences. Psalm 137 also instructed the collective that Jewish memory was synonymous with the metaphorization of Jerusalem; poetic activity had indeed, then, become a kind of embalming fluid that preserved the City as Woman in suspended animation. And, again, if the only clear biblical exception to this is the Song of Songs, the midrashic mind had to work overtime to enrich the embalming fluid for that text.

Jerusalem as woman—or for that matter, the Land itself as object of male Jewish desire—was never more pronounced than in the Zionist Age of Return.[39] But, as we shall see, Jerusalem as Woman returns in Amichai's late poetry in more daring ways as claims of possession intensify in the public sphere.

The Terrible *Ḥad Gadya* Machine: Goats, Sons,
and Fathers in the Breach

The closer the poet himself comes to the physical center of holiness and the more the political conflict over borders is hijacked by a holy war over the Sacred Center, the more endangered are the flesh-and-blood men and women in the "narrow in-between." Still, the self and the profane are never sacrificed in the name of the collective or the sacred; distance is always measured in the space between two humans, even if—*especially if*—between them they frame the Temple Mount. The place where Amichai lived out his last decades with his wife Hana provided a constant reminder of that challenge. Invoked by the prophet Isaiah as a topos of eschatological domesticity (Is. 32:18), Mishkenot sha'ananim or "Peaceful Habitations" is located on the seam between East and West Jerusalem, in one of the earliest Jewish neighborhoods to be built outside the walls of the Old City in the mid-nineteenth century.[40] Not far from Gay Ben Hinom, but facing Mount Zion and abutting a valley called Brekhat ha-Sultan, Birket es-Sultan, or Sultan's Pool, Mishkenot sha'ananim underwent gentrification and attracted artists and writers after 1967. What may have been a water reservoir as early as the time of Herod, Sultan's Pool, with its brambles and rocks, one of the open wounds in the "wounded city," became for Amichai a kind of no-man's-land, closer to Foucault's "heterotopia" or Soja's "thirdspace,"[41] where the voices of a Jewish father and an Arab shepherd could meet in their search for a son and a goat:

> An Arab shepherd is searching for his goat on Mount Zion
> and on the opposite hill I am searching
> for my little boy.
> An Arab shepherd and a Jewish father
> both in their temporary failure.
> Our two voices meet above the Sultan's Pool
> in the valley between us. Neither of us wants
> the child or the goat to get caught in the wheels
> of the terrible *Ḥad Gadya* machine . . .

The "terrible *Ḥad Gadya* machine" refers to the fanciful—and macabre—Passover ditty, an Aramaic version of "She Swallowed a Fly," that recounts successive persecutions starting with the poor little (scape)goat and concluding with divine intervention.[42] In Amichai's poem, the shepherd and the father indeed find the goat and the son, respectively, and their voices "came back inside us, laughing and crying." But the knowledge that the search for a "goat" or a "son" "has always been the beginning / of a new religion" in this region continues to undermine the sense of relief.[43] What will the "new religion" be this time? This poem, written in the cautiously hopeful decade following the '67 war, suggests that such encounters could actually bind ancient and contemporary wounds and lead to a better gospel, one that plays out in profane spaces, making room not only for the diasporic self but also—especially—for the Muslim neighbor.

A similar encounter, this time between the speaker and an Arab shopkeeper in the Old City on Yom Kippur, a few months after the war, evokes another father-and-son pairing:

> On Yom Kippur in 1967, the Year of Forgetting, I put on
> my dark holiday clothes and walked to the Old City of Jerusalem.
> For a long time I stood in front of an Arab's hole-in-the-wall shop,
> not far from the Damascus Gate, a shop with
> buttons and zippers and spools of thread
> in every color and snaps and buckles.
> A rare light and many colors, like an open Ark.
>
> I told him in my heart that my father too
> had a shop like this, with thread and buttons.
> I explained to him in my heart about all the decades
> and the causes and the events, why I am now here
> and my father's shop was burned there and he is buried here.
>
> When I finished, it was time for the Closing of the Gates prayer.
> He too lowered the shutters and locked the gate
> and I returned, with all the worshipers, home.[44]

This silent encounter between an Arab and a Jewish Israeli in the Old City on the holiest day of the Jewish calendar, the image of the "buttons and zippers and spools of thread / in every color and snaps and buckles," from which a "rare light and many colors" emanate, like the "open Ark" in synagogues all over the city and all over the world, provide another chronotope of human grace—but only if covered with a dose of "forgetting" (the Hebrew acronym for the year 1967 spells out "you will forget"). The elision between then and now, between the Gates of Heaven, the gates of the buttons-and-thread shops "here" and "there," and the gates of the city are tentative, fleeting, and fragile.

As with the stone lions that connect and protect the homes of the child and the adult while eliding the terrible war that destroyed the former, here too a fearful symmetry and a wonderful wordless compassion connect and elide the wars each of these mute interlocutors has suffered and seem to equalize both pain and possibility. But there is more. The silence at the heart of this poem, which Glenda Abramson, Ranen Omer-Sherman, and Chana Kronfeld dwell upon, implicates the speaker in what Kronfeld interprets as the "general failure to ask forgiveness for the suffering caused to the Palestinian Other." She calls the symmetries or analogies between the two characters, between the "Holy Ark containing the Torah in the synagogue and the Palestinian's hole-in-the-wall shop," even "between God and the shopkeeper," "scandalously sacrilegious," even as the poem eventually would get defanged and added to the "celebratory nationalist canon."[45] My own demurral from this concern over cooptation may be a naïve faith in the power of the subversive voice to make itself heard even above the chorus of praise and self-congratulation. In this sense, Amichai can be read alongside his contemporary, the poet Dan Pagis, whose most subversive poems were also embraced by the suffocating forces of commemoration and cooptation but still manage to preserve their unnerving power.[46]

In addition to neighbors who don't speak each other's language but seek for common ground, there are in these poems, as we have seen, fathers and sons (and generic "children" who sometimes include daughters)—and a few mothers too. A number of readers have noted that Amichai eschews the more common oedipal struggles in favor of the soft caress across generations.[47] In the previous chapter, we recalled Gershom Scholem's ominous challenge to the coming generations, his warning in 1926, in a letter to Franz Rosenzweig on the future of the Hebrew language, of the "apocalyptic thorn" of divine speech that inheres even in secularized modern Hebrew.[48] We then recalled Jacques Derrida's belated and somewhat ambivalent response to that letter in the 1980s, reflected in the question he directed at the very generations who inherited the Hebrew that Scholem had warned us about. Derrida admits, in mischievous language that recalls Bialik's, that "we have committed a profanation by extracting the sacred language from the sacred text. We have let it out into the street and into everyday life . . . Iconoclasm and idolatry at the same time, if that is possible." He then asks what insights Scholem's prophecy might afford into the youth of "Israel today."[49]

Amichai implicitly responds to this question and to the larger question of the fate of the ephemeral, "profaned" quotidian by invoking his tenth-century Hebrew predecessor, Shmuel Ha-nagid. What he offers is not the "apocalyptic thorn" or the Grim Reaper, but one's own progeny as *compassionate and forgiving* arbiters of the future. In a late poem, his speaker relates bringing his children to "Tel Gat," the mound where he had fought his early battles:

> I brought my children to the mound
> Where once I fought battles,
> So they would understand the things I did do
> And forgive me for the things I didn't do.

The speaker then recalls that other soldier-poet who sat on a mound before battle some ten centuries ago:

> I brought my children to the mound
> And we sat there, "on its back and its side"
> As in the poem by Shmuel Ha-Nagid in Spain,
> Like me, a man of hills and a man of wars
> Who sang a lullaby to his soldiers before the battle.
> Yet I did not talk to my heart, as he did,
> But to my children. To the mound, we were the resurrection,
> Fleeting like this springtime, eternal like it too.[50]

And yet. As we saw, Amichai's earlier poems had indeed reflected the promise of filial reconciliation of ancestral grievances, of the tempering and filtering of sacred yearnings through human encounters, of heterotopias as meeting places between embattled neighbors or anxious fathers. But in the closing decade of the twentieth century and of his life, as the political horizon shortened and the landscape of holiness became, once again, a battleground, even the children's lives were on the line again. To meet this challenge, Amichai honed his poetry into a testament more searing than soothing. Managing still to preserve his metaphysical celebration of the quotidian—a twentieth-century version of Blake's world seen in a grain of sand and heaven in a wild flower—he exposes with no less clarity the local shame, humiliation, and distortion of the human image that Jerusalem perpetrates in the name of holiness. Never has the abandon with which Amichai celebrated the created world—physical and metaphysical, sacred and profane, elevated and humble—been so endangered as it was at the end of his life, culminating in the last collection, *Open Closed Open*, published shortly before his death. And never has the "literary archaeology" I am performing been more consequential.

Comedy and Compassion: The Akeda Revisited

As with Agnon, the Binding of Isaac and the Song of Songs are the constitutive texts that Amichai continues to reclaim and repurpose. Whenever sons are sacrificed, the poet now tells us, whenever the terrible Ḥad Gadya machine becomes the *akeda* machine, the one who is really sacrificed is Abraham's "third son," "Yivkeh":

> Three sons had Abraham, not just two.
> Three sons had Abraham: Yishma-El, Yitzhak and Yivkeh.
> First came Yishma-El, "God will hear,"
> next came Yitzhak, "he will laugh,"

and the last was Yivkeh, "he will cry."
No one has ever heard of Yivkeh, for he was the youngest,
the son that Father loved best,
the son who was offered up on Mount Moriah.
Yishma-El was saved by his mother, Hagar,
Yitzhak was saved by the angel,
but Yivkeh no one saved.
When he was just a little boy, his father
would call him tenderly, Yivkeh,
Yivkeleh, my sweet little Yivkie—
but he sacrificed him all the same.
The Torah says the ram, but it was Yivkeh.
Yishma-El never heard from God again,
Yitzhak never laughed again,
Sarah laughed only once, then laughed no more.
Three sons had Abraham,
Yishma, "will hear," Yitzhak, "will laugh," Yivkeh, "will cry."
Yishma-El, Yitzhak-El, Yivke-El,
God will hear, God will laugh, God will cry.[51]

Amichai's moral legacy is enshrined in this late poem. Whereas, as we saw, most modern Israeli invocations of the akeda subtract some element from the story—the rescuing God or Angel is usually the one that is AWOL[52]—Amichai *adds* two characters: the overlooked other son, Ishmael, and the invented son, Yivkeh. In an earlier poem, he focused on the ram, the "real hero of the akeda."[53] But here he seems to be demonstrating more than his usual poetic profligacy: facing Mount Moriah, he transforms an internal, hermetic encounter between Israel and its God into a porous, morally and politically accountable, dialogue that must, in the first instance, embrace the discarded other, Ishmael, and in the final instance embrace the *principle of compassion* that has always been sacrificed to the visions of the uncompromising father and his competing sons.[54]

On September 28, 2000, five years after Yitzhak Rabin was assassinated and six days after Amichai died, Ariel Sharon slaughtered Yivkeh once again by staging the triumphalist appearance on the Temple Mount that would spark the bloody Second Intifada. We have already seen how the gaze that moves from every-and-any-place in Jewish Geography to *The Place, Har ha-bayit*, swallows all other places and threatens to obliterate the synoptic gaze. Even if he didn't live to see its most hideous current manifestations, Amichai signaled, especially in his last work, a change in poetic language to reflect the change on the ground—and offered a new poetics, or a more urgent and desperate version of his earlier poetic vision and practice.

"This rough magic I here abjure": The Song Undone

I have bedimmed
The noontide sun, called forth the mutinous winds,
And twixt the green sea and the azured vault
Set roaring war. To the dread rattling thunder
Have I given fire, and rifted Jove's stout oak
With his own bolt. The strong-based promontory
Have I made shake, and by the spurs plucked up
The pine and cedar. Graves at my command
Have waked their sleepers, oped, and let 'em forth
By my so potent art. But this rough magic
I here abjure, and when I have required
Some heavenly music—which even now I do—
To work mine end upon their senses, that
This airy charm is for, I'll break my staff,
Bury it certain fathoms in the earth,
And deeper than did ever plummet sound
I'll drown my book.

SHAKESPEARE, *The Tempest*, 5.1.41–57

Like Shakespeare's magician in his valedictory address, Yehuda Amichai, in his final role as poet of Jerusalem, interrogates his own "potent art." "In Jerusalem everything is a symbol," he reminds us in one of the last poetic cycles of his last book.[55] This cycle appears at first as a reprise of earlier, unfettered ways of imagining Jerusalem, leaving "some heavenly music" to do its work upon our senses: Jerusalem is "forever changing her ways," he announces, and then mobilizes a range of conceits to represent those changes: "Jerusalem is like an Atlantis that sank into the sea"; "Jerusalem is a merry-go-round"; "sometimes Jerusalem is a city of knives." Amichai's symbolic language was his major import from the wisdom learned in Diaspora into the claustrophobic space of Return. But the symbols themselves now carry more toxicity, and the project has become even more consequential. No one image, however elaborate, can contain Jerusalem—each captures but a facet of the city *and, when literalized, releases its toxins*. It turns out that "Jerusalem is like an Atlantis" where "everything is submerged and sunken"; Jerusalem is a "merry go round" where you "can't get off"; "Jerusalem is a city of knives" where "even the hopes for peace are sharp."[56]

In these revisited images, symbolic practice itself will become suspect. First, Amichai had to reveal the specific danger in the image of Jerusalem as Woman that had been inherent in the poetics of memory from the earliest iterations of the Hebrew imagination, and that would haunt any period defined as the "end-time": the inevitable consequences of total recall. Indeed, his early post-'67 embrace was a memory bank of sanguine, whimsical representations of the beguiling female Jerusalem—the "City [that] plays hide and seek among her names," beckoning to all her lovers, naming them one by one, in descending historical order: "Yerushalayim, Al-Quds, Salem, Jeru, Yeru, all the while / whispering her first, Jebusite name: Y'vus, / Y'vus, Y'vus, in the dark." An eroticized encounter with all her conquerors makes her weep "with longing: Aelia Capitolina, Aelia, Aelia. / She comes to any man who calls her / at night, alone. But we know / who comes to whom."[57]

Do we know? In his last two volumes, Amichai uncovered the connection between the poetic appropriations of the city over the centuries and the potentially vengeful political stirrings of a literalizing male imagination vis-à-vis the female object of his fealty. The feminization of Jerusalem had given birth in its primordial moments to an ecstatic fantasy of erotic possession, and the poetics of memory would give rise to a vengeful form of total recall; both are conflated in Yehuda Amichai's final poetic pronouncements:

> ... The Greater Land of Israel is like a fat and heavy woman,
> And the State of Israel like a young woman,
> Supple and narrow-waisted.
> But in the one and in the other as well
> Jerusalem is always the nakedness ...
> The insatiable nakedness of the land.
> The writhing, shrieking desire
> That will never finish till Messiah comes.[58]

The biblical Hebrew word 'erva, here rendered as "nakedness" (though often invoked in the Bible in connection with forbidden forms of sexual intercourse), and the word ha-evyona, connoting libido or sexual desire, are among the most explicit sexual references in Amichai's oeuvre.[59] And the juxtaposition of the young, supple, and narrow-waisted State of Israel with the fat and heavy woman who represents ha-aretz ha-shlemah, the Whole or Greater Land of Israel—the nationalist-religious designation for what is referred to internationally as Israel-Palestine—is his most explicit political pronouncement. But, as we saw, even in the early, euphoric moment after 1967, the poet had already expressed discomfort with the engorged figure of "united" Jerusalem:

> They're burning the photos of the divided Jerusalem
> and the beautiful letters of the beloved,
> who was so quiet.
>
> The noisy old dowager, all of her,
> with her gold and copper and stones,
> has come back
> to a fat legal life.

> But I don't like her.
> Sometimes I remember the quiet one.[60]

By 1998, in Amichai's valedictory volume, this noisy old dowager had become the shrieking center of insatiable desire. In another poem in that volume, it is her self-regarding, incommensurable pose that isolates her and condemns her to eternal solitude. For one last time, the poet breathes life into her iconic, immutable self, again through the alchemy of sexual desire or *evyona*. Recalling the succession of historical lovers who abandoned her, he also recalls the rhetorical history of her solitude ("How doth the City sit solitary that was full of people," Lam. 1:1):[61]

> If Jerusalem is a woman, does she know desire?
> When she cries out, is it from pleasure
> or pain? What is the secret of her appeal?
> When does she open her gates willingly and when is it rape?
> All her lovers abandon her, leaving her
> with the wages of love—necklaces, earrings,
> towers and houses of prayer
> in the English, Italian, Russian, Greek, Arab styles,
> wood and stone, turrets and gables, wrought-iron gates,
> rings of gold and silver, riots of color. They all give her
> something to remember them by, then abandon her.
> I would have liked to talk to her again, but I lost her
> among the dancers. Dance is total abandon.
> Jerusalem sees only the skies above her
> and whoever sees only the skies above—
> not the face of her lover—truly does lie solitary.
> Sit solitary, stand solitary, and dance all alone.[62]

"When does she open her gates willingly and when is it rape?" Indeed, this land-locked, self-regarding city, hospitable or lascivious, inviolable or ravaged, has generated many sexual fantasies. In the early twentieth century, James Joyce's Leopold Bloom contemplated the Holy Land as "a barren land, bare waste . . . Dead: an old woman's: the grey sunken cunt of the world."[63] Not yet dead in Amichai's late twentieth-century gaze, but both self-regarding and insatiable.

Recapitulating all the stages of his own encounter with the beloved city—the "wages of love," the gates, the towers, and the houses of prayer, the languages and hallowed intersections of the prayerful and the pedestrian—the poet of Jerusalem finally admits to having "lost her / among the dancers." He warns us, his compatriots, and all the generations to come, of the dangers of that terrible solitude, of the engorged self who is configured as the "bedrock" of her own existence.

If the most radical expression of the poet's last reckoning is with the similes and metaphors trained on Jerusalem and the Land of Israel, its final iteration is a head-on confrontation with that other magician of metaphor, Amichai's "predecessor," King Solomon, the "author" of the Song of Songs.

As we saw in our discussion of the Song, there is no appeal or address in
that text, as in other biblical texts, to Jerusalem *as* metaphor, as an other, an oppositional figure. Rather, the entire poetic enterprise comes from within, from
an intimate, unmediated inscription of body on landscape and of landscape on
body. Again, two cardinal elements of the biblical text, which were occluded
over centuries of interpretive acrobatics, are the central *status of metaphor*, or
more commonly, of simile, in the exchange between the two major speakers,
and the *absence of the Deity and of physical sites of holiness* in the city specifically identified in the very first verse as Jerusalem under the reign of Solomon.
We saw that the king who presides over and authorizes this text, the one who is
credited elsewhere in the Hebrew Bible with building the "house to the Name
of God" on Mount Moriah, is not represented in his Song by even one edifice
that can be identified as the Temple—and this in a document replete with details of the flora and fauna, the architecture and populace, of Jerusalem.

Amichai's Solomon puts up a desperate defense against the actions of
those latter-day zealots who are intent on rebuilding that House on Mount
Moriah. In response to the literalizers who ground the rabbinic images in
concrete places in order to seal their exclusive, proprietary claim on the city,
and for the sake of his own project of a nonproprietary return of the Hebrew
body to the Hebrew landscape, the modern poet of Jerusalem sends "Solomon" back for one more task—which will prove to be impossible:

The singer of the Song of Songs sought his beloved so long and hard
that he lost his mind and went looking for her with a simile map
and fell in love with the images he himself had imagined.
He went down to Egypt, for he had written "to a mare among Pharaoh's chariots
I compare thee," and he went up to Gilead to see her flowing hair,
for he had written "Thy hair is like a flock of goats flowing down
Mount Gilead," and he went up to the Tower of David, for it says
"Like the Tower of David is thy neck," and he got as far as Lebanon and found
no peace, for it says "Thy nose is like the Tower of Lebanon that looks out
toward Damascus" . . .
And he dashed off to the desert, for it says "Who is that rising
from the desert like pillars of smoke." And the Bedouin thought
he was one of the crazy prophets, and he thought
he was King Solomon. And he is still wandering, a fugitive and a vagabond
with the mark of Love on his forehead. And sometimes he happens upon

the loves of other couples in other times; he even got as far as our home
with its broken roof on the border between Jerusalem
and Jerusalem. And we never even saw him because we
were in each other's arms. He is still wandering, shouting
"You are beautiful, my bride," as if from within a deep sack
of oblivion. And whoever wrote "Love is as fierce as death"—
he understood his own simile only at the end,
understood and loved and died (the metaphor blew up with its meaning).[64]

In Hebrew the last line is: "Ha-nimshal hitpotzetz 'im ha-mashal." That is,
binding a freely contracted trope in the fetters of a *mashal* and a *nimshal*, of
the parable and its exegesis, proved to be, for those living after 1967 "between
Jerusalem and Jerusalem," literally an explosive act. The poet's final gesture is
to separate himself even from Solomon, the poet "with the mark of Love on
his forehead," who has nonetheless become so blindsided by the reified power
of his own images that he can no longer see the couple making love under a
dilapidated roof in the open wound that divides the Holy City. Like Prospero
on his island, Amichai's King Solomon must actually relinquish his powers of
enchantment because they have come to endanger the simple witness to the
power of human love under broken roofs on the border between sanity and
insanity.

What we may have here is a final separation not so much between the poet
of modern Jerusalem and the putative poet of the Song as between Amichai
and the King Solomon who was coopted by the midrashic turn in ancient
times and the literalizing turn in our time. If in the earlier, more sanguine,
poems, Jerusalem was a "port city on the shore of eternity"; if she opened
her gates and beckoned to all her lovers to "come" and make their claim,
while closing the window for privacy; now, in his last testament, the poet reveals what will happen when the imagination is territorialized and defeated,
the gates closed, all other lovers and contenders banished, so that Jerusalem
will sit truly alone, utterly *un-figured*. If Jerusalem is bedrock, compared to
nothing but herself, abolishing comparison and substitution as acts of world-
embracing compassion, as the forces that could bring *Yivkeh* to life, then love
is abolished and we are all Isaacs with no ram or angel in sight.

So, again like Prospero, Yehuda Amichai at the end of his life, in the guise
of King Solomon, had to bury his "rough magic . . . certain fathoms in the
earth, / And deeper than did ever plummet sound . . . drown [his] book." But,
like Shakespeare's play, the book itself survived and the magic is reawakened
every time we turn its pages.

Coda

Anger vanished from their faces and every speech is soft and good, and from every house and every courtyard shine many candles, and the whole city is like a palace adorned with candles and lights. Here a lamp is lit and there a lantern. Here a bowl of olive oil and there pure white candles. Here two candles *for* [*ke-neged*] remember the Sabbath day and keep the Sabbath day, and two tablets of the Covenant, and there ten candles *for* the Ten Commandments. Here seven candles *for* the seven days, and there twelve candles *for* the twelve Tribes of Israel.

S. Y. AGNON, description of Sabbath preparations in the Old City of
Jerusalem circa 1912, *Only Yesterday* (emphases mine)[1]

This book opened with a survey of the configurations of sacred space as they traveled through the Hebrew Bible, until they came to rest on the Temple Mount in Jerusalem. The story and the rock that cements the story congeal in the akeda, the Genesis narrative misread throughout Jewish history as template of sacrificial tragedy. They separate in the storylines and verses of the Song of Songs as poetic fancy and erotic love relocate the sacred to the human plane— though this text too would be subject to a kind of systematic misreading.

Jews would live for two millennia after the destruction of the "Second" Temple in a mediated relation to the sacred center, through interpretive acrobatics and cultic practices that nourished the imaginative faculties. "Two candles *for* [*ke-neged*] the two tablets of the Covenant, twelve *for* the twelve tribes of Israel." As we saw in chapter 5, the Hebrew word *ke-neged*, or *mi-neged*, "for" or "opposed to," is a Mishnaic term signifying not only a form of substitution for the main thing, the thing signified—the two tablets, the seven days, the twelve tribes—but also distance itself; the textual comparative basis for an argument also denotes a spatial relation to what is on the other side. The term is even used for positioning oneself toward (*ke-neged*) the sacred center, even in the Holy Land, even in Jerusalem, and even while standing where the Temple stood. All of Israel, no matter where they may be, are oriented to One Place (*le-makom ehad*).[2] Such symbolic language, explicitly acknowledging its own surrogate status, also saves its speakers from idolatry.

And yet the yearning for an unmediated reconnection with the center would remain a strong subterranean force. The mimetic project and spatial representations of the sacred were interrogated in the twelfth century by Maimonides in the *Guide* that would serve generations of perplexed readers and provide clues for recalibrating those muscles. In the verses of centuries of liturgical poets, as in the philosophical deliberations of the greatest of medieval thinkers, the magnetic pull of Jerusalem as the site of divine immanence would be invoked along with the surrogate strategies that validate distance.

Modern Temptations: The Rock and the Story

The rock and the story continue to ground the Jewish passion. First, the rock itself, where Isaac was "bound," where the Temple once stood, where Mohammed's step was imprinted before he rose to heaven: In the early prestate community referred to in Zionist parlance as the Yishuv, the Temple Mount had more or less the same status as it had throughout two thousand years of Diaspora, as Jews had relative access to but no sovereignty over the site. In the passage quoted above from Agnon's epic novel, as in other passages, diasporic acts of mediation are practiced even in the shadow of the ruined temple. Much of the tension that came to a head in 1929 between Muslims and Jews centered on Jerusalem, the Wailing Wall or Al Buraq, and the Temple Mount or Haram al Sharif; still, well into the 1920s, Jewish and even Zionist folk art persisted in presenting an eclectic and mediated view of present opportunities along with eschatological projections. A Rosh Hashana (New Year's) greeting from 1925 by the craftsman Moshe Mizrahi can stand in for hundreds of such artifacts (see fig. 10).[3]

The iconography is layered and inclusive, representing a popular concatenation of visions for the future. The flag on the top of a somewhat stylized Dome of the Rock (where the Crescent should be) says "mekom [ha-] mikdash," or "place of [the] Temple." There are a number of biblical verses and illustrations, including a reference to the akeda and the priestly blessing. There are doves of peace with greetings in their beaks. But the most interesting element, which is barely decipherable even when we enlarge the image, is the writing on the mosque meant, presumably, to be the "place holder" for the Temple. The passage is from Isaiah's eschatological projections—when God, the speaker, "will bring them to My holy mountain and give them joy in My house of prayer. Their burnt offerings and sacrifices shall be welcome on My altar; For My house a house of prayer shall be called for all the peoples" (Is. 56:7). The "them" in the first verse refers to "all the peoples" in the second—all those who will accept God's dominion in the end of days—but the phrase "all the peoples" doesn't appear in the inscription on this card.

Naturally, the Hebrew reference to sacrifices and burnt offerings was not exactly pleasing to the Muslims whose Koranic inscriptions it supplants.

FIGURE 10. Moshe Mizrahi, New Year's card (1925). Image courtesy of William Gross.

Although in the ongoing conflict over the Temple Mount, this image and others like it enraged the Muslim community, and, as Hillel Cohen shows, this
kind of supersessionism actually contributed to the riots of 1929,[4] one can,
in a more generous frame of mind, regard such acts as subliminally evoking
an "end of days" scenario in which the shadow text will be restored and all
competing religious visions reconciled.

Such negotiations with sacred texts and with history continued to evolve in modern Israel as they had over two millennia. Between the declaration of the State in 1948 and the Israeli victory over East Jerusalem and the West Bank in 1967, a kind of "diasporic distance" prevailed. But the wisdom and humility gained during all that time have now been endangered. Since 1967, along with the loss of space between Jews and their Sacred Center—or, in the words of Jacques Derrida, the loss of the space between the "family hearth and the sacrificial fire"[5]—has come the loss of the ethical mandate that informs the mimetic project. Over the past half century, Jerusalem has shifted from the disputed center of a political conflict over borders, a centrifugal movement outward to putative boundaries, to the center of a holy war, a centripetal thrust into the vortex of sacrifice.

Sovereignty Inc.

Even if one accepts the argument I have been making—that just as the original akeda did not signify the accomplished sacrifice, the Temple Mount as conceived and as constructed did not signify the *confined presence* of the Divine but rather designated the place for human appellation and affirmation of the Divine—still, there is no disputing their status as the holiest story and the holiest site in Judaism. When it comes to the physical space, that fact should make it even less amenable to claims of political sovereignty. Israeli philosopher Avi Sagi argues that the moment the Israeli flag was raised over the Temple Mount during the 1967 War constituted a dramatic displacement of its inherent sanctity. "A holy space [such as the Temple Mount] cannot, as such, be subject to human sovereignty, since that is its nature—a holy space is under the absolute rule of God . . . [Turning the Temple Mount into] yet another device for demonstrating the power of the [Israeli sovereign means that] God has vanished to be replaced by human beings as the divine sovereign."[6] The dilemma, as we have seen, goes back to the ancient kings of Israel, starting with David and Solomon. In our time, Sagi's words resonate with those of another king, Hussein of Jordan, who spoke before the US Congress in July 1994, in that sanguine moment when peace between the Israelis, the Palestinians, and other Arab neighbors seemed imminent:

> My religious faith demands that sovereignty over the holy places in Jerusalem reside . . . with God and God alone . . . Religious sovereignty should be accorded to all believers of the three Abrahamic faiths, in accordance with their religions. In this way, Jerusalem will become the symbol of peace and its embodiment, as it must be for both Palestinians and Israelis when their negotiations determine the final status of Arab East Jerusalem.[7]

Just over a year later, on September 4, 1995, Hussein's counterpart, then-Israeli
Prime Minister Yitzhak Rabin, would commemorate "3000 years" of Jewish
connection to the Temple Mount by declaring his (rather naïve) faith in a
united Jerusalem under Jewish sovereignty that accorded rights to all religious traditions. He arrived at his pledge of tolerance and peace through reference to millennia of Jewish history and legend:

> Mr. Speaker, Mayor of Jerusalem, sons and daughters of Jerusalem:
> Jewish legend tells us that at the moment that King David was about to dig
> the foundations of the Holy Temple, the groundwaters rose and threatened to
> flood and destroy Jerusalem, the land of Israel and the entire world.
> The legend goes that King David then rose and cast into the turbulent
> waters a shard on which the Ineffable Name of God was written and the waters
> immediately receded. The People of Israel were assured safety in their land
> and on their soil.
> If it were only possible to repeat that feat today, I would write on that shard
> two words of love to Jerusalem, to the land of Israel. One word tolerance. The
> other peace.[8]

Note that the ancient reference is to the "Ineffable Name" and not the "Ineffable Presence." Rabin's speechwriters knew their sources. But note also the
Israeli prime minister's substitution of tolerance and peace for the Name Itself. And yet it turned out that despite Hussein's reference to the God of the
three monotheistic religions as the true sovereign, and Rabin's reference to
Jerusalem as the "eternal" capital of a city presided over by a benevolent deity
and administered by a tolerant Jewish government, time was not on the side
of either head of state. The rock that had absorbed so much blood over two
millennia would repel all visions of benign sovereignty. Yitzhak Rabin would
be assassinated just two months after his speech—and Hussein, whose own
days were numbered, would eulogize his friend at the funeral in Jerusalem
with the weight of unfulfilled history on his bent shoulders.[9]

The discussion of the real position of "Jewish history" or "the sources"
vis-à-vis Jerusalem depends, of course, on which strand of Zionism one cherishes.[10] Tomer Persico argues that Zionism recovered its own religious lineage
at the very moment it conquered "Judea, Samaria," and the Temple Mount:

> Its underlying driving force of messianism is revealed, even as the Western
> liberalism it had imagined was its foundation is shaken. Unsurprisingly, the
> religious Zionist public, which since Rabbi Abraham Isaac Kook had claimed
> just that—that Zionism in its essence was, in fact, not secular at all but the
> actual fulfillment of the prophecies for the Jewish End of Days—is happy to
> claim ownership and leadership of the journey up the Mount.[11]

Somewhat like Yeshayahu Leibowitz before him, Persico is confirming, in the idiom of internal religious debates, the argument that I have been making throughout these pages in my focus on the poetic idiom: namely, that since 1967, Israeli claims to sovereignty over the sacred constitute a redefinition of the Judaism that has evolved from the time of the destruction of the Second Temple (and in some respects, even from the destruction of the First Temple). Messianic temptations appeared from time to time during the long journey officially defined as "Exile," but they were overcome by more pragmatic procedures and ethical values; this may be the governing force behind Maimonides's *Guide of the Perplexed*. Perplexity allows for space between the self and the Ultimate Other. Contrary to what Persico identifies as the demise of "secular" Zionism in the current upsurge of messianic fervor, there are still expressions of a vibrant secular culture especially in the coastal regions of Israel, and of tolerant, inclusive forms of Judaism and ecumenical religious sensibilities in Jerusalem herself. But the loudest voices and the most dangerous acts belong to those who have erased distance and substitution, reconfiguring two thousand years of negotiating the ethics and praxis of distance from the sacred.

To Remember Is to Forget: S. Y. Agnon and Yehuda Amichai

"If I forget thee O Jerusalem . . ." (fig. 11).[12] Over the course of this book, I have focused on the three salient elements of that much-cited pledge from Psalm 137: the singular speaking subject, the contingencies and frailties of memory, and the ultimate object of fealty—the Holy City as remote, desired, female, other. The memory practices that served the Jews of the far-flung diasporas were intricate—and they would be imported into modern Jerusalem. As poetic strategies reflecting religious practices, they can be summed up in the image of the citron from S. Y. Agnon's story "Ha-yerahmielim" that I cited in chapter 5: during a year of scarcity, the Jewish towns of Poland were each allocated only a piece of the "etrog," the ritual citron for Sukkoth, instead of the whole fruit that customarily arrived from the Holy Land. Of that piece, each community made jam which literally "preserved" the metonymic fruit of the Holy Land.[13] That is, as symbol of the symbol, a bare taste of the fruit sufficed to evoke the memory of, and the longing, for Zion.[14] Hebrew literature's Nobel laureate embraces such mimetic practices and the value of mediation itself in the most consequential spaces—and, indeed, even in the Old City of Jerusalem "herself" and in the "Holy of Holies" on the Temple Mount.

In addition to the metonymic qualities of diasporic Judaism that could be imported into the Holy City, cultural crossroads provided ongoing encounters with other forms of monotheism. Although these were often portrayed

FIGURE 11. Relief on the wall of the Central Bus Station in Jerusalem (2019). "If I forget thee, O Jerusalem, may my right hand forget." Photograph by Jan Kuehne.

as inimical, Jerusalem could also provide a platform for surprising acts of reconciliation.

In "Ma'aglei tzedek" (Circles of Justice), one of Agnon's most enchanting and enigmatic stories, Jerusalem appears as the inclusive theological site of compassion and mercy. First published in 1923, the story invokes in its title the well-known verse from Psalm 23: "Yanheni be-ma'aglei tzedek le-ma'an shmo," "He leads me on the pathways of justice for His Name's sake." "Ma'aglei tzedek" has been variously translated as paths or pathways of justice or righteousness.[15] But the literal image of intertwining *circles* is particularly poignant in this context. Agnon's narrative follows a poor vinegar maker ("Vinegar, Son of Wine")[16] as he stumbles through a series of misunderstandings with the priests of the Polish village in which he lives; as a result, he is cast into prison for a theft he did not knowingly commit. There, alone, in chains and near death, he is visited by a Christ figure who transports him on his back to Jerusalem. The description of their flight exhibits a kind of ecumenism rare in Hebrew literature and utterly unique in Agnon's oeuvre. The reference to "that man" (*oto ha-ish*) recalls a talmudic epithet for Jesus:

The old man embraced the neck of *that man* as the latter turned and faced in the direction of Jerusalem. On their first flight *that man* stopped smiling. On their second flight the old man's fingers turned cold. On their third flight he felt that he was embracing cold stone. His heart melted and his hands waxed weak. He was set loose and fell to the ground. On the morrow when his captors came in, he was not to be found.

That night a knocking was heard on the door of the Kolel in Jerusalem. Those who went outdoors saw a flight of angels which had come from the exile bearing a mortal form, which that very night they took and buried, in keeping with the custom in Jerusalem not to hold over the dead. (Emphases mine)[17]

This text resonates richly with passages from the Gospels as well as from the Talmud and later sources.[18] But the systemic cognitive dissonance between Jews and Christians, which accounts for the vinegar maker's obliviousness, the priests' and judges' ignorance—as well, perhaps, as the blindness of Jerusalem's Jews to That Man, who appears to them as a flight of angels—is replicated in many of the commentaries on this story.[19] I want to focus on what I see as the heart of the narrative, which generations of readers have either overlooked or dismissed: the figure of Jesus as he appears to the poor vinegar maker—not as Jesus the Christ, not even as Jesus the suffering Jew, but as Jesus the compassionate one. What the Jewish residents of the village and the Polish representatives of both the Church and the judiciary fail to enact—justice as empathy and compassion—is embodied in this figure, who answers the vinegar maker's prayers by transporting him to Jerusalem. In this act, That Man performs as a vessel far more miraculous than the kerchief on which Agnon's Hananiah made his journey to the Land of Israel in another story.[20] Not one hermetic circle but many circles ("ma'aglei tzedek") intersect here to create a porous and therefore complete reconciliation, fulfilling both Isaiah's vision of an ingathering of nations and the vision in Psalm 23 of divine comfort in the face of death.[21]

The history of the interpretation of this story remains a sign, I believe, of our own blindness to unlikely agents of redemption in the poor city of Jerusalem. What is still missing, of course, in this rare vision of reconciliation in the prose of Jerusalem's storyteller is some Muslim agent of or partner in human redemption. Perhaps he is to be found in the Arab father looking for his goat on Mt. Zion, opposite the home of the poet of Jerusalem, or the shopkeeper in the Old City, the poet's silent interlocutor, who closes his button and thread shop as the Gates close on Yom Kippur? Their silence would yield to a brief moment of dialogue during the 1980s and early '90s, when resolution of the conflict seemed within reach.[22]

Indeed, while it takes some detective work to uncover instances of religious reconciliation in Agnon's prose, Yehuda Amichai consistently preserved diasporic encounters and the ethics and poetics of mediation—even more urgently after 1967 and in physical proximity to the Western Wall. Moral sanity is a confection of memory mediated by distance—and seasoned, necessarily, with a healthy dose of amnesia. As we saw, Amichai taught his readers that "the best way to preserve memory is to conserve it inside forgetting, / so not even a single act of remembering will seep in / and disturb memory's eternal rest."[23]

These principles and practices would become more consequential with every passing decade. In the three years between the Israeli victory over East Jerusalem in 1967 and his death in 1970, Agnon wrestled with his own ambivalence about proximity to the sacred. Amichai lived for thirty more years, confronting these challenges head-on. And for a short while his unlikely partner in this enterprise was Paul Celan.

"Say that Jerusalem is . . ."

Paul Celan visited Jerusalem in October 1969, just months before his death. He spent many hours with Yehuda and Hana Amichai in their home in Mishkenot Sha'ananim, overlooking East Jerusalem and Sultan's Pool—that rocky, bramble-laden space of tense encounters where Yishmael and Yivke could still seek common ground. After Celan's return to Paris, the two poets exchanged a few letters in which they revealed to each other the burdens of their respective poetic patrimonies. Celan expressed his envy over Amichai's rootedness in the ground of Israel and the Hebrew language; he contrasted this with his own weightless, "pneumatic," presence in the world as the last representative of the Jewish "spirit" in Europe.[24] Amichai, in turn, wrote wistfully that such groundedness enslaved him to the demands of the hour and an ongoing accountability to local and ancient history.[25] Most of this exchange, in person and in writing, was conducted in German, the native tongue of both poets.

Na'ama Rokem explores the exchange between Celan and Amichai and the profound effect they had on each other, including the focus on Celan's "pneuma" contrasting with Amichai's groundedness. Years after Celan's death, Amichai wrote a poem for him, which foregrounds this exchange:

> Paul Celan. Toward the end, the words grew
> fewer inside you, each word
> so heavy in your body
> that God set you down like a heavy load

for a moment, perhaps, to catch
His breath and wipe His brow.
Then He left you and picked up a lighter load,
another poet. But the last bubbles
that rose from your drowning mouth
were the final concentration, the frothy concentrate
of the heaviness of your life.[26]

Poems and poetic fragments written during the last months before Celan's suicide were published posthumously by his childhood friend and probable lover, the Israeli writer Ilana Shmueli. Celan revealed there his own profound connection to but also his ambivalence about Jerusalem, the conflict between the "pneuma" in which he lived and the hard rock reality of the Holy City. His words are a fitting coda to the passions and perplexities that fill the pages of this book.

"Sag, dass Jerusalem ist . . . ," writes Celan in one of his last poetic fragments. "Say that Jerusalem is . . ."[27] Imagining the City, which Celan and Shmueli toured together, alternately as the source of light that emanates from the buried Temple, "Das Leuchten . . . / eine Goldboje, aus / Tempeltiefen" (A golden buoy, from / Temple's depths), and as a kind of metastasized cancer that threatens the entire body, "Tochtergeschwulst einer Blendung im All" (daughter metastasis / of a glare in space),[28] the poet looks warily into the open future.

Celan's unfinished sentence, like Amichai's vision of a layered, open-gated, and reconciled Jerusalem, is echoed in the capacious conclusion to Agnon's story of Jewish yearning and Christian grace as the interlocking circles of an endless journey. They can speak for so many of us who have loved Jerusalem from afar—but, up close, have been suffocated by the single-mindedness of those who could love her only by possessing her.

Sag, dass Jerusalem ist . . .

Acknowledgments: Ancient Debts and Ongoing Gratitude

This book has had a long gestation. It began in 1967 when, as a young graduate student in the English department at Brandeis University, I found myself gravitating to the "foreign fields" of Near Eastern and Judaic Studies, and specifically to the prominent Austro-Hungarian-born scholar of medieval philosophy Alexander Altmann. Professor Altmann was teaching a seminar on Maimonides's *Moreh ha-nevokhim* (*Guide of the Perplexed*), using the original Arabic and the medieval Hebrew translation as well as the English translation by Shlomo Pines that had recently been published by the University of Chicago Press, with an introduction by Leo Strauss. I became fascinated by the Rambam's theories—and uses—of metaphor in that text, and with the usual *hutzpah* of a graduate student who thinks that she has discovered a new continent, I proposed writing a seminar paper on the topic. In his quiet but enabling way, Professor Altmann treated my proposal with gravity and encouraged me to undertake the project. He had by then taken me under his wing and into his home, with the graciousness that characterized his engagement with the world. I was to discover, quickly, that I was not really equipped for the trek; that, besides, much work had been done on this very subject, while I had no purchase on medieval Jewish philosophy or poetics. So, adopting a strategy I would later see with my own students—at least those who had bitten off more than they could chew—I began to evade my dear professor in the corridors and grounds of campus. But a few months later, he caught me and told me with a knowing smile that he was giving me an A for the course and that I could hand in the paper whenever I was ready. More months went by. He finally caught me again and told me, in Hebrew, that he was letting me off the hook. "Ani poter otakh," he said.

Need I say it? Of all the seminar papers I wrote as a graduate student at Brandeis, this unwritten paper is the one that has lived inside me for over fifty years. Professor Altmann is no longer with us; were I as pious as Agnon's character Tehila, I might have simply taken this writ of obligation to my grave. But although I am only a little less perplexed now than I was then, I am somewhat wiser and more intrepid. Anyway, the evasion is over: the chapter in this book on *Moreh ha-nevokhim* is for him.

There are two other Maimonides-related debts that cannot be collected in this life. My other partner in all things medieval and many things modern, my "secret sharer," was Kalman Bland, professor of religious studies and medieval Jewish philosophy at Duke University. Friend of my youth, and companion throughout life, he saved me from many pitfalls as I was working on Maimonides's poetics and constructing an imaginary dialogue between the Great Eagle and Israel's Nobel laureate. Kal died suddenly, in the middle of our conversation, and before he could read the final version, but I hope that something of his spirit, his wisdom, and his humor has entered these pages. And finally: Joel Kraemer, whose mighty biography of Maimonides inspired me to indulge my heterodox instincts, was gracious enough to read one of the final drafts of that chapter. He too did not live to see the final product. These scholars are hardly responsible for my mistakes or misreadings. But I do mean that chapter as a small tribute to their scholarship and their *Menschlichkeit*.

A few more posthumous debts must be discharged. Chana Bloch and Alan Mintz enriched my life and are no longer alive to agree or disagree with my claims. Readers of my chapter on the Song of Songs will quickly discern that virtually every page is inflected by Chana's erudition and poetic soul. But my debt to her goes far beyond her scholarship and translations to the myriad ways her own poetry—its wit and courage—accompanied me in many of the pathways of adult life. Alan and I lived parallel lives for over fifty years, and his erudition and presence enriched my life, especially as our mutual passion for Agnon informed the past two decades and as our work came to be complementary. His sudden death left a hole in the souls of many; I would like to believe that he would receive this book as homage to our ongoing conversations.

Geoffrey Hartman, cherished mentor and friend, read an early draft of *Figuring Jerusalem* and wrote to me on January 4, 2015, already ill with the Parkinson's that would cut his life short: "What we do as humanistic scholars, has not, and apparently cannot, change matters by the kind of wisdom we try to convey . . . [But] we do come across literary archaeologies that gladden mind and heart despite the sadness they bring as realia." That blessing and that challenge have accompanied me through the final phases of this project.

Shortly before this book went to the publisher, another shocking death turned an acknowledgment into a loving eulogy. David Ehrlich was my beloved student, interlocutor on all things Jerusalem, all things literary, all things human. It would have been appropriate to launch this book in Tmol Shilshom, the literary café named after Agnon's great novel, which David turned from a dream into a "mikdash me'at," a temple to literature and the sister arts that nurtured writers and would-be writers, readers and consumers of good books, good conversation, good food and wine.

And for the living, my gratitude knows no bounds: To Ilana Pardes, whose work on Agnon and on the Song of Songs has enlarged my own perceptions and projects for decades, and whose generosity with colleagues and students has helped to make the Department of General and Comparative Literature at the Hebrew University—my last home before retirement—a smorgasbord of intellectual discovery, inflected by true caring. To Vivian Liska, whose embrace of the world of Jewish and European literature and philosophy, combined with boundless hospitality, has enriched the intellectual and cultural life of Jerusalem over most of the past decade and created a skyway between Hebrew University and her Institute of Jewish Studies at the University of Antwerp. Vivian's sharp mind is matched only by her kindness and ability to listen and empathize, and I have come to rely on her as friend and interlocutor on all matters of the heart and mind.

Robert (Uri) Alter has been my mentor on the page for over half a century, and a dear friend for almost forty years. He taught me, and countless others, to read Hebrew differently; his early work on biblical poetics and biblical narrative opened up the Hebrew Bible to generations of new readings inflected by literary sensibilities, and his translation of the entire Hebrew Bible, completed only in 2019, has already become a classic. In his work on modern Hebrew literature he showed us how, beginning in Europe, long before the establishment of the enterprise that was to become the State of Israel, Hebrew writers of the nineteenth century created a virtual street and a virtual city. And while doing all this, Uri's fascination with literature in the real cities of Western and Eastern Europe never abated; some of the most fascinating work on Sterne, Flaubert, Proust, Nabokov, and Kafka was done while he was presumably doing other things. Though I was too old to be his student, Uri always seemed to know which corner I should turn before I had quite reached it. He has influenced and blessed all my endeavors; in his presence, one always feels like an only child, even as the sibling chain spreads far and wide. Together, he and his late wife, Carol Cosman, translator and writer, have nourished body and soul during my sojourns "at the end of the West."

Dan Miron has been a champion of my work since the 1980s and even intervened on my behalf at a crucial moment when my institutional status was in jeopardy. He has been a companion and an enabler as well as one of the most knowledgeable readers and scholars of Hebrew, Yiddish, and European literature.

Jeffrey Saks has been an interlocutor and precious source for all things related to Agnon. He and Oreet Meital, the director of Beit Agnon, have granted a vibrant afterlife to the Jerusalem home of Israel's Nobel laureate.

During the years that this project was forming, I was fortunate to receive the endorsement of two institutions—in addition to the ongoing support of deans, colleagues, and students at Hebrew University. Being chosen a Guggenheim Fellow in 2007 provided the vote of confidence and the financial support that allowed me to take time off from my teaching duties to launch the book. And my last years before retirement were nurtured by my fellowship at Scholion, the Research Center at Hebrew University; I wish to thank its two directors, Yisrael Yuval and Danny Schwartz, as well as my colleagues in the research group "Jews and Cities."

Other companions along the way include colleagues and current and former students: Michal Ben-Naftali, Amos Goldberg, Ariel Zinder, Galili Shachar, Almog Behar, Rachel Elior, Amnon Raz-Krakotzkin, Daniel Boyarin, Shuli Barzilai, Elizabeth Freund, Ruth Ginsburg, Shlomith Rimmon-Kenan, Marianne Hirsch, Leo Spitzer, Susannah Heschel, Susan Suleiman, Miriam Cooke, Bruce Lawrence, Omer Bartov, Nitza Ben-Dov, Nitza Peremen-Drori, Na'ama Rokem, Tova Rosen, Tamar Hess, Anita Norich, James Young, Jan Kuehne, Ben Pollock, Hanna Soker-Schwager, Hana Wirth-Nesher, and Hava Schwartz.

To others whose presence helps to keep me sane: Donald and Linda Zisquit, for professional and personal counsel, for poetry and art, for vodka and heart; Eva Katz, Nomi Chazan, Lily Galili, Connie and David Greene, Dorothy and David Harman, for good work in the world and for always being by my side; my spiritual companions in the quest for a just Jerusalem, Ruth Schulman, Sara Avitzour, Steve Copeland, Veronica and Elliot Cohen, Paula and Rabbi Levi Weiman-Kelman, Rabbi Oded Mazor, Rabbi Naamah Kelman-Ezrachi and Elan Ezrachi, Rabbi Susan Silverman, and Yosef Abramowitz; my beloved teacher and intrepid warrior for peace and justice, Alice Shalvi.

For lifelong, world-embracing friendship "in good times and in better times": Anita Claire Fellman, Judy Graubart, Jerry Weinstein, Trudy Bulkley, Davi-Ellen and Bruce Chabner, Elaine Cohen. For conversation, compassion, and conviction: Natalie and Chandler Davis, Avrom Udovitch and Lucette Valensi, Froma Zeitlin, Jeremy and Vicky Zwelling, and Judith Wechsler.

To my "village" in New Hampshire: Cindy Johnson, my preacher and my heart's confessor on weekly circumambulations of Lake Kezar, and her help-meet, Jeff Maguire, for wisdom spiced with humor and tireless dedication to the education of young and old alike; Carlton Bradford, for the best rendition of "Danny Boy" and for insights undimmed by ninety-five years of life on this planet; Gail Matthews, for sunshine even on rainy days.

Yehuda Amichai was a friend and neighbor in the alleyways, valleys, streets, and salons of Jerusalem; his poetry continues to illuminate the lives of generations of this city's inhabitants. Over the twenty years since Yehuda's death, Hana Amichai has proved not only a worthy and generous custodian of her husband's legacy, but a dear friend and companion.

Sometimes, if we're lucky, family and professional colleagues overlap. To the Fishbane family, my deep appreciation: my beloved sister Mona, for profound insights into the human psyche, and for a lifetime of sisterhood; Michael (Buzzy) Fishbane, my brother-in-law, for decades of stimulating conversation, in person and in print. Buzzy and I bring different sensibilities to some of the same texts, but the dialogue has been challenging and inspiring ever since we were fellow graduate students at Brandeis. And to the Fishbane sons, Eitan and Elisha, for illuminating other corners of the Jewish textual world. Eitan and I have shared joy and sorrow, a love of Hebrew in all its incarnations, a love of poetry, and, above all, a love of Jerusalem. To Jane Flint, sister-in-law-and-in-love. Finally, to the memory of my parents and my brother, Ira, who forged the world in hard iron and delicate silver and strummed his way through many dark hours.

Always, before the beginning and after the end, my work is blessed by the eye, the mind, and the heart of my "soul sister," Chana Kronfeld. Nothing I do would be possible without the conversation that traverses continents and time zones and has lasted for many decades. Chana taught us all how to read the Hebrew and Yiddish modernists with a new eye, and her ongoing work on the Song of Songs has made my own chapter much richer and deeper. My posthumous dialogue with Yehuda Amichai would not be possible without her insights and readings, articulated in *The Full Severity of Compassion*. But her fingerprints are all over this book.

And then there is Mati Senkman, my "Man Friday," without whom none of my work over a dozen years would have seen the light of day. Former student, tour guide through Israel and through the labyrinth of bibliographic and academic arcana: no problem is too great for him to solve. I am forever in his debt.

My enormous gratitude to the editors at the University of Chicago Press, especially to Alan G. Thomas for years of encouragement, and to Randolph Petilos for solving every practical problem and soothing overwrought nerves with practical solutions and virtual cappuccinos. And to Barbara Mann and Adriana X. Jacobs, my two wonderful readers, whose sharp eyes and keen minds made the final version of this book so much richer. To the production team: Brian Chartier, Lisa Hein, Meredith Nini, Christine Schwab. And to Susan Tarcov, copyeditor extraordinaire, who, as luck would have it, was the young copyeditor on my first book, *By Words Alone*, published by this press in 1980; forty years later, her unerring eye has grown only sharper and her understanding heart only deeper.

The feeling of being accompanied is what has made this entire journey worthwhile. My children and stepchildren, their spouses and all our grand-children provided the love, the conversation, and the distractions that car-ried me from day to day. Even when virtual meetings replaced face-to-face encounters over this past year, watching the little ones grow and their parents navigate the challenges of this time has only made me more grateful.

Figuring Jerusalem is dedicated to my beloved husband, Bernard Avishai, first and last reader of my work, my partner in consciousness. He joined me in the middle of my life's journey and helped me to reclaim the New England I had left behind, while rediscovering Jerusalem as a "port city on the shore of eternity." He is the taste of coffee in the morning and martinis in the evening. He is the prose and the poetry of my life.

I have written the last draft of this book during global crises in health and public governance. The cease-fire that followed eleven days of hostilities be-tween the Israeli government and Hamas, in May 2021, may hold, but it will not heal the wounds that have been exposed and explored here. In Geoffrey Hartman's words, no writer can hope to "change matters," but we can offer some new formulations of what lies beneath and beyond the "realia." I have offered here my own "literary archaeology" as a piece of the ongoing endeav-ors, and cherished values, of so many interlocutors, the living, the dead, and (dare we hope?) the unborn.

*

The many lines of poetry by Yehuda Amichai in English translation are reprinted by permission of Hana Amichai. Amichai's "Jerusalem 1967," "Not like a Cypress," and "An Arab Shepherd Is Searching for His Goat on Mount Zion" are from *The Selected Poetry of Yehuda Amichai*, edited and translated by Chana Bloch and Stephen Mitchell, © 1986, 1996, 2013 by Chana Bloch and Stephen Mitchell, published by the University of California Press. Poems by Yehuda Amichai from *Open Closed Open*, © 2000, translated by Chana Bloch and Chana Kronfeld, published by Harcourt, are reprinted by permis-sion of Chana Kronfeld. Haim Gouri's "Heritage" is reprinted by permission of Yael Gouri. Dan Pagis's "Written in Pencil in the Sealed Railway-Car," © Dan Pagis and ACUM, is reprinted from *Points of Departure*, translated by Stephen Mitchell (Jewish Publication Society, 1981). And Amichai's "If I Forget Thee, Jerusalem," translated by Assia Gutmann, is reprinted from *The Poetry of Yehuda Amichai*, edited by Robert Alter (Farrar, Straus and Giroux, 2015). My thanks to all for allowing me to quote these poems.

Notes

Prologue

1. "Jerusalem, Jerusalem, Why Jerusalem?," no. 11, trans. Chana Bloch and Chana Kronfeld, from *Open Closed Open*, in *The Poetry of Yehuda Amichai*, ed. Robert Alter (New York: Farrar, Straus and Giroux, 2015), 503–4.

2. Yehuda Amichai, "Yerushalayim yerushalayim lama yerushalayim?," no. 11, *Patuaḥ Sagur Patuaḥ, Shirei Yehuda Amichai* (Tel Aviv and Jerusalem: Schocken, 2002), 5:280.

3. For a succinct discussion of the political conundrum that is contemporary Jerusalem, and the various plans to resolve it, see Gershon Baskin, "The Jerusalem Problem: The Search for Solutions," *Palestine-Israel Journal* 8, no. 1 (2001): 6–11. He explains that the "Holy Basin" is the rather loose term adopted in Israeli parlance for the entire area, including all of the Old City, the Ophel, the City of David, and the Mount of Olives.

4. Scores of historical studies and demographic and political monographs have appeared in the past half century alone. A representative list would contain such items as surveys of Jerusalem since 1967, its municipal life, political challenges, social fabric, and cultural and religious roadblocks and opportunities, as well as information on the archaeology, history, and architectural layers of construction in Jerusalem, on the Temple Mount, on art, photography, film, and poetry—in and of Jerusalem—and on the challenges of everyday life. It would include listings for essays on more theological or theopoetic dimensions of Jerusalem, as well as samples of imaginative representations of Jerusalem in Israeli literature, in addition to the writers we will consider here, especially the fictive evocations of the sacred center in Jerusalem and the resonances of past glory and destruction in apocalyptic fantasy that have appeared in recent years.

5. James Carroll, *Jerusalem, Jerusalem: How the Ancient City Ignited Our Modern World* (Boston: Houghton Mifflin Harcourt, 2011), 1.

6. For a survey of accounts of the "Jerusalem Syndrome," as fantasy and reality, from the nineteenth century to the end of the twentieth, see Eliezer Witztum and Moshe Kalian, "The 'Jerusalem Syndrome'—Fantasy and Reality: A Survey of Accounts from the Nineteenth Century to the End of the Second Millennium," *Israel Journal of Psychiatry and Related Sciences* 36, no. 4 (1999): 260–71. "The so-called 'Jerusalem Syndrome' [relates to] behavioral phenomena observed in eccentric and psychotic tourists with religious delusions . . . visiting the Holy City" (260). The authors' conclusion is that these visitors were "already guided by a delusionary system

derived from their religious belief and cultural background" when they "set out for their journey to the Holy City" (260).

7. As Yair Zakovitch points out, these accounts can also be attributed to the varying political agendas of the authors or redactors of these verses. "The First Stages of Jerusalem's Sanctification under David: A Literary and Ideological Analysis," in *Jerusalem: Its Sanctity and Centrality to Judaism, Christianity, and Islam*, ed. Lee I. Levine (New York: Continuum, 1999), 17–18, 16–35. For the Josephus reference, see *Antiquities of the Jews*, in *The Works of Flavius Josephus*, trans. William Whiston (Baltimore: Armstrong & Berry, 1834), bk. 7, chap. 3, 143.

8. For a popular account of this claim, see Kanan Makiya, *The Rock: A Tale of Seventh-Century Jerusalem* (New York: Pantheon Books, 2001), 182, 322–25. In the Muslim version of the cosmic drama, the rock, like the foundation stone in midrashic accounts, must be held in place by superhuman effort in order to prevent it from detaching from its moorings. The rock and the space around it thus become a dizzying arabesque or echo chamber of competing stories. Yet there is evidence that "the earliest Arabic name for Jerusalem [before *al-Quds*] is *Madinat Bayt al-Maqdis* . . . City of the Temple," taken from the Hebrew word for the Temple, *beit ha-mikdash* (Makiya, *The Rock*, 291). In constructing his own fanciful narrative of seventh-century Jerusalem, Makiya looks for parallels or reverberations in the different traditions that are tributes and not exclusive counterclaims. See also Angelika Neuwirth on the significance of Jerusalem both as the first *qibla*, or direction of prayer, in Islam and as eschatological geography. "The Spiritual Meaning of Jerusalem in Islam" in *City of the Great King: Jerusalem from David to the Present*, ed. Nitza Rosovsky (Cambridge: Harvard University Press, 2013), 93–116. On Jesus's complex relation to the Temple, see Haviva Pedaya, "Temurot ba-kodesh ha-kodashim: Min ha-shulayim la-mercaz" [Changes in the Holy of Holies: From the Periphery to the Center], *Mada'ei ha-yahadut* [Jewish Studies] 37 (1996): 53–110. See also Pedaya, "The Divinity as Place and Time and the Holy Place in Jewish Mysticism," in *Sacred Space: Shrine, City, Land*, ed. Benjamin Z. Kedar and R. J. Zwi Werblowsky (New York: New York University Press, 1998), 84–111.

9. See Sidra DeKoven Ezrahi, *Booking Passage: Exile and Homecoming in the Modern Jewish Imagination* (Berkeley: University of California Press, 2000).

10. Among the most influential contemporary analyses of the implicit and explicit dialogue between Jews and Christians from ancient times through the Middle Ages are found in the work of Daniel Boyarin and Israel Yuval. See Boyarin, *Borderlines* (Philadelphia: University of Pennsylvania Press, 2004); and Yuval, *Two Nations in Your Womb* (Berkeley: University of California Press, 2006). For one of the earliest post-Holocaust arguments for a more literal reading of the akeda story, see Shalom Spiegel, *The Last Trial: On the Legends and Lore of the Command to Abraham to Offer Isaac as a Sacrifice*, trans. Judah Goldin (New York: Jewish Lights Classic Reprint, 1993); and see my elaboration of this in chapter 1, below.

11. See Burke O. Long, *Imagining the Holy Land: Maps, Models, and Fantasy Travels* (Bloomington: Indiana University Press, 2003). For a Protestant-American version of the Temple as transportable and reproducible site of holiness, see the Holy Land models at the Chautauqua Institution founded in New York in 1874.

12. See Moshe Idel's exploration of the "prophetic" or "ecstatic" brand of mysticism that regarded the human body as the "true analogue of the Land of Israel." Eventually this led to Kabbalistic and Hassidic notions of personal salvation and symbolic rather than concrete connections with the Sacred Center. Idel, "The Land of Israel in Medieval Kabbalah," in *The Land of Israel: Jewish Perspectives*, ed. Lawrence Hoffman (Notre Dame: University of Notre Dame Press, 1986), 176–81. Quoted in DeKoven Ezrahi, *Booking Passage*, 48–49.

13. Almost nothing about Agnon's life, except the date of his death, is indisputable. He manipulated his birthdate to coincide with the Ninth of Av, when, according to popular belief, the Messiah will be born. This is the way Wikipedia puts it: "Officially, his date of birth on the Hebrew calendar was 18 Av 5648 (July 26), but he always said his birthday was on the Jewish fast day of Tisha' B'av, the Ninth of Av"—i.e., July 17. https://en.wikipedia.org/wiki/Shmuel_Yosef _Agnon. As for publication dates, 1908 marks the publication of his first Hebrew story, "Agunot," though he had published some youthful poems and stories in Yiddish and Hebrew while still in his hometown of Buczacz, Galicia. See Dan Laor, Hayei Agnon (Jerusalem: Schocken, 1998), 19. Agnon won the Nobel Prize for literature in 1966.

14. As part of her advocacy for the "revolutionary Amichai," Chana Kronfeld exposes and critiques the ubiquity and free appropriation of Amichai's poetry, in both Israeli and American Jewish ritual contexts. See The Full Severity of Compassion: The Poetry of Yehuda Amichai (Stanford: Stanford University Press, 2016), 25–80. And see the distinction that Israeli author David Grossman makes between Amichai's success in articulating the most intimate, personal experiences of his reader and the public appropriation or hijacking of his poetry for official ceremonial occasions. "[Amichai's] words have become part of my interior monologue, and not mine alone." Quoted in Kronfeld, Full Severity of Compassion, 28, 303n10.

15. See Sidra DeKoven Ezrahi, "Jerusalem Divorced Family's Home as Inspiration for Israeli-Palestinian Peace," Haaretz, February 27, 2016, https://www.haaretz.com/israel-news/.premium .MAGAZINE-no-clean-divorce-for-israel-and-palestine-1.5409395. Among the many books on layers of architecture and life in contemporary Jerusalem, inflected by deep historical knowledge and personal passion, two are worth noting here: Elan Ezrachi, Shfuya ba-halomah: ge'ut ve-shefel be-50 shnot ihud yerushalayim [Awakened Dream: 50 Years of Complex Unification of Jerusalem] (Herzliya: Albatross, 2017); and Adina Hoffman, Till We Have Built Jerusalem: Architects of a New City (New York: Farrar, Straus and Giroux, 2016). For a different personal and poignant Hebrew vision of Israelis and Palestinians in Jerusalem, from 1967 to 2017, see the book by veteran journalist Nir Hasson, Urshalim: Yisraelim u-falastini'im bi-yerushalayim 1967–2017 [Urshalim: Israelis and Palestinians in Jerusalem, 1967–2017] (Tel Aviv: Sifriat aliyat ha-gag, 2017). The political and literary work of Meron Benvenisti and the radio broadcasts of Eliezer Yaari have richly informed the lives of Jerusalemites over many decades. See, for example, Benvenisti, City of Stone: The Hidden History of Jerusalem (Berkeley: University of California Press, 1996); and Yaari, Mi-pa'am le-fa'am [Every So Often]. Photographs: Alex Levac (Hod ha-sharon: Agam Books, 2020). And among the many fictional writers who grew up in the old sections of the divided city and have struggled to navigate the new, engorged reality, see the fiction of Haim Be'er, including his "Bildungsroman," Havalim, translated as The Pure Element of Time (Waltham: Brandeis University Press), 2012.

16. See below, chapter 7.

17. See Amichai, "An Arab Shepherd Is Searching for His Goat on Mt. Zion," trans. Chana Bloch, Poetry of Yehuda Amichai, 274. Shirei Yehuda Amichai, 3:274. For a discussion of this poem, see below, chapter 7.

18. "Songs of Zion the Beautiful," no. 24, trans. Chana Bloch, in Poems of Jerusalem and Love Poems, a Bilingual Edition (New York: Sheep Meadow Press, 1988), 69–71. I prefer this translation of the poem to the more euphonious translation by Robert Alter in his edition of Amichai's poetry. Shirei eretz tzion yerushalayim, no. 24, Shirei Yehuda Amichai, 3:21.

19. "Songs of Zion the Beautiful," no. 23, trans. Chana Bloch, in Poems of Jerusalem and Love Poems, 69–71. Amichai, Shirei eretz tzion yerushalayim, no. 23, Shirei Yehuda Amichai, 3:20.

20. For an analysis of Psalm 137 and the latter-day emergence of the generally repressed verses with which it concludes, see DeKoven Ezrahi, "By the Waters of Babylon: The Amnesia of Memory [on Psalm 137]," in *Psalms in/on Jerusalem*, ed. Ilana Pardes and Ophir Münz-Manor, in the series Perspectives on Jewish Texts and Contexts, ed. Vivian Liska (Berlin: De Gruyter, 2019), 153–64.

21. Amichai, "Jerusalem, Jerusalem, Why Jerusalem?," no. 26, trans. Chana Bloch and Chana Kronfeld, *Poetry of Yehuda Amichai*, 508–9. Amichai, "Yerushalayim yerushalayim lama yerush-alayim?," no. 26, *Shirei Yehuda Amichai*, 5:287.

22. Ariel Hirschfeld, *Rishimot ʿal makom* [Local Notes] (Tel Aviv: Am Oved, 2000), 15.

23. Tomer Persico, "The End Point of Zionism: Ethnocentrism and the Temple Mount," *Israel Studies Review* 32, no. 1 (Summer 2017): 107. Persico tackles the reappearance of the Temple Mount in its many iterations in contemporary Israeli politics and religious practice. His point of departure is Scholem's warning from 1926 about (what Persico calls) the "messianic Eros and Zionism's susceptibility to its allure, particularly when the Jewish people are again in the Land of Israel" (105). He then traces the evolution of Jerusalem's status in Zionist thought and practice before and after 1948, and since 1967, drawing a distinction between the settlement project for mainstream religious Zionism—"Temple matters [were] far more remote from the heart of the public" (108)—and the status of the Temple Mount in underground messianist movements.

24. First articulated in 1994 and repeated many times since. See Serge Schmemann, "Incidents and Arguments Add to Arab-Israeli Friction," *New York Times*, September 25, 1996, https://www.nytimes.com/1996/09/25/world/incidents-and-arguments-add-to-arab-israeli -friction.html.

25. On this see Kronfeld, "Living on the Hyphen: The Necessary Metaphor," in *Full Severity*, 225–26. And see below, chapter 6.

26. Amichai, "The Singer of the Song of Songs," "The Bible and You, the Bible and You, and Other Midrashim," no. 32, trans. Chana Bloch and Chana Kronfeld, *Poetry of Yehuda Amichai*, 434–35. See below, chapter 7.

27. Mark Twain, *Innocents Abroad* (Hartford, CT: American Publishing Company, 1869), chapter 53, https://www.gutenberg.org/files/3176/3176-h/3176-h.htm.

Introduction

1. In Hebrew: "Leylot she-ʿasiti ʿim Ḥasidim ve-anshei maʿaseh be-ḥatzot layla etzel ha-kotel ha-maʿaravi ʿeynayim natnu li lirot et artzo shel ha-kadosh barukh hu she-natan lanu et ha-ʿir *she-shiken shmo ʿaleha . . .*," emphasis mine. I have slightly emended the official translation. Nobel Prize Banquet speech, December 10, 1966, http://www.nobelprize.org/nobel_prizes /literature/laureates/1966/agnon-speech_he.html.

2. Amichai, "Jerusalem 1967," no. 21, translated by Amichai and Ted Hughes, *Poems of Jerusalem and Love Poems*, 61; *Shirei Yehuda Amichai*, 2:21.

3. For a summary of the various historical processes and accounts that conflate the "second temple" and the "third temple," see Pamela Berger, *The Crescent on the Temple: The Dome of the Rock as Image of the Ancient Jewish Sanctuary* (Leiden: Brill, 2012). For a succinct discussion of this process and its ramifications, see Simon Goldhill, *The Temple of Jerusalem* (Cambridge: Harvard University Press, 2005).

4. Robert Alter translates *be-korvatam* as "when they came forward before the Lord." He comments: "This is the verb regularly used for coming before the divine presence in the sanctuary. When the act is unauthorized, the implication of the verb is 'to encroach.'" Alter, trans.,

The Hebrew Bible (New York: W. W. Norton, 2019), 1:421n1. All biblical translations are by Alter, unless otherwise specified.

5. According to Maimonides, the Priests pronounced the Tetragrammaton during the sacerdotal blessing; at some point this practice was discontinued and the Priests "ceased mentioning *the articulated name* [*ha-shem ha-mefurash*] in the *Sanctuary* because of the corruption of the people." A twelve-letter word and then a forty-two-letter word was substituted, denoting the various attributes of God. *The Guide of the Perplexed*, trans. Shlomo Pines, introductory essay by Leo Strauss (Chicago: University of Chicago Press, 1963), I:62, p. 151.

6. Just how human even the High Priest is acknowledged to be is demonstrated by long talmudic passages that detail the possible bodily emissions and sinful behavior or even intent on the part of the High Priest in the days leading up to Yom Kippur. Versions of such passages are interspersed in intriguing and problematic ways among the pedestrian struggles of an otherwise unremarkable New York Jew in the months leading up to 9/11 in Ruby Namdar's Hebrew novel *The Ruined House*, trans. Hillel Halkin (New York: Harper Collins, 2017).

7. See the talmudic epithet for the Divine as "Ha-makom," or The Place. Gen. R. 65:9.

8. See Elhanan Reiner, "Destruction, Temple and Holy Place," in *Streams into the Sea: Studies in Jewish Culture and Its Context*, ed. Rachel Livneh-Freudenthal and Elchanan Reiner (Tel Aviv: Alma College, 2001), 147. And see Alter's translation of the edifice in Genesis 28:12 as "ramp." The references suggest an association with the "Mesopotamian ziggurat, and so the structure envisioned is probably a vast ramp with terraced landings." Alter, *Hebrew Bible*, 1:100n12.

9. A comparative study by Yair Zakovitch and Avigdor Shinan of this passage and the Tower of Babel narrative (Gen. 11:1–9) underscores the ongoing dialogue with Babylonian culture. "Babel" presumably refers to the Babylonian designation "Bab-ilu," gate of God, or "Bab i-lanu," gate of the gods. Jacob's plural and then singular versions of "House of God" ("beit elohim," "beit el," Gen. 28:17–19) could be a grammatical echo of that ongoing dialogue. But the differences between the two narratives are also underscored in Zakovitch's and Shinan's essay. The Tower of Babel narrative as polemic with the tower-temple to the god Marduk gives way to the story of the ladder in Jacob's dream; it will resonate in the midrashic narratives of Arauna and David, eventuating in the establishment of Jerusalem as the apotheosis of divine habitation. *Lo kakh katuv ba-tana"kh* [Once Again: That's Not What the Good Book Says] (Tel Aviv: Mishkal-Yedioth ahronot and Chemed, 2004), 67–72. English translation: *From Gods to God: How the Bible Debunked, Suppressed or Changed Ancient Myths and Legends*, trans. Valerie Zakovitch (Lincoln: University of Nebraska Press, 2012). Later, "Bethel" would be conflated with the Temple of Solomon by those Christian pilgrims who visited the Dome of the Rock, now called Templum Domini. See Berger, *Crescent*, 78.

10. Ismar Schorsch, "Behind God's Names," *Jewish Theological Seminary*, November 20, 1993, http://www.jtsa.edu/behind-gods-names.

11. It is, of course, anachronistic to impute clear tenses to biblical Hebrew; the implication is not of tense but of aspect, a process that has not yet been completed.

12. One should take notice, throughout these passages, of the primacy of the oral exchange between Moses and God, even when the challenge is for visual representation. While it is the voice of God that is hypostasized into His presence in later (Second Temple), postbiblical, apocryphal, Hellenistic, and rabbinic discourse (see the rabbinic "bat kol" [echo; lit., daughter of a voice]), Azzan Yadin argues that "the concept of a mediating, hypostatic voice exists in earlier strata of the Hebrew Bible as well." Yadin, "קול [Voice] as Hypostasis in the Hebrew Bible," *Journal of Biblical Literature* 122, no. 4 (Winter 2003): 601.

13. On this see the prologue, above.

14. My translation differs slightly from Alter's.

15. The reference is to an ancient Israelite or Ephraimite site of holiness and sanctuary that had been obliterated. There are many references to Shiloh in the Hebrew Bible (see I Sam. 1–3) and a lively discussion among scholars about its history. What is fairly certain is that it had been destroyed long before Jeremiah's quotation of the divine exhortation regarding Jerusalem. See Donald G. Schley, *Shiloh: A Biblical City in Tradition and History* (Sheffield, UK: JSOT Press, 1989, 2009), 196.

16. For a discussion of the Temple to the "Name of God," see Goldhill, *The Temple*, 23. For an earlier discussion and elaboration of some of the issues raised in this chapter, see Sidra DeKoven Ezrahi, " 'To what shall I compare thee?' Jerusalem as Ground Zero of the Hebrew Imagination," *PMLA*, special issue, "Cities," ed. Patricia Yaeger, 122, no. 1 (January 2007): 220–34.

17. On the image of water flowing from the site of the Temple as an apocalyptic element connected both to the vision of ultimate "repair" and to the primordial waters of creation, see Pedaya, "Temurot."

18. I have used here the JPS translation: Jerusalem as a "city without walls" is glossed in the next phrase: "so many shall be the men and cattle it contains" (Zech. 2:8). The Hebrew word is *perazot*, which designates an unwalled settlement. See also the Anchor Bible translation and the gloss by Carol L. Meyers and Eric M. Meyers on this passage as implying God's selection of Jerusalem as the sacred center of Judah, the sign of which will be the city's very vulnerability: "Jerusalem itself will be fortified, albeit with God's protection rather than stone walls." *Haggai, Zechariah 1–8. The Anchor Bible: A New Translation with Introduction and Commentary*, ed. Carol L. Meyers and Eric M. Meyers (New York: Doubleday, 1987), 149, 150, 154, 155. The Temple is not mentioned but implied in this passage as the locus of God's earthly presence that radiates out to encompass the whole city. The book of Zechariah combines a pragmatic and spirited vision of the reconstruction that is already underway with increasingly eschatological visions as developments on the ground sour. See also the putative "boundaries" of the Land— from Damascus in the north to the Jordan River in the east, to the Wadi [of Egypt] in the south and the 'Great Sea' in the west—in Ezekiel 47. The confusion of eschatological and political visions is not, then, a modern invention. I wish to thank Eric Meyers and Rabbi Steve Sager for illuminating the biblical and talmudic records of the life of Jerusalemites in the wake of the destruction of the First and Second Temple, respectively. To this picture should be added the very different—more militant and exclusive—focus of Nehemiah, who claims to have been sent from the Persian court to Jerusalem in order to build and fortify the "wall." Alter refers to the first-person references in the book that bears his name and the catalogues of other names as properties of a "memoir," possibly written at the end of the fifth century BCE by a member of the Persian court. *The Writings. The Hebrew Bible*, 3:xliv, 803–5.

19. This strange amnesia or fantasy about the dimensions of the sites of holiness will be repeated in the Gospels. On the shifting topography of holiness, see Maurice Halbwachs: "Whatever epoch is examined, attention is not directed toward the first events, or perhaps the origin of these events, but rather toward the group of believers and toward their commemorative work. When one looks at the physiognomy of the holy places in successive times, one finds the character of these groups inscribed." "The Legendary Topography of the Gospels in the Holy Land," in *On Collective Memory*, ed. and trans. Lewis A. Coser (Chicago: University of Chicago Press, 1992), 234–35. This pathbreaking essay was, evidently, initiated after Halbwachs visited the Convent of Our Lady of Sion in Jerusalem. "In Jerusalem, according to [historian Vincent] Lemire,

Halbwachs learned that space and sacred memory are interrelated," and this insight inspired his "Legendary Topography." Quoted in Menachem Klein, "Jerusalem's Alternative Collective Memory Agents," *Israel Studies Review* 35, no. 1 (Spring 2020): 1, https://www.berghahnjournals .com/view/journals/israel-studies-review/35/1/isr350102.xml.

20. Goldhill, *The Temple*, 42. Again, the construction of temple surrogates or simulacra is one of the most enduring mimetic traditions in Judaism, Christianity, and Islam. The Jewish synagogue that flourished both while the Second Temple was standing and after its destruction continues to be referred to as *mikdash me'at* or "miniature temple." See DeKoven Ezrahi, *Booking Passage*, 3–23. On the mystical concept of the temple, rooted in Ezekiel's vision and evolving into a kind of place/time continuum, and on the transactions between geographical and human centers of holiness, see Pedaya, "Divinity as Place," 84–111.

21. Victor Avigdor Hurowitz, "Tenth Century BCE to 586 BCE: The House of the Lord (Beyt YHWH)," in *Where Heaven and Earth Meet: Jerusalem's Sacred Esplanade*, ed. Oleg Grabar and Benjamin Z. Kedar (Austin and Jerusalem: University of Texas Press and Yad Ben Zvi, 2009), 32–34.

22. The move from reference to the Temple to reference to the "Temple Mount" as sacred center coincides with the sensibility of the rabbis of the post–Second Temple period, according to Yaron Z. Eliav, *God's Mountain: The Temple Mount in Time, Place, and Memory* (Baltimore: Johns Hopkins University Press, 2005), 190–236. Both Eliav and Goldhill emphasize the holiness of the Temple Mount as a designation of absence. "The space of [the Temple's] absence has attracted the hopes and aspirations of millions of people over the centuries, and continues to fuel the most intense feelings in the Middle East and beyond . . . The Temple, lost and reconstructed, yearned for and mourned for, pictured and sung about, is above all else a monument of the imagination." Goldhill, *The Temple*, 15, 18.

23. For a sober, engaged, but scholarly discussion of Helena's "discovery," see James Carroll, *Constantine's Sword: The Church and the Jews. A History* (New York: Mariner's Books, 2002), 197ff.

24. Alter's translation, "heartland," does not quite capture the corporeal reference. The phraseword "*omphalos* [navel] of the world" (*tabur ha-aretz*), in reference to Jerusalem, from Ezek. 38:12, is only one instance of the metaphoric rendering of the world as human body.

25. Again, on the primordial waters of creation, see Pedaya, "Temurot."

26. I have modified Alter's translation somewhat.

27. Tikva Frymer-Kensky, "Zion, the Beloved Woman," in *In the Wake of the Goddesses: Women, Culture, and the Biblical Transformation of Pagan Myth* (New York: Fawcett Columbine, 1992), 174. As Frank S. Frick points out, the feminine designation is evidence that such social structures were considered to be "nurturers of their inhabitants . . . Although the dominant image of protection in the Hebrew Bible may be that of military might, the fundamental awareness of maternal care permeates the concept of cities as female." "Mother/Daughter (NRSV, Village) as Territory," in *Women in Scripture: A Dictionary of Named and Unnamed Women in the Hebrew Bible, the Apocryphal/Deuterocanonical Books, and the New Testament*, ed. Carol Meyers (Grand Rapids: Eerdmans, 2000), 532–33.

28. Elaine Follis goes so far as to claim that the poetic designation "daughter [of]" is "*hellenosemitic*" and that both Jerusalem and Athens, more or less concurrently (sixth–fifth centuries BCE), were so designated not just because it was a conventional collective personification of a city's inhabitants but also because these cities were "divinely favored, the centers of their respective civilizations, close to the heart of the God of Heaven. And both were regarded in figurative

language as the daughter of that high god." "The Holy City as Daughter," in *Directions in Biblical Poetry*, ed. Follis (Sheffield, UK: JSOT, 1987), 182.

29. Yehuda Halevi, "Tzion ha-lo tishali" or "Ode to Zion," in *The Penguin Book of Hebrew Verse*, ed. T. Carmi (Harmondsworth: Penguin, 1981), 18. For an elaboration of this subject, see DeKoven Ezrahi, *Booking Passage*, 40ff.

30. "In the case of banal, even dead, metaphor, the tension with the body of our knowledge disappears," says Paul Ricoeur. *The Rule of Metaphor: Multidisciplinary Studies of the Creation of Meaning in Language*, trans. Robert Czerny (Toronto: University of Toronto Press, 1977), 214. For a longer discussion of this in the context of Maimonides's poetics, see chapter 3, below.

31. For the designation of a diasporic place of worship as "mikdash me'at," or small temple, following Ezek. 11:16 and referring specifically to the Babylonian exile, see Megillah 29a.

32. Available at Sefaria: https://www.sefaria.org/Megillah.31b?lang=bi (accessed July 9, 2021).

33. There were Karaite "Mourners of Zion," *avelei tzion*, through the twelfth century (although remnants of the sect exist till this day in Israel, Turkey, the US, and Europe). On the Rambam's description of how one rends one's garments when approaching the site of the ruined Temple, and the likelihood that he met a few of the remaining *avelei tzion* when he visited Jerusalem, see Joel Kraemer, *Maimonides: The Life and World of One of Civilization's Greatest Minds* (New York: Doubleday, 2008), 138–39.

34. For Moshe Idel's elaboration of this phenomenon, see the prologue, above.

35. Among the most significant instances of messianic fervor accompanied by acts of pilgrimage that took place around the time of Maimonides were that of Yehuda Halevi and that of a group of European rabbis who went to the Holy Land a few years after Maimonides's death: "In the year 4971 (1211 CE), God inspired the rabbis of France and England to go to Jerusalem," writes Ibn Verga; "they numbered more than three hundred." Yitzhak Baer and Azriel Shochat, eds., *Shevet Yehudah* (Jerusalem: Bialik, 1946/47), 147.

36. Yakov Z. Meyer, "Parashat Vayakhel-Pekudei / Moses as Literary Contractor," *Haaretz*, March 12, 2015, http://www.haaretz.com/weekend/portion-of-the-week/.premium-1.646614; Yakov Z. Meyer, "Parashat Tzav / When Texts Supplant Sacrifice," *Haaretz*, March 26, 2015, http://www.haaretz.com/weekend/portion-of-the-week/.premium-1.649055.

37. The presumption that the prayer for the State of Israel that contains this reference was written by S. Y. Agnon has been refined by recent evidence, which suggests that he only did light editing on the text composed by Chief Rabbi Herzog. On this see below, chapter 5.

38. Agnon, Nobel Prize Banquet speech. This subject recurs several times in Agnon's fiction. See, for example, stories from the volume *Ha-esh ve-ha-'etzim* [The Fire and the Wood]. And see below, chapter 5.

Chapter One

1. Interview with Leah Goldberg, A. B. Yaffe, *Pegishot 'im Leah Goldberg* [Meetings with Leah Goldberg] (Tel Aviv: Tcherikover, 1984), 142. Please note that the English spelling of her forename as "Leah" or "Lea" is a convention of the specific translator; my preference, where not otherwise specified, is for "Leah."

2. Mark Twain, *Innocents Abroad* (Hartford, CT: American Publishing Company, 1869), https://www.gutenberg.org/files/3176/3176-h/3176-h.htm.

3. Textual and physical evidence coincides only from the first century BCE with remains of the so-called Second Temple that Herod rebuilt and refashioned—which is why, as we have

already seen, many scholars refer to three and not two temples. For a cogent journalist account of the history and status of the Temple Mount, after a violent incident on October 13, 2014, see Elon Gilad, editor and writer at *Haaretz*, "The History of the Temple Mount: Where Gods Collide," *Haaretz*, November 19, 2014, http://www.haaretz.com/archaeology/.premium-1.627324.

4. After the Bar Kokhba revolt, the so-called Third Jewish Revolt, there was a general ban on Jews living in Jerusalem, though the Talmud refers to a small "Holy Congregation in Jerusalem." Samuel Safrai, "Holy Congregation in Jerusalem," *Scripta Hierosolymitana* 23 (1972): 62–78. The last attempt in Roman antiquity to encourage Jews to rebuild their Temple was under the Emperor Julian; a year later, in 363 CE, just after such efforts had begun, the project came to an abrupt end when Julian was killed in battle. Yoram Tsafrir, "70–638: The Temple-less Mountain," in Grabar and Kedar, *Where Heaven and Earth Meet*, 86. In addition, early Church sources, including the account of the "Pilgrim from Bordeaux" and Jerome's commentaries, refer to a pilgrimage made by Jews once a year, probably on Tisha` B'av, a precedent for the Karaites, or *avelei tzion*, in the ninth to eleventh centuries. On the Jewish presence in Jerusalem in the first centuries of the Common Era, see Oded Irshai, "The Christian Appropriation of Jerusalem in the Fourth Century: The Case of the Bordeaux Pilgrim," *Jewish Quarterly Review* 99, no. 4 (Fall 2009): 465–86. Tsafrir adds that the "triumph of Christianity was expressed in neglect of the Temple Mount [in favor of the Holy Sepulchre], both in mind and in practice." Tsafrir, "70–638," 87.

5. For a description of Jerusalem at this time, and beyond, and the history of the relations between the Catholic Church and the Jews, see James Carroll, *Constantine's Sword: The Church and the Jews, A History* (New York: Mariner's Books, 2002).

6. See Michael Avi-Yonah, *The Madaba Mosaic Map* (Jerusalem: Israel Exploration Society, 1954), 18; Dan Bahat, "A New Suggestion for the Dating of the Madaba Map," *Ariel* 116 (1996): 74–77.

7. The Dome of the Rock was built around 691 and Al Aqsa mosque around 705. For the many iterations of this process, beginning with the "loose confederation of Arab clans and tribes" in the early period, through the Umayyad period leading to dominance by the Abbasid and into the Fatimid periods, see Andreas Kaplony, "635/638–1099: The Mosque of Jerusalem (Masjid Bayt Al-Maqdis)," in Grabar and Kedar, *Where Heaven and Earth Meet*, 100–131; see also Berger, *The Crescent*, 33ff.

8. Benjamin Z. Kedar and Denys Pringle, "1099–1187: The Lord's Temple (Templum Domini) and Solomon's Palace (Palatium Salomonis)," in Grabar and Kedar, *Where Heaven and Earth Meet*, 133. Berger writes that in medieval images of Christological scenes in or near the Temple that date from or represent the presence of the Crusaders, a salient structure "with an onion dome similar to that on the Dome of the Rock" features "a cross [that surmounts] that dome." This is meant to be a "reincarnation" of Solomon's temple, a "structure thought of as having existed during Jesus' time." Berger, *The Crescent*, 81.

9. Joshua Prawer, *The History of the Jews in the Latin Kingdom of Jerusalem* (Oxford: Clarendon Press, 1988), 142. See also below, chapter 3; Kraemer, *Maimonides*, 138ff., 515nn34, 35; and Maimonides, *Letters and Essays of Moses Maimonides*, ed. Isaac Shailat (Jerusalem: Ma`aliyot, 1987–88), 1:225; quoted in Kedar and Pringle, "1099–1187," 135–36, 398n5. The source is a letter published in 1600.

10. On these rulers, and their policies vis-à-vis the Jews and others as regards access to the Temple Mount, see essays by Michael Hamilton Burgoyne, Donald P. Little, and Amnon Cohen in Grabar and Kedar, *Where Heaven and Earth Meet*, 150–230.

11. See the coda, below.

12. For a summary of the evolving sanctity of the Mount of Olives, in tandem with sites and stories of Jesus's ascension in early Christianity, see Reiner, "Destruction," 149–51. "This tradition [the ascent of the *shekhina* to the Mount of Olives] assumed the pattern of pilgrimage and holy place no later than 326 CE, the year in which Helen, Constantine's mother, consecrated the Church of the Ascension on the site." Ibid., 150. For a contemporary dramatic invocation of the Mount of Olives as competing or complementary site, see the Hebrew film *Ha-har* (The Mountain), dir. Yaelle Kayam, 2015, https://www.imdb.com/title/tt4917622/.

13. DeKoven Ezrahi, *Booking Passage*, 237, 317n3.

14. Buried with her is the unfinished *plot* of her life with her long-deceased intended, Shraga. See ibid., 101. One of the first readers to call attention to this was Eddy Zemach, "Be-kefel dmut" [Doppelgänger], *Moznaym* 62, nos. 7–8 (1988): 43–49.

15. Although, as Elhanan Reiner argues, it appears that in dialogue with Christian practices, Jewish pilgrimage continued to the Mount of Olives instead of or en route to the Wailing Wall, it also appears that, "beginning at least in the 12th century, Jewish attitudes to the destruction changed completely . . . [Influenced probably by the customs of the Karaites], the ceremonies on the Mount of Olives were no longer observed, and mourning for the Temple was essentially the main, if not only, content of pilgrimage to Palestine at the time, as we see from Judah Halevi's poems written on his way there . . . The idea of the destruction as a cosmic event, cutting history into two, or more precisely, three, became the fundamental historical conception of traditional Judaism." "Overt Falsehood and Covert Truth: Christians, Jews and Holy Places in Twelfth Century Zion" [Heb.], *Zion* 63, no. 2 (1998): 152.

16. See DeKoven Ezrahi, *Booking Passage*, 33–35, 254nn3, 4, 254–55n5. On this see also the following sources: Eli Barnavi, "The Karaites: A Medieval Jewish Sect," *My Jewish Learning*, http://www.myjewishlearning.com/article/the-karaites-a-medieval-jewish-sect/3/ (accessed July 9, 2021); Reiner, "Overt Falsehood," 159; Reiner, "Destruction," 138–52; and Daniel al-Kumisi, "Appeal to the Karaites of the Dispersion to Come and Settle in Jerusalem," in *Karaite Anthology*, ed. Leon Nemoy (New Haven: Yale University Press, 1952), 37.

17. The esplanade of the Temple Mount is approximately 37.1 acres; see Grabar and Kedar, introduction to *Where Heaven and Earth Meet*, 9. For an elaboration of the history and ramifications of this site, see Amnon Cohen, "Haram-i Serif, the Temple Mount under Ottoman Rule," in ibid., 210–30; and Yitzhak Reiter and Jon Seligman, "1917 to the Present: Al-Haram al Sharif/ Temple Mount (Har Habayit) and the Western Wall," in ibid., 231–74; and see also Yehoshua Ben-Arieh, *'Ir be-re'i ha-tkufa: Yerushalayim ba-meah ha-19* [The City in Its Historical Context: Jerusalem in the Nineteenth Century] (Jerusalem: Yad Ben Tzvi, 1977), 27.

18. For a detailed account of the evolution of the Temple Mount and of the Waqf's history and authority from Ottoman times till the present, as well as the political ramifications of the current situation, see Yitzhak Reiter, *The Eroding Status-Quo: Power Struggles on the Temple Mount*, trans. Amy Erani (Jerusalem: Jerusalem Institute for Policy Research, 2017), especially 7–17 and 25–29; and see Dov Lieber, "Amid Temple Tumult, the Who, What and Why of Its Waqf Rulers," *Times of Israel*, July 20, 2017, https://www.timesofisrael.com/amid-temple-mount-tumult-the-who-what-and-why-of-its-waqf-rulers/. For an older account, see Michael Dumper, "Muslim Institutional Development in Jerusalem: The Role of Waqfs," *Journal of Islamic Jerusalem Studies* 2, no. 1 (Winter 1998): 21–38.

19. These videos were taken down soon after they were posted.

20. Here is the "timeline" of those events: "After Summer of War, an Autumn of Terror," *Haaretz*, December 25, 2014, https://www.haaretz.com/terror-timeline-1.5340133.

21. See Tomer Persico, "Why Rebuilding the Temple Would Be the End of Judaism As We Know It," *Haaretz*, November 13, 2014, http://www.haaretz.com/news/features/.premium -1.626327; Tomer Persico, "The Temple Mount and the End of Zionism," *Haaretz*, November 28, 2014, 8–10, http://www.haaretz.com/news/features/.premium-1.628929. And see Bradley Burston, "Hanukah in a Dark Israel: There's More Than One Way to Defile a Temple," *Haaretz*, December 16, 2014, 6, https://www.haaretz.com/.premium-hanukkah-in-a-dark-israel-1.5347517.

22. Nir Hasson, "Temple Mount Custodian Lost Control. It's in Israel's Interest to Assist," *Haaretz*, March 12, 2019, https://www.haaretz.com/israel-news/.premium-temple-mount-custodian-lost -control-it-s-in-israel-s-interest-to-aid-it-1.7018424. For a sample of articles written during the escalations on the Temple Mount in late winter and spring of 2019, see Amira Hass, "Beyond the Holiness of Israel's Security Forces," *Haaretz*, February 26, 2019, https://www.haaretz.com/opinion /.premium-beyond-the-holiness-of-israel-s-security-forces-1.6965282; Nir Hasson, "Why Israel and Jordan Are Clashing Over the Temple Mount," *Haaretz*, February 24, 2019, https://www.haaretz.com /israel-news/.premium-why-israel-and-jordan-are-clashing-over-the-temple-mount-1.6962043; Nir Hasson, "Temple Mount Tensions Continue as Israeli Police Officers Refuse to Remove Shoes at Disputed Prayer Site," *Haaretz*, March 9, 2019, https://www.haaretz.com/israel-news/.premium -israeli-police-refuse-to-remove-shoes-at-disputed-temple-mount-prayer-site-1.7002612.

23. Usually labeled the "Sacrifice of Isaac" in Christian art, prefiguring the Crucifixion, the topos has possibly its most compassionate visual rendering in Rembrandt's *The Sacrifice of Abraham*, with its focus on the pathos of the sacrificing father. Note the angel's embrace of Abraham, who, in turn, lovingly covers Isaac's eyes. The rock at the base of the etching anchors the three monotheistic religions: identified traditionally as the foundation rock on Mount Moriah that connects earthly and supernal realms, it forms the base of the altar in the Holy of Holies in Solomon's Temple and the centerpiece of the Dome of the Rock.

24. Genesis Rabbah was edited between the fourth and the sixth century in Palestine; *Mimesis* was written in Istanbul and first published in Switzerland in 1946.

25. Like generations of readers and students of the Bible, and as will be clear from the following analysis, I have been schooled in Robert Alter's literary approaches to the Bible, starting with *The Art of Biblical Narrative* (New York: Basic Books, 1981), followed by *The Art of Biblical Poetry* (New York: Basic Books, 1985), and culminating in his magisterial annotated translation of the entire Hebrew Bible (2019).

26. The reference in the Koran is to the sacrifice of an unspecified son; it is not clear but traditionally understood to be referring to Ishmael (there are, however, disagreements). See Ayaz Afsar, "A Comparative Study of the Intended Sacrifice of Isaac/Ishmael in the Bible and the Quran," *Islamic Studies* 46, no. 4 (Winter 2007): 483–98; and David J. Zucker, "Ishmael and Isaac: Parallel, Not Conflictual Lives," *Scandinavian Journal of the Old Testament* 26, no. 1 (2012): 1–11.

27. See Hillel Cohen, *Tarpa"t: Shnat ha-efes ba-sikhsukh ha-yehudi-'aravi* [1929: The Zero Hour of the Jewish-Arab Conflict] (Jerusalem: Keter Books, 2013), 108. For more detailed sources on this subject, see Ghulām Murtaza Azād, "Isra' and M'iraj: Night Journey and Ascension of Allah's Apostle Muhammad (S. A. W. S.)," *Islamic Studies* 22, no. 2 (Summer 1983): 63–80; and Christiane Gruber, "Al-Buraq," *Encyclopaedia of Islam*, 3rd ed. (Leiden: Brill, 2012), 40–46.

28. It should also be noted that the midrashic material that elaborates on such discussions would have been available to the compilers of the Koranic tradition; many Islamic scholars argue that the sources are rabbinic. See Norman Calder "From Midrash to Scripture: The Sacrifice of Abraham in Early Islamic Tradition," in *The Qur'an: Formative Interpretation*, ed. Andrew

Rippin (Aldershot, UK: Ashgate, 1999), 87. See also Mishael Caspi and T. Greene, eds., *Unbinding the Binding of Isaac* (Lanham, MD: University Presses of America, 2007), 72.

29. The debate over Aristotle's definition of comedy among classicists and theorists of comedy and humor is an ongoing, and lively, one. See, for example, Leon Golden, "Aristotle on Comedy," *Journal of Aesthetics and Art Criticism* 42, no. 3 (Spring 1984): 283–90, http://www.jstor.org /stable/429709.

30. The connection is, however, very tenuous. "Though traditional exegesis," writes Robert Alter, "supported by the reference to the Mount of the Lord at the end of the tale, identifies this with Jerusalem, the actual location remains in doubt." Alter, *Hebrew Bible*, 1:72.

31. Again, it is important to emphasize that the "literal" readings I am proposing here and in the next chapter on the Song of Songs are actually *literary* readings meant to unearth the tropes and rhetorical patterns that prevail in both texts from under the parabolic readings to which they have been subjected. It is these parabolic or allegorical readings that have in turn been literalized and recruited for historical exigencies.

32. See Hava Schwartz, "The Return to the Monument: The Looming Absence of the Temple," *Israel Studies Review: An Interdisciplinary Journal* 32, no. 1 (Summer 2017): 48–66; Rafi Greenberg and Yonatan Mizrahi, "Mi-Silwan le-Har ha-bayit: Ḥafirot arkhiyologiot ke-emtza'i li-shlita. Hitpatḥuyot—bi-kfar Silwan u-va-'ir ha-'atika shel yerushalayim be-shnat 2012" [From Silwan to the Temple Mount: Archaeological Digs as Means of Control. Developments in the Village of Silwan and the Old City of Jerusalem in 2012], *Emek Shaveh* (2013).

33. Even here, of course, the notion of the "original" Hebrew Bible is very fraught. The earliest extant version of many of the books of the Bible is the Dead Sea Scrolls.

34. J. William Whedbee, *The Bible and the Comic Vision* (Minneapolis: Fortress Press, 2002), 7; Northrop Frye, *Fables of Identity: Studies in Poetic Mythology* (New York: Harcourt, Brace and World, 1963), 25. I am grateful to Avivah Zornberg for first calling Whedbee's work to my attention. For a similar, though somewhat abridged, version of the argument presented here, see DeKoven Ezrahi, "Literary Archaeology at the Temple Mount: Recovering the Comic Version of the Sacrifice of Isaac," *MLA* (July 2016), https://profession.mla.org/literary-archaeology-at-the -temple-mount-recovering-the-comic-version-of-the-sacrifice-of-isaac/.

35. For reference to "Isaac's ashes," see Lev. Rabbah 36:5; Taanit 16a; see also Jon Levinson, *The Death and Resurrection of the Beloved Son* (New Haven: Yale University Press, 1995), 192–99.

36. Of the many pictorial representations of Christian appropriation of the akeda as prefiguring the Crucifixion, there is at least one, I believe, that gestures to the preempted sacrifice: Rembrandt's 1655 etching, called, appropriately, *The Sacrifice of Abraham*, with Isaac's eyes covered by Abraham's own hand even as the compassionate angel forestalls the deed by holding the same arm. See figure 1 on p. 34.

37. Terry Eagleton, *Sweet Violence: The Idea of the Tragic* (Oxford: Blackwell, 2003).

38. Scott Cutler Shershow, *Laughing Matters: The Paradox of Comedy* (Amherst: University of Massachusetts Press, 1986), 20. For an elaboration of this argument, see DeKoven Ezrahi, "After Such Knowledge, What Laughter?," *Yale Journal of Criticism* 14, no. 1 (2001): 287–313.

39. Following upon midrashic elaborations on lacunae or inconsistencies in the text, modern scholars see possible traces of a suppressed tragedy—the "actual" sacrifice of Isaac—in the Hebrew Bible itself. They do not, however, go so far as to acknowledge the ensuing comedy. See, for example, Michael Fishbane, *Inner-Biblical Exegesis: Biblical Interpretation in Ancient Israel* (Oxford: Clarendon Press, 1985), 182.

40. In his early work on biblical narrative, Robert Alter developed the insights of former biblical scholars, including Martin Buber and Franz Rosenzweig, through their translations, into the significance of repetitions of a "leitmotif" in biblical narratives. Alter notes the "network of connections," for example, between the "life-threatening trial in the wilderness [that] first occurs to Abraham's older son, Ishmael (Genesis 21), then to his younger son, Isaac, whom Abraham seems commanded to slaughter (Genesis 22)"—and of course the miraculous intervention that saves both their lives. By the same token, the "Leitwort" or word that appears repeatedly, often in different constructions, signals a deeper thematic thrust. *Art of Biblical Narrative*, 180–82.

41. For bibliography and references to instances of laughter connected to Isaac's life, see David J. Zucker, "Isaac: A Life of Bitter Laughter," *Jewish Bible Quarterly* 40, no. 2 (2012): 105–10, http://jbq.jewishbible.org/assets/Uploads/402/jbq_402_isaaclaughter.pdf. Those readings that do note the laughter usually ascribe it to an ironic, rather than a comic, reflex.

42. Alter, *Hebrew Bible*, 1:55.

43. Whedbee, *The Bible and the Comic Vision*, 76.

44. Alter, *Hebrew Bible*, 1:55.

45. Alter, *Hebrew Bible*, 1:58.

46. This is also a powerful example of what Alter calls "narration through dialogue." *Art of Biblical Narrative*, 69.

47. Whedbee, *The Bible and the Comic Vision*, 76. Meir Shalev says that the incredulous laughter of Sarah and Abraham is the first—and also the *last*—laughter in the Bible. I do not agree that it is the last, but certainly laughter is the dominant motif in this narrative. It is, says Shalev, also the first instance of "Jewish humor"—humor born of danger. Shalev, *Reshit* [In the Beginning] (Tel Aviv: Am Oved, 2008), 213.

48. See Philip Roth, "The Conversion of the Jews," in *Goodbye, Columbus and Five Short Stories* (New York: Vintage/Random House, 1987), 137–59. And see below.

49. Alter, *Hebrew Bible*, 1:69.

50. See Alter's explication of the frequent and powerful use of conjunctives such as "and" in the paratactic structure of the Bible, which he renders faithfully in his own translations. Alter, *The Art of Bible Translation* (Princeton: Princeton University Press, 2019), 4–7, 27–31.

51. Northrop Frye, *Anatomy of Criticism* (New York: Atheneum, 1968), 179; quoted in Whedbee, *The Bible and the Comic*, 84.

52. Each of these phrases, each of these lacunae that Erich Auerbach taught us was "fraught with background," has, of course, generated reams of commentary. *Mimesis: The Representation of Reality in Western Literature*, trans. Willard R. Trask (Princeton: Princeton University Press, 1953), 12. My own "naïve," literary approach attempts to stay close to the text by consciously blotting out centuries of interpretation.

53. See Alter's comment on this: "The meaning of the verb here is clearly sexual, implying either fondling or actual sexual 'play.' It immediately follows the name 'Isaac,' in which the same verbal root is transparently inscribed . . . Perhaps there is some suggestion that the generally passive Isaac is a man of strong physical appetites." Alter, *Hebrew Bible*, 1:90.

54. Whedbee assures us that God always has the "last laugh." *The Bible and the Comic*, 76. This could be a version of the cynical Yiddish proverb, *Der mensch tracht, un gott lacht*. The version of divine laughter that I am espousing here is far more benign.

55. See René Girard, *The Scapegoat*, trans. Yvonne Freccero (Baltimore: Johns Hopkins University Press, 1986). An important distinction should be made between this principle of substitution as essential to the topos of sacrifice and what Giorgio Agamben calls "homo

sacer"—common life that is deemed universally "sacred" and therefore "may be killed but not sacrificed." *Homo Sacer: Sovereign Power and Bare Life*, trans. Daniel Heller-Roazen (Stanford: Stanford University Press, 1998), 114–15.

56. Spiegel, *Last Trial*, 68–69. On the idea of "temurah" and Spiegel's essay, as part of a seminal essay on the akeda in Israeli literature, see Ruth Kartun-Blum, *Profane Scriptures: Reflections on the Dialogue with the Bible in Modern Hebrew Poetry* (Cincinnati: Hebrew Union College Press, 1999), 21, 92n7.

57. As we will see later, the talmudic term "mi-neged" or "ke-neged," which literally means "across from" or "in opposition to," conveys in the rabbinic and postrabbinic imagination both distance and substitution. See below, chapter 5 and coda.

58. If the Jews have a credo or a doxology it is this. See DeKoven Ezrahi, "After Such Knowledge," 306–7.

59. Kafka, "Abraham." From a letter to Robert Klopstock, Franz Kafka, *Briefe 1902–1924* (Frankfurt: S. Fischer Verlag, 1966), 332. Translated as "Abraham," in *The Basic Kafka*, introduction by Erich Heller (New York: Washington Square Press, 1979), 172. Kafka shared his thoughts on Kierkegaard with a few other friends, including Max Brod.

60. Although Kafka does not spell it out in this context, the figure of beggar as would-be Messiah, with his sources in the Talmud, appears frequently in modern Jewish literature. See S. Y. Agnon's novel *Bilvav yamim* and his short story "Lefi ha-tza'ar ha-sakhar," and the discussions of this figure in DeKoven Ezrahi, *Booking Passage*, 89, 274n13; and see Galili Shachar, *Gufim ve-shemot: kri'ot be-sifrut yehudit ḥadasha* [Bodies and Names: Readings in Modern Jewish Literature] (Tel Aviv: Am Oved, 2016), 128–31, 249–54. See also the epilogue to Shachar's book, specifically on the akeda, "Teshuvot Avraham" [Abraham's Answers], 298–335.

61. John Caputo, *Against Ethics: Contributions to a Poetics of Obligation with Constant Reference to Deconstruction* (Bloomington: Indiana University Press, 1993), ix, 15, 21.

62. For a longer discussion of Caputo, Kafka, and Derrida in the context of the akeda, see DeKoven Ezrahi, "From Auschwitz to the Temple Mount: Binding and Unbinding the Israeli Narrative," in *After Testimony: The Ethics and Aesthetics of Holocaust Narrative*, ed. Susan Suleiman, Jakob Lothe, and James Phelan (Columbus: Ohio State University Press, 2012), 291–313, especially 302–10.

63. Robert Arnold Darrow, "Kierkegaard, Kafka, and the Strength of 'The Absurd' in Abraham's Sacrifice of Isaac," MA thesis, Wayne State University, 2005, https://corescholar.libraries .wright.edu/etd_all/18/.

64. Gilles Deleuze and Felix Guattari, "Kafka: Toward a Minor Literature: The Components of Expression," *New Literary History* 16, no. 3 (Spring 1985): 605–6. See also Deleuze and Guattari, *Kafka: Toward a Minor Literature* (Minneapolis: University of Minnesota Press, 1986). And see Roberto Calasso, *K*, trans. Geoffrey Brock (New York: Alfred A. Knopf, 2005), 300–301.

65. Jacques Derrida, *The Gift of Death*, trans. David Wills (Chicago: University of Chicago Press, 1995), 85–88, emphasis mine.

66. Ibid., 85.

67. Carey Perloff, "Tragedy Today," *PMLA* 129, no. 4 (October 2014): 833. For a more specific connection with the cultural context of our discussion, see Perloff's discussion of photos of atrocities in the Middle East, including from Iraq, which prompt her to wonder "how we [might] apply the ethical arguments of Greek tragedy to shed light, for example, on the divisive tribalism of the contemporary Middle East?" In this context, where each ethnicity "believes it has the prior claim and the deepest sense of victimization, is the sacrifice of an individual to this cycle of

vendetta tragic or foolish? This is the question of the modern Elektra . . . We long for the catharsis of tragedy, for the quest for meaning that defines Greek dramaturgy" (831–33).

68. Derrida, *Gift*, 88.

69. Quoted in Calasso, *K*, 300–301.

70. Maimonides, *Guide of the Perplexed*, I:18, p. 44.

71. Ibid., pp. 44–45.

72. Ibid., p. 45. On this, see below, chapter 3. Hebrew: "Ein hefresh bein heyot ha-ish be-merkaz ha-aretz o ba-ʿelyon she-ba-galgal ha-teshiʿi (ilu haya efshar)—she-hu lo yirhak min ha-shem hena ve-lo yikrav lo sham." *Sefer moreh ha-nevokhim*, trans. Rabbi Yehuda Ibn Tibbon (Jerusalem: Monson, 1960), I, chap. 18, p. 35.

73. For a brief discussion in Hebrew of the paradigms of war (*milḥama*) and catastrophe (*ḥurban*), from biblical through modern iterations, see Sidra [DeKoven] Ezrahi, "Ha-milḥama ba-sifrut ha-ʿivrit" [War and Catastrophe in Jewish Culture], in *Zman Yehudi ḥadash: Tarbut Yehudit be-ʿidan ḥiloni* [New Jewish Time: Jewish Culture in a Secular Epoch], vol. 3, ed. Dan Miron and Hannan Hever (Jerusalem: Keter, 2007), 206–9. One of the first critical readings of the history of Hebrew lamentation literature, and its modern iterations, including the poetry of Shaul Tchernichovsky, is Alan Mintz's *Hurban: Responses to Catastrophe in Hebrew Literature* (New York: Columbia University Press, 1984).

74. "On the Slaughter," in Carmi, *Penguin Book of Hebrew Verse*, 512–13. Mintz's long discussion of Bialik's Kishinev poems ignited a new scholarly interest in the subject. *Hurban*, 129–54. See also the Hebrew volume that "revisits" Bialik's long poem "In the City of the Slaughter" on the centenary of its original publication: *Be-ʿir ha-harega—Bikur meʿuḥar bimlot meah shana la-poema shel Bialik*, ed. Michael Gluzman, Hannan Hever, and Dan Miron (Tel Aviv: Resling, 2005). For a more recent discussion of the events themselves as well as responses in the press and in Jewish/Hebrew literature and culture, see Steven J. Zipperstein, *Pogrom: Kishinev and the Tilt of History* (New York: Liveright, 2018).

75. Carmi, *Penguin Book of Hebrew Verse*, 565. Hebrew: "Yerusha," *Shoshanat ha-ruḥot* (Tel Aviv: Ha-kibbutz ha-meuchad, 1960), 28.

76. Ruth Kartun-Blum's short book on this subject was one of the earliest and covered a wide range of Hebrew writers, including Gouri, Yitzhak Lamdan, Nathan Alterman, T. Carmi, Tuvia Ruebner, Amir Gilboa, David Avidan, S. Yizhar, and Avot Yeshurun; the illustrations by Menashe Kadishman give a glimpse of the presence of the akeda also in the plastic arts in contemporary Israel. *Profane Scriptures*, 15–62.

77. Hanoch Levin, "The Akeda (The Binding)," trans. Donny Inbar, in *Queen of Bathtub* (Tel Aviv: Cameri Theater, 1970), http://www.sjsu.edu/people/victoria.harrison/courses/JWSS111/s1/Hanoch-Levin-Binding-and-Creation.pdf. On this, and on the other version of an akeda poem in that play, spoken by Isaac in his "grave," see Kartun-Blum, *Profane Scriptures*, 55–58.

78. Yitzhak Laor, "Ha-metumtam ha-ze Yitzhak," "Ha-metumtam ha-ze Yitzhak (Girsa meʿuḥeret)," *Shirim 1974–1992* (Tel Aviv: Ha-kibbutz ha-meuchad, 2002), 278, 120. English translation is my own.

79. Kartun-Blum, *Profane Scriptures*, 5, 91n6.

80. As Grossman's "Stabat mater," Gluzman claims, this novel embodies a concept of Jewish/Israeli history that is "korbanit be-mahuta," that is, sacrificial/martyrological in its essence. Michael Gluzman, "Im lo tihiyeh yerushalayim: ʿal Isha boraḥat mi-besora" [If Jerusalem Ceases to Exist: On *To the End of the Land* by David Grossman], *Haaretz*, May 5, 2008, https://www.haaretz.co.il/literature/1.1322595. Iris Milner's well-argued position is that even as it ostensibly

resists the "militaristic agenda and rhetoric," including the topos of the akeda, the novel remains within that inescapable paradigm. Like other literary works, she claims, Grossman's novel "'perform[s]' post-trauma" that produces "an aporia, a hole in the symbolic order." And yet Milner regards Avram and Ora as typical representatives of a "previous generation of 'Isaacs'—sons and daughters brought to the altar by a previous generation of 'Abrahams' . . . The former Isaac [the character Avram] now becomes the father of one." "Sacrifice and Redemption in *To the End of the Land*," *Hebrew Studies* 54 (2013): 324–25, 331–32. One could argue that the trauma paradigm has competed with and in some quarters replaced the akeda paradigm in contemporary Israeli culture; both, however, rhyme in reflecting Gouri's conclusion that the sons are born in every generation with a "knife in their hearts."

81. Yael Feldman, *The Glory and the Agony: Isaac's Sacrifice and National Narrative* (Stanford: Stanford University Press, 2010), 14, 315–17.

82. David Grossman, *To the End of the Land*, trans. Jessica Cohen (New York: Knopf, 2010), 62–63.

83. Ibid., 246.

84. See Yehuda Amichai's presentation of Jerusalem as place-time: "I've come back to this city where names / are given to distances as if to human beings / and the numbers are not of bus-routes / but: 70 After, 1917, 500 / B.C., Forty-eight. These are the lines / you really travel on." "Jerusalem 1967," no. 2, trans. Stephen Mitchell, *Poetry of Yehuda Amichai*, 81.

85. Mount Herzl is the military cemetery, with its rows of identical graves of the young soldiers who gave up their lives for the country; Yad Vashem, the memorial to the dead in the Holocaust, is perched on a hilltop that occludes the traces in the valley below of the Arab village of Deir Yassin, many of whose inhabitants were massacred in 1948. One guide at Yad Vashem lost his job because he pointed this out to a group of yeshiva students in 2009.

86. Quoted in Kartun-Blum, *Profane Scriptures*, 92n1, from Mordechai Omer, *Upon One of the Mountains: Jerusalem in Israeli Art* (Jerusalem: Genia Schreiber Gallery, 1988), 127.

87. Kadishman indeed had a profound fascination with the substitution motif of the akeda, having sculpted and painted many rams that signify the akeda as the human sacrifice that did not happen. His artwork also graces the cover of the present volume; the Wailing Wall covered with splashes of color reflects our primary argument: namely, that it is distance from the sacred that will save us all from the terrible fires of sacrifice—and that art, mimesis, is itself a form of distancing.

88. DeKoven Ezrahi, "From Auschwitz to the Temple Mount," 303–4.

89. A. B. Yehoshua, *Mr. Mani*, trans. Hillel Halkin (San Diego: Harcourt Brace, 1993), 318. There are other versions of this Mani's death in the novel.

90. A. B. Yehoshua, "Mr. Mani and the Akeda," trans. Rivka Hadari and Amnon Hadari, *Judaism* 50 (Winter 2001): 61–65.

91. As we saw in the introduction, in rabbinic Hebrew, the word *makom*, or Place, came to refer to God.

92. What I identify as the comic undercurrent of the akeda in *Tmol shilshom* is, however, rare also in Agnon's oeuvre, as can be seen by comparing it with a pictorial representation of the akeda in the home of the narrator of his long story "Hadom ve-kiseh" [Footstool and Chair], published posthumously. In this rambling and rather surreal narrative, the narrator and his daughter are in the throes of leaving their rented lodgings when an old "akeda" painting commemorating a historical catastrophe is uncovered hanging on the wall, though somewhat

damaged: what is missing is the ram. This small vignette actually creates an ekphrastic represen-tation of the element that has been removed, as we have seen, in most renderings of the akeda: i.e., the "happy end." S. Y. Agnon, *Lifnim min ha-ḥoma* [Within the Wall] (Jerusalem: Schocken, 1975), 128–30. See below, chapter 5.

93. Dan Pagis, "Brothers," in *Points of Departure*, bilingual ed., trans. Stephen Mitchell, introduction by Robert Alter (Philadelphia: Jewish Publication Society, 1981), 5. I have emended the translation somewhat. Pagis died in 1986; a posthumous collection of his poetry, including a hitherto unpublished manuscript of prose-poems, was published in 1991. On the absence of the akeda topos in his writing, and the "message" of the nonsectarian humanity of the First Family, see DeKoven Ezrahi, "Dan Pagis—Out of Line: A Poetics of Decomposition," *Prooftexts* 10, special anniversary issue (May 1990): 335–63.

94. Pagis, "Written in Pencil in the Sealed Railway-Car," in *Points of Departure*, 23.

95. Cyclical reading of this poem is common practice at memorial sites like Yad Vashem and on memorial occasions such as Holocaust Remembrance Day. That this is also educational policy has been repeatedly confirmed for me on those occasions when I have led seminars for teachers at Yad Vashem; asked to recite the poem, these teachers, like their students, inevitably attach the last words to the first—even though they cannot parse grammatically—clearly resisting the open-ended appeal with its stark lack of closure.

96. Salo W. Baron, "Newer Emphases in Jewish History," *Jewish Social Studies* 25, no. 4 (October 1963): 235–48.

97. Philip Roth, *Goodbye Columbus* (New York: Houghton Mifflin, 1959), 140–42, 146, 155, 157–58. The story was first published in the *Paris Review* in 1958. For a discussion of the resonances of the akeda in the enacted scene as well as in the name of the teacher, Mr. *Bind*er, see Theoharis C. Theoharis, "For with God All Things Are Possible: Philip Roth's 'The Conversion of the Jews,'" *Journal of the Short Story in English* 32 (Spring 1999): 2–6.

98. For a more comprehensive discussion of Roth and of the "urban congregation" he helped to celebrate in America, see DeKoven Ezrahi, "Philip Roth: Writing the American Jewish Century," in *Makers of Jewish Modernity: Thinkers, Artists, Leaders, and the World They Made*, ed. Jacques Picard, Jacques Revel, Michael Steinberg, and Idith Zertal (Princeton: Princeton University Press, 2016), 597–612. For an excerpt, see https://www.tabletmag.com/sections/arts-letters/articles/in-defense-of-philip-roth.

99. Woody Allen, "The Scrolls." This is an excerpt from the complete text, which was first published in the *New Republic*, August 31, 1974, https://newrepublic.com/article/113899/scrolls-woody-allen.

100. Oh, God said to Abraham, "Kill me a son."
   Abe said, "Man, you must be puttin' me on."
   God said, "No." Abe say, "What?"
   God say, "You can do what you want, Abe, but
   The next time you see me comin', you better run."
   Well, Abe said, "Where d'you want this killin' done?"
   God said, "Out on Highway 61 . . ."
      https://www.youtube.com/watch?v=8hr3Stnk8_k.

101. For an elaboration of this argument, see DeKoven Ezrahi, "America as the Theatre of Jewish Comedy: From Sholem Aleichem to Grace Paley," *Studia Judaica* 13 (2005): 74–82; and, specifically on Sholem Aleichem, see DeKoven Ezrahi, *Booking Passage*, 103–30.

102. Ephraim of Bonn is the most familiar example of a survivor-paytan (liturgical poet) whose "akeda" is also a typological witness to the massacre he survived in the town of York in 1190. See the poem itself with commentary in Spiegel, *Last Trial*, 139–52.

Chapter Two

The quotation in the chapter's title is from Song of Songs 6:4. *The Song of Songs, A New Translation*, by Ariel Bloch and Chana Bloch, with an introduction ("In the Garden of Delights") by Chana Bloch and commentary by Ariel Bloch, afterword by Robert Alter (New York: Random House, 1995), 93. Unless otherwise indicated, I am using this translation throughout—and I dedicate this chapter to the memory of Chana Bloch.

1. From the website of the Judaica Collection at the Yale University Library: "This calligraphic masterpiece, 11-inch-high piece of parchment . . . contains the entire biblical Song of Songs in Hebrew micrography (written in tiny letters). It is signed by the Lithuanian artist/scribe, Baruch ben Shemariah, 1794. It renders the entire Song of Songs as a work of art, in letters that are at once text and illumination. Shir (song) is the central word around which the text revolves. The crown, labeled 'crown of kingship' perhaps refers to the Song's opening statement that its author is King Solomon." November 5, 2013, http://campuspress.yale.edu/judaicacollection/2013/11/05/song-of-songs/.

2. Ariel Bloch elaborates on this in his scientific commentary on the Song. Ariel Bloch and Chana Bloch, trans., *The Song of Songs: A New Translation*, 158. For an earlier iteration of some of the arguments offered in this chapter, see DeKoven Ezrahi, " 'To what shall I compare thee?,' " 225–26.

3. Admittedly, I am rather slyly referring here to S. Y. Agnon's posthumous work *A City in Its Fullness* [*'Ir u-meloah*], which will be discussed in chapter 5. My argument there is that contemporary Jerusalem and Agnon's native Polish town of Buczacz actually rhyme in their many iterations in his prose—and that they are both nonpolitical spaces. In chapter 4, I will argue that the Song of Songs is a constitutive but enigmatic intertext in many of Agnon's iconic stories.

4. I can attest that teaching the Song of Songs "naïvely," that is, without its exegetical resonances, is virtually impossible in any modern Hebrew-speaking environment; whenever I ask my Israeli students, who come from backgrounds ranging from secular to ultra-Orthodox, to read and relate to the uninflected text, most of them are simply unable to rid their minds of such deeply ingrained voices. By the same token, as we shall see, the verses and properties of the Song permeate the external landscape, as well as the ritual, scientific, and popular cultures—especially poetry and song—in contemporary Israel.

5. See my discussions of these repercussions in *Booking Passage*, 144–45, 261n44; and in " 'To what shall I compare thee?,' " 223. It is possible to read Lamentations as the default version of the flourishing city depicted in Song of Songs, a dystopic version of functional social order. For a whimsical, Marxist-inspired version of this insight, see Roland Boer, *Knocking on Heaven's Door: The Bible and Popular Culture* (London: Routledge, 1999), 125.

6. Ilana Pardes, *The Song of Songs: A Biography* (Princeton: Princeton University Press, 2019).

7. Ibid., 1.

8. Alter, "Afterword," in A. Bloch and C. Bloch, *Song of Songs*, 131. See also Alter's earlier discussion of the Song in *Art of Biblical Poetry*, 185–203; and the short introduction to his own translation, "To the Reader," in *Strong as Death Is Love: The Song of Songs, Ruth, Esther, Jonah, and Daniel* (New York: W. W. Norton, 2015).

9. See Yair Zakovitch's argument, below, for a more dynamic intrabiblical dialogue between Song of Songs and certain passages in the prophetic books and Proverbs. This resonance also informs the textual connections drawn between the Song and the revelation at Sinai in the rabbinic tradition; see discussion of Boyarin, below. On the iterations of the "dove" image in the midrashic literature, see Pardes, *Song of Songs*, 31–35.

10. "Like the hyperbolic reference to an ivory tower in 7:5," such images "symbolize workmanship of the highest order, evoking a master architect," writes Ariel Bloch. But they also corroborate the relatively late dating and the cultural sources of the entire Song: "Since there is nothing in the Bible about a tower of David . . . this may be yet another indication of elements of popular folklore in the Song." A. Bloch and C. Bloch, *Song of Songs*, 172–73. On the tower image in other verses in the Song, and the different avenues of interpretation that such an image invites, see below.

11. C. Bloch, "In the Garden of Delights," introduction to A. Bloch and C. Bloch, *Song of Songs*, 10–11. On Solomonic references in the Song that are both biblical and extrabiblical in origin, see also A. Bloch, commentary, A. Bloch and C. Bloch, *Song of Songs*, 190.

12. See the introduction above.

13. The other scrolls are Ruth, Lamentations, Ecclesiastes, and Esther.

14. Private communication, January 12, 2018. For an articulation of the idea originally floated by Chaim Rabin, see Abraham Mariaselvam, *The Song of Songs and Ancient Tamil Love Poems: Poetry and Symbolism* (Rome: Editrice Pontificio Istituto Biblico, 1988), especially part 1, 26–86, part 3, 153–239, and appendix 1, 279–86.

15. See Chana Bloch and Ariel Bloch's summary of the scholarship based on linguistic and stylistic peculiarities of the text. "In the Garden of Delights," 15, 19, 21–27. Ariel Bloch cites material that "is clearly Midrashic in nature" and could "certainly have left its imprint on the Song, even though the Midrash itself was committed to writing only at a much later date." A. Bloch and C. Bloch, *Song of Songs*, 161. As we shall see, this remains a dynamic investigation within the scholarly community.

16. Talmy Givón, "The Drift from VSO to SVO in Biblical Hebrew: The Pragmatics of Tense-Aspect," in *Mechanics of Syntactic Change*, ed. Charles N. Li (Austin: University of Texas Press, 1977), 188; cited in Chana Kronfeld, *On the Margins of Modernism: Decentering Literary Dynamics* (Berkeley: University of California Press, 1996), 99.

17. Alter, "Afterword," in A. Bloch and C. Bloch, *Song of Songs*, 119.

18. See Ariel Bloch's discussion of this trope, A. Bloch and C. Bloch, *Song of Songs*, 166–68. Yair Zakovitch takes issue with this translation, insisting that the reference is indeed to a veil, and not to a plait of hair; he goes on to elaborate on the "veiled" or slantwise nature of many of the encounters between the would-be lovers. *The Song of Songs: Riddle of Riddles*, trans. Valerie Carr Zakovitch (London: T&T Clark, 2018), 67–68.

19. The saying, commonly attributed to H. N. Bialik, that "reading in translation is like kissing the bride through a veil," was probably adopted from a European folk adage. Bialik's statement was actually somewhat different—and may reflect his own occasional mixing of kinship and eros: "whoever knows Judaism through translation is like a person who kisses his mother through a handkerchief." H. N. Bialik, "Nation and Language" [Heb.], in *Devarim she-be-'al peh* [Oral Tradition] (Tel Aviv: Dvir, 1935), 1:15–20, http://benyehuda.org/bialik/dvarim02.html.

20. For a whimsical articulation of the gender-inflected nature of the language, see Hebrew poet Yona Wallach's allusion to Hebrew as a "sex maniac." "Hebrew," in *Wild Light*, trans. Linda Zisquit (New York: Sheep Meadow Press, 1997), 6–8.

21. Pardes, *Song of Songs*, 148–50.

22. See Richard N. Soulen, "The *Wasfs* of the Song of Songs and Hermeneutic," *Journal of Biblical Literature* 86, no. 2 (June 1967): 183–90, https://www.jstor.org/stable/3263272. After surveying the various scholarly attempts to read Song of Songs as a version, or perversion, of the *wasf* form, Soulen concludes in the spirit of the Song: "In short, a *wasf* is not a thought problem 'easily solved': it is a celebration of the joys of life and love and at the same time an invitation to share that joy. Only from this perspective is the intent of the poet preserved and the object of love not made grotesque and ludicrous." Ibid., 190.

23. C. Bloch, "In the Garden of Delights," 3–4.

24. Alter, "Afterword," in A. Bloch and C. Bloch, *Song of Songs*, 121. Alter's own translation, as part of his monumental translation of the entire Hebrew Bible, differs from that of the Blochs but is indebted to it. As I have already indicated, in this chapter, unless otherwise specified, I am using not Alter's but the Blochs' translation.

25. Pardes, *Song of Songs*, 2.

26. "The . . . mountains mentioned in this verse are symbols of inaccessibility and danger, and at the same time of majestic, primeval beauty. But the Shulamite and her lover are not in the mountains of Lebanon, close to the dwellings of lions and leopards. This fantasy scene is not unlike the one in 8:5, where the two of them are 'coming up' together from the wilderness." A. Bloch and C. Bloch, *Song of Songs*, 174. In the reference to Ein Gedi, Alter suggests that the reader remains "a little unsure" whether the image of the lover as a "sheaf of henna blossoms / in the vineyards of Ein Gedi" (1:14) implies that the "blossoms are merely from Ein Gedi . . . or whether, metaphor exfoliating into literal landscape, that is where the lovers embrace." Alter, "Afterword," in A. Bloch and C. Bloch, *Song of Songs*, 121.

27. The full verse, in the Bloch translation, is "Kiss me, make me drunk with your kisses! / Your sweet loving / is better than wine" ("Yishakeini mi-neshikot pihu / ki tovim dodekha mi-yayin"). Ibid., 44–45. Here the elision is between kissing and wine pouring/drinking. See A. Bloch and C. Bloch, *Song of Songs*, 137.

28. Alter, "Afterword," in A. Bloch and C. Bloch, *Song of Songs*, 119 (see above). In *The Art of Biblical Poetry*, Alter enumerates some of the "poetic principles" that shape the Song: "narrativity," "originality" of metaphoric invention, and "innovative imagery" as well as creative uses of parallelism hardly found elsewhere in the Hebrew Bible. *Art of Biblical Poetry*, 185–93.

29. In her analysis and critique of feminist interpretations of the Song, Fiona C. Black goes so far as to consider some of the imagery under the rubric of the grotesque. "Unlikely Bedfellows: Allegorical and Feminist Readings of Song of Songs 7:1–8," in *The Song of Songs: A Feminist Companion to the Bible*, 2nd series, ed. Athalya Brenner and Carole R. Fontaine (Sheffield, UK: Sheffield Academic Press, 2000), 120ff. One other scholar, Leroy Waterman, went so far as to "conclude that the purpose of the Song was to humiliate Solomon by depicting him as . . . rebuffed by a humble if not downright ugly girl from the north . . . to create ridiculous parallels to a ridiculous physical appearance." Soulen, "Wasfs," 185.

30. A. Bloch and C. Bloch, *Song of Songs*, 153; see also Ariel Bloch's discussion of the verb *d-m-h* on 143; and, for other examples, see Song, 2:17, 8:14. This is what Alter calls "the artifice of metaphorical representation," by which the poet "call[s] our attention to his exploitation of similitude." Alter, *Art of Biblical Poetry*, 193.

31. Alter, *Art of Biblical Poetry*, 195.

32. C. Bloch, "In the Garden of Delights," 19.

33. Phyllis Trible, "Depatriarchalizing in Biblical Interpretation," *Journal of the American Academy of Religion* 41, no. 1 (March 1973): 30–31. See Pardes's discussion of the pathbreaking feminist readings of Trible and others. *Song of Songs*, 163–66.

34. Carol Meyers, "Gender Imagery in the Songs of Songs," *Hebrew Annual Review* 10 (1986): 217, 220; essay reprinted in Brenner and Fontaine, *Feminist Companion to the Song of Songs*, 197–212. On the subject of the mother's house, see also Phyllis Trible, *God and the Rhetoric of Sexuality* (Philadelphia: Fortress Press, 1978), 158.

35. Franz Rosenzweig, *Star of Redemption*, trans. William W. Hallo (Boston: Beacon Press, 1964), 201. Quoted in Ilana Pardes, *Agnon's Moonstruck Lovers: The Song of Songs in Israeli Culture* (Seattle: University of Washington Press, 2014), 65.

36. Zali Gurevitch, *Kol Dodim: 'Al leshon ha-ahava shel shir ha-shirim* [The Sound of Love: On Erotic Language in the Song of Songs] (Tel Aviv: Bavel, 2013), 120–21.

37. Yair Zakovitch, *Shir ha-shirim, mikra le-yisrael: perush mada'i la-mikra* [Song of Songs, Israel's Scriptures: Scientific Interpretation of the Bible] (Tel Aviv and Jerusalem: Am Oved and Magnes Press, 1992). The entire volume presents an excellent balance of biblical scholarship and literary sensibility and the introduction lays out the structural, historical, and exegetical issues in the composition, canonization, and different appropriations of the Song. Ibid., 3–42.

38. Zakovitch, *Song of Songs: Riddle of Riddles*, 95.

39. Ibid., 82.

40. Ibid., 83.

41. Alter, "Afterword," in A. Bloch and C. Bloch, *Song of Songs*, 121–22.

42. Ibid., 125.

43. Ibid.

44. Ibid., 130.

45. Brenner, "'My' Song of Songs," in Brenner and Fontaine, *Song of Songs*, 159.

46. "Amar rabi 'Akiva, ḥas ve-shalom, lo neḥlak adam mi-yisrael 'al shir ha-shirim she-lo tetamei et ha-yadayim, she-ein kol ha-'olam kulo keda'i ka-yom she-natan bo shir ha-shirim le-yisrael, she-kol ha-ketuvim kodesh, ve-shir ha-shirim kodesh kodashim." Available at Sefaria: https://www.sefaria.org.il/Mishnah_Yadayim.3.5?lang=bi&WITH=all&lang2=en (accessed July 9, 2021).

47. David Stern, "Ancient Jewish Interpretation of the Song of Songs in a Comparative Context," in *Jewish Biblical Interpretation and Cultural Exchange: Comparative Exegesis in Context*, ed. Natalie B. Dohrmann and David Stern (Philadelphia: University of Pennsylvania Press, 2008), 96. C. Bloch, more tongue-in-cheek, considers Rabbi Akiva's claim that the Song of Songs is the "holy of holies" to be the "denial of denials . . ." "In the Garden of Delights," 28.

48. Rachel Elior, "The Garden of Eden Is the Holy of Holies and the Dwelling of the Lord," *Studies in Spirituality* 24 (2014): 90.

49. Alter says that the "continuous celebration of passion and its pleasures makes this the most consistently secular of all biblical texts." *Art of Biblical Poetry*, 185. Taken, of course, from the Latin *saeculum*, referring to those elements of world that are not the church, "secular" roughly corresponds to *ḥalal* in ancient and modern Hebrew. For a short exposition of this subject, see Zali Gurevitch, *Ha-'ivrit 'al pinu* [Travels in Hebrew] (Jerusalem: Carmel, 2017), 53–58.

50. C. Bloch, "In the Garden of Delights," 30.

51. See, again, Brenner, who cites the inherent "singability" of the Song of Songs, as attested to by the "humming noise" that accompanies modern Israeli teaching of the Song and

its ubiquity in popular musical culture. "'My' Song of Songs," in Brenner and Fontaine, *Song of Songs*, 158, 161.

52. C. Bloch, "In the Garden of Delights," 30.

53. Ibid., 3. Elior mentions parallels between the oils and incense in the Song of Songs and at least one apocryphal story of the Garden of Eden, inviting a comparison between the two texts that take place in gardens. "Garden of Eden," 90.

54. C. Bloch, "In the Garden of Delights," 30.

55. Trible, "Depatriarchalizing," 42, 46–48.

56. Michael Fishbane, introduction to *The JPS Bible Commentary: Song of Songs. The Traditional Hebrew Text with the New JPS Translation* (Philadelphia: Jewish Publication Society, 2015), xix.

57. Fishbane elaborates: "In Jewish tradition, these four types of interpretation—peshat, derash, remez, and sod—are known by the (slightly scrambled) acronym of PaRDeS . . . According to one famous analogy (recorded in the Zohar): peshat is the outer (textual) garment of Scripture; derash is its (more concealed cultural) body (with its theologies and laws); remez is the (inner) soul of this 'textual being' (with hints of religious quest and truth); and sod is the supernal supersoul (of Scripture, its ultimate divine dimension)." Introduction to *The JPS Bible Commentary*, xxxviii. As Ariel Bloch explains, "pardes," a loan-word from Persian, meaning enclosed park or garden, took on the meaning "orchard" probably in the third century BCE, which is approximately when the Song would have been composed. A. Bloch and C. Bloch, *Song of Songs*, 177; also see H. L. Ginsberg, "Introduction to the Song of Songs," in *The Five Megilloth and Jonah* (Philadelphia: Jewish Publication Society, 1969), 52.

58. Fishbane, introduction to *The JPS Bible Commentary*, 266ff.

59. This is the way the editors describe their translation of the Song of Songs under "Product Description" on the Artscroll website: http://www.artscroll.com/Books/9780899060088.html (accessed July 9, 2021).

60. Fishbane, introduction to *The JPS Bible Commentary*, 268. The original text of the Song is marked by italics.

61. Ibid., 288–89.

62. Ha-rav Yosef-Dov Halevi Soloveitchik, "U-vikashtem mi-sham" [And you have inquired into it], in *Ish ha-halakha—galui ve-nistar* [The Man of Halakha—Revealed and Concealed] (1944; Jerusalem, 1979, 1991–92), 120. http://www.torahleadership.org/categories/shirhashirimtransyi1.pdf.

63. Fishbane, introduction to *The JPS Bible Commentary*, 51. The Blochs' translation of this verse reads as follows: "You are beautiful, my king, / and gentle. Wherever we lie / our bed is green. / Our roofbeams are cedar, / our rafters fir" (53).

64. Three rabbis (R. Yuda in the name of R. Simon and R. Yohanan) said "'It was spoken at Sinai' [and] R. Meir said, 'It was spoken at the Tent of Meeting . . .' The rabbis said, 'In the Eternal Temple.'" Shir ha-shirim Rabbah 1.2. See on this David Stern's elaboration of Tamar Kadari's insights. Stern, "Ancient Jewish Interpretation of the Song of Songs," 94. The Temple would be reinserted into the text also in the Zohar, where Rabbi Yose is reported as saying that "this song was aroused by Solomon when the Temple was built and all worlds were consummated, above and below, in single perfection." Terumah 2:143a; quoted in Pardes, *Song of Songs*, 84–85, 241n36.

65. In the category of "remez": "Just as breasts sustain a suckling with milk . . . these men sustained Israel with the teachings of Torah" (Shir ha-shirim Rabbah 4.1). Fishbane, introduction to *The JPS Bible Commentary*, 110. And see Rashi's transfiguration of the word *shorerekh* (Song 7:3), generally translated as navel or vulva, to "lishkat ha-gazit," the hall or chamber of "hewn stones"

that sits in the "navel of the world." This hall, where the Sanhedrin sat, was said to have been po-sitioned half inside and half outside the sanctuary. Rashi, *The Megilloth and Rashi's Commentary with Linear Translation*, trans. Avraham Schwartz and Yisroel Schwartz (New York: Hebrew Linear Classics, 1983), 131–32. For wonderful feminist readings of this passage, see Athalya Brenner, "'Come Back, Come Back, the Shulammite' (Song of Songs 7:1–10): A Parody of the wasf Genre," in *On Humour and Comic in the Hebrew Bible*, ed. Athalya Brenner and Y. T. Radday (Sheffield, UK: Almond Press, 1990), 245–46. And for a fascinating critique of the feminist celebration of the language of the Song, alongside medieval Jewish and Christian allegorical renderings, in-cluding Rashi's, see Black, "Unlikely Bedfellows," 104–27; on the image of "shorerekh" and other female body parts, see 109–10. She prefers, along with Brenner, to view the female persona as sometimes "ridiculous, comical" or even grotesque. Acknowledging that her reading will "likely affect readers who are enamoured with the Song, its beauty of language and idyllic view of love," Black concludes that "affecting readers is what the Song does best." Ibid., 127–29.

66. See Fishbane's explanation of the "derash" of verses 1:13–14, which we considered above through the Blochs' translation and Alter's endorsement. Using the JPS translation, "My beloved to me is a bag of myrrh (tzeror ha-mor) / Lodged between my breasts," Fishbane explains that these words "articulate the intimate relationship between Keneset Yisrael and her [divine] Be-loved (dodi) . . . According to Rabbi Azariah, tzeror ha-mor refers to Abraham." Introduction to the *JPS Bible Commentary*, 48.

67. See A. Bloch and C. Bloch, *Song of Songs*, 196–98. The use of the generic pronoun, "ha-shulamith," the Shulamite, reveals that it is not a proper name. Ariel Bloch makes the convincing argument that "The Shulamite lives in 'the city,' as Jerusalem is called, a walled metropolis with streets and squares" (3:2–3, 5:70). A. Bloch and C. Bloch, *Song of Songs*, 198.

68. Sometimes there would appear to be a level of topographical historical conscious-ness at work here. For example, David Stern writes that "for the rabbis . . . and specifically for R. Yohanan and his disciples, the 'daughters of Jerusalem' refer to the outlying, presumably Gen-tile cities or colonies of Jerusalem, a metropolis (literally 'mother-city' with daughters), whom Jerusalem addresses in 1:6." "Ancient Jewish Interpretation of the Song of Songs," 105.

69. See Stern's citation of Scholem and Lieberman's exploration of the possible connection between the esoteric doctrine in "Shiur Komah" ("The Measurements of the [Divine] Body"—part of the "heikhalot literature" of the second–third centuries CE) and the description by the maiden of her lover's body; in this case the hyperbolic imagination of the divine measurement seems to know no bounds as what Philip S. Alexander calls "a mental mandala, an aid to mysti-cal contemplation that gave the mystic something on which to focus at the climax of his ecstasy, and allowed him to prolong the moment of his mystical contemplation of God." Quoted in Stern, "Ancient Jewish Interpretation of the Song of Songs," 95.

70. As I will elaborate below, I am adopting Daniel Boyarin's distinction between parable and allegory.

71. For a comprehensive exploration of the poetic sensibilities in the Zohar, see Eitan Fishbane, *The Art of Mystical Narrative: A Poetics of the Zohar* (Oxford: Oxford University Press, 2018).

72. Tamar Kadari, "'Friends Hearken to Your Voice': Rabbinic Interpretations of the Song of Songs," in *Approaches to Literary Readings of Ancient Jewish Writings*, ed. Klaas Smelik and Karolien Vermeulen (Leiden: Brill and University of Antwerp, 2014), 183.

73. The assumption of a male speaker is not an oversight on Kadari's part. The speaker, apprehended as "Knesset Yisrael," while figured as God's bride, is, in talmudic parlance, the male subject of the nation. Daniel Boyarin looks at the homoerotic implications of the talmudic

forum as no less normative than the heterosexual. See *Carnal Israel: Reading Sex in Talmudic Culture* (Berkeley: University of California Press, 1993).

74. Kadari, "'Friends Hearken to Your Voice,'" 196.

75. Ibid., 192.

76. *Avot d-Rabbi Natan*, version A, ed. Solomon Schechter (1887; New York: Jewish Seminary of America, 1950), 2; quoted in Stern, "Ancient Jewish Interpretation of the Song of Songs," 90.

77. Ibid.

78. Daniel Boyarin, "The Song of Songs, Lock or Key: The Holy Song as a Mashal," in Boyarin, *Intertextuality and the Reading of Midrash* (Bloomington: Indiana University Press, 1990), 109–10. One of the prooftexts Boyarin brings for the argument that connects Shir ha-shirim Rabbah with Exodus is an elaboration of the image we considered earlier, "my dove in the clefts of the rock." Ibid., 111–12.

79. Julia Kristeva, *Tales of Love*, trans. Leon S. Roudiez (New York: Columbia University Press, 1987), 95. Quoted from DeKoven Ezrahi, "'To what shall I compare thee?,'" 226. David Stern, in comparing early Jewish with early Christian readings, beginning with Origen, claims that while "there is very little that is explicitly erotic . . . about the rabbinic allegorical reading . . . the major thrust of Origen's reading . . . was to kindle his 'fallen' human reader's spiritually erotic 'God-love' and to 'leave cold earth-love behind.'" Stern, "Ancient Jewish Interpretation of the Song of Songs," 104.

80. Jon Whitman, ed., *Interpretation and Allegory: Antiquity to the Modern Period* (Boston: Brill-Leiden, 2000), 4, 18. See especially his discussion of the turns represented in the work of Kant and Frye in his introduction, "A Retrospective Forward: Interpretation, Allegory and Historical Change," 3–32.

81. Yehuda Halevi, "Zion Won't You Ask," *Yehuda Halevi: Poems from the Diwan*, trans. Gabriel Levin (London: Anvil Press, 2002), 101.

82. Private communication, March 2020. Kronfeld's current study focuses on the Song as the model that enables both the inversion of the prophetic metaphor and the insistence on the literal voice and subjectivity of a woman speaker (with the land or city as the vehicle, rather than the tenor). See "The Land as Woman: Esther Raab and the Afterlife of a Metaphorical System," *Prooftexts: A Journal of Jewish Literary History*, forthcoming.

83. Alter presents the poetic form of Lamentations, which "is unique among books of the Bible . . . Might it be a mnemonic to facilitate public recitation?" Introduction to Robert Alter's translation of Lamentations. *Hebrew Bible*, 3:643.

84. See also Micha, Isaiah, etc. For an elaboration of this insight, see DeKoven Ezrahi, *Booking Passage*, 144–45, 261n44; and DeKoven Ezrahi, "'To what shall I compare thee?,'" 223. As we saw above, Zakovitch's recent work challenges the more or less consensual dating of the prophetic books and Song of Songs. For my purposes, his claim that much of the Song was actually the precedent to which many of the prophetic and other texts were responding only reinforces the dialogical connection between them. This is especially salient in regard to the image of the City as Woman or Woman as City vs. Woman in the City.

85. Kronfeld, private communication, March 2020.

86. Available at Come and Hear: http://www.come-and-hear.com/sanhedrin/sanhedrin_104 .html (accessed July 9, 2021). This is a trope that will appear in Agnon's writing; see "Ha-mitpaḥat," in *Elu ve-elu*, new ed. (Jerusalem: Schocken, 1998), 206. And see chapter 5, below.

87. Piyyut has also become integral to written and performed music in contemporary Israel. See for example the website An Invitation to Piyut, which includes scholarly discussions of classical piyyut as well as contemporary compositions and performances: http://old.piyut.org.il.

88. Meshullam ben Kalonymus, "Afik renan ve-shirim le-nos'ei 'al nesharim." See *Mahzor kolel ha-tefilot ve-ha-piyyutim le-khol mo'adei El* [Prayerbook with Prayers and Piyyutim for All the Holidays], ed. Meir Ha-Levi Letteris (Prague: Gottlieb Haase, 1847), 7:217–27. Many of these piyyutim have been recovered or authenticated through material found in the Cairo Geniza.

89. Meir Ha-levi Letteris, or Max Letteris (1800–1871), who edited one of the most reliable nineteenth-century editions, was descended from a family of printers from Amsterdam; he became a scholar, a "maskil," and a poet, living in Berlin, Prague, and Vienna, while editing manuscripts and working in the printing business for a living.

90. The different translations and explications of this seemingly simple verse reveal the divisions even among modern scholars and practitioners of piyyut. Ariel Zinder suggests the following rough translation: "He will hurry and deliver me / From those who plow me and break me / And restore me to the place I hope for [or: the place He cares for]." Private communication, February 28, 2019. Almog Behar, as we have seen, offers a very different translation and interpretive stance that privileges the house of study: Private communication, February 4, 2018. I am grateful to them both for their help and for sharpening the dichotomies in interpretation. Yona Frankel, who edited a more contemporary edition of this mahzor, glosses "neveh midrashi" as the "place the Lord requires": "ha-makom asher ha-kadosh barukh hu doresh oto"—an extrapolation from Ps. 23:2. *Mahzor Pesah* (Jerusalem: Koren, 1993), 77.

91. See Fishbane, introduction to *The JPS Bible Commentary*, xlviii–li. He explains that the rabbinic interpretations incorporated in such piyyutim are "all keyed to the core cycle of events around Passover: the exodus from Egypt; the crossing of the sea; the song sung in celebration; the wandering in the desert; and the revelation at Sinai. The Song is the verbal matrix of this praise." Ibid., l. For discussions of piyyutim on Song of Songs, see also Pardes, *Song of Songs*, 71–81.

92. See DeKoven Ezrahi, "The Poetics of Pilgrimage: Yehuda Halevi and the Uncompleted Journey," in *Booking Passage*, especially 38–51.

93. Yehuda Halevi, "Zion Won't You Ask," 101.

94. "Your Words Are Scented with Perfume of Myrrh" [Devarekha be-mor 'over rekuhim], in Raymond P. Scheindlin, *The Song of the Distant Dove: Judah Halevi's Pilgrimage* (Oxford: Oxford University Press, 2008), 193. This poem appears in a cluster that Scheindlin calls poems of "argumentation," reflecting mainly Halevi's internal struggles with his own doubts, written in the period leading up to his pilgrimage. See ibid., 91–93.

95. Ibid., 91.

96. Quoted in Fishbane, introduction to *The JPS Bible Commentary*, 274, 307n73.

97. In Ariel Bloch's reading, images such as "the mountain of myrrh" and "hill of frankincense" are associated with the Shulamite throughout the Song (3:6, 4:6, 4:14). Commentary, A. Bloch and C. Bloch, *Song of Songs*, 173.

98. Pardes, *Agnon's Moonstruck Lovers*, 14–15. For a longitudinal view of eros in Jewish culture, see David Biale, *Eros and the Jews: From Biblical Israel to Contemporary America* (New York: Basic Books, 1992), especially as relates to Hassidic and Maskilic appropriations of the Song of Songs in highly eroticized and transgressive ways, 143–44, 161–62, 170; as well as early Zionist appropriations of the poem, 189–90. And for a discussion of the Song in the context of Zionism's gendered figures, see Michael Gluzman, *Ha-guf ha-tzioni: Le'umiyut, migdar u-miniyut ba-sifrut ha-'ivrit ha-hadasha* [The Zionist Body: Nationalism, Gender, and Sexuality in Modern Hebrew Literature] (Tel Aviv: Ha-kibbutz ha-meuchad, 2007), especially his discussion of the transition from the biblical-maskilic image of the nation as a woman to the Zionist image of the nation as a masculine body, 14–15.

99. Pardes, *Agnon's Moonstruck Lovers*, 15, 133. This book reviews the permutations of the Song in modern Hebrew culture beginning in the Haskalah or Enlightenment, speculating on its contemporaneity: nothing "would be more natural than for Solomon, the great women-lover, to ask one of the female singers of his court to gather for him the best of current Israelite poetry . . ." Ibid., 62–63, 134. Although my inquiry in the second half of this book is limited to the work of Agnon and Amichai, the Song may be the most animating biblical text in modern Hebrew culture. Writers as diverse as Haviva Pedaya, Haim Be'er, and David Grossman give current expression to the centrality of this text, as do the musical and artistic cultures of our time.

100. Rosenzweig, *Star of Redemption*, 199, 201; Gurevitch, *Kol Dodim*, 22. "The poem is earthly, the gaze is always trained on what is before the eyes," writes Gurevitch: "body, vegetation, landscape, human eyes. Never in Song of Songs is there a glance that moves upwards to the . . . world beyond. Longing is always contained within the world itself, and it animates the imagination, even without [reference to] the heavens above, the ceiling of the universe, the Supernal King" (102).

101. See, for example, Pardes's analysis of resonances of the Song in American culture, from Walt Whitman to Toni Morrison. *Song of Songs*, 172–218.

102. On this, and on Anselm Kiefer's paintings of "Shulamith" and "Margarete" in the context of the Holocaust and Celan's poem, see DeKoven Ezrahi, "The Grave in the Air: Unbound Metaphors in Post-Holocaust Poetry," in *Probing the Limits of Representation: Nazism and the Final Solution*, ed. Saul Friedlander (Cambridge: Harvard University Press, 1992), 259–76; see also Gurevitch's reference to "Shulamith" and "Todesfuge" in the moving coda to his monograph on Shir ha-shirim: *Kol Dodim*, 169–70.

103. Kronfeld, *On the Margins*, 92.

104. Ibid., 101–2. Similarly, in these texts, as Kronfeld shows, an "autoerotic experience—'by night on my bed' (Song of Songs 3:1)—or erotic dream—'I sleep, but my heart waketh' (Song of Songs 5:2)—may constitute the 'event' which the poems obliquely describe. In Fogel's poem ["At the End of the Day"], what is presented syntactically as the narrative climax (in stanzas three and four) may in fact be a highly suggestive linguistic correlative to the speaker's own sexual climax: U-feta' az itar mi-yetsu'i / U-ve-yadai a'amtsem [et shaday] el ḥazi . . . / Gam raḥmi yir'ad ('And suddenly then I (will) leap(ed) from my bed / And with my hands I (will) clench(ed) [my breasts] to my chest / breast. . . . / And my womb (will) shudder(ed).') A very similar reading could be provided for the metaphorical depiction of the Shulamite 'opening to' her lover, her fingers dripping with sweet smelling myrrh 'upon the handles of the lock' (Song of Songs 5:5–6)." Ibid., 100–101.

105. Alter, "Afterword," in A. Bloch and C. Bloch, *Song of Songs*, 129.

106. Kronfeld, *On the Margins*, 100.

107. Roland Barthes, *A Lover's Discourse: Fragments*, trans. Richard Howard (New York: Hill and Wang, 1979).

108. Ariel Hirschfeld, "'Ha-ḥeder Ha-yarok shel Shir Ha Shirim" ["The Green Room" of Song of Songs], *Haaretz*, April 11, 2017, https://www.haaretz.co.il/literature/.premium-1.4009931; see also Ariel Hirschfeld, "Nafshi Yatsah Bidvaro" [How I Wanted Him When He Spoke], *Haaretz*, April 17, 2017, https://www.haaretz.co.il/literature/.premium-1.4024012.

109. Gurevitch, *Kol Dodim*, 82ff.

110. Fishbane, introduction to *The JPS Bible Commentary*, xxi–xxii ff.

111. Brenner, "'My' Song of Songs," in Brenner and Fontaine, *Song of Songs*, 162 and passim.

112. For an English version of this letter, translated by Gil Anidjar, see Jacques Derrida, *Acts of Religion*, ed. Gil Anidjar (New York: Routledge, 2002), 226–27. For Jacques Derrida's response

to the letter, see "The Eyes of Language: The Aiyss and the Volcano," in ibid., 189–226. For an extensive discussion of the repercussions of Scholem's letter, especially in Hebrew culture, see the special issue "Koaḥ meshiḥi ḥalash: teologia politit, dat ve-ḥiloniut ba-sifrut ha-ʿivrit" [A Weak Messianic Power: Political Theology, Religion, and Secularism in Hebrew Literature], *Mikan* 14, ed. Hanna Soker-Schwager (March 2014); and DeKoven Ezrahi, *Shlosha paytanim* [Three Poets of the Sacred Quotidian] (Jerusalem: Mossad Bialik, 2020). And see below, chapter 6.

113. East Jerusalem, captured by Israel in 1967, was immediately incorporated into the municipal jurisdiction of West Jerusalem; it was officially declared part of "unified Jerusalem" by the "Jerusalem Law" passed by the Knesset in 1980. This of course remains contested in the international community.

114. Among the many scholarly studies of the historical, political, philosophical, and religious aspects of this subject, see particularly the work of Haviva Pedaya, *Merḥav u-makom: Masa ʿal ha-lo-mudaʿ ha-teologi-politi* [Expanses: Essay on the Theological and Political Unconscious] (Tel Aviv: Ha-kibbutz ha-meuchad, 2011); Yaron Eliav, *God's Mountain*; and Motti Inbari, *Jewish Fundamentalism and the Temple Mount: Who Will Build the Third Temple?*, trans. Shaul Vardi (Albany: SUNY Press, 2009). And, for recent explorations of the subject, see the essays in Yoram Peri, ed., "Changing Perspectives on the Temple Mount," special issue of *Israel Studies* 32, no. 1 (Summer 2017): 1–122. See also Noa Ḥazan and Avital Barak, eds., *Ha-har, ha-kipa ve-ha-mabat: har ha-bayit ba-tarbut ha-ḥazutit ha-yisraelit* [The Mountain, the Dome, and the Gaze: The Temple Mount in Israeli Art] (Haifa: Pardes, 2017).

115. Alter, "Afterword," in A. Bloch and C. Bloch, *Song of Songs*, 131.

116. Agnon's writing covers most of the twentieth century, and his posthumously published work—some of which contained implicit knowledge of the insidious forces that he had not quite brought to the surface in the prose published during his lifetime—continued to appear for many years after his death. Focusing on resonances of the Song in his work, I will enlarge on Pardes's claim that Agnon's stories complicate the allegorical turn in modern Hebrew writing. See below, chapter 4.

117. In one of the earliest feminist readings of this text, as we have already seen, Carol Meyers brings this image as "a reversal of the stereotypical gender association." "Gender Imagery," 215.

118. See Zakovitch's gloss on the series of exchanges between the Shulamite and her brothers which ends with the wall image—and which he reads as one of the primary riddle structures in the Song. The brothers speculate on how developed their sister is: "We have a little sister, / Whose breasts are not yet formed. / What shall we do for our sister / When she is spoken for? / If she be a wall, / We will build upon it a silver battlement . . ." "The little sister," Zakovitch writes, "hears out her brothers and solves their riddles, cleverly choosing between the various interpretations: 'I am a wall,' she replies, choosing the meaning of wall as an emblem of chastity; then she informs them she has a lover: 'So I became, in his eyes, as one who finds peace.'" Zakovitch, *Song of Songs*, 40–42.

119. "Jerusalem, Jerusalem, Why Jerusalem?," no. 18, *Poetry of Yehuda Amichai*, 506. *Shirei Yehuda Amichai*, 5:283.

Chapter Three

I wish to thank Professor Alexander Altmann for first igniting my interest—some fifty-four years ago—in the poetics of sacred space as expressed in the Rambam's great work. Next, I am indebted more than I can say to Professors Kalman Bland and Joel Kraemer for their generous help, over several years, with this chapter—in which I have waded, with much enthusiasm, and trepidation, into the deep waters of medieval Jewish (and Arab) philosophy and poetics. All three of them died before they could see the fruits of their generosity. The mistakes are, of course, my own. The "private communication" I cite with Kalman was through email exchanges that ranged from 2006 until the summer of 2017; he died in the middle of our conversation on the Rambam and so much more. This chapter is in many respects a tribute to our sustained dialogue and is dedicated to his memory.

1. Of the various English translations of the title—Guide *of*, *to*, or *for*, the Perplexed—"of" is the most accurate. There remains a certain ambiguity in both Arabic and Hebrew originals; it is not quite clear whether it is the addressee who is "perplexed" or whether, by extension, every rational being is (potentially) in that state of religious doubt or confusion. The Arabic original, *Dalalāt al-Hairin*, like the title, *Moreh ha-nevokhim*, given by Hebrew translator Ibn Tibbon during Maimonides's lifetime, can mean either *of* or *for* as a genitive form with no preposition. M. Friedlander's 1881 translation, *Guide for the Perplexed*, persists in other modern renditions into English. The most authoritative English translation for our age is that of Shlomo Pines, *Guide of the Perplexed*, which leaves the question of the perplexed subject *and* object somewhat unresolved. *Guide of the Perplexed*, trans. Shlomo Pines, introductory essay by Leo Strauss (Chicago: University of Chicago Press, 1963). I am also using a more modern Hebrew translation: Yosef ben David Kapach, trans., *Rabbeinu Moshe ben Maimon, Moreh Nevokhim, tirgem le-'ivrit bi'er ve-hikhin 'al pi kitvei yad ve-defusim* (Jerusalem: Mossad ha-rav Kuk, 1977). Unless otherwise noted, I am using these translations throughout.

2. Epistle Dedicatory, *Guide*, I, p. 4.

3. Kraemer, *Maimonides*, 360. For a discussion of the pupil whom Leo Strauss calls the *Guide*'s primary "addressee," see Strauss, introduction, *Guide*, vol. 1, pp. xvii, xix.

4. Menachem Lorberbaum, *Nutzahnu be-ne'imuto: Torat ha-elohut ke-poetika be-yitzira ha-yehudit ha-andalusit* [Dazzled by Beauty: Theology as Poetics in Hispanic Jewish Culture] (Jerusalem: Yad Izhak Ben-Zvi and the Hebrew University of Jerusalem, 2011), 54. Lorberbaum presents a beautiful, and sustained, discussion of the place of poetic and literary imagery in the *Guide*, as well as a consideration of the Rambam's own poetic language; see, especially, 51–121. In the English abstract, Lorberbaum argues against the "categorical distinctions between poetics and philosophy" in Maimonides's world and specifically in his work. Ibid., v.

5. The discussion is, of course, not limited to the *Guide*, but relates to the larger issue of idolatry that Maimonides addresses in *Mishneh Torah Hilkhot 'Avoda Zara* and other places that we cannot engage with here but have been explored by many scholars.

6. As Kraemer pointed out to me, "love of God plays a role in Maimonides' theology, even in a Sufi way, with the Sufi/erotic term ishq [cognate to *heshek* in Hebrew]." Private communication, March 28, 2011.

7. This principle "Ein mukdam u-me'uhar ba-torah" (there is no "before" or "after" in the Torah) is attributed to different sources, as early as the second century CE, though there is ongoing discussion over its origin among Talmud scholars.

8. See, on this, DeKoven Ezrahi, *Booking Passage*, 33–51.

9. "Eleikhem ishim ekra ve-koli el bnei adam" (Unto you, *ishim*, I call, and my voice is to *bnei adam*, Prov. 8:4). James Arthur Diamond explains that *ishim* are figured here as those who possess an active intellect and understand philosophical concepts; *bnei adam* are the multitude who cannot—so the Torah speaks or gives voice to the language of *bnei adam* (*dibra torah bilshon bnei adam*)—for their sake. *Maimonides and the Hermeneutics of Concealment: Deciphering Scripture and Midrash in the Guide of the Perplexed* (Albany: SUNY Press, 2002), 7–8.

10. Kraemer, *Maimonides*, 360.

11. Ibid., 237.

12. Folk saying, provenance unclear.

13. 1215–16 CE, corresponding to 4976 since the Creation. Sinai is the midpoint; from Sinai till 1215 signals the time till the final restoration. See Kraemer, *Maimonides*, 236. As it happened, that day would come—and go—only eleven years after Maimonides's death.

14. The marble bust of Maimonides, rendered by Brenda Putnam, hangs, along with those of twenty-two other figures, in the United States House of Representatives. As stated on the official website of the Architect of the Capitol: "The 23 marble relief portraits over the gallery doors of the House Chamber in the US Capitol depict historical figures noted for their work in establishing the principles that underlie American law. They were installed when the chamber was remodeled in 1949–1950." https://www.aoc.gov/art/relief-portrait-plaques-lawgivers/maimonides (accessed July 9, 2021).

15. As for the claim that Moses was the only prophet who did not speak in parables, see Strauss's counterclaim that if it is an article of faith that the Torah is the word of God transmitted through Moses, then the poetic conceits that abound there originate from him as well. Introduction to *Guide*, vol. 1, pp. xxxvi ff.

16. For an enlightening discussion of Maimonides's image of the "filigree," see Lorberbaum, *Nutzaḥnu*, 56.

17. The inference is that a logical argument can be articulated in language that is both fitting and of inherent beauty. In both Hebrew and Arabic rhetoric of the Middle Ages, the silver filigree and not the content is the poetic achievement. See, on the evolution and intricacies of medieval Hebrew (and Arabic) poetics, Dan Pagis, *Hebrew Poetry of the Middle Ages and the Renaissance* (Berkeley: University of California Press, 1991). For an expanded Hebrew version, see Dan Pagis, *Ha-shir dabur ʿal ofanav: Meḥkarim u-masot ba-shira ha-ʿivrit shel yemei ha-beinayim*, ed. Ezra Fleischer (Jerusalem: Magnes Press, 1993).

18. Strauss, introduction to *Guide*, vol. 1, p. xl.

19. Rambam, *Sefer moreh ha-nevokhim*, trans. Rabbi Yehuda Ibn Tibbon (Jerusalem: Monson, 1960), I, chap. 18, p. 35. Pines's translation of the term *melitzim* as "preachers" is problematic, both because of its Christian and ecclesiastical resonances and because it does not capture the essence of the term in Hebrew; the "melitz" is one who is a master of rhetorical flourish—and in theological terms, the "melitz yosher" is the intercessor between humans or even between the human and the divine spheres (Job 33:23). Nevertheless, Maimonides is signaling his own ambivalence or caution toward such rhetorical practitioners.

20. Rambam, *Sefer moreh ha-nevokhim*, trans. Ibn Tibbon, I, chap. 59, p. 89.

21. "ʿAd she-ḥibru devarim, ketzatam—kefira gemura, u-ketzatam—yesh bahem min ha-shtut ve-hefsed ha-dimyon, ma she-raʾui le-adam she-yishak ʿalav lefi tivʿo ke-she-yishmaʿ, ve-yivkehu ʿim ha-hitbonenut." Ibid.

22. Lorberbaum's main argument is that "theological articulation is understood [by poets Ibn Gabirol and Yehuda Halevi, as well as by the philosopher Maimonides] as a form of poetics." *Nutzaḥnu*, v.

23. Quoted in Norman Roth, "Maimonides on Hebrew Language and Poetry," in *Maimonides, Essays and Texts: 850th Anniversary* (Madison: Hispanic Seminary of Medieval Studies, 1985), 117.

24. Ibid., 115.

25. On this see Lorberbaum, *Nutzaḥnu*, 60–61.

26. Even such prophets as Baruch son of Neriah "find no vision from the Lord . . . because they were in Exile." They may hear the voices but do not see the visions. *Guide* II:32–33, pp. 362, 364. The reference to Baruch son of Neriah is from Jer. 36:4. A vision, as Kalman Bland explains it, entails seeing something that comes from inside as if it comes from the outside. Private communication. See the following chapters on Agnon, who often claims that his inspiration comes from nighttime "visions."

27. Abraham Joshua Heschel argues that Maimonides regarded prophecy not only as possible in *Galut*, but as harbinger of the messianic age; indeed, Heschel continues, Maimonides probably thought of himself as prophet, as his disciples in their turn thought of themselves. For a discussion of Heschel's complex relation to and apprehension of Maimonides, which reflects the complexities and ambiguities in the oeuvre of *both* philosophers, as well as Heschel's identification with the medieval philosopher, see Michael Marmur, "Heschel's Two Maimonides," *Jewish Quarterly Review* 98, no. 2 (Spring 2008): 230–54. Marmur argues that "Heschel's Maimonides is a man who undergoes change . . . from scholarly detachment to social involvement and from abstraction to concrete action"—and that this amounts to a "heroic tale." Ibid., 251–52.

28. Mordechai Z. Cohen, "Logic to Interpretation: Maimonides' Use of al-Fârâbî's Model of Metaphor," *Zutot: Perspectives on Jewish Culture* 2 (2002): 104–13. In this short essay and in his longer work, Cohen cites a number of Maimonides's acknowledged and unacknowledged predecessors and interlocutors, including Saʿadia Gaon, al-Fârâbî, Moses Ibn Ezra, and Abraham Ibn Ezra. He sets up a cross-generational Hebrew conversation on biblical metaphor in his *Three Approaches to Biblical Metaphor: From Abraham Ibn Ezra and Maimonides to David Kimhi* (Leiden: Brill, 2003).

29. Cohen, *Three Approaches*, 213. One of the ambient influences on Maimonides's thinking, that of Averroes or Ibn Rusd, arrives at the metaphorical act through the implied syllogism based on Aristotle's poetics. A metaphor is actually a condensed syllogism or enthymeme; the logic is the same except that in metaphor, the common property that holds the syllogism together is implied and the pleasure is in the recognition of that missing part. See Salim Kemal, *The Philosophical Poetics of Alfarabi, Avicenna and Averroes: The Aristotelian Reception* (London: Routledge, 2010).

30. Cohen, *Three Approaches*, 212–13. This is what contemporary theorists call "lexicalized metaphor."

31. These passages from the *Guide* are quoted in Cohen, "Logic to Interpretation," 106–7.

32. Cohen, *Three Approaches*, 16–22.

33. Cohen, "Logic to Interpretation," 110. But there are other approaches to biblical and postbiblical imagery that allow for "ocular desire" untarnished by either repetition or exegetical dismissal—i.e., that claim that the images remain "undead"—and that challenge the so-called aniconic impulses in Judaism. See Daniel Boyarin, "The Eye in the Torah: Ocular Desire in Midrashic Hermeneutic," *Critical Inquiry* 16, no. 3 (Spring 1990): 532–50; and Kalman P. Bland, *The Artless Jew: Medieval and Modern Affirmations and Denials of the Visual* (Princeton: Princeton University Press, 2000).

34. Cohen, "Logic to Interpretation," 110–11. In this context, the violated categories are the linguistic categories of al-Fârâbî and of Maimonides's own earlier distinctions in *The Treatise on Logic*. Moshe Halbertal and Avishai Margalit go even further in arguing that not only figurative language but all "linguistic representations" are suspect in Maimonides's view and that he "devotes most of Part I of *The Guide of the Perplexed* to liberating the reader from the hold of language" itself. Moshe Halbertal and Avishai Margalit, *Idolatry*, trans. Naomi Goldblum (Cambridge: Harvard University Press, 1992), 62.

35. Some of the inconsistencies between Maimonides's early writing, in the *Mishneh Torah*, for example, or in his *Treatise on Logic* and the *Guide*, or within the *Guide* itself, between the "lexicographic" chapters and their summaries, are accounted for by the critics in different ways. One assumption is that there are distinct units, like the "lexicographic" unit, that were written at different times. See M. Z. Cohen, *Three Approaches*, 212–13. In any event, the *Guide* as finally redacted by Maimonides contains the unresolved contradictions which, at the very least, suggest the author's own struggle and profound ambivalence.

36. Cohen, "Logic to Interpretation," 108.

37. Ricoeur, *Rule of Metaphor*, 253. See also Eva Feder Kittay, *Metaphor: Its Cognitive Force and Linguistic Structure* (New York: Oxford University Press, 1990), 89. Much of this research builds on the work of George Lakoff. See Lakoff and Mark Johnson, *Metaphors We Live By* (Chicago: University of Chicago Press, 1980). See also Barbara Dancygier and Eve Sweetser, *Figurative Language* (Cambridge: Cambridge University Press, 2014).

38. The book of Lamentations is attributed traditionally to the prophet Jeremiah, but its poetic discourse and the function of poetic tropes are quite different from those in the book of Jeremiah. See on this, above, chapter 2.

39. Bland, *Artless Jew*, 5–6. The aniconic assumptions, Bland claims, can be attributed to much later influences: "If it were not for Kant and Hegel, the denial of Jewish art would not have been invented." Ibid., 5. Reaching similar conclusions, but focusing on biblical and midrashic material, Daniel Boyarin asserts that "it is an absolutely unexamined axiom that 'Hebraic impulses' must be toward an invisible God, who does not show Himself to humankind and only speaks that they may hear." "Eye in the Torah," 533. He goes on to argue that it was Greek influence on or polemic with Judaism that largely brought about the repression of the visual.

40. On this see, for example, Gary Alan Long, whose primary concern, like that of Maimonides, is for figuration in regard to representations of divinity. But "if figuration was used knowingly for topics not concerned with deity, I do not think it altogether unlikely that it was used knowingly for deity," he writes. "Dead or Alive? Literality and God-Metaphors in the Hebrew Bible," *Journal of the American Academy of Religion* 62, no. 2 (Summer 1994): 522. As we have seen in previous chapters, Robert Alter's pathbreaking study *The Art of Biblical Poetry* remains a touchstone for literary inquiry into biblical texts in the late twentieth and early twenty-first centuries.

41. *MT, Hilkhot Yesodei ha-Torah* 7:3 quoted in M. Z. Cohen, *Three Approaches*, 120. My emendations or additions to the translation are in brackets.

42. Sometimes similes are even labeled as *meshalim*; see *Guide* I:1, p. 23; III:2, p. 419; I:49, p. 110; III:7, p. 429. See also counterexamples in II:36, p. 370, or II:47, pp. 408–9, where Maimonides refers to "things said in a figurative way" through similes or metaphors as opposed to parables. On this see Cohen, *Three Approaches*, 119–21.

43. As we saw, *Makom* designating God is postbiblical—and Maimonides never mentions this. See Strauss, introduction to *Guide*, vol. 1, p. xxxi.

44. One could add the burning bush to Mount Sinai as sacred space accessible to or approachable by only one person, Moses, who is by definition immune to the dangers of bringing strange fire or engaging in idolatrous practice or speech.

45. Hebrew: Kapach, *Rabbeinu Moshe ben Maimon*, 403–4; Rambam, *Sefer moreh ha-nevokhim*, trans. Ibn Tibbon, III, chap. 51, p. 64.

46. Kraemer interprets these passages in a nonracist spirit, arguing that these final chapters of the *Guide* "concern the ideal of human perfection. Although the matrix is Jewish, the significance is human and universal." *Maimonides*, 398.

47. Yehuda Halevi, *The Kuzari*, trans. Hartwig Hirschfeld (London: George Routledge and Son, 1969), bk. 2, para. 20.

48. See above, chapter 1.

49. See a full translation and discussion of this poem in Scheindlin, *Song of the Distant Dove*, 63–65.

50. Ibid., 64–65.

51. See Jonathan Z. Smith, *Map Is Not Territory: Studies in the History of Religion* (Chicago: University of Chicago Press, 1978), xii ff., 128, 137, 142 and passim.

52. See DeKoven Ezrahi, *Booking Passage*, 33–51.

53. See above, chapter 1.

54. This is the view of Joshua Prawer, historian of the Crusader period. Prawer, *History of the Jews*, 142n37, 143n38. For Kraemer's reservations on this assertion, see *Maimonides*, 137–39; and see above, chapter 1.

55. Maimonides, *Commentary on the Mishnah*, Tractate Middot, catalogue 38, fols. 294v–295, Bodleian Libraries, University of Oxford (MS Poc.295). David Kraemer reproduces this diagram in his concise essay on Maimonides and Jerusalem for the catalogue of the exhibition on Jerusalem in the early Middle Ages at the New York Metropolitan Museum of Art (September 26, 2016–January 8, 2017). As he writes, "one of the many areas of dispute among those who study [Maimonides's] legacy is his relationship to Jerusalem." This essay focuses on two dimensions—the scanty record of the Rambam's visit to Jerusalem and his attitudes toward the city as reflected in his legal writings, specifically the laws of the "Chosen House" in his *Mishneh Torah*. "Maimonides and Jerusalem," *Jerusalem 1000–1400: Every People under Heaven*, ed. Barbara Drake Boehm and Melanie Holcomb (New Haven: Yale University Press, 2016), 82–83, 96.

56. The status of the *shekhinah* as holy emanation is a complex subject in itself, but it does suggest both that holiness inheres in that place and that the place itself is portable.

57. This subject, which would be elaborated in the *Guide*, appears in Maimonides's earliest work, his *Commentary on the Mishnah*, where the third of his thirteen articles of faith is "that God is incorporeal, without image or form." See Kraemer, *Maimonides*, 181–82.

58. Ibid., 398.

59. S. Y. Agnon, "Tehila," first published in Hebrew in the literary journal *Me'asef Davar* in 1949; republished in *'Ad hena* (1951; Jerusalem: Schocken, 1972), 183. Translated by Walter Lever in *Firstfruits: A Harvest of 25 Years of Israeli Writing*, ed. James A. Michener (Greenwich, CT: Fawcett, 1973), 62. Translation slightly emended. Quoted and discussed in DeKoven Ezrahi, *Booking Passage*, 101, 278n47.

60. Maimonides did not reject the martyr, who was already sanctified in much of the literature that preceded him, especially in the Talmud, but he offered the alternative, also going back to rabbinic times, as respectful of the imperative to *choose life*. See Kraemer, *Maimonides*, 104ff.

61. See, again, Girard, *Scapegoat*; and see above, chapter 1.

62. Kraemer, *Maimonides*, 114–15.

63. On Massada and its legacy, see Yael Zerubavel, *Recovered Roots: Collective Memory and the Making of Israeli National Tradition* (Chicago: University of Chicago Press, 1995), 62–63. We already glimpsed Spiegel's reproduction and discussion of Ephraim of Bonn's poetic reaction to the horrors in the Rhineland in the twelfth century through the topos of the akeda: *Last Trial*, 139–52. See chapter 1, above.

64. "Moses ben Maimon practiced Islam in Fez and eventually left and sailed to Acre. We do not know whether he was already a practicing Muslim when he came to Fez." Kraemer,

Maimonides, 123. See his chapter 7, "Did Maimonides Convert to Islam?" for a summary of the controversy and the evidence that Kraemer and others deem conclusive.

65. For a discussion of what Chana Kronfeld translates as "the wisdom of camouflage" (*ḥokhmat ha-hasva'a*), as it is expressed in the poetry of Yehuda Amichai, see *Full Severity*, 103–8.

66. On this see Kraemer, *Maimonides*, 115. Among the many Maimonides scholars who have tackled the subject of conversion or living under camouflage, see Abraham Joshua Heschel on "Fez [as] predestined for a life in hiding" and a "dress rehearsal . . . for the Spanish tragedy of the Marranoes to come." *Maimonides: A Biography*, trans. Joachim Neugroschel (New York: Farrar, Straus and Giroux, 1983), 15.

67. Private communication.

68. "Normative" is Avinoam Rosenak's term; he suggests that there may be an inherent contradiction between Maimonides's "normative position," his insistence that the Holy Land is made holy through human action, and the notion that Mount Moriah retains its sacred immanence. Avinoam Rosenak, "Halakhah, Thought and the Idea of Holiness in the Writings of Rabbi Chaim David Halevi," in *Creation and Re-creation in Jewish Thought: Festschrift in Honor of Joseph Dan on the Occasion of His Seventieth Birthday*, ed. Rachel Elior (Tübingen: Mohr Siebeck, 2005), 319. "Anthropological," again, is Kraemer's term. *Maimonides*, 398.

69. For a comprehensive consideration of Maimonides's positions on the Holy Land and on Jerusalem, see Isadore Twersky, "Maimonides and Eretz Yisrael: Halakhic, Philosophic and Historical Perspectives," in *Perspectives on Maimonides*, ed. Joel Kraemer (London: Littmann Library of Jewish Civilization, 1996), 257–90. By contrast with Yehuda Halevi and Nahmanides, Twersky writes, "if we come to search out [in Rambam's writings] an indubitable proto-Zionist inclination . . . we shall ultimately be disappointed." Politics and sovereignty can be deduced from his thinking, he continues, but with limits: "Maimonides' Messianic scenario shows that the political dimension was of central importance. Jewish sovereignty—although not aggressive or expansionist—is crucial." Ibid., 261, 285. That last caveat is, I believe, more significant than Twersky acknowledges. For a connection between this essay and Agnon's prose, see below, chapter 5.

70. Like many of Maimonides's so-called dictates, this too is not unambiguous. While "anthropologizing" sacrifice, he also adverts, in the *Mishneh Torah*, to the common article of faith that the messianic age would herald the resumption of sacrifice. But the most important aspect of Israel's return to the Land is, as we shall see below, not to conquer other people, but to live at peace.

71. In his discussion, at the end of the *Guide*, of the commandments regarding sacrifice, and specifically regarding wine and song, Maimonides acknowledges the "utility of pilgrimage" when the Temple is standing. But he doesn't explicitly encourage pilgrimage for the purpose of settling the land (*Guide* III:46, p. 592). "By not encouraging settlement in the Land of Israel as a religious obligation, Maimonides . . . differed from Judah ha-Levi" and from Nahmanides (1194–1270), writes Kraemer. *Maimonides*, 140. Many scholars believe that Maimonides may have undertaken his own pilgrimage to atone for the sin of conversion. He did write, in *Epistle on Conversion*, that it is preferable to go to Eretz Yisrael than to continue to live a covert life under Muslim rule in exile.

72. For a discussion of this phenomenon, see Alexandra Cuffel, "Call and Response: European Jewish Emigration to Egypt and Palestine in the Middle Ages," *Jewish Quarterly Review* 90, nos. 1–2 (July–October 1999): 61–102. Cuffel argues that sources deciphered from the Cairo

Geniza broaden the profile of those who made the trip to the Holy Land in the thirteenth century; not only rabbinic households and scholars but people of various ranks were among those who went on pilgrimage or even settled in Palestine. Cuffel's tentative conclusion, subject to further research, is that messianic currents were more powerful as engines of immigration for Jews from northern Europe than from southern Europe.

73. As should be apparent by now, the two scholars who have most influenced my work are Joel Kraemer and Mordecai Z. Cohen. Kraemer's magisterial biography of Maimonides not only encompasses the vast areas and centuries of research on the "Great Eagle," but also presents the material in a manner accessible to the contemporary reader and sensitive to the intellectual and ethical issues of our time. Cohen has written extensively on Maimonides's poetics based on a profound understanding not only of the medieval philosopher's own system but also of the cultural influences that helped to shape it.

74. See, for example, Arieh Bruce Saposnik, "Wailing Walls and Iron Walls: The Wailing Wall as Sacred Symbol in Zionist National Iconography," *American Historical Review* 120, no. 5 (December 2015): 1653–81. For references to the ongoing work of Tomer Persico on this subject, see the prologue, above, and the coda, below.

75. See DeKoven Ezrahi, "From Auschwitz to the Temple Mount," 291–313.

76. *Mishneh Torah*, Kings and Their Wars, 12:5. Quoted in Kraemer, *Maimonides*, 568n212. Kraemer shows how this was probably borrowed from Aristotle's notion of the hereafter. Ibid., 356, 323.

77. The contemporary Israeli philosopher whose halakhic positions on these subjects reflect, mutatis mutandis, some of the concerns we have raised in this chapter is Yeshayahu Leibowitz. After 1967, he took a strong stand in favor of the separation of religion and state and against messianic claims based on proximity to the sacred; he came to regard the pseudomessianic forces that emanated from the school of R. Zvi Yehuda Kook and those focused on the Wailing Wall and the Temple Mount as nothing less than idol worship. For an overview of his thinking on these subjects, including references to the Rambam, see Haim O. Rechnitzer, "Redemptive Theology in the Thought of Yeshayahu Leibowitz," *Israel Studies* 13, no. 3 (Fall 2008): 137–59. For an example of his fiery rhetoric, see Leibowitz's reference to the "Disco-Weeping Wall" in his essays collected as "The Six Day War" in *Judaism, Jewish People, and the State of Israel* [Heb.] (Tel Aviv: Schocken, 2005), 404–5. See also Leibowitz, "Ha-Rambam: Ha-adam ha-avrahami" [Maimonides: The Abrahamic Man], *Be-terem* 211 (1955): 20–22, http://leibowitz .co.il/about.asp?id=59#_edn1; and "Ha-geula ha-meshiḥit be-mishnato shel ha-Rambam" [Messianic Redemption in Maimonides's Thought], in Yeshayahu Leibowitz, *Emuna, historia ve-'arakhim: ma'amarim ve-hartsa'ot* [Religion, History, and Values: Articles and Lectures] (Jerusalem: Akademon, 1982), 89–101, http://www.leibowitz.co.il/leibarticles.asp?id=68. The significant differences that remain between Leibowitz and the Rambam, which are not only attributable to the existential, philosophical, and political differences between twelfth-century Morocco and Egypt and twentieth-century Jerusalem, are clearly beyond the scope of my project.

78. See Strauss, introduction to *Guide*, vol. 1, pp. xiii–xiv.

79. Leo Strauss, *Persecution and the Art of Writing* (Chicago: University of Chicago Press, 1952), 24–26, 31, 33, 36–37, 55–56, 57–58ff.

80. Sarah Stroumsa, "The Politico-Religious Context of Maimonides," in *The Trias of Maimonides / Die Trias des Maimonides: Jewish, Arabic, and Ancient Culture of Knowledge*, ed. G. Tamer (Berlin: De Gruyter, 2005), 264. Stroumsa presents here and in her other work a different approach to the philosophical and existential context of Maimonides's life and work

from that of Strauss. Defining Strauss's project mainly as a concern for "political theory," in which Maimonides, following the Platonic model of the philosopher-king, views "the prophet as the ideal statesman," Stroumsa argues for a more balanced understanding between different Islamic influences and Hellenistic ones—and of the nuances within the Arabic world generally and among Arabic philosophers more specifically. Most significant for our exploration of Maimonides's discussion of anthropomorphic language in the Bible is Stroumsa's argument that "Maimonides, just like the Almohads, identified true monotheism with a non-corporeal perception of God, and he included this understanding among the thirteen principles . . . of faith, the belief in which are preconditions for belonging to the Jewish people. Maimonides was not, of course, the first Jewish thinker to reject anthropomorphism, but none of his predecessors had defined this article of faith as the condition sine qua non for salvation . . . It is most probable that in this approach he followed the Almohads, [who also presented] a living model: a political regime which, despite the fact that it persecuted Maimonides' own people, presented some traits with which Maimonides could identify." Ibid., 257–58, 263, 268. See also Sarah Stroumsa, *Maimonides in his World: Portrait of a Mediterranean Thinker* (Princeton: Princeton University Press, 2012).

81. See DeKoven Ezrahi, *Booking Passage*.

82. Maimonides and Pines, quoted and discussed in Marmur, "Heschel's Two Maimonides," 253–54.

83. There were, of course, as we have seen, *avelei tzion*, Karaite "Mourners of Zion," through the twelfth century; on Rambam's description of how to rend one's garments when approaching the site of the ruined Temple, and the likelihood that he met a few of the remaining *avelei tzion*, see Kraemer, *Maimonides*, 138–39.

Chapter Four

1. S. Y. Agnon, Nobel Prize Banquet speech, December 10, 1966, http://www.nobelprize.org/nobel_prizes/literature/laureates/1966/agnon-speech.html. A different version of this genealogical claim appears in Agnon's story "The Sense of Smell" (Ḥush ha-re'aḥ), though in that text the names of specific sages are omitted. Shmuel Yosef Agnon, "The Sense of Smell," trans. Arthur Green, in *A Book That Was Lost and Other Stories*, ed. Alan Mintz and Anne Golomb Hoffman (New York: Schocken, 1995), 139–46.

2. There is much discussion of Kafka's influence on Agnon, who wrote in a letter to literary scholar Dov Sadan that "Kafka is not at the root of my soul [*eino mi-shoresh nishmati*], and that whoever is not at the root of my soul I do not absorb, even if he is as large as the ten elders who composed the book of Psalms." *Me-'atzmi el 'atzmi* [Between Me and Myself] (Jerusalem: Schocken, 2000), 255–56. But see Gershom Scholem's comment on this: "I am certain that Agnon read Kafka. I have no doubt, and Agnon denied this with a [kind of] injured stubbornness [*a shanut ne-'elevet*]. We were all certain of it and were surprised: why does he deny this. It was a bit silly." Dan Miron, interview with Scholem on Agnon in *Retzifut u-mered: Gershom Scholem be-omer u-ve-si'aḥ* [Continuity and Rebellion: Gershom Scholem in Conversation], ed. Avraham Shapira (Tel Aviv: Am Oved, 1994), 85. Among the critical studies that connect the two writers, see Hillel Barzel, *Bein Agnon le-Kafka* [Between Agnon and Kafka] (Ramat Gan: Bar Oryan, 1972).

3. This visit of Agnon's to the home of his publisher, Shlomo Zalman Schocken, was in August 1938. Agnon, *Me-'atzmi el 'atzmi*, 23.

4. S. Y. Agnon, *Ba-ḥanuto shel mar Lublin, 1962–1968* (Jerusalem: Schocken, 2001), 41; see also 184. *In Mr. Lublin's Store*, trans. Glenda Abramson, afterword by Haim Be'er (New Milford,

CT: Toby Press, 2016), vii–xxii. Indeed, the most revealing of the numerous references to Maimonides in Agnon's oeuvre may be in this novel, where the narrator relates that he annually commemorates the 20th of Teveth (circa mid-January), the anniversary of the Rambam's death, by dividing his day of contemplation into three parts, each devoted to studying another of his major texts: one third for "*Sefer ha-halakhot*" (presumably the reference is to *Sefer ha-mitzvot*, or Book of Commandments), one third for his commentary on the Mishnah (*Perush ha-mishnayot*), and the final third for *Moreh ha-nevokhim*. On the missed connections to the Rambam in this story, see Haim Be'er, "Ha-mafte'aḥ le-havanat *Ba-ḥanuto shel mar Lublin, me-et Agnon*" [The Key to Understanding Agnon's *In Mr. Lublin's Store*], *Haaretz*, August 12, 2016, https://www.haaretz .co.il/literature/study/.premium-1.3037102. Further, in a conversation with the Hebrew scholar A. M. Habermann, Agnon claims that he underwent a religious revival while praying in the synagogue in Egypt where the Rambam was said to have prayed. A. M. Habermann, "Siḥot ʿim S. Y. Agnon" [Conversations with Agnon], in *Masekhet sofrim ve-sifrut* [On Writers and Literature] (Jerusalem: Reuben Mas, 1976), 131. I am grateful to Rabbi Jeffrey Saks, the director of research at Beit Agnon, for a number of these references—and for ongoing conversations on many things related to Agnon's oeuvre and the immense scholarship surrounding it.

5. See the introduction above.

6. On this see above, chapter 1.

7. S. Y. Agnon, "The Tale of the Scribe," trans. Isaac Franck, in *A Book That Was Lost and Other Stories*, 176. Hebrew: S. Y. Agnon, "Aggadat ha-sofer," *Elu ve-elu* (Jerusalem: Schocken, 1972), 139. For an early account of the evolution of this story, and its enthusiastic reception by Gershom Scholem and Walter Benjamin in Germany in 1917, see Laor, *Ḥayei Agnon*, 112–13; and see Arnold Band, *Nostalgia and Nightmare: A Study in the Fiction of S. Y. Agnon* (Berkeley: University of California Press, 1968), 63–66; and Michal Arbel, "Ha-ketiva ke-matzeva: romantika ve-historiosophia be-sippurav shel S. Y. Agnon" [Writing as Epitaph: Romanticism and Philosophy of History in the Narratives of S. Y. Agnon], *Mikan* 2 (July 2001): 66–73.

8. See for example Ariel Hirschfeld's discussion of the clashing discourses in this story. *Likro et S. Y. Agnon* [Reading Agnon] (Tel Aviv: Aḥuzat Bayit, 2011), 63–89.

9. Pardes, *Agnon's Moonstruck Lovers*; Shachar, *Gufim ve-shemot*.

10. For a range of the exegetical suggestions that have accompanied these and other midrashlike constructions in Agnon, see the work of Dov Sadan, Gershon Shaked, Samuel [Shmuel] Werses, and, more recently, Nitza Ben-Dov, Michal Arbel, Ariel Hirschfeld, and Galili Shachar.

11. On this see "Yehuda Halevi and the Uncompleted Journey," in DeKoven Ezrahi, *Booking Passage*, 33–51.

12. David Stern, introduction to "The Tale of the Menorah," in Agnon, *Book That Was Lost*, 233.

13. See on this Yahil Tzaban, who claims that Agnon wrote for the "mefarshim," the commentators or scholars, and tucked all kinds of hints in his fictions to keep them busy. "Neged Agnon: O zehu ha-matsaʿ shel ha-bayit ha-yehudi" [Against Agnon; or, This Is the Platform of the Jewish Home], *Haaretz*, March 24, 2017, https://www.haaretz.co.il/literature/.premium -1.3948333. Of the many commentators who attempt to decipher the enigmas in an Agnon narrative, Galili Shachar is in my reading more of a "fellow traveler" through the mysterious tunnels than a detective devoted to exposing the "solution" to the "riddle." Shachar, *Gufim ve-shemot*.

14. Laor, *Ḥayei Agnon*.

15. Dov Sadan, ʿ*Al Shai Agnon: Masa ʿiyyun ve-ḥeker* [Studies in Agnon] (Tel Aviv: Hakibbutz ha-meuchad, 1973), 66. See Nitza Ben-Dov's elaboration of this argument in *Ahavot*

lo me'usharot: tiskul eroti, omanut va-mavet bi-yetzirat Agnon [Unhappy/Unapproved Loves: Erotic Frustration, Art, and Death in Agnon's Fiction] (Tel Aviv: Am Oved, 1997), 377–80.

16. Richard Eastman, "The Open Parable: Demonstration and Definition," *College English* 22 (October 1960): 15–18. Cited in Avraham Holtz, "Ha-mashal ha-patu'aḥ ke-mafte'aḥ le-sefer ha-ma'asim shel Shai Agnon" [The Open Parable as Key to S. Y. Agnon's *Book of Deeds*], *Ha-sifrut* 4 (1973): 303. See also a discussion of the open parable in Wayne Booth, *The Rhetoric of Fiction*, 2nd ed. (Chicago: University of Chicago Press, 1983), 286n8. And see below, the relevance of this insight to Walter Benjamin's reading of Kafka's allegorical structures.

17. Raphael's abstinence is, then, a sin against the very foundation of holiness in the Diaspora. See Boyarin, *Carnal Israel*, especially 107–33.

18. S. Y. Agnon, "Agunot," in *Book That Was Lost*, 35–36. In Hebrew: "'Agunot," *Elu ve-elu* (Jerusalem: Schocken, 1972), 405. This story, Agnon's first published Hebrew narrative, which appeared in Palestine in 1908 in the Hebrew periodical *Ha-Omer* (vol. 2, no. 1), underwent revisions in 1921 and 1931. The English translation by Baruch Hochman is of the 1951 text and was first published in 1975 in *Modern Hebrew Literature*, edited with introductions by Robert Alter (New York: Behrman House, 1975), 183–94; see Alter's introduction to the story, 179–82. It was then anthologized in Agnon, *A Book That Was Lost and Other Stories*. For the first thorough English exposition of the publishing history of this text, see Band, *Nostalgia and Nightmare*, 54–57. For a summary of the many textual references, early and late medieval midrashic texts, mystical allusions, etc., in the opening paragraph and throughout the text, see Gershon Shaked, "Midrash and Narrative: Agnon's 'Agunot,'" in *Midrash and Literature*, ed. Geoffrey H. Hartman and Sanford Budick (New Haven: Yale University Press, 1968), 285–303; and Hillel Barzel, *Sipurei ahava shel Shmuel Yosef Agnon* [S. Y. Agnon's Love Stories] (Ramat Gan: Bar Ilan University Press, 1975), 92–97.

19. David Stern argues persuasively that the introductory passage is "not so much a midrash as an 'aggadic homily [derasha]' modelled on the medieval *ma'aseh*" (the "quintessential literary form of medieval Hebrew literature")—and suggests that this is the "critical category for correctly appreciating the meaning of this enigmatic story." In the case of aggadic homily, the exemplum that "exemplifies a moral tale" usually refers to an actual—or presumably actual—historical event and not a "mere fiction (like a *mashal*)." Nonetheless, there is inevitably a misfit between the homily or lesson and the story itself; "the pious and traditional moral frames of the *ma'asim* are variously at odds with the profane and morally ambiguous worlds actually depicted in their narratives." Agnon would have applied these contradictions self-consciously. Additionally, Stern argues, along with others, "Agunot" is "about redemption (or, more accurately, the failure of redemption) and about the relationship of the artistic vocation to redemption." "Agnon from a Medieval Perspective," in *History and Literature: New Readings from Jewish Texts in Honor of Arnold Band*, ed. William Cutter and David C. Jacobson (Providence: Brown Judaic Studies, 2002), 176–82. Such a "pseudo-midrash," an authorizing fiction posing as a classical source, is a topos that Sholem Aleichem invokes as comic ploy in *Tevye the Dairyman*. As Hillel Halkin puts it, "in traditional Jewish terms . . . Tevye is not nearly so erudite as the uninformed reader, or some of his own unversed acquaintances, may think . . . When he wishes to quote a line of Talmud to Layzer Wolf, he has to make it up out of whole cloth." Introduction to *Sholem Aleichem, Tevye the Dairyman and The Railroad Stories*, trans. Hillel Halkin (New York: Schocken, 1987), xxviii.

20. Shaked, "Midrash and Narrative," 287. Anne Golomb Hoffman and Alan Mintz call "Agunot" Agnon's "signature story." *Book That Was Lost*, 31.

21. Agnon, "Agunot" [Heb.], p. 405.

22. See Ariel Hirschfeld's discussion of God's "quotation" of this phrase in His address to Knesset Yisrael—as well as other classical appropriations of this text, through kabbalistic traditions. Hirschfeld, "A Source and Oblivion—Story, Folk and Folktale in Agnon's Writing," *Jerusalem Studies in Jewish Folklore—Textures: Culture, Literature, Folklore, for Galit Hasan-Rokem* 28 (2013): 532–35.

23. "La-merḥakim yikḥu oto / raba hi ha-nedunya / rotzeh hu mar aviv kakha / u-mi yavo ʾimo bi-trunya." Hochman's translation of Friedele's song is masterful but does not capture the bitterness camouflaged in an Aramaically flavored, poetically naïve ditty where "nedunya" (dowry) rhymes with "trunya" (complaint): "They have borne him far away / to wed a dowered maiden, / His father did not care to know / Our hearts were heavy laden" (E 45, H 113).

24. The narrator's plea—"ʾad matai te'agena ha-neshamot she-be-ʿolamkha" (Till when shall the souls that dwell in Thy kingdom suffer the death of this life in bereavement, E 40, H 109)—the dream itself, and the reference to visions are, indeed, not unusual in Agnon's fiction. For an interesting discussion of the gothic motif and figures in Agnon's oeuvre, see Karen Grumberg, *Hebrew Gothic: History and the Poetics of Persecution* (Bloomington: Indiana University Press, 2019).

25. From Hochman's translation of *ʾagunot*, one could surmise that the "forsaken in love" could be men or women; Agnon's proto-feminist reference, containing possibly an implied critique of the halakhic position on the "ʿaguna" or abandoned wife, is lost in this translation.

26. The most salient example of this, and, I believe, the only major instance in Agnon's oeuvre in which a real 'tikkun' or repair is accomplished, is in his novella *Bilvav yamim* (1934), in which the main character, Hananiah, is detained on his way to the Holy Land with a group of pilgrims, because he must release a particular "ʿaguna." See DeKoven Ezrahi, *Booking Passage*, 81–102.

27. On the recitation of Song of Songs in the Passover service, see above, chapter 2.

28. The term "shoshanim" has been variously and often interchangeably translated as lilies, roses, or the more generic "flowers." In the Blochs' translation of Song of Songs, the lover (m.) is described as having "gone down to / his garden . . . . to graze and to gather lilies" (6:2). See Pardes citing Rashi's exegesis of the Torah as a "Rose" in her discussion of "Tale of the Scribe." *Agnon's Moonstruck Lovers*, 88.

29. Stern, "Ancient Jewish Interpretation of the Song of Songs," 100; I have also used Stern's rather than the Blochs' translation here for the biblical text.

30. This image also resonates with that of the Torah itself as a bride/beautiful woman in mystical sources, making the encounter with Miriam even more transgressive.

31. In the short discussion of this story in her evocative study of the Song of Songs in Israeli literature, Pardes claims that Rafael, and Rechnitz in the story "Shvuat emunim," are "so trapped in their passion for their work that they lose touch with the women whom they love." *Agnon's Moonstruck Lovers*, 88–89, 167n47. Hirschfeld talks about the conflict and contiguity in this story and in "Agunot" between art and eros. *Likro et S. Y. Agnon*, 71. See also Alan Mintz and Anne Golomb Hoffman's introduction to this story in their collection of Agnon's stories, *A Book That Was Lost and Other Stories*, 164; and Hoffman's discussion elsewhere of this story, and her claim that "there are subtle indications that his [Rafael's] excess is not simply to be understood as piety." *Between Exile and Return: S. Y. Agnon and the Drama of Writing* (Albany: SUNY Press, 1991), 34.

32. Hirschfeld offers a very different reading of the immersion in cold water. He also speculates on parallels between Rafael and Agnon himself, who dedicated the story to his wife Esther (!!). *Likro et S. Y. Agnon*, 64.

33. See Fishbane, *JPS Bible Commentary*, 110; and see the Hebrew of Shir ha-shirim Rabbah. On this see above, chapter 2.

34. Shaked, "Midrash and Narrative," 296.

35. Pardes, *Agnon's Moonstruck Lovers*, 15. See above, chapter 2.

36. Agnon, "Va-terev ḥokhmat Shlomo," in *'Ad hena* (Jerusalem: Schocken, 1972); trans. Mordecai Beck, *Ariel—Israel Review of Arts and Letters* 92 (1993): 278–79. Quoted in Pardes, *Song of Songs*, 225–29.

37. Pardes, *Song of Songs*, 229.

38. Quoted in C. Bloch, "In the Garden of Delights," 3, 14–15. See also Alter's earlier chapter on Song of Songs, "The Garden of Metaphor," *Art of Biblical Poetry*, 185–203.

39. In his discussion of Yehuda Halevi, Michael Fishbane embraces the "kiss of God" as the ultimate mingling with the divine after one has shuffled off the mortal coil. "For [Yehuda] Halevi and similar seekers, life in this world is a torment of false desire, a web of entanglements in which the face of pleasure is the receding image of God, and from which only death can bring release." *The Kiss of God: Spiritual and Mystical Death in Judaism* (Seattle: University of Washington Press, 1994), 11, 20. For my very different reading of Halevi's poetic and theological quest, see DeKoven Ezrahi, *Booking Passage*, 46–51. But of course Fishbane is drawing on an established tradition for which "mitat neshika" (death by a kiss) is applied to those righteous individuals who are rewarded with a painless death. See the last strophe of Chana Bloch's poem "The Face of Death," written when she was dying of cancer: "I refuse to turn my eyes away. / I am choosing day by day to see / even as I am seen, till the last face-to-face / when I am taken with a kiss." Quoted in Chana Kronfeld, "My Chana," *Shofar* 36, no. 2, tribute issue for Chana Bloch (Summer 2018): 10.

40. Bland, *Artless Jew*, 79.

41. On this image, and also on Dan Pagis's elaboration of the image, see above, chapter 3.

42. Walter Benjamin, "Some Reflections on Kafka," from "Letter to Gerhard Scholem," June 12, 1938, in *Illuminations*, trans. Harry Zohn, ed. Hannah Arendt (New York: Schocken, 1968), 144. There have of course been nearly as many subsequent translations, interpretations, and elaborations of this text, which was originally published in Germany in 1955 and first published in English in 1968, as of the Kafka narrative itself. See, for example, Howard Eiland, *Walter Benjamin: A Critical Life* (Cambridge: Belknap Press, 2014), 602. And see Vivian Liska, who reads Benjamin's presentation of the parable, or the aggadah, somewhat differently, as part of an ongoing polemic with the Pauline turn in contemporary thought, represented currently by Giorgio Agamben. *German-Jewish Thought and Its Afterlife: A Tenuous Legacy* (Bloomington: Indiana University Press, 2016), 57–65. She argues for the "necessary complementarity" of the law (*halakha*) with narrative (*aggadah*), which "is itself the notion of justice upheld by Judaism." Ibid., 65.

43. Fishbane, introduction to *The JPS Bible Commentary*, 51. See above, chapter 2.

Chapter Five

1. "Maimonides and Eretz Yisrael" is an English version of the Hebrew essay Twersky published twenty years earlier. Yitzhak Tversky, "Ha-Rambam ve-Eretz Yisrael: hebetim hilkhati'im, philosophi'im ve-histori'im," in *Tarbut ve-ḥevra be-toldot Yisrael bi-yemei ha-benayim: Kovetz ma'amarim le-zikhro shel Haim Hillel Ben-Sasson* [Medieval Jewish Culture and Society: Essays in Memory of Haim Hillel Ben-Sasson], ed. Reuven [Robert] Bonfil, Menahem Ben-Sasson,

and Joseph Hacker (Jerusalem: Mercaz Zalman Shazar, 1988), 353–81. The above quote is from 377–79.

2. Taken from the story "Ha-yeraḥmielim" [The Yerahmiels]. S. Y. Agnon, *Korot bateinu* (Jerusalem: Schocken, 1979), 48–49, 56–57. Although this posthumous collection of fictionalized, semi-autobiographical stories, mainly referring to Agnon's family and communal history, contains tales written as early as the immediate postwar period, "Ha-yeraḥmielim" was evidently written in 1969. See Laor, *Ḥayei Agnon*, 20, 519–22, 629–30. See also Laor, "La'asot sefer yoḥasin le-zar'o: *Korot Bateinu* me-et S. Y. Agnon," *Haaretz*, July 13, 1979, 21–24.

3. There is a significant and consequential misspelling—or deliberate misrepresentation—in Twersky's English version of the title of Agnon's story as "*beiteinu*" or "our house"—which would signify the only House worthy of its name for Twersky: the Beit ha-mikdash or Holy Temple. The word in Agnon's text and in the Song of Songs is "*bateinu*" which refers to "our houses," though "our roofbeams" in the Song camouflage that.

4. Agnon, *Korot bateinu*, 59–62.

5. We will soon add Yehuda Amichai's voice to this confection, as his recipe for "preserves" includes the merciful ingredient of forgetting to the implacable imperative to remember. See the coda, below.

6. S. Y. Agnon, Nobel Prize Banquet speech, December 10, 1966, http://www.nobelprize.org/nobel_prizes/literature/laureates/1966/agnon-speech.html.

7. Baruch Kurzweil was the most prominent representative of a more traditional embrace of Agnon. *Masot 'al sipurei Shai Agnon* [Essays on the Stories of S. Y. Agnon] (Jerusalem: Schocken, 1962).

8. The sense of surrogacy in the writing of the modern paytan or scribe is underscored in a number of Agnon's stories, such as "Ha-siman" and "Lefi ha-tza'ar ha-sakhar." See DeKoven Ezrahi, "Agnon Before and After," *Prooftexts* 2, no. 1 (January 1982): 78–94; and see Shachar, *Gufim ve-shemot*.

9. See Dan Miron, "Mi-mashal le-sipur toladi: petiḥa le-diyun bi-*tmol shilshom*" [From Parable to Chronicle: Preliminary Discussion of *Tmol shilshom*], in *Kovetz Agnon* II, ed. Emuna Yaron et al. (Jerusalem: Magnes Press, 2000), 94.

10. As we saw in the preceding chapter, Dov Sadan was one of the first of Agnon's contemporaries to acknowledge the tentative nature of every hermeneutic act, and to suggest, slyly, that every commentator write in parenthesis at the top of his exegesis an admonition to both himself and his readers: "(For the time being)." Precisely because *Tmol shilshom* is less dense with classical intertexts than a novella like *Bilvav yamim* or a story like "Tehila" or "'Ido ve-'eynam," the riddle is less an exegetical exercise and therefore remains even more mysterious.

11. T. W. Adorno, *Aesthetic Theory* (London: Routledge, 1984), 173, 177, 179. In conflating distinct domains, both riddles and enigmas "produce change in the world," according to Galit Hasan-Rokem and David Shulman. The first invite attempts to reach closure and resolution through "disambiguating and disentangling" those domains; the second allow for a more open-ended engagement with mystery. *Untying the Knot: On Riddles and Other Enigmatic Modes* (New York: Oxford University Press, 1996), 5.

12. This novel and the wide array of interpretive strategies are discussed in greater detail in my essay "Sentient Dogs, Liberated Rams, and Talking Asses: Agnon's Biblical Zoo—or Rereading *Tmol shilshom*," *AJS Review* 28, no. 1 (April 2004): 105–35. There I relied on my close analysis of the novel; here I am focusing more on the moves that relate to Agnon's complex engagement with Jerusalem and the poetics that serve those moves.

13. S. Y. Agnon, *Tmol shilshom* (1945-46; Jerusalem: Schocken, 1971); English translation: *Only Yesterday*, trans. Barbara Harshav (Princeton: Princeton University Press, 2000). Unless otherwise noted, I am using this translation throughout.

14. Michael André Bernstein, *Foregone Conclusions: Against Apocalyptic History* (Berkeley: University of California Press, 1994), 9-41, passim, especially 16. I am, admittedly, applying this term rather freely, as Bernstein's critique is of teleological historiography, history understood as determined from its endpoints. But I am arguing that, published in the immediate wake of the Holocaust, this novel was structured to invite such readings—and that such readings have only solidified over the decades.

15. Agnon, in his letter to Kurzweil, which we will discuss below, says that the story is "about a man and about a dog" (*shel ish ve-shel kelev*). Agnon to Kurzweil, January 28, 1946. Lilian Dvi-Guri, ed., *Kurzweil-Agnon-UZG: Correspondence* (Ramat Gan: Bar Ilan University Press, 1977), 18-21.

16. So named because the principal of the "Alliance Israel" French school read the letters that spell dog (*kelev* in Hebrew) on his back "as was his wont from left to right." "Well then," confides the narrator to the reader, "we can call him Balak, too. And what was his name, perhaps he had a name and it sank and perhaps he didn't have a name . . ." (E 303, H 291-92). Agnon, as is *his* wont, takes liberties with orthography here, exchanging the letter "kuf" in Balak's name for the "kaf" in *kelev* (dog). And "Balak" has actually appeared by name a few pages before this etymological disquisition (E 299, H 288).

17. Although there were many alterations in the original story as the akeda became a topos of Jewish, Christian, and Muslim imagination, perhaps the *only constant* in these traditions, as I argued in chapter 1, is also the most significant act of "misreading" of the biblical text: the actual sacrifice of Isaac. In Agnon's novel, the misreading starts with the principal of the Alliance Israel school and extends to all those inhabitants of Jerusalem who literalize the text on the dog's back.

18. On Kafka's meditation on Abraham, and on Hanoch Levin's play *Malkat Ambatia*, with its second, melancholy, akeda poem as the only nonsatirical element in the drama, see above, chapter 1. For Kierkegaard's surprising fictional exercises, see *Fear and Trembling*, in *The Kierkegaard Reader*, ed. Jane Chamberlain and Jonathan Rée (Oxford: Blackwell, 2001), 81-83.

19. From Kafka's letter to Robert Klopstock, June 1921. See above, chapter 1.

20. *Rav roman—Masternovel—*is the title and subject of Boaz Arpali's book. Arpali compares Isaac, among others, to Karl in Kafka's *Amerika. Rav roman: hamisha ma'amarim 'al Tmol shilshom me-et S. Y. Agnon* [Masternovel: Five Essays on *Tmol Shilshom* by S. Y. Agnon] (Tel Aviv: Ha-kibbutz ha-meuchad, 1998).

21. Avraham Holtz claims that *Tmol shilshom* belongs to the genre of "documentary fiction." "Hitbonenut be-firtei *Tmol shilshom*" [Reflecting on the Details: *Tmol shilshom*], in *Kovetz Agnon*, ed. Emuna Yaron et al. (Jerusalem: Magnes Press, 1994), 178-221.

22. On Isaac as candidate for the average hero of modern tragedy, see Miron's discussion of the influences of Flaubert and Tolstoy in "Bein shtei neshamot: ha-analogia ha-faustit bi-*tmol shilshom* le-shai agnon" [Between Two Souls: The Faustian Analogy in S. Y. Agnon's *Tmol Shilshom*], in *Mi-vilna li-yerushalayim* [From Vilna to Jerusalem], ed. David Asaf, Israel Bartal, et al. (Jerusalem: Magnes Press, 2002), 549-608. Miron goes through all the possible permutations of the novel, from tragedy through satire to social realism, montage, melodrama, and then comes back to his initial claim that the novel is a tragic-epic. "Bein shtei neshamot," 591. An expanded version of this essay appeared recently in book form as *Bein shtei neshamot: ha-analogia ha-faustit bi-tmol shilshom le-shai agnon: ba'ayat ha-tragedia ha-modernit* [Between Two Souls:

The Faustian Analogy in S. Y. Agnon's *Tmol Shilshom*: The Dilemma of Modern Tragedy] (Jerusalem: Mossad Bialik, 2020). See also Miron, "Mi-mashal le-sipur toladi," 87–159. Gershon Shaked, Arpali, and many others have argued for some version of the Greek tragic paradigm as informing *Tmol shilshom*. See Arpali, *Rav roman*, 104–11.

23. Avraham Band, "Ha-ḥet ve-ʿonsho bi-*Tmol shilshom*" [Crime and Punishment in *Tmol shilshom*], *Molad* 1, n.s., 24 (1967–68): 75–78. Dostoevsky's novel, alluded to here, can itself be considered a "rav-roman" or polygeneric novel, through the prism that Mikhail Bakhtin offers of the "polyphonic novel." *Problems of Dostoevsky's Poetics*, ed. and trans. Caryl Emerson (Minneapolis: University of Minnesota Press, 1984), 178 and passim.

24. In his ongoing explorations of *Tmol shilshom* as a tragic-epic novel, Miron drops references to the akeda as amplifying the tragic idea—without further explanation: "The story places *akedat yitzhak* and not the faith of Abraham as the principal myth of the period." "Bein shtei neshamot," 600. See also his claim that the story can be read both as an "absurd akeda" and as a "mystical akeda," without further elaboration. "Mi-mashal le-sipur toladi," 93. See also, on the akeda motif in *Tmol shilshom*, the work of Sarah Hagar and Hillel Weiss.

25. Søren Kierkegaard, *Fear and Trembling*, trans. Alastair Hannai (New York: Penguin, 2005), 53. Jacques Derrida's response is that there is no question: Abraham is a murderer. See above, chapter 1.

26. Bernstein, *Foregone Conclusions*, 95–119.

27. See chapter 1, above.

28. Baruch Kurzweil, who hailed the novel as "the most important and successful experiment in the field of the social novel in our modern literature," did admit, in a private exchange of letters with Agnon, his bafflement over the irreconcilable appearance of the dog Balak in Isaac's story. Kurzweil's letter and Agnon's response opened the door to decades of critical debate over the genesis and unity of the text. Kurzweil, *Masot*, 104. See also Boaz Arpali's question of how the story of the dog Balak fits into a "social-psychological novel" (*roman ḥevrati-psychologi*) featuring Isaac. "Balak ki-fshuto u-khe-midrasho" [Balak as Literal and as Midrash], in *Kovetz Agnon II*, ed. Emuna Yaron et al. (Jerusalem: Magnes Press, 2000), 167.

29. See Laor, *Ḥayei Agnon*, 370.

30. Robert Alter, *Hebrew and Modernity* (Bloomington: Indiana University Press, 1994), 73; and see his *The Invention of Hebrew Prose: Modern Fiction and the Language of Realism* (Seattle: University of Washington Press, 1988). Alter also cites exceptions in the Books of Esther, Daniel, Jonah, etc. "Introduction to the Old Testament," in *The Literary Guide to the Bible*, ed. Robert Alter and Frank Kermode (Cambridge: Harvard University Press, 1987), 30. See also Dan Miron's claim that the novel was, for Agnon, an "alien genre" in which he nevertheless toiled, with great success. "Domesticating a Foreign Genre: Agnon's Transactions with the Novel," *Prooftexts* 7, no. 1 (January 1987): 19ff.

31. Amos Oz, *The Silence of Heaven: Agnon's Fear of God*, trans. Barbara Harshav (Princeton: Princeton University Press, 2000), 75, 63.

32. I am, as will be increasingly apparent, giving far more credit to Isaac as a man of imagination than most readers. Miron insists that as a "*baʿal dimyonot*, Isaac was unable to distinguish between preconceived notions and fantasy." "Mi-mashal le-sipur toladi," 129.

33. As we saw, the much-quoted opening of Agnon's first story under his pseudonym (1908) can be read as a manifesto for all the fiction to come; see Agnon, "Agunot," *Book That Was Lost*, 183, and my discussion above, chapter 4. The end of Eden is, then, the beginning of fiction.

34. The narration, spanning the period roughly from 1908 to 1911, is characterized by the accuracy of many of its descriptive passages, the presence of such explicitly historical figures as

Y. H. Brenner and A. D. Gordon, and such thinly disguised figures as Hemdat (Agnon's literary and biological progeny). See Oz's summary of the critical consensus in decoding the identity of such figures. Oz, *Silence of Heaven*, 177. Still, to the persistent critical question of whether *Tmol shilshom* is a "novel of the Second Aliyah," a novel of the "Zeitgeist," Oz responds: "If a computer were asked to create a composite character embodying the characteristic sociological profile of the people of the Second Aliya, the product would not be Isaac." Ibid., 98–99. In a way, though, a human computer *did* create the sociological profile. We note, with some impatient page turning, that the history-laden passages are more what Harshav calls "categories and catalogues" than a realistic, "novelistic" evocation of place and time. Harshav, introduction to Agnon, *Only Yesterday*, xx. The overdetermined rhetoric of Zionist and religious messianism is matched by the overstuffed catalogues of historical fact and the overcrowded gatherings in Hebrew-speaking cafés.

35. Hirschfeld reflects early twenty-first-century reflexes in conflating the Zionist story with traditional Jewish theodicy. *Likro et S. Y. Agnon*, 151–64.

36. The reigning principle here might be captured in the Hebrew phrase "he-ḥalom ve-shivro," whose biblical meaning is the dream and its exposition or interpretation (Judg. 7:15). The phrase began to acquire different dimensions when it was appropriated by Eliezer Ben Yehuda in 1917 as the (Zionist) dream and its fulfillment. "He-ḥalom ve-shivro-ha-ʾidan ha-rishon" [The Dream and Its Meaning], in *He-ḥalom ve-shivro: mivḥar ktavim be ʾinyanei lashon* [The Dream and Its Meaning: A Selection of Writings on Language], ed. Reuven Sivan (Jerusalem: Bialik, 1978), https://benyehuda.org/read/5692. But in popular Israeli culture it has come to signify the very opposite—the dream and its default, or dystopic, mode. The motif of the dream is ubiquitous in Zionist parlance—from Herzl's "if you will it, it is not a dream," through Ben Yehuda to Rachel Bluwstein's poem "Ve-ulai," which incorporates the hallucinatory element in the dream state: "were you real or did I dream a dream?" *Anthology of Modern Hebrew Poetry*, trans. A. C. Jacobs (Jerusalem: Institute for the Translation of Hebrew Literature and Israel Universities Press, 1966), https://pij.org/articles/536. On the different iterations of Herzl's dream metaphor, see DeKoven Ezrahi, *Booking Passage*, 3, 91, 243.

37. In a contemporary review of the novel, Leah Goldberg described Kumer sympathetically as a "funnel" or "sieve" through which the characteristics of the generation flow. Quoted from *Mishmar* (February 22, 1946) in Laor, *Ḥayei Agnon*, 373, 685n10. This was reflected in Oz's reading, which I cited above.

38. I am using Harshav's translation even though *baʿal ha-dimyonot* can be translated, as it is elsewhere, as "man of imagination," as *baʿal* denotes ownership; the point, however, is well taken in this passage, which contrasts divine and human agency.

39. Everett Fox, trans., *The Five Books of Moses* (New York: Schocken, 2000), 777; the reference is to Martin Buber's *Moses: The Revelation and the Covenant* (New York: Harper and Brothers, 1958).

40. Fox and Alter both translate "malakh" in Num. 22:23 as "messenger": "And the ass saw the Lord's messenger stationed in the road." Alter, *Hebrew Bible*, 1:559.

41. "In [Num.] 22:21–35 the redactor has included the folktale of Balaam's talking ass . . ." James S. Ackerman, "Numbers," in Alter and Kermode, *Literary Guide to the Bible*, 86.

42. Tzvetan Todorov, *The Fantastic: A Structural Approach to a Literary Genre*, trans. Richard Howard (Ithaca: Cornell University Press, 1973), 25, 33. For both a survey of the vast critical literature on this subject and her own compelling theory, see Rosemary Jackson, *Fantasy: The Literature of Subversion* (London: Routledge, 1981).

276 NOTES TO PAGES 153-157

43. At times Miron refers to *Faust* as "model" and at times as "analogue." In any case, he claims that whereas parallels to other texts are specific and sporadic (*nekudati*), *Faust* is structurally integral (*tavniti*) to the novel. "Bein shtei neshamot," 560, 574. Among the many other interpretations offered over the years are those of Avraham Band, "Ha-ḥet ve-'onsho bi-*Tmol shilshom*," 77; Arpali, *Rav roman*, 16. See also Meshulam Tuchner, who argues that Balak is Isaac's suffering alter ego. *Pesher Agnon* [Interpreting Agnon] (Ramat Gan: Massada, 1968), 62-80. Eli Schweid claims that it is not the dog who is an "animal reflection" of the man, but Isaac who is "a human reflection of the dog." "Kelev ḥutzot—ve-adam: 'iyyun be-*Tmol shilshom* le-Shai Agnon" [Stray Dog—and a Man: Studies in *Tmol shilshom*], *Molad* 11 (December–January 1958): 387.

44. "O im balak eyno ela netakh basar na' she-zarak Agnon li-mevakrav she-yevashluhu kakh she-ye'arev le-ḥikam ve-yishtalev 'im hashkafat 'olamam." Ben-Dov, *Ahavot lo me'usharot*, 378.

45. Fox, *Five Books of Moses*, 769.

46. Alter, *Art of Biblical Narrative*, 104-6. Alter brings a quote from the Midrash—"You have humiliated me! If I had a sword in my hand, I would kill you" (Ba-Midbar Rabbah 20:21)—to demonstrate that this commentary "shrewdly notes the irony of Balaam's wanting a sword to kill an ass when he has set out to destroy a whole nation with his words alone," while the angel stands in the wings, "sword in hand."

47. The seeming slippage in which the Midrash refers to "Parashat Balaam" may not be a mistake so much as a rabbinic recognition that the story is really about Balaam, not Balak. The Balaam/Balak trail also leads us to the Zohar, where connections between Balaam and the canine theme developed in Agnon's novel become clear. See Hillel Barzel, "Diyokano shel kelev: 'iyyun mashveh: 'kelev ḥutzot' mi-tokh *tmol shilshom* le-shai agnon u-meḥkarav shel kelev lefi kafka" [Profile of a Dog: Comparative Study of Agnon and Kafka], *Karmelit* 14-15 (1968): 161-73. Barzel also shows that it is not only Isaac who has an ancestor in the novel *Hakhnasat kalah*; Balak, he claims, is the great-grand-dog [*nin*] of the dog encountered by R. Yudel Hasid.

48. The phrase "she divided herself into many sections" not only emphasizes the land's agency (over and against its inhabitants) but also has the slang meaning, borrowed from Yiddish, of pretending to be divided (*machn zikh* means to make oneself, to pretend).

49. A similar passage represents the pilgrims' arrival at the Western Wall in Agnon's novella *Bilvav yamim* and in the story "Tehila." This is discussed in DeKoven Ezrahi, *Booking Passage*, 94.

50. Hoffman takes these two passages in a very different direction, namely, as evidence of Isaac's search for "maternal presence" as part of his oedipal struggle. *Between Exile and Return*, 139-41.

51. "U-mi she-eino yakhol le-khaven et ha-ruḥot mekhavnim liban lifnei ha-makom u-mitpalelim she-ne'emar ve-hitpalelu el ha-shem; haya 'omed be-ḥu"l yekhaven et libo ke-neged eretz yisrael she-ne'emar ve-hitpalelu el ha-shem derekh artzam; haya 'omed be-eretz yisrael yekhaven et libo ke-neged yerushalayim she-ne'emar ve-hitpalelu el ha-'ir ha-zot; ha-'omdim bi-yerushalayim mitpalelim ke-neged beit ha-mikdash she-ne'emar ve-hitpalelu el ha-bayit ha-ze; ha-'omdim ba-mikdash yekhavnu et liban ke-neged beit kodshei ha-kodashim she-ne'emar ve-hitpalelu el ha-makom ha-ze; nimtze'u ha-'omdim le-tzafon peneihem la-darom ha-'omdim ba-darom peneihem la-tzafon ha-'omdim ba-mizraḥ peneihem la-ma'arav ha-'omdim ba-ma'arav peneihem la-mizraḥ ve-nimtze'u kol yisrael mitpalelim le-makom eḥad." *Mishnah, maskekhet zerayim, tosefta brakhot gimel: tet zayin* (2002), https://www.mechon-mamre.org/b/f/f11.htm. See the coda below for a broader discussion of this passage.

52. Ricoeur, *Rule of Metaphor*, 205–6.

53. In this he is closer to the craftsman Yohanan Lightfoot (nicknamed Sweetfoot, "ha-regel ha-metukah"). Lightfoot's father was a painter of Russian Orthodox icons, and he himself is a master "craftsman" (E 72–77, H 71–77). See Eddy Zemach, who argues that the true artisan or craftsman (*uman*) in *Tmol shilshom* is Lightfoot. Zemach provides a fascinating reading of the entire novel through Sweetfoot and the tension between shoes (feet) and hats, between the upper and the lower spheres. "Ha-regel ha-metukah: mikra be-*tmol shilshom*" [Sweetfoot: A Reading of *Tmol shilshom*], in Eddy Zemach, *Kria tama: 'Iyyunim be-sifrut 'ivrit* [Readings in Hebrew Literature] (Tel Aviv: Ha-kibbutz ha-meuchad, 1990), 25–39 (originally published in *Haaretz*, 1963); and Zemach, "Ba-'avur na'alayim" [For the Sake of Shoes], in *Kria tama*, 62–70.

54. Miron argues that Agnon's "transactions with the novel" were never fully resolved. "Like all who attempt *tikkun* or religious reformation of the world, [Agnon] put himself in the heart of the danger, where he was most apt to be hurt," claims Miron. What that meant, continues Miron, was that he could only go so far in realizing the form of the modern novel: "Accepting the wholeness offered by eros and poetry" as "possible fulfillment" for "*l'homme moyen sensuel*" who appears in later novels like *Guest for the Night*, *Only Yesterday*, and *Shira* would have meant a kind of "exile" from the "personal spiritual source of Agnon's life and art." Miron, "Domesticating," 19, 25–26.

55. On *midat ha-hishtavut* in Hassidic texts, see Rachel Elior, *Ḥarut 'al ha-luḥot: ha-maḥshava ha-ḥasidit, mekoroteha ha-misti'im vi-yesodoteha ha-kabali'im* [Incised in the Tablets] (Tel Aviv: Misrad ha-bitahon, 1999), 150–64, especially the discussion of the tzaddik in his mediation between the material and the spiritual worlds, 162–63.

56. Ricoeur, *Rule of Metaphor*, 227.

57. Of course, not every equation is figurative. The tenor and the vehicle in this sentence are taken from the same semantic field, a field that literally refers to Isaac's profession. But the construct itself will lead to something even more consequential.

58. I Kings 19:12. It is not in the earthquake, not in the whirlwind, not in the fire, but in the "still, small voice" that God manifests Himself to Elijah in this passage. Alter translates this as "a sound of minute stillness." See Yair Zakovitch, "Kol demama daka: Tzura ve-tokhen be-Malakhim 1, 19:12" [A Still Small Voice: Structure and Content in I Kings 19:12], *Tarbiz* 51, no. 3 (1983): 329–46. As a man of peace, Isaac Kumer is a worthy vessel of this message.

59. I am grateful to my colleague Galit Hasan-Rokem for first calling my attention to the resonances of the akeda in this passage.

60. Balak becomes what Hoffman calls "a wandering text . . . a writing cut loose, 'demonic' in its randomness." *Between Exile and Return*, 128–29. See also Arbel, "Ha-ketiva ke-matzeva"; and Arbel, *Katuv 'al 'oro shel kelev: 'al tefisat ha-yetzira etsel Shay Agnon* [Written on the Dog's Skin: S. Y. Agnon, Concepts of Creativity and Art] (Jerusalem: Keter and Ben Gurion University, 2006), 151, 198–254 and passim.

61. Hoffman, *Between Exile and Return*, 128.

62. Reb Fayish, Shifra's father, is an exemplar of those literalists who believe their strict earthly acts will hasten the coming of the Redeemer: "Reb Fayish [the ritual slaughterer] could have enjoyed his life and filled his belly with meat, but he was fonder of a tiny bit of Wild Ox in the World-to-Come than of all the living animals and birds in This World, and was rigorous about disqualifying meat as unfit even in cases when most legal rabbinical opinions would have permitted it" (E 331, H 315). Because he lives in a state of messianic anxiety, Reb Fayish can

find—and give—no comfort in this world. It is only when he has been neutralized, paralyzed by his own encounter with Balak, that his literal-mindedness ceases to interfere with Isaac's chances for fulfillment as artist and as lover.

63. Miron evocatively cites Magritte's "Ceci n'est pas une pipe" to demonstrate the difference between Isaac's act and the self-consciously mimetic artistic enterprise. "Bein shtei neshamot," 559.

64. "Dam klavim," dog's blood, or *pshakrev*, is a common Polish/Russian curse that also migrated to Yiddish.

65. On "ko'aḥ ha-medameh," or the imaginative faculty, in both Agnon and Maimonides, see chapter 4.

66. See above, chapter 1. On Jewish messianism in its comic mode, and the distinction between deferred and "anxious" messianism, see DeKoven Ezrahi, "After Such Knowledge," 287–313. And see Oz's definition of "true messianism" as belonging "to the grammatical and emotional sphere of the future." *Silence of Heaven*, 102.

67. Spiegel, *Last Trial*, 69. See above, chapter 1.

68. For a sanitized version of how "Um Juni" became Kibbutz Degania, see Center for Israel Education, "First Kibbutz in Israel Is Established," https://israeled.org/degania-alef-established-as-first-kibbutz-in-israel/ (accessed July 9, 2021). For a more balanced account, see Rachel S. Havrelock, "Pioneers and Refugees: Arabs and Jews in the Jordan River Valley," in *Understanding Lives in the Borderlands: Boundaries in Depth and in Motion*, ed. William Zartman (Athens: University of Georgia Press, 2010), 198–99.

69. Laor, *Ḥayei Agnon*, 685n7.

70. See Slavoj Žižek on Lacan and the Real: "the hidden/traumatic underside of our existence or sense of reality, whose disturbing effects are felt in strange and unexpected places: the Lacanian Sublime." Marek Wieczorek, "The Ridiculous, Sublime Art of Slavoj Žižek," introduction to Slavoj Žižek, *The Art of the Ridiculous Sublime: On David Lynch's Lost Highway* (Seattle: University of Washington Press, 2000), viii. Balak is the vessel through which the *Unheimliche* can be expressed as the space emptied by the withdrawal of the divine presence, or, in the language of Hélène Cixous, the place of "signs without significance." Cixous's position is paraphrased by Jackson in *Fantasy*, 68.

71. Ariel Hirschfeld comes close to a reading that would privilege the "fantastic," but he resolves the doubt inherent in the fantastic in favor of the more peremptory mode of the grotesque. Hirschfeld, "'Ivut ha-merḥav bi-groteska bi-*tmol shilshom*" [Distortion of Space as Grotesque in *Tmol shilshom* by S. Y. Agnon], *Jerusalem Studies in Hebrew Literature* 2 (1982): 50ff. Eli Schweid's reading comes close to Hirschfeld's; he hears in the novel's conclusion a mad shriek that echoes in the cosmic vacuum, with no hope for any human or divine resolution beyond the horizon of the novel. "Kelev ḥutzot," 388. Hirschfeld's definition of the "grotesque" is based in part on that of W. Kayser, with whom Bakhtin strenuously disagrees. Bakhtin's far more capacious, "novelistic," application of the grotesque, especially the subcategory of "realist grotesque," with its roots in the "culture of folk humor and the carnival spirit," as opposed to Kayser's presentation of the "gloomy, terrifying . . . romantic and modernist grotesque," is, again, more consistent with the view I am endorsing here. Bakhtin, *Rabelais and His World*, trans. Helene Iswolsky (Bloomington: Indiana University Press, 1984), 46–58.

72. Miron puts this as the most crucial question in the novel. "Bein shtei neshamot," 592. See also Arpali, one of the few who acknowledge that the narrative, read as a string of contingencies without its terrible and unpredictable conclusion, could be emplotted as comedy. *Rav roman*, 11.

73. Agnon to Kurzweil, January 28, 1946. Dvi-Guri, *Kurzweil-Agnon-UZG*, 20.

74. Agnon, *Lifnim min ha-ḥoma*, 128–30.

75. See on this Sidra DeKoven Ezrahi, "S. Y. Agnon's Jerusalem: Before and After 1948," *Jewish Social Studies* 18, no. 3 (Spring/Summer 2012): 139.

76. The term itself is revealing, as it signifies a state of disrepair or entropy.

77. See the inscription to the foreword by Alan Mintz to his magisterial volume on *'Ir u-meloah*: "I am building a City," Alan Mintz and Jeffrey Saks, eds., *A City in Its Fullness* (New Milford, CT: Toby Press, 2016), xv.

78. Epigraph. Ibid., vii. From S. Y. Agnon, *'Ir u-meloah* (Jerusalem: Schocken, 1973). See also Omer Bartov, *Anatomy of a Genocide: The Life and Death of a Town Called Buczacz* (New York: Simon & Schuster, 2018). Note that even though Agnon fairly consistently called it a "city" (*'ir*), Bartov refers to Agnon's Buczacz, as I do, as a "town" and a "shtetl." See *Anatomy of a Genocide*, 4–5, 19–22, 27, 35, 289–90, 297–98.

79. For a sampling of the work on this subject over the past few decades, see Dan Miron, "The Literary Image of the Shtetl," *Jewish Social Studies*, n.s., 1, no. 3 (Spring 1995): 1–43; David G. Roskies, "The Shtetl in Jewish Collective Memory," in *The Jewish Search for a Useable Past* (Bloomington: Indiana University Press, 1999); Barbara Kirshenblatt-Gimblett, introduction to the reissued edition of Mark Zborowski and Elizabeth Herzog, *Life Is with People: The Culture of the Shtetl* (New York: Schocken, 1995), 62; Samuel Kassow, "Shtetl," in *YIVO Encyclopedia of Jews in Eastern Europe*, http://www.yivoencyclopedia.org/article.aspx/shtetl#author (accessed July 9, 2021). And, finally, see Jeffrey Shandler, *Shtetl: A Vernacular Intellectual History*, vol. 5 (New Brunswick, NJ: Rutgers University Press, 2014).

80. Bartov, *Anatomy of a Genocide*, 4–5, 19–22, 27, 35, 289–90, 297–98 and passim. Buczacz was also the hometown of Bartov's mother. I am grateful to Bartov for his work and his generosity.

81. See, for example, S. Y. Agnon, *Polin: Sippurei aggadot* [Poland: Tales] (Tel Aviv: Hedim, 1925); and see, on the origins of the town, Avidov Lipsker, "Yisud Buczacz: Mofet, Kedusha ve-ashma be- *'Ir u-meloah* le-Shay Agnon" [The Founding of Buczacz: Template, Sanctity, and Guilt in *A City in Its Fullness* by S. Y. Agnon], *Maḥshavot 'al Agnon*, vol. 1 (Ramat Gan: Bar Ilan University, 2015), 59–96. A version of this legend opens the permanent exhibition in the Polin museum in Warsaw. See a vivid description of this by the exhibition's curator, Barbara Kirshenblatt-Gimblett: "Materializing History: Time and Telos at POLIN Museum of the History of Polish Jews," Cornell University, Jewish Studies Program, May 15, 2017, https://www.cornell.edu/video/barbara-kirshenblatt-gimblett-time-telos-polin-museum-history-polish-jews (minute 24:45).

82. Lipsker, "Yisud Buczacz," 88–89. "Ha-siman" was first published in 1944 but, like so many of Agnon's narratives, went through later iterations.

83. See, on both stories, DeKoven Ezrahi, "Agnon Before and After," 78–94.

84. For a brief discussion of "Tehila," see above, chapter 3.

85. Agnon, "Lifnim min ha-ḥoma," in *Lifnim min ha-ḥoma* (Jerusalem: Schocken, 1975), 49, my translation. For a longer analysis of the anachronism in such stories, and of the interesting parallels between Agnon's Jerusalem and his hometown, see Sidra DeKoven Ezrahi, "The Shtetl and Its Afterlife: Agnon in Jerusalem," *AJS Review* 41, no. 1 (April 2017): 133–54, https://agnonhouse.org.il/wp-content/uploads/2017/05/shtetl_and_its_afterlife_agnon_in_jerusalem-1.pdf.

86. This translated quote and the above translation from Agnon's *'Ir u-meloah* are by Omer Bartov, *Tales from the Borderlands: Making and Unmaking the Past* (New Haven: Yale University Press, forthcoming).

87. Agnon, "Chapters for the Book of State," trans. Sara Daniel, Isaac Franck, and Jules Harlow, in *The Orange Peel and Other Satires*, ed. Jeffrey Saks (London: Toby Press, 2015), 125–69. I am also going in a very different direction from that of Hannan Hever, who argues that the principle of "deferred messianism" is so central to Agnon's theological vision that Zionist institutions and politicians cannot even approximate it. Hever, "Perakim le-sefer ha-medina me-et Shay Agnon" [Chapters for the Book of State by S. Y. Agnon], *Mikan* 14 (March 2014): 168–99.

88. In a longer essay on this subject I buttress the argument by reference to a number of voices in urban theory, including Jurgen Habermas in an earlier generation and Edward Soja more recently. "Shtetl and Its Afterlife," 139–40.

89. Based on meticulous comparison of the relevant documents, Yoel Rappel has argued persuasively that the attribution of this prayer to Agnon is inaccurate and that the prayer for the safety of the State with its messianic attribution was indeed composed by Chief Rabbi Herzog and only shown to Agnon for editing, which he did very lightly. See Yoel Rappel, "Zehuto shel meḥaber ha-tefila li-shlom ha-medina" [The Identity of the Writer of the Prayer for the Safety of the State], in *Et Shivat Tzion Hayinu ke-ḥolmim*, ed. R. Benyamin Lau and Yoel Rappel (Jerusalem: Koren, 2013), 355–61.

90. On this, see DeKoven Ezrahi, "Shtetl and Its Afterlife," 140.

91. Laor, *Ḥayei Agnon*, 611.

92. Here is the original: "Le-faresh pasuk shel be-ḥarbi u-ve-kashti be-tzelota u-ve-ota vadai she-ein anu rotzim be-ḥaravot u-ve-keshatot . . . ke-she-hitḥila parshat ha-kotel ʿamadeti mishtomem le-ota ʿgevuraʾ she-heru ʿgiboreinuʾ ve-dibarti ʿim kama manhigim ve-hokhahti otam bi-devarim, amarti lahem ma atem ʿosim, haniḥu yedeikhem mi-ze . . . u-ke-she-hayiti be-yeshivat ha-vaʿad ha-leumi (paʿam aḥat be-ḥayai) ve-raʾiti et shapaʿat ha-gevura shel giborei ha-noʿamim ḥafatzti litzʿok haniḥu yedeikhem mi-ze, ela she-mitivʿi ani neḥba el ha-kelim ve-kol ha-yamim hayiti mitztaʿer she-lo ʿamadeti ba-paretz . . . ve-ha-shem yigdor pirtzat ʿamo ve-yiten lanu et ha-ḥayyim ve-et ha-shalom." S. Y. Agnon, *Me-ʿatzmi el ʿatzmi* (Jerusalem: Schocken, 1975), 414. Some of this letter is quoted in Hillel Cohen, "What the 1929 Palestine Riots Teach Us about Today's Violence," *+972 Magazine*, October 16, 2015, http://972mag.com /what-the-1929-palestine-riots-teach-us-about-todays-violence/112830/.

Chapter Six

1. "Gods Change, Prayers Are Here to Stay," no. 19, *Open Closed Open*, trans. Chana Bloch and Chana Kronfeld, *Poetry of Yehuda Amichai*, ed. Robert Alter, 414–15. The Hebrew word *tallit* is rendered in this translation as *tallis*—the more familiar-familial Yiddish pronunciation.

2. Amichai, *Shirei Yehuda Amichai*, 5:155.

3. On the "paytanim" and the Song of Songs, see above, chapter 2. For a Hebrew elaboration of this argument, see DeKoven Ezrahi, "Yehuda Amichai: paytan shel ha-yomyom" [Yehuda Amichai: Sacred Poet of the Quotidian], *Mikan* 14 (Spring 2014): 143–67; expanded in DeKoven Ezrahi, *Shlosha paytanim* [Three Poets of the Sacred Quotidian] (Jerusalem: Mossad Bialik, 2020).

4. Kronfeld, *Full Severity*. Except where otherwise noted, I will avail myself of the translations into English of Amichai's poetry by many hands that appear in *The Poetry of Yehuda Amichai*.

5. The term "cultural claustrophilia" was, presumably, coined by Arthur Koestler, in reference to the prestate and nascent State of Israel. *Promise and Fulfillment: Palestine, 1917–1949* (New York: Macmillan, 1949), 330.

6. There are many illuminating studies of alternate spaces in Hebrew literature; a very partial list would include the work of Barbara Mann on Tel Aviv as incubator of private dramas; Jordan D. Finkin on time and space in Jewish modernisms; Shachar Pinsker on coffeehouses as secular sanctuaries for Jewish intellectuals in nineteenth- and twentieth-century Europe and Palestine; Naama Tsal on space and home in the fictions of Yehoshua Knaz and Ronit Matalon; Hanna Soker-Schwager on alternative spaces in the work of Ya'akov Shabtai. To this one could add the fictions of David Grossman, who probes inner sancta in Jerusalem itself as well as entering into Palestinian spaces in journalism and fiction. One of the earliest anthropological forays into the subject of "place" and "Place" was the essay by Zali Gurevitch and Gideon Aran, "'Al ha-makom" [On Place], *Alpayim* 4 (1991): 9–44. A version appeared in English as "The Land of Israel: Myth and Phenomenon," *Studies in Contemporary Jewry* (1994): 195–210. And see Zali Gurevitch, "The Double Site of Israel," in *Grasping Land: Space and Place in Contemporary Israeli Discourse and Experience*, ed. Eyal Ben-Ari and Yoram Bilu (Albany: SUNY Press, 1997), 203–16.

7. H. N. Bialik, "'Al shniyut bi-yisrael" [On Duality in Israel], talk delivered in Berlin in 1922, in *Devarim she-be-'al peh*, vol. 1 (Tel Aviv: Dvir, 1935), 39.

8. H. N. Bialik, "The Sacred and the Secular in Language," talk delivered to the "Legion for the Protection of the Language," Tel Aviv, August 1927, trans. Jeffrey M. Green. H. N. Bialik, *Revealment and Concealment: Five Essays*, afterword by Zali Gurevitch (Jerusalem: Ibis, 2000), 89. Note that I translate *gdud* as "battalion"; both "legion" and "battalion" are accurate and reflect the premilitary mindset of early Zionist rhetoric.

9. H. N. Bialik, "There Passed by Me" [Ḥalfa 'al panai], trans. Zali Gurevitch, in "Eternal Loss: An Afterword," in Bialik, *Revealment and Concealment*, 132–33. Gurevitch's essay is very useful for understanding the inherent dualism or "metaphysical exile . . . exile [even] from himself" in Bialik's poetics. Ibid., 115. On this subject see also Ariel Hirschfeld, *Kinor 'Arukh: Lashon ha-regesh be-shirat Hayim Nahman Bialik* [A Tuned Violin: The Language of Emotion in the Poetry of Hayim Nahman Bialik] (Tel Aviv: Am Oved, 2011), 12.

10. "Lashon hagigit" in the original, which denotes language that is ceremonial and celebratory. Bialik, "Sacred and the Secular," 90.

11. H. N. Bialik, "Ḥevlei Lashon" [Language Pangs], in *'Ivriya*, 1905; reprinted in *Ha-Shilo'aḥ* 18 (1907), https://benyehuda.org/bialik/xevlei_lashon.html; in *Kol kitvei H. N. Bialik* [Complete Writings of H. N. Bialik] (Tel Aviv: Dvir, 1938), 185–90. Trans. Chana Kronfeld and Eric Zakim; quoted and discussed in Kronfeld, *On the Margins*, 83–86 and 248nn9, 10. Bialik's essay is fascinating in its assertions and also in its internal contradictions. Although he is not unambivalent about the consequences of such a process, he asserts the necessity for what Chana Kronfeld calls an "organistic account of language." *On the Margins*, 85.

12. Bialik arrived in Tel Aviv in 1924. He did continue to write poems for children, as well as the cycle "Shirei yatmut" [Orphaned Poems]. See http://benyehuda.org/bialik/bia101.html. There have been a number of interesting insights into Bialik's silence. See, for example, Sheila Jelen, "Bialik's Other Silence," *Hebrew Studies Journal* 44 (2003): 65–86. And see Amichai's playful reference to Bialik's silence in chapter 7, below.

13. See, for example, Bialik, "'Al saf beit ha-midrash" [On the Threshold of the Study House, 1894], in *Kol Shirei Bialik* (Tel Aviv: Dvir, 1956), 32–35, https://benyehuda.org/read/5532.

14. This short letter was "rediscovered" in 1985 and has continued to generate lively debate among scholars and writers throughout the Jewish world, including Stéphane Mosès and Jacques Derrida. For a more thorough treatment of this in the context of Amichai's poetry, see

the chapter "Yehuda Amichai: Paytan shel ha-yomyom," in DeKoven Ezrahi, *Shlosha paytanim*, 96–101.

15. See Derrida, "Eyes of Language," *Acts of Religion*, 206–7, 215. Because Derrida would not have been familiar with most of the Hebrew texts we are discussing, especially those of Bialik, he might not have been as troubled by the sacred/profane dichotomy.

16. Ibid., 212.

17. The following argument, and its expanded version in the chapter on Amichai in my Hebrew volume, *Shlosha paytanim*, differ from that of Boaz Arpali, who insists that Amichai works as a "dialectical" poet to create "secular poetry." Although our ethical and political positions are similar, especially on Jerusalem, this marks a cardinal difference in our approaches to his poetics. See Boaz Arpali, "Yerushalayim ḥatranit: Yerushalayim ke-tsomet mefarek mitosim be-shirat Yehuda Amichai" [Subversive Jerusalem: Jerusalem as Crossroads of Dismantled Myths in the Poetry of Yehuda Amichai], *Dapim le-meḥkar be-sifrut* 14–15 (2005): especially 293–94. See also Arpali, "On the Political Significance of Amichai's Poetry," in *The Experienced Soul: Studies in Amichai*, ed. Glenda Abramson (Boulder, CO: Westview Press, 1997), 27–50.

18. Leah Goldberg, "Tel Aviv, 1935," trans. Adriana X. Jacobs, in "Ha-masa' ha-katzar be-yoter" [The Shortest Journey], in *'Im ha-layla ha-ze* [With This Night] (Bnai Brak: Sifriat Poalim, 1964), http://teachgreatjewishbooks.org/1-poem-tel-aviv-1935-leah-goldberg-1964. For a discussion of the sea as trope in modern Hebrew literature, see Hannan Hever, *El Ha-ḥof ha-mekuveh: Ha-yam ba-tarbut ha-'ivrit ha-modernit* [To the Desired Shore: The Sea in Modern Hebrew Culture] (Jerusalem: Van Leer Institute and Ha-kibbutz ha-meuchad, 2007).

19. Mikhail M. Bakhtin, *The Dialogic Imagination: Four Essays*, ed. Michael Holquist, trans. Caryl Emerson and Michael Holquist (Austin: University of Texas Press, 1981), 6–8.

20. Ibid., 11.

21. Ibid., 23.

22. Ibid.

23. Amichai, "And Who Will Remember the Rememberers?," no. 10, trans. Chana Bloch and Chana Kronfeld, *Poetry of Yehuda Amichai*, 525. *Shirei Yehuda Amichai*, 5:307–8.

24. This is Tova Rosen's point in her essay "Kemo ba-shir shel Shmuel Ha-nagid: Bein Shmuel Ha-nagid le-Yehuda Amichai" ["As in Shmuel Ha-nagid's Poem": Between Shmuel Ha-nagid and Yehuda Amichai], *Meḥkarei yerushalayim be-sifrut 'Ivrit*, no. 15 (1995): 106–83. And see John Donne, "The Anniversarie," in *John Donne: The Conservative Revolutionary*, ed. N. J. C. Andreasen (Princeton: Princeton University Press, 1967), 219–20, 223. On Stevens and Rilke as metaphysical poets, see Jennifer Anna Gosetti-Ferencei, "Immanent Transcendence in Rilke and Stevens," *German Quarterly* 83, no. 3 (Summer 2010): 275–96. For discussions of Amichai's affinity with medieval Hebrew poets, see Kronfeld, *Full Severity*, 8, 19, 120, 124–25. See also David Fishelov, "Amichai: A Modern Metaphysical Poet," *Orbis Litterarium* 47 (1992): 178–91; and Shimon Sandbank, "Li-va'ayat ha-shir ha-kal" [The Problem of the Simple Poem], *Siman Kriah* 12–13 (February 1981): 331–34.

25. Or "Zelda," as she was known in the familiar, condescending nomenclature by which some women writers were allowed into the Hebrew canon. In some cases, however, as Wendy Zierler has shown, the mononym was deliberately adopted by women writers as a rejection of the patrilineal affiliation. See Wendy I. Zierler, *And Rachel Stole the Idols: The Emergence of Modern Hebrew Women's Writing* (Detroit: Wayne State University Press, 2004), especially the introduction, 1–15. When many of these writers "seized upon the personal as a vehicle of expression, they often did so as a subversive means of gaining access to the public and national language of Hebrew representation so long denied women" (12). On the poet Zelda, see 264–71.

26. From Amichai, "I Foretell the Days of Yore," no. 8, *Open Closed Open*, trans. Chana Bloch and Chana Kronfeld, *Poetry of Yehuda Amichai*, 438. *Shirei Yehuda Amichai*, 5:187.

27. Emily Dickinson, "Some Keep the Sabbath Going to Church," in *Final Harvest: Emily Dickinson's Poems*, ed. Thomas H. Johnson (Boston: Little, Brown, 1961), 66; Wallace Stevens, "Sunday Morning," *The Collected Poems of Wallace Stevens* (New York: Alfred A. Knopf, 1993), 66–70.

28. David Grossman, "Amichai va-anaḥnu" [Amichai and Us], *Haaretz*, October 22, 1999. Quoted in Kronfeld, *Full Severity*, 28. See the prologue above.

29. *Shirei Yehuda Amichai*, 1:86. I am using Chana Bloch and Chana Kronfeld's translation, which is slightly different from Alter's translation. Kronfeld, *Full Severity*, 89. Kronfeld's analysis of Amichai's "rhetoric of autobiography" in this canonic poem/prayer is enlightening. Ibid., 89–92.

30. Kronfeld, *Full Severity*, 225–66. Kronfeld argues for Amichai practicing irony as dialogical and open; irony, as she invokes it, is not sarcasm but the recognition of a gap in knowledge. Private communication, March 31, 2019.

31. From Amichai, "Late Marriage," trans. Chana Bloch, *Poetry of Yehuda Amichai*, 363. *Shirei Yehuda Amichai*, 4:202.

32. James Wood, "Like a Prayer: The Poetry of Yehuda Amichai," *New Yorker*, January 4, 2016, 74.

33. From Amichai, "Late Marriage," *Poetry of Yehuda Amichai*, 363.

34. "Beynayim," *Shirei Yehuda Amichai*, 5:37. "Between," trans. Chana Bloch, *Poetry of Yehuda Amichai*, 379; and see Kronfeld's discussion of this poetic principle in *Full Severity*, 108–9, 325n84, 225–32.

35. "I Wasn't One of the Six Million," no. 6, trans. Chana Bloch and Chana Kronfeld, *Poetry of Yehuda Amichai*, 491; "Ani lo hayiti eḥad mi-sheshet ha-milionim. U-ma meshekh hayai? Patu'aḥ sagur patu'aḥ," no. 1, *Shirei Yehuda Amichai*, 5:126. See, on this, Kronfeld, *Full Severity*, 231.

36. Kronfeld, *Full Severity*, 225.

37. "Not like a Cypress," trans. Stephen Mitchell, *Poetry of Yehuda Amichai*, 30; *Shirei Yehuda Amichai*, 1:98–99.

38. "On the one hand, the speaker [in this poem, who is never specified] wants to remain unnoticed, hidden, almost passive. On the other, he wishes to make his presence all-encompassing, comingling with and reaching out to as many people as possible," writes Kronfeld. *Full Severity*, 99.

39. From "Travels," trans. Ruth Nevo, *Poetry of Yehuda Amichai*, 133–34. *Shirei Yehuda Amichai*, 2:150–51.

40. The "Palmach" (acronym for "plugot ha-mahatz" or fighting forces) was the elite force of the Haganah, the underground army of the Yishuv (Jewish community), founded in 1941.

41. For more discussion of the presence of "Little Ruth" (Ruth Hanover) in Amichai's life and writing, see Kronfeld, *Full Severity*, 13–14; and Nili Scharf Gold, *Yehuda Amichai: The Making of Israel's National Poet* (Waltham: Brandeis University Press, 2008), especially 74–100. And see the essays published in Germany and then in Israel as Yehuda Amichai, *Bein milḥama le-ahava: ha-meshorer Yehuda Amichai* [Between War and Love: The Poet Yehuda Amichai], translated from German by Hana Livnat, ed. Renata Eickmeyer and Edith Reim (Ramat Gan: Rimonim, 2016), 74–111. See also Hana Amichai, "Little Ruth, My Personal Anne Frank," *Haaretz*, October 22, 2010, https://www.haaretz.com/1.5129177.

42. As Ranen Omer-Sherman writes, "for many, [Amichai] stands apart as the quintessential poet of connections between seemingly disparate realms and identities, demonstrating a deep commitment to make some kind of coherence out of all the violent and random contingencies that shape the fragile fabric of human lives." "Yehuda Amichai's Exilic Jerusalem," *Prooftexts* 26, nos. 1–2 (Winter/Spring 2006): 220.

43. From "Travels," trans. Stephen Mitchell, *Poetry of Yehuda Amichai*, 134. *Shirei Yehuda Amichai*, 2:151.

44. So far as I know there were no copies of the drawing in Würzburg, though Dürer lived and worked there for a time.

45. "God's hand is in the world / like my mother's hand in the guts of the slaughtered chicken / on Sabbath eve." "Yad elohim ba-'olam," no. 1, *Shirei Yehuda Amichai*, 1:80; trans. Stephen Mitchell, *Poetry of Yehuda Amichai*, 24.

46. "Gam ani nikhnas ve-yotze tamid kemo le-tokh dirot ḥadashot / derekh sivkhot barzel she-hen shel zikaron." "Mas'ot Binyamin ha-shlishi." *Shirei Yehuda Amichai*, 2:144. "I too / am always coming and going, as if into new apartments / through the barbed wire entanglements of memory." "Travels of Benjamin III," trans. Ruth Nevo, *Poetry of Yehuda Amichai*, 129.

47. Here Bakhtin singles out Dostoevsky as exemplar of heteroglossia. With Dostoevsky, he writes, "one is dealing not with a *single* author-artist who wrote novels and stories, but with a number of philosophical statements by *several* author-thinkers—Raskolnikov, Myshkin, Stavrogin, Ivan [Karamazov], the Grand Inquisitor, and others . . . *A plurality of independent and unmerged voices and consciousnesses, a genuine polyphony of fully valid voices is in fact the chief characteristic of Dostoevsky's novels.*" *Problems of Dostoevsky's Poetics*, 5–6, emphasis in original.

48. "In the elegance of this house, at the end of its gable, one can spot a figure of a tired old lion. The lion was the symbol of the Zendler [Sandel] Family's pharmacy. Theodore Zendler built a house which had a great influence on the Jerusalemite landscape. Zendler was an engineer, architect, and contractor and left many edifices." Aviva and Shmuel Bar-Am, "A German Colony in Jerusalem," *Times of Israel*, April 6, 2013, http://www.timesofisrael.com/a-german-colony-in-jerusalem/.

49. From "Travels," trans. Ruth Nevo, *Poetry of Yehuda Amichai*, 110. "Arayot-even shel gishrei 'ir yalduti shamru / 'aleinu 'im arayot even shel ha-bayit ha-yashan bi-yerushalayim." *Shirei Yehuda Amichai*, 2:118.

50. "Sometimes I want to go back / to everything I had, as in a museum, / when you go back not in the order / of the eras, but in the opposite direction, against the arrow, / to look for the woman you loved. / Where is she? The Egyptian Room, / the Far East, the Twentieth Century, Cave Art, / everything jumbled together, and the worried / guards calling after you: you can't go against the eras! Stop! / The exit's over here! You won't learn from this, / you know you won't. You're searching, you're forgetting." Amichai, from "Travels of the Last Benjamin of Tudela," trans. Stephen Mitchell, *The Selected Poetry of Yehuda Amichai*, trans. Chana Bloch and Stephen Mitchell (Berkeley: University of California Press, 1996), 67–68. The translation in Alter's edition is slightly different. *Poetry of Yehuda Amichai*, 117. *Shirei Yehuda Amichai*, 2:128–29. See Kronfeld's discussion of this section and Amichai's temporal freedoms and the "rhetorical and philosophical system[s] they illustrate." *Full Severity*, 112–14.

51. Unlike Nili Gold, who claims that this is a form of suppression that needs to be uncovered, most Amichai scholars see it as a poetic and existential decision with far-reaching implications. See Kronfeld, *Full Severity*, 10, 295n24.

52. On Wurzburg and its bridge in ruins in 1945, see Geoff Walden, "Würzburg, Part 2: Würzburg during the War," July 20, 2000, on his website The Third Reich in Ruins, http://www.thirdreichruins.com/wurzburg2.htm.

53. Yehuda Amichai, *Not of This Time, Not of This Place*, trans. Shlomo Katz (New York: Harper & Row, 1968). *Lo me-'akhshav lo mi-kan* (Jerusalem: Schocken, 1963).

54. In an interview with Kronfeld, the poet explained that "there was something traumatic about that year, and about having spent it in America. Trauma is an explosion [*hitpotzetzut*]

which brings to the surface completely different materials." The "'explosion,'" explains Kronfeld, "is one of the metaphors Amichai uses repeatedly to express the ways historical crises destabilize the geological layers that make up the 'archaeology of the self.'" *Full Severity*, 14, 51. Amichai himself defined "Travels" as a "poema," an archaic form combining elements of the travelogue and the epic. See *Full Severity*, 14, 298n50.

Chapter Seven

1. Yehoshua, *Mr Mani*, 265–66. *Mar Mani* (Tel Aviv: Ha-kibbutz ha-meuchad, 1993), 255.

2. Amichai, from "Travels," trans. Stephen Mitchell, *Selected Poetry of Yehuda Amichai*, 71. The translation by Ruth Nevo is slightly different. *Poetry of Yehuda Amichai*, 121–22. *Shirei Yehuda Amichai*, 2:134. Throughout these chapters, wherever translations are from a source other than Alter's edition, it is either because that poem was omitted from the collected volume, or because of a stated preference for another version.

3. Amichai, from "Travels," trans. Stephen Mitchell, *Selected Poetry of Yehuda Amichai*, 71. *Shirei Yehuda Amichai*, 2:134.

4. Omer-Sherman, "Yehuda Amichai's Exilic Jerusalem," 229. In another post-'67 poem, Amichai's speaker refers to the "scribbled wishes stuck between the stones of the Wailing Wall: bits of crumpled, wadded paper. / And across the way, stuck in an old iron gate half hidden by jasmine: 'Couldn't make it, I hope you'll understand.'" "Jerusalem, 1985," trans. Chana Bloch, *Selected Poetry of Yehuda Amichai*, 169. *Shirei Yehuda Amichai*, 4:170. Omer-Sherman writes, "Rather than mistake the stones for 'holy,' [these poems] take . . . us into the charged spaces around them, in which the homely scraps of hopeful prayers reside" (229).

5. "Jerusalem, Jerusalem, Why Jerusalem?," no. 2, trans. Chana Bloch and Chana Kronfeld, *Poetry of Yehuda Amichai*, 500. *Shirei Yehuda Amichai*, 5:275.

6. Referred to as the "separation barrier" by the Israeli authorities; the length of the barrier varies according to different sources, but it is somewhere between 160 and 200 km. "The 202 km segment of the barrier that surrounds Jerusalem, built alternately as a concrete wall and a chain-link fence, was named 'the Jerusalem envelope' . . . The route of the barrier was indeed determined in relation to the municipal boundaries of Jerusalem, but also in relation to the [Jewish] settlements that surround the city," built after 1967. "The Separation Barrier," 'Ir Amim, https://www.ir-amim.org.il/en/issue/separation-barrier (accessed July 9, 2021).

7. In a discussion and elaboration of Maurice Halbwachs's concept of "collective memory," and in his own work on Holocaust memorial sites throughout Europe and the United States, James Young coined the term "*collected* memory." "The result has been a shift away from the notion of a national 'collective memory' to what I would call a nation's 'collected memory.' Here we recognize that we never really shared each other's actual memory of past or even recent events, but that in sharing common spaces in which we collect our disparate and competing memories, we find common (perhaps even a national) understanding of widely disparate experiences and our very reasons for recalling them." James Young, *The Stages of Memory: Reflections on Memorial Art, Loss, and the Spaces Between* (Amherst: University of Massachusetts Press, 2016), 15. For an earlier iteration of this, see James Young, *At Memory's Edge: After-Images of the Holocaust in Contemporary Art and Architecture* (New Haven: Yale University Press, 2002), 210.

8. "Jerusalem, Jerusalem, Why Jerusalem?," no. 9, trans. Chana Bloch and Chana Kronfeld, *Poetry of Yehuda Amichai*, 503.

9. Amichai, "Yerushalayim, Yerushalayim, Lama Yerushalayim?," no. 9. *Shirei Yehuda Amichai*, 5:279.

10. Recall that the poet spent several months in the United States in 1967–68 and referred to "Travels" as a "poema." See above, chapter 6. Taking their cue from him, Israeli critics typically refer to it as an autobiographical "poema." See Boaz Arpali, *Ha-perahim ve-ha-agartal; shirat Amichai: mivne, mashma'ut, poetika* [The Flowers and the Urn: Amichai's Poetry, 1948–1968] (Tel Aviv: Siman Kria/Ha-kibbutz ha-meuchad, 1986), 161–64. See also Glenda Abramson, who reads "Travels" alongside T. S. Eliot's "Four Quartets." *The Writing of Yehuda Amichai: A Thematic Approach* (Albany: SUNY Press, 1989), 18–20.

11. "Travels," trans. Stephen Mitchell, *Poetry of Yehuda Amichai*, 131. "Lif amim / ani roeh et Yerushalayim bein shnei anashim / ha-'omdim le-yad halon u-mash'irim revah / beinehem." *Shirei Yehuda Amichai*, 2:147.

12. "Travels," trans. Stephen Mitchell, *Selected Poetry of Yehuda Amichai*, 61. The translation is slightly different in Alter's edition. The poet is addressing his own younger heart in the second person singular, "Libkha le-'olam lo yilmad le-emod merhakim / Ha-rahok beyoter bishvilo hu ha-etz ha-karov be-yoter / sefat ha-midrakha, penei ha-ahuva . . ." *Shirei Yehuda Amichai*, 2:118.

13. And: "When I lie on my back, / the bones of my legs are filled / with the sweetness / of my little son's breath." "Travels," trans. Stephen Mitchell, *Selected Poetry of Yehuda Amichai*, 86. The translation is slightly different in Alter's edition. *Shirei Yehuda Amichai*, 2:158.

14. See Kronfeld, *Full Severity*, 271–75; and see Kronfeld, *On the Margins*, chap. 6, "Yehuda Amichai: On the Boundaries of Affiliation," 143–58.

15. *Selected Poetry of Yehuda Amichai*, 79, trans. Stephen Mitchell. The translation in Alter's edition is slightly different. "Ze haya yakhol lihiot shir halel / la-el ha-matok ve-ha-medume shel yalduti. / Ze haya be-yom shishi, u-malakhim shehorim mil'u et 'emek ha-matzleva, ve-kanfeyhim / hayu batim shehorim u-makhtzavot netushot. / Nerot shabbat 'alu ve-yardu kemo oniyot." *Shirei Yehuda Amichai*, 2:147–48.

16. *Selected Poetry of Yehuda Amichai*, trans. Stephen Mitchell, 80. *Shirei Yehuda Amichai*, 2:148.

17. "Yehuda Ha-Levi," trans. Stephen Mitchell, *Poetry of Yehuda Amichai*, 14; see also "Travels," ibid., 125–26; "Jewish Travel: Change Is God and Death Is His Prophet," no. 2, ibid., 483. *Shirei Yehuda Amichai*, 1:30, 2:140, 5:252.

18. "Mas'ot Binyamin ha-aharon mi-tudela," *Shirei Yehuda Amichai*, 2:139. "The Travels of the Last Benjamin of Tudela," trans. Ruth Nevo, *Poetry of Yehuda Amichai*, 125. On Bialik, and his poetic silence, see above, chapter 6.

19. Aviya Kushner, "How One Nation Mourns a Poet," *Partisan Review* 68, no. 4 (Fall 2001): 613–14. Quoted in Omer-Sherman, "Yehuda Amichai's Exilic Jerusalem," 233.

20. From "Jerusalem 1967," no. 21, trans. Stephen Mitchell, *Poetry of Yehuda Amichai*, 88. *Shirei Yehuda Amichai*, 2:21. See the introduction above.

21. "Ve-el ot tashuv: topographia omanutit be-'emek refaim," street project by artist Arik Caspi to commemorate the thirteenth anniversary of the death of Yehuda Amichai, Sept. 1–Nov. 1, 2013, http://poetryplace-festival.org/2013/exhibition.php. The initiative for such street art came from Gilad Meiri and Noa Shakargy.

22. Again, for the history of this house and of the neighborhood, see https://www.jerusalem-love.co.il/?page_id=2215. As a longtime resident of this neighborhood, I have my own layered history with another house. See prologue and Sidra DeKoven Ezrahi, "Jerusalem Divorced Family's Home as Inspiration for Israeli-Palestinian Peace," *Haaretz*, February 27, 2016, updated

April 10, 2018, https://www.haaretz.com/israel-news/.premium.MAGAZINE-no-clean-divorce
-for-israel-and-palestine-1.5409395.

23. "Evening Promenade on Valley of the Ghosts Street," no. 1, trans. Chana Bloch and
Chana Kronfeld, *Poetry of Yehuda Amichai*, 457. *Shirei Yehuda Amichai*, 5:215.

24. "I define 'wounded cities' as densely settled locales that have been harmed and structured by particular histories of physical destruction, displacement, and individual and social
trauma resulting from state-perpetrated violence." Karen Till, "Wounded Cities: Memory-Work
and a Place-Based Ethics of Care," *Political Geography* 31, no. 1 (2012): 6.

25. II Kings 21:1–9; Jer. 19; II Chr. 33:1–9.

26. "Houses (Plural); Love (Singular)," no. 4, *Poetry of Yehuda Amichai*, 464. "Garnu be-gey
ben hinom be-shetah hefker bi-yerushalayim ha-mehuleket . . ." "Batim batim ve-ahava ahat,"
no. 4, *Shirei Yehuda Amichai*, 5:224. See also Yehuda Amichai, "I Lived for Two Months in Quiet
Abu Tor," trans. Stephen Mitchell, *Poems of Jerusalem and Love Poems*, bilingual ed. (New York:
Sheep Meadow Press, 1966), 25; "Mas'ot Binyamin ha-aharon mi-tudela," *Shirei Yehuda Amichai*,
2:140–41. And see Amichai, "Zikaron be-Abu tor" [A Memory from Abu Tor], which invokes a
liminal zone of dangerous meetings between soldiers from both sides, and the prayer space of
an old synagogue. *Shirei Yehuda Amichai*, 3:345.

27. See, for example, the Hebrew murder mystery by Yiftach Ashkenazi, set in that space: *Gay
ben-hinom* [Gehenna] (Hevel Modi'in Industrial Park: Kinneret, Zmora, Dvir, 2019); and see the
apocalyptic novels by Dror Burstein, *Tit* [translated as Muck], trans. Gabriel Levin (New York:
Farrar, Straus and Giroux, 2018); and Zvi Jagendorf, *Coming Soon: The Flood* (London: Halban,
2018), an English novel set in no-man's-land in divided Jerusalem—a roman à clef that invokes
many of Amichai's friends and fellow poets during the early 1960s. On this geopolitical space and
the subsequent efforts of a number of artists to commemorate it in 2011, see Nir Hasson, "Reclaiming Jerusalem's No Man's Land," *Haaretz*, October 30, 2011, https://www.haaretz.com/1.5204736.

28. See the introduction above. For a discussion of the messianic vision of waters flowing
from the Temple Mount, see Pedaya, "Temurot," 53–110.

29. "Jerusalem 1967," no. 21, trans. Stephen Mitchell, *Poetry of Yehuda Amichai*, 88. *Shirei
Yehuda Amichai*, 2:21. The dedication of this poem cycle—"to my friends Dennis, Arieh, and
Harold"—embraces Amichai's fellow poets, scholars, and writers Dennis Silk, Arieh Sachs, and
Harold Schimmel, who were central figures in the Jerusalem bohemia of the 1960s and '70s. See,
for example, Dennis Silk's *Retrievements: A Jerusalem Anthology* (Jerusalem: Israel Universities Press, 1968), which covers an eclectic range of voices, ancient, medieval, and modern, and
includes translations of Amichai by Silk, Sachs, and others as well as drawings by Ivan Schwebel
and photographs by Susie Abelin.

30. See the prologue above for a discussion of this term.

31. Omer-Sherman, "Yehuda Amichai's Exilic Jerusalem," 222. Italics in original.

32. See my discussion of this passage from Isaiah as inscribed on the Dome of the Rock in
Jewish New Year's Greetings, in the coda, below.

33. Tikva Frymer-Kensky, *Studies in Bible and Feminist Criticism* (New York: Jewish Publication Society, 2010), 117.

34. For an elaboration of this argument, see DeKoven Ezrahi, "By the Waters of Babylon,"
153–64.

35. See prologue, above.

36. "If I Forget Thee, Jerusalem," trans. Assia Gutmann, Amichai, *Poems of Jerusalem and
Love Poems*, 7–8; reprinted in *Poetry of Yehuda Amichai*, 144. *Shirei Yehuda Amichai*, 2:197. I

have changed Gutmann's translation considerably; the most crucial change relates to one word. In both the original volume, *Akhshav be-ra'ash* and the five-volume collected poems, the word *sha'ar* (gate) appears in the third line of the second strophe; Assia Gutmann translates this as "hair" (*se'ar*), which would put the diacritical point on the left side of the letter *shin*. Although this would strengthen the "hair" motif that, as Kronfeld shows, runs through much of Amichai's poetry (see *Full Severity*, 25ff.), there is, as far as I can tell, no documentary evidence except for Gutmann's translation for this variation, and it is probable that Amichai did not catch the error when the translation appeared, even though he had corresponded with Gutmann on various issues of translation. Hana Amichai corroborated my hunch in a private conversation.

37. Alter, *Hebrew Bible*, 3:313–14.

38. For explorations of the endangered present tense in Hebrew fiction, see Ya'akov Shabtai, *Past Continuous*, trans. Dalya Bilu (New York: Overlook Press, 1985). Hebrew: *Zikhron Devarim* (Bnai Brak: Ha-kibbutz ha-meuchad, 1977). And see David Grossman, *The Book of Intimate Grammar*, trans. Betsy Rosenberg (New York: Picador, 2002). Hebrew: *Sefer ha-dikduk ha-penimi* (Bnai Brak: Ha-kibbutz ha-meuchad, 1991).

39. This subject has been widely explored in the critical literature, and is the subject of ongoing research by Chana Kronfeld. Perhaps its most dramatic early expression and the most terrifying in its political-theological implications is Uri Zvi Greenberg's poem "Bi-zkhut em u-vena vi-yerushalayim" [By the merit (For the sake) of a mother and her son and Jerusalem]. As I noted elsewhere, the bereaved human mother concedes her place to "Jerusalem" in the knowledge that her martyred son is no longer in his grave, that his body has been accepted as a sacrifice and has sanctified the soil into which it has been absorbed. The city personified as mother earth, as lover and wife, receives the body of the young soldier; the woman "Jerusalem," who first competes with and then supplants the mother, acquires mystical substantiation and sacramentalization that supersedes and at the same time cancels her own status as a poetic, flexible sign. "Bizkhut em u-vena vi-yerushalayim," *Uri Zvi Greenberg: Kol Ketavav*, vol. 7 (Jerusalem: Mossad Bialik, 1994), 57–59. See DeKoven Ezrahi, *Booking Passage*, 21; and "'To what shall I compare thee?,'" 226–27.

40. "Mishkenot sha'ananim" abuts and is often referred to as "Yemin Moshe" because of the central role that Moses Montefiore played in the development of the neighborhood in the late nineteenth century. Recently, the Montefiore windmill was reactivated, and it again revolves in Jerusalem's winds.

41. Michel Foucault's invoking of "heterotopia" as spatial reference is traced to a talk he gave in March 1967 that was published posthumously in October 1984. "Of Other Spaces: Heterotopias," trans. Jay Miskowiec, from *Architecture, Mouvement, Continuité*, no. 5 (1984): 46–49, https://foucault.info/documents/heterotopia/foucault.heteroTopia.en/. See also Edward Soja, *Thirdspace: Journeys to Los Angeles and Other Real-and-Imagined Places* (Hoboken, NJ: Blackwell, 1996).

42. This song may be medieval; it first appears in a Haggadah from the late sixteenth century. See Cecil Roth, *The Haggadah, A New Edition* (London: Soncino Press, 1959), 85. For a subversive contemporary rendition of this song, see Chava Alberstein, "Had Gadya," released in 1989 during the first Intifada: https://www.youtube.com/watch?v=DHdVYy5B6JM.

43. "An Arab Shepherd Is Searching for His Goat on Mt. Zion," trans. Chana Bloch, *Poetry of Yehuda Amichai*, 274. *Shirei Yehuda Amichai*, 3:274.

44. "Jerusalem 1967," no. 5, trans. Stephen Mitchell, *Poetry of Yehuda Amichai*, 83. *Shirei Yehuda Amichai*, 2:13–14.

45. For a long, detailed analysis of this poem and its resonances in the public culture, see Kronfeld, *Full Severity*, 44–48; and see Omer-Sherman, "Yehuda Amichai's Exilic Jerusalem," 223–27; and Abramson, *Writing of Yehuda Amichai*, 130–31. For Abramson's broader discussion of Jerusalem, see ibid., chap. 6, 124–43.

46. For a discussion of the subversive force of even Pagis's most "canonical" poem, "Written in Pencil in the Sealed Railway-Car," see DeKoven Ezrahi, *Booking Passage*, 161–63.

47. See Dan Miron's essay commemorating the fifth anniversary of Amichai's death and arguing that Amichai was one of the few writers of his generation who didn't wage an oedipal war against their fathers or The Fathers. "Yeled tov u-malei ahava" [A Good and Loving Boy], *Haaretz: Tarbut ve-sifrut*, October 12, 2005, 2, http://www.haaretz.co.il/literature/1.1050312. And see Chana Kronfeld's claims not only that Amichai's women and mother figures, including "literary mothers" like Leah Goldberg, create a softer alternative to the patrilineal vector, but also that, independent of the autobiographical facts, the "poetic Amichai had a 'good mother.'" *Full Severity*, 155. For a discussion of the larger theoretical issues raised by the presence and procession of women and the figures who substitute for male agency in Amichai's poetry and poetics, see ibid., 156–63.

48. Scholem's short letter to Rosenzweig was, as we noted in the previous chapter, "rediscovered" in 1985 and has continued to generate lively debate among scholars and writers throughout the Jewish world, including Jacques Derrida.

49. Derrida, "Eyes of Language," *Acts of Religion*, 212.

50. Amichai, "Tel Gat," *Yehuda Amichai: A Life of Poetry, 1948–1994*, trans. Benjamin Harshav and Barbara Harshav (New York: Harper Collins, 1994), 409. *Shirei Yehuda Amichai*, 5:11. For a discussion of Amichai's literary genealogy leading through medieval Hebrew poets such as Ha-nagid, and Tova Rosen's very persuasive argument about this connection, see above, chapter 6, and DeKoven Ezrahi, *Shlosha paytanim*, 118–24.

51. "The Bible and You, the Bible and You, and Other Midrashim," no. 6, trans. Chana Bloch and Chana Kronfeld, *Poetry of Yehuda Amichai*, 426. For other akeda poems in Amichai's last book of poetry, see ibid., nos. 19, 20, 430; "Jewish Travel: Change Is God and Death Is His Prophet," no. 5, 485. *Shirei Yehuda Amichai*, 5:171, 177, 254.

52. See above, chapter 1.

53. "The Real Hero," trans. Chana Bloch, *Poetry of Yehuda Amichai*, 313. *Shirei Yehuda Amichai*, 4:21.

54. Recruiting compassion into this story will also leave room for the comic principle that, I have argued, is the real message of the akeda. It is again, as Bakhtin taught us, the view from up close. See above, chapter 6.

55. "Jerusalem, Jerusalem, Why Jerusalem?," no. 7, *Poetry of Yehuda Amichai*, 502. *Shirei Yehuda Amichai*, 5:278.

56. "Jerusalem, Jerusalem, Why Jerusalem?," nos. 5, 6, 19, trans. Chana Bloch and Chana Kronfeld, *Poetry of Yehuda Amichai*, 501–2, 506. *Shirei Yehuda Amichai*, 5:277–78, 283–84.

57. "Jerusalem 1967," no. 8, trans. Stephen Mitchell, *Poetry of Yehuda Amichai*, 84. *Shirei Yehuda Amichai*, 2:15.

58. "The Land Knows," trans. Robert Alter, *Poetry of Yehuda Amichai*, 405. *Shirei Yehuda Amichai*, 5:134.

59. Benjamin and Barbara Harshav's translation is far more sexually blatant, rendering *'erva* as "cunt" and *evyona* as "throbbing and screaming orgasm." Amichai, *Yehuda Amichai: A Life of Poetry*, 464. See also *evyona* as soul. "I. Heb. Evyônâ, 'Soul,'" *American Journal of Semitic Languages and Literatures* 32, no. 2 (1916): 141–42, http://www.jstor.org/stable/528344.

60. "Songs of Zion the Beautiful," no. 24, trans. Chana Bloch, in Amichai, *Poems of Jerusalem and Love Poems*, 69–71. I prefer this translation to the more euphonious translation by Robert Alter in his edition of Amichai's poetry. *Shirei Yehuda Amichai*, 3:21. See prologue, above.

61. Alter's translation is slightly different: "How she sits alone / the city once great with people."

62. "Jerusalem, Jerusalem, Why Jerusalem?," no. 13, trans. Chana Bloch and Chana Kronfeld, *Poetry of Yehuda Amichai*, 504–5. *Shirei Yehuda Amichai*, 5:281.

63. James Joyce, *Ulysses* (Mineola: Dover Publications, 2002), 59. See DeKoven Ezrahi, *Booking Passage*, frontispiece.

64. "The Bible and You, the Bible and You, and Other Midrashim," no. 32, trans. Chana Bloch and Chana Kronfeld, *Poetry of Yehuda Amichai*, 434–35. *Shirei Yehuda Amichai*, 5:182–83.

Coda

1. Agnon, *Only Yesterday*, 271. Agnon, *Tmol shilshom*, 262. See above, chapter 5, for a discussion of the novel and of this passage.

2. For a discussion of the relevant talmudic text, Masekhet Berakhot 3:17, see above, chapter 5. The positioning of the worshipper vis-à-vis the Holy of Holies in the Temple depends on where he (m.) is located in the universe, but the worldwide community of worshippers is imagined as all inclining toward the Sacred Center. See also above, chapter 1.

3. Moshe Mizrahi—later Ben-Yitzhak Mizrahi, still later Sofer—was born in Teheran before 1870 and died in 1940; he is buried on Mount of Olives. Mizrahi was one of the craftsmen of Jerusalem that Agnon describes in *Tmol shilshom*. My thanks to Eli Osheroff for his stimulating lecture in which he presented this card in a more recent context: as the back jacket of a polemic pamphlet by Yehuda Etzion, *'Alilot ha-mufti ve-ha-doktor: ha-si'aḥ ha-yehudi-muslemi be-nosei har ha-bayit 'al reka' pera 'ot tarpa"t* [The Plots of the Mufti and the Doctor: the Jewish-Muslim Discourse on the Temple Mount in Light of the Riots of 1929] (Beit El: Sifriyat Beit El, 2014). The "Doctor" referred to is Zionist leader Haim Arlosoroff, and the pamphlet by Etzion is part of the ongoing polemic initiated by the thorough investigation of the events of "tarpa"t" (the riots of 1929) by Hillel Cohen, *Tarpa"t*. A detailed description of the iconographic elements of this card is available in Berger, *Crescent*, 353–58.

4. Comparing the riots of October 2015 to those of 1929, which also centered on the Temple Mount and its environs, Hillel Cohen wrote:

> It makes me think of Rabbi Abraham Isaac Kook, known in Hebrew as HaRav Avraham Yitzchak HaCohen Kook. In 1929, during the terrible massacres in Hebron and Safed, while people were being lynched in Jerusalem and murdered all over the country, Kook was the chief rabbi of Mandatory British Palestine . . . Contrary to the image that has become associated with his teachings among a substantial segment of the religious-Zionist community, the rabbi's worldview was anchored in a universalist approach. He contended that the Jewish people were sacred because sanctity is embedded deep down within *every* human being. The role of the Jewish people, in his view, is to raise humanity to a higher level by raising itself higher and taking the rest of humanity with it. Kook took a similar attitude to the Land of Israel and the Temple Mount as its heart. It is the epicenter of the universe where the glory of God is revealed . . . But the rabbi's greatest strength—the lucid vision of his mysticism that encompassed both the sanctity of the Jewish people and that of the Temple's location—was also his great blind spot.

Two days before the massacre in Hebron, a day before the acts of lynching and attacks in Jerusalem, the British turned to the leaders of the Arab and Jewish communities in Palestine, asking them to call on their respective communities to exercise restraint and refrain from further inflaming the situation. The Arab leadership took upon itself to do so, even if perhaps only perfunctorily. Rabbi Kook, however, responded to the British appeal in the negative. (Cohen, "What the 1929 Palestine Riots Teach Us")

5. Derrida, *Gift of Death*, 88. See above, chapter 1.

6. Avi Sagi, "Keeping God on the Temple Mount," *Haaretz*, April 18, 2018, http://www .haaretz.com/misc/article-print-page/.premium-1.681883.

7. Quoted in Enrico Molinaro, *The Holy Places of Jerusalem in the Middle East Peace Agreements: The Conflict between Global and State Identities* (Brighton, UK: Sussex Academic Press, 2009), 17.

8. Yitzhak Rabin, "Inauguration of Jerusalem 3000 Festivities," Israeli Ministry of Foreign Affairs, September 4, 1995, https://mfa.gov.il/MFA/MFA-Archive/1995/Pages/ADDRESS%20BY% 20PRIME%20MINISTER%20YITZHAK%20RABIN%20INAUGURATI.aspx.

9. See "Eulogy for the Late Prime Minister and Defense Yitzhak Rabin by His Majesty King Hussein of Jordan," November 6, 1995, https://mfa.gov.il/mfa/mfa-archive/1995/pages/rabin%20 funeral-%20eulogy%20by%20king%20hussein.aspx. Rabin's and Hussein's visions for Jerusalem were, of course, not identical, as can be seen in the difference between the king's assumption of a tolerant and benign deity as sovereign over the Temple Mount and the prime minister's assumption of a tolerant and benign Israeli government as sovereign over the Temple Mount. But there was room for cautious optimism during those few years referred to as the "Oslo Process."

10. For a detailed discussion of this subject, see the essay by Yitzhak Beer, "Dangerous Liaison: The Dynamics of the Rise of the Temple Movements and Their Implications" (Jerusalem: 'Ir Amim, 2013), http://www.ir-amim.org.il/sites/default/files/Dangerous%20Liaison-Dynamics%20 of%20the%20Temple%20Movements.pdf, especially pp. 53ff. For a longer consideration of the history of such contested sites, and the possibilities for resolution, see also Yitzhak Reiter, *Contested Holy Places in Israel-Palestine: Sharing and Conflict Resolution* (London: Routledge, 2017).

11. Persico, "End Point of Zionism," 114.

12. In figure 11, note that the letter *nun* from "yemini" (my right hand) has been dislodged. Note also that the Montefiore windmill in the center of the relief looks like a skull and crossbones. Finally, note that the dome is prominent on Dome of the Rock, in contrast to some current representations by the Israeli government and Jerusalem municipality, where such interdenominational architectural elements have been effaced. See Nir Hasson and Olivier Fitoussi, "Jerusalem Municipality Removes Dome of the Rock from Temple Mount Drawing," *Haaretz*, June 14, 2019, https://www.haaretz.com/israel-news/jerusalem-municipality-erases-dome-of-the-rock-from -temple-mount-drawing-1.7369163.

13. Taken from the story "Ha-yeraḥmielim," 59–62. See above, chapter 5.

14. As a meditation on memory, the piece of citron acts in the precincts of the Hebrew imagination not unlike Proust's madeleine in the personal sphere.

15. "Pathways of justice" is Robert Alter's translation. Alter, *Hebrew Bible*, 3:71. The *JPS* translation, curiously, is "straight paths," even though the Hebrew, "ma'aglei tzedek," clearly delineates *circles* of *justice* or righteousness, or at least circular motion constituting righteousness or justice. The KJV also misses the circularity as it renders this phrase "paths of righteousness." "Circles of Justice" is my own translation of the story's title. In Amiel Gurt's translation, quoted below, the title is "Paths of Righteousness."

16. See references to Vinegar, Son of Wine—*ḥometz ben yayin*—in the Talmud as signifying not only economic but also moral degeneration (ex., the son of Shimeon bar Yochai). Bava Metsia 83b. Popular culture adopted the phrase as a rather unflattering idiom—or curse.

17. "Paths of Righteousness, or the Vinegar Maker," trans. Amiel Gurt, in Agnon, *Book That Was Lost*, 197.

18. For an elaboration of these sources and a longer discussion of this story, see DeKoven Ezrahi, "S. Y. Agnon's Jerusalem," 146–47. It is significant that this early story was written while Agnon was in Germany.

19. In some fundamental ways, it was Agnon's detractors, those who blamed him for sympathy for the *goyim* and regarded this story as an invitation to their savior to defile the premises of Hebrew prose, who, I believe, got the story "right." His supporters claimed, for the most part, that the story was an ironic, grotesque, or satiric attack on Jewish faith in Gentile intentions. For an elaboration of these arguments, see ibid., 151–52n53.

20. See Agnon, *Bilvav yamim*; on this, see DeKoven Ezrahi, *Booking Passage*, 81–102.

21. See the interpretation of the circularity in "ma'aglei tzedek" in the commentary on Ps. 23 by R. Meir Leibush ben Yehiel Michal Weiser (Ha-malbi'm): "Be-ma'aglei tzedek hu ha-derekh ha-sibuvi she-sovev be-'igul 'ad she-yagi'a el meḥoz ḥeftzo, rotzeh lomar ma she-natiti min ha-derekh ha-yashar el ha-ma'agal haya be-ma'aglei tzedek ki tzedek yikra'uhu le-raglo be-tahalukhot eleh." *Mikra'ei kodesh*, vol. 8, *Nevi'im u-ktuvim* (Vilna: Hotza'at aḥim Re'em, 1890), 42. Free translation: "In the pathways of righteousness [*be-ma'aglei tzedek*] signal the circular path that [one] follows until he arrives at the place of his desire, that is, when I have strayed from the straight path into circularity it was for the [sake] of righteousness because just and righteous are one's steps in these journeys."

22. One of the first of the modern Hebrew writers to incorporate the Arab voice—as well as the discarded Yiddish voice—was Avot Yeshurun. See Avot Yeshurun, *The Syrian-African Rift and Other Poems*, trans. Harold Schimmel (Philadelphia: Jewish Publication Society, 1980). Marginalized for much of his lifetime, he has reemerged in recent years as harbinger of a short-lived dialogue that included such bilingual Palestinian writers as Anton Shammas and Mahmoud Darwish. See Shammas, *Arabesques*, trans. Vivian Eden (Hebrew, 1986; Berkeley: University of California Press, 2001). A beautiful exchange between Darwish and Yeshurun's daughter, Helit Yeshurun, also signaled a more sanguine moment in modern Israeli literature. Darwish, *Palestine as Metaphor*, trans. Amira el-Zein and Carolyn Forché (Northampton, MA: Interlink, 2019). The chapter "I Don't Return, I Arrive" was first published in Hebrew in *Hadarim* 12 (Spring 1996), 91–145. "When I read Hebrew, I remember place," Darwish admits in that conversation. "Language brings the landscape with it." Ibid., 144.

23. Amichai, "And Who Will Remember the Rememberers?," no. 10, trans. Chana Bloch and Chana Kronfeld, *Poetry of Yehuda Amichai*, 525. *Shirei Yehuda Amichai*, 5:307–8. See above, chapter 6.

24. "Perhaps I am one of the last who must live out to the end the destiny of the Jewish spirit in Europe," Celan wrote as early as 1948 to relatives living in Israel. The word he uses is "pneumatisch." John Felstiner, "Writing Zion," *New Republic*, June 5, 2006, https://newrepublic.com/article/65477/writing-zion. The term "pneumatisch/e" as noun or adjective appears frequently in Celan's writing. See Norman Manea, who refers to "the pneumatic Celan." Introduction to *The Correspondence of Paul Celan and Ilana Shmueli*, trans. Susan H. Gillespie (New York: Sheep Meadow Press, 2010), iii. And see Lydia Koëlle, *Paul Celans pneumatisches Judentum: Gott-Rede und menschliche Existenz nach der Shoah* (Mainz: Matthias-Grünewald-Verlag, 1997).

25. Cited in Hana Amichai, "Ha-kfitza bein ha-ʿadayin ve-ha-kvar lo" [The Leap between What Still Exists and What Has Not Yet Come], *Haaretz*, April 5, 2012, https://www.haaretz.co.il /misc/1.1679553. For a more extensive discussion of this, see DeKoven Ezrahi, *Shlosha paytanim*, 32–35.

26. "Names, Names, in Other Days and in Our Time," no. 10, trans. Chana Bloch and Chana Kronfeld, *Poetry of Yehuda Amichai*, 497. *Shirei Yehuda Amichai*, 5:270. "Thus," concludes Na'ama Rokem, "in Amichai's imagined parting from Celan, the last thing that Amichai allows himself to see is a guise of pneuma, the breath that Celan had spoken of in Jerusalem." Rokem, "German-Jewish Encounters in the Poetry of Yehuda Amichai and Paul Celan," *Prooftexts* 30, no. 1 (2010): 114.

27. Ilana Shmueli, *Sag, dass Jerusalem ist. Uber Paul Celan: Oktober 1969–April 1970* (Eggingen: Edition Isele, 2000; 2nd, expanded ed., 2010). This volume was first published in 1995 in *Jüdischer Almanach des Leo Baeck Instituts*. An enlarged Hebrew version was published in 1999 and an English version was later published under the title *Say That Jerusalem Is*. Most of the poetic texts cited by Shmueli are fragments of unpublished poems that punctuated their correspondence.

28. Ilana Shmueli, *The Correspondence of Paul Celan and Ilana Shmueli*, trans. Susan H. Gillespie (New York: Sheep Meadow Press, 2010), 22, 25.

Bibliography

Abramson, Glenda. *The Writing of Yehuda Amichai: A Thematic Approach.* Albany: SUNY Press, 1989.

Adorno, T. W. *Aesthetic Theory.* London: Routledge, 1984.

Afsar, Ayaz. "A Comparative Study of the Intended Sacrifice of Isaac/Ishmael in the Bible and the Quran." *Islamic Studies* 46, no. 4 (Winter 2007): 483–98.

Agamben, Giorgio. *Homo Sacer: Sovereign Power and Bare Life.* Trans. Daniel Heller-Roazen. Stanford: Stanford University Press, 1998.

Agnon, S. Y. *'Ad hena* [This Far]. Jerusalem: Schocken, 1972.

———. "Aggadat ha-sofer" [The Tale of the Scribe]; "*'Agunot.*" In *Elu ve-elu* [These and Those]. Jerusalem: Schocken, 1972.

———. "Agunot." Trans. Baruch Hochman. In *Modern Hebrew Literature*, ed. Robert Alter, 183–94. New York: Behrman House, 1975.

———. "Agunot." In Agnon, *A Book That Was Lost and Other Stories*, ed. Alan Mintz and Anne Golomb Hoffman. New York: Schocken, 1995.

———. "And Solomon's Wisdom Excelled." Trans. Mordechai Beck. *Ariel: Israel Review of Arts and Letters* 92 (1993): 277–82.

———. *Ba-ḥanuto shel mar Lublin, 1962–1968* [In Mr. Lublin's Store]. Jerusalem: Schocken, 2001.

———. *Bilvav yamim: sippur aggadah shel S. Y. Agnon* [In the Heart of the Seas: A Legend by S. Y. Agnon]. From "Sippurim shel Eretz Yisrael" [Stories from the Land of Israel]. In *Elu ve-elu* [These and Those]. New ed. Jerusalem: Schocken, 1998.

———. *A Book That Was Lost and Other Stories.* Ed. Alan Mintz and Anne Golomb Hoffman. New York: Schocken, 1995.

———. *The Bridal Canopy* [Hakhnasat kalah]. Trans. I. M. Lask. New York: Literary Guild of America, 1937.

———. "Chapters for the Book of State." Trans. Sara Daniel, Isaac Franck, and Jules Harlow. In *The Orange Peel and Other Satires*, ed. Jeffrey Saks, 125–69. London: Toby Press, 2015.

———. *A City in Its Fullness.* Trans. and ed. Alan Mintz and Jeffrey Saks. New Milford, CT: Toby Press, 2016.

———. *Elu ve-elu* [These and Those]. Jerusalem: Schocken, 1972; new ed., 1998.

———. *Hakhnasat kalah* [The Bridal Canopy]. Jerusalem: Schocken, 1974.

————. "Ha-siman" [The Sign]. In *Ha-esh ve-ha-'etsim*. Jerusalem: Schocken, 1998.

————. *In Mr. Lublin's Store*. Trans. Glenda Abramson. Afterword by Haim Beer. New Milford, CT: Toby Press, 2016.

————. *In the Heart of the Seas: A Story of a Journey to the Land of Israel*. Trans. I. M. Lask. New York: Schocken, 1947.

————. *'Ir u-meloah* [A City in Its Fullness]. Jerusalem: Schocken, 1973.

————. *Korot bateinu* [The Rafters of Our Home; Chronicles of Our Homes]. Jerusalem: Schocken, 1979.

————. "Lefi ha-tza'ar ha-sakhar" [According to the Struggle the Reward.] In *Ha-esh ve-ha-'etsim*. Jerusalem: Schocken, 1998.

————. *Lifnim min ha-ḥoma* [Within the Wall]. Jerusalem: Schocken, 1975.

————. *Me-'atzmi el 'atzmi* [Between Me and Myself]. Jerusalem: Schocken, 2000.

————. Nobel Prize Banquet speech, December 10, 1966. http://www.nobelprize.org/nobel_prizes/literature/laureates/1966/agnon-speech.html.

————. *Only Yesterday*. Trans. Barbara Harshav. Introduction by Benjamin Harshav. Princeton: Princeton University Press, 2000.

————. *Oreaḥ nata la-lun* [A Guest for the Night]. Jerusalem: Schocken, 1939.

————. *Polin: Sippurei aggadot* [Poland: Tales]. Tel Aviv: Hedim, 1925.

————. "The Sense of Smell." In Agnon, *A Book That Was Lost and Other Stories*, ed. Alan Mintz and Anne Golomb Hoffman, 139–46. New York: Schocken, 1995.

————. "The Tale of the Scribe." Trans. Isaac Franck. In Agnon, *A Book That Was Lost and Other Stories*, ed. Alan Mintz and Anne Golomb Hoffman, 176. New York: Schocken, 1995.

————. "Tehila." *Me'asef Davar* (1949); *'Ad hena* [This Far]. Jerusalem: Schocken, 1972.

————. "Tehila." Trans. Walter Lever. In *Firstfruits: A Harvest of 25 Years of Israeli Writing*, ed. James A. Michener. Greenwich, CT: Fawcett, 1973.

————. *Tmol shilshom* [Only Yesterday]. Jerusalem: Schocken, 1971.

————. "Va-terev ḥokhmat Shlomo" [And Solomon's Wisdom Excelled]. In *'Ad hena* [This Far]. Jerusalem: Schocken, 1972.

Alberstein, Chava. "Ḥad Gadya." YouTube, 1989. https://www.youtube.com/watch?v=DHdVYy5B6JM.

al-Kumisi, Daniel. "Appeal to the Karaites of the Dispersion to Come and Settle in Jerusalem." In *Karaite Anthology*, ed. Leon Nemoy, 35–38. New Haven: Yale University Press, 1952.

Allen, Woody. "The Scrolls." *New Republic*, August 31, 1974. https://newrepublic.com/article/113899/scrolls-woody-allen.

Alter, Robert. *The Art of Bible Translation*. Princeton: Princeton University Press, 2019.

————. *The Art of Biblical Narrative*. New York: Basic Books, 1981.

————. *The Art of Biblical Poetry*. New York: Basic Books, 1985.

————. *Hebrew and Modernity*. Bloomington: Indiana University Press, 1994.

————, trans. *The Hebrew Bible*. New York: W. W. Norton, 2019.

————. *The Invention of Hebrew Prose: Modern Fiction and the Language of Realism*. Seattle: University of Washington Press, 1988.

————, trans. *Strong as Death Is Love: The Song of Songs, Ruth, Esther, Jonah, and Daniel*. New York: W. W. Norton, 2015.

Alter, Robert, and Frank Kermode, eds. *The Literary Guide to the Bible*. Cambridge: Harvard University Press, 1987.

Amichai, Hana. "Ha-kfitza bein ha-'adayin ve-ha-kvar lo" [The Leap between What Still

Exists and What Has Not Yet Come]. *Haaretz*, April 5, 2012. https://www.haaretz.co.il/misc /1.1679553.

———. "Little Ruth, My Personal Anne Frank." *Haaretz*, October 22, 2010. https://www.haaretz .com/1.5129177.

Amichai, Yehuda. *Bein milḥama le-ahava: ha-meshorer Yehuda Amichai* [Between War and Love: The Poet Yehuda Amichai]. Translated from German by Hana Livnat. Ed. Renata Eickmeyer and Edith Reim. Ramat Gan: Rimonim, 2016.

———. *Lo me-ʿakhshav lo mi-kan.* Jerusalem: Schocken, 1963.

———. *Not of This Time, Not of This Place.* Trans. Shlomo Katz. New York: Harper & Row, 1968.

———. *Poems of Jerusalem and Love Poems.* Bilingual ed. New York: Sheep Meadow Press, 1988.

———. *The Poetry of Yehuda Amichai.* Ed. Robert Alter. New York: Farrar, Straus and Giroux, 2015.

———. *The Selected Poetry of Yehuda Amichai.* Trans. Chana Bloch and Stephen Mitchell. Berkeley: University of California Press, 1996.

———. *Shirei Yehuda Amichai.* 5 vols. Jerusalem: Schocken, 2002.

———. *Yehuda Amichai: A Life of Poetry, 1948–1994.* Trans. Benjamin Harshav and Barbara Harshav. New York: Harper Collins, 1994.

Arbel, Michal. "Ha-ketiva ke-matzeva: romantika ve-historiosophia be-sippurav shel S. Y. Agnon" [Writing as Epitaph: Romanticism and Philosophy of History in the Narratives of S. Y. Agnon]. *Mikan* 2 (July 2001): 66–73.

———. *Katuv ʿal ʿoro shel kelev: ʿal tefisat ha-yetzira etsel Shay Agnon* [Written on the Dog's Skin: S. Y. Agnon: Concepts of Creativity and Art]. Jerusalem: Keter and Ben Gurion University, 2006.

Arpali, Boaz. "Balak ki-fshuto u-khe-midrasho" [Balak as Literal and as Midrash]. In *Kovetz Agnon II*, ed. Emuna Yaron et al., 160–212. Jerusalem: Magnes Press, 2000.

———. *Ha-peraḥim ve-ha-agartal; shirat Amichai: mivne, mashmaʿut, poetika* [The Flowers and the Urn: Amichai's Poetry, 1948–1968]. Tel Aviv: Siman Kria/Ha-kibbutz ha-meuchad, 1986.

———. "On the Political Significance of Amichai's Poetry." In *The Experienced Soul: Studies in Amichai*, ed. Glenda Abramson, 27–50. Boulder, CO: Westview Press, 1997.

———. *Rav roman: ḥamisha maʿamarim ʿal Tmol shilshom me-et S. Y. Agnon* [Masternovel: Five Essays on *Tmol Shilshom* by S. Y. Agnon]. Tel Aviv: Ha-kibbutz ha-meuchad, 1998.

———. "Yerushalayim ḥatranit: Yerushalayim ke-tsomet mefarek mitosim be-shirat Yehuda Amichai" [Subversive Jerusalem: Jerusalem as Crossroads of Dismantled Myths in the Poetry of Yehuda Amichai]. *Dapim le-meḥkar be-sifrut* 14–15 (2005): 293–320.

Ashkenazi, Yiftach. *Gay ben-hinom* [Gehenna]. Hevel Modiʿin Industrial Park: Kinneret, Zmora, Dvir, 2019.

Auerbach, Erich. *Mimesis: The Representation of Reality in Western Literature.* Trans. Willard R. Trask. Princeton: Princeton University Press, 1953.

Avi-Yonah, Michael. *The Madaba Mosaic Map.* Jerusalem: Israel Exploration Society, 1954.

Azād, Ghulām Murtaza. "Israʾ and Mʿiraj: Night Journey and Ascension of Allah's Apostle Muhammad (S. A. W. S.)." *Islamic Studies* 22, no. 2 (Summer 1983): 63–80.

Baer, Yitzhak, and Azriel Shochat, eds. *Shevet Yehudah.* Jerusalem: Bialik, 1946/47.

Bahat, Dan. "A New Suggestion for the Dating of the Madaba Map." *Ariel* 116 (1996): 74–77.

Bakhtin, Mikhail. *The Dialogic Imagination: Four Essays.* Trans. Caryl Emerson and Michael Holquist. Austin: University of Texas Press, 1981.

———. *Problems of Dostoevsky's Poetics.* Trans. and ed. Caryl Emerson. Minneapolis: University of Minnesota Press, 1984.

———. *Rabelais and His World*. Trans. Helene Iswolsky. Bloomington: Indiana University Press, 1984.

Band, Arnold. *Nostalgia and Nightmare: A Study in the Fiction of S. Y. Agnon*. Berkeley: University of California Press, 1968.

Band, Avraham. "Ha-ḥet ve-'onsho bi-*Tmol shilshom*" [Crime and Punishment in *Tmol shilshom*]. *Molad* 1, n.s., 24 (1967–68): 75–78.

Barnavi, Eli. "The Karaites: A Medieval Jewish Sect." *My Jewish Learning*. http://www.myjew ishlearning.com/article/the-karaites-a-medieval-jewish-sect/3/. Accessed July 9, 2021.

Baron, Salo W. "Newer Emphases in Jewish History." *Jewish Social Studies* 25, no. 4 (October 1963): 235–48.

Barthes, Roland. *A Lover's Discourse: Fragments*. Trans. Richard Howard. Foreword by Wayne Koestenbaum. New York: Hill and Wang, 1979.

Bartov, Omer. *Anatomy of a Genocide: The Life and Death of a Town Called Buczacz*. New York: Simon & Schuster, 2018.

———. *Tales from the Borderlands: Making and Unmaking the Past*. New Haven: Yale University Press, forthcoming.

Barzel, Hillel. *Bein Agnon le-Kafka* [Between Agnon and Kafka]. Ramat Gan: Bar Oryan, 1972.

———. "Diyokano shel kelev: 'iyyun mashveh: 'kelev ḥutzot' mi-tokh *tmol shilshom* le-shai 'agnon u-meḥkarav shel kelev lefi kafka" [Profile of a Dog: Comparative Study of Agnon and Kafka]. *Karmelit* 14–15 (1968): 161–73.

———. *Sipurei ahava shel Shmuel Yosef Agnon* [S. Y. Agnon's Love Stories]. Ramat Gan: Bar Ilan University Press, 1975.

Baskin, Gershon. "The Jerusalem Problem: The Search for Solutions." *Palestine-Israel Journal* 8, no. 1 (2001): 6–11.

Be'er, Haim. "Ha-mafte'aḥ le-havanat *Ba-ḥanuto shel mar Lublin, me-et Agnon*" [The Key to Understanding Agnon's *In Mr. Lublin's Store*]. *Haaretz*, August 12, 2016. https://www.haaretz .co.il/literature/study/.premium-1.3037102.

———. *The Pure Element of Time*. Trans. of *Ḥavalim* by Barbara Harshav. Waltham: Brandeis University Press, 2012.

Beer, Yitzhak. "Dangerous Liaison: The Dynamics of the Rise of the Temple Movements and Their Implications." Jerusalem: 'Ir Amim, 2013. http://www.ir-amim.org.il/sites/default/files /Dangerous%20Liaison-Dynamics%20of%20the%20Temple%20Movements.pdf.

Ben-Arieh, Yehoshua. *'Ir be-re'i ha-tkufa: Yerushalayim ba-meah ha-19* [The City in Its Historical Context: Jerusalem in the Nineteenth Century]. Jerusalem: Yad Ben Tzvi, 1977.

Ben-Dov, Nitza. *Ahavot lo me'usharot: tiskul eroti, omanut va-mavet bi-yetzirat Agnon* [Unhappy/Unapproved Loves: Erotic Frustration, Art, and Death in Agnon's Fiction]. Tel Aviv: Am Oved, 1997.

Benjamin, Walter. "Some Reflections on Kafka." From "Letter to Gerhard Scholem," June 12, 1938. In *Illuminations*, trans. Harry Zohn, ed. Hannah Arendt, 141–47. New York: Schocken, 1968.

Ben Maimon, Moses. See under Maimonides; for Hebrew translations, see under Ibn Tibbon and Kapach.

Benvenisti, Meron. *City of Stone: The Hidden History of Jerusalem*. Berkeley: University of California Press, 1996.

Ben Yehuda, Eliezer. "He-ḥalom ve-shivro-ha-'idan ha-rishon" [The Dream and Its Meaning]. In *He-ḥalom ve-shivro: mivḥar ktavim be'inyanei lashon* [The Dream and Its Meaning: A Selection of Writings on Language], ed. Reuven Sivan. Jerusalem: Bialik, 1978. https://ben yehuda.org/read/5692.

Berger, Pamela. *The Crescent on the Temple: The Dome of the Rock as Image of the Ancient Jewish Sanctuary*. Leiden: Brill, 2012.

Bernstein, Michael André. *Foregone Conclusions: Against Apocalyptic History*. Berkeley: University of California Press, 1994.

Biale, David. *Eros and the Jews: From Biblical Israel to Contemporary America*. New York: Basic Books, 1992.

Bialik, H. N. "'Al saf beit ha-midrash" [On the Threshold of the Study House, 1894]. In *Kol Shirei Bialik*, 32–35. Tel Aviv: Dvir, 1956. https://benyehuda.org/read/5532.

———. "'Al shniyut bi-yisrael" [On Duality in Israel]. Talk delivered in Berlin in 1922. *Devarim she-be-'al peh*, vol. 1, 39. Tel Aviv: Dvir, 1935.

———. "Ḥevlei Lashon" [Language Pangs]. In *'Ivriya* (1905); reprinted in *Ha-shilo'aḥ* 18 (1907). Reprinted in *Kol kitvei H. N. Bialik* [Complete Writings of H. N. Bialik], 185–90. Tel Aviv: Dvir, 1938.

———. "Nation and Language" [Heb.]. In *Devarim she-be-'al peh* [Oral Tradition]. Tel Aviv: Dvir, 1935. http://benyehuda.org/bialik/dvarim02.html.

———. *Revealment and Concealment: Five Essays*. Afterword by Zali Gurevitch. Jerusalem: Ibis, 2000.

Black, Fiona C. "Unlikely Bedfellows: Allegorical and Feminist Readings of Song of Songs 7:1–8." In *The Song of Songs: A Feminist Companion to the Bible*, 2nd series, ed. Athalya Brenner and Carole R. Fontaine. Sheffield, UK: Sheffield Academic Press, 2000.

Bland, Kalman P. *The Artless Jew: Medieval and Modern Affirmations and Denials of the Visual*. Princeton: Princeton University Press, 2000.

Bloch, Ariel, and Chana Bloch, trans. *The Song of Songs: A New Translation*. Afterword by Robert Alter. New York: Random House, 1995.

Bluwstein, Rachel. "Ve-ulai." Trans. A. C. Jacobs. In *Anthology of Modern Hebrew Poetry*. Jerusalem: Institute for the Translation of Hebrew Literature and Israel Universities Press, 1966. https://pij.org/articles/536.

Boer, Roland. *Knocking on Heaven's Door: The Bible and Popular Culture*. London: Routledge, 1999.

Booth, Wayne. *The Rhetoric of Fiction*. 2nd ed. Chicago: University of Chicago Press, 1983.

Boyarin, Daniel. *Borderlines*. Philadelphia: University of Pennsylvania Press, 2004.

———. *Carnal Israel: Reading Sex in Talmudic Culture*. Berkeley: University of California Press, 1993.

———. "The Eye in the Torah: Ocular Desire in Midrashic Hermeneutic." *Critical Inquiry* 16, no. 3 (Spring 1990): 532–50.

———. "The Song of Songs, Lock or Key: The Holy Song as a Mashal." In *Intertextuality and the Reading of Midrash*, ed. Boyarin, 105–16. Bloomington: Indiana University Press, 1990.

Brenner, Athalya, and Carole R. Fontaine, eds. *A Feminist Companion to the Song of Songs*. 2nd ser. Sheffield, UK: Sheffield Academic Press, 2000.

Brenner, Athalya, and Y. T. Radday, eds. *On Humour and Comic in the Hebrew Bible*. Sheffield, UK: Almond Press, 1990.

Buber, Martin. *Moses: The Revelation and the Covenant*. New York: Harper and Brothers, 1958.

Burstein, Dror. *Tit* [Muck]. Trans. Gabriel Levin. New York: Farrar, Straus and Giroux, 2018.

Burston, Bradley. "Hanukah in a Dark Israel: There's More Than One Way to Defile a Temple." *Haaretz*, December 16, 2014. https://www.haaretz.com/.premium-hanukkah-in-a-dark-israel -1.5347517.

Calasso, Roberto. *K*. Trans. Geoffrey Brock. New York: Alfred A. Knopf, 2005.

Calder, Norman. "From Midrash to Scripture: The Sacrifice of Abraham in Early Islamic Tradition." In *The Qur'an: Formative Interpretation*, ed. Andrew Rippin, 81–108. Aldershot, UK: Ashgate, 1999.

Caputo, John. *Against Ethics: Contributions to a Poetics of Obligation with Constant Reference to Deconstruction*. Bloomington: Indiana University Press, 1993.

Carmi, T. *The Penguin Book of Hebrew Verse*. Harmondsworth: Penguin, 1981.

Carroll, James. *Constantine's Sword: The Church and the Jews, A History*. New York: Mariner's Books, 2002.

———. *Jerusalem, Jerusalem: How the Ancient City Ignited Our Modern World*. Boston: Houghton Mifflin Harcourt, 2011.

Caspi, Mishael, and T. Greene, eds. *Unbinding the Binding of Isaac*. Lanham, MD: University Presses of America, 2007.

Cohen, Amnon. "Haram-i Serif, the Temple Mount under Ottoman Rule." In *Where Heaven and Earth Meet: Jerusalem's Sacred Esplanade*, ed. Oleg Grabar and Benjamin Z. Kedar, 210–30. Austin and Jerusalem: University of Texas Press and Yad Ben Zvi, 2009.

Cohen, Hillel. *Tarpa"t: Shnat ha-efes ba-sikhsukh ha-yehudi-'aravi* [1929: The Zero Hour of the Jewish-Arab Conflict]. Jerusalem: Keter Books, 2013.

———. "What the 1929 Palestine Riots Teach Us about Today's Violence." *+972 Magazine*, October 16, 2015. http://972mag.com/what-the-1929-palestine-riots-teach-us-about-todays-violence/112830/.

Cohen, Mordechai Z. "Logic to Interpretation: Maimonides' Use of al-Fârâbî's Model of Metaphor." *Zutot: Perspectives on Jewish Culture* 2 (2002): 104–13.

———. *Three Approaches to Biblical Metaphor: From Abraham Ibn Ezra and Maimonides to David Kimhi*. Leiden: Brill, 2003.

Cuffel, Alexandra. "Call and Response: European Jewish Emigration to Egypt and Palestine in the Middle Ages." *Jewish Quarterly Review* 90, nos. 1–2 (July–October 1999): 61–102.

Dancygier, Barbara, and Eve Sweetser. *Figurative Language*. Cambridge: Cambridge University Press, 2014.

Darrow, Robert Arnold. "Kierkegaard, Kafka, and the Strength of 'The Absurd' in Abraham's Sacrifice of Isaac." MA thesis, Wayne State University, 2005. https://corescholar.libraries.wright.edu/etd_all/18/.

Darwish, Mahmoud. "I Don't Return, I Arrive." *Hadarim* 12 (Spring 1996): 91–145.

———. *Palestine as Metaphor*. Trans. Amira el-Zein and Carolyn Forché. Northampton, MA: Interlink, 2019.

DeKoven Ezrahi, Sidra. "After Such Knowledge, What Laughter?" *Yale Journal of Criticism* 14, no. 1 (2001): 287–313.

———. "Agnon Before and After." *Prooftexts* 2, no. 1 (January 1982): 78–94.

———. "America as the Theatre of Jewish Comedy: From Sholem Aleichem to Grace Paley." *Studia Judaica* 13 (2005): 74–82.

———. *Booking Passage: Exile and Homecoming in the Modern Jewish Imagination*. Berkeley: University of California Press, 2000.

———. "By the Waters of Babylon: The Amnesia of Memory [on Psalm 137]." In *Psalms in/on Jerusalem*, ed. Ilana Pardes and Ophir Münz-Manor, 153–64. Berlin: De Gruyter, 2019.

———. "Dan Pagis—Out of Line: A Poetics of Decomposition." *Prooftexts* 10, special anniversary issue (May 1990): 335–63.

———. "From Auschwitz to the Temple Mount: Binding and Unbinding the Israeli Narrative." In *After Testimony: The Ethics and Aesthetics of Holocaust Narrative*, ed. Susan Suleiman, Jakob Lothe, and James Phelan, 291–313. Columbus: Ohio State University Press, 2012.

———. "The Grave in the Air: Unbound Metaphors in Post-Holocaust Poetry." In *Probing the Limits of Representation: Nazism and the Final Solution*, ed. Saul Friedlander, 259–76. Cambridge: Harvard University Press, 1992.

———. "Ha-milḥama ba-sifrut ha-'ivrit" [War and Catastrophe in Jewish Culture]. In *Zman Yehudi ḥadash: Tarbut Yehudit be-'idan ḥiloni* [New Jewish Time: Jewish Culture in a Secular Epoch], vol. 3, *Literature and the Arts*, ed. Dan Miron and Hannan Hever, 206–9. Jerusalem: Keter, 2007.

———. "Jerusalem Divorced Family's Home as Inspiration for Israeli-Palestinian Peace." *Haaretz*, February 27, 2016. https://www.haaretz.com/israel-news/.premium.MAGAZINE -no-clean-divorce-for-israel-and-palestine-1.5409395.

———. "Literary Archaeology at the Temple Mount: Recovering the Comic Version of the Sacrifice of Isaac." *MLA* (July 2016). https://profession.mla.org/literary-archaeology-at-the -temple-mount-recovering-the-comic-version-of-the-sacrifice-of-isaac/.

———. "Philip Roth: Writing the American Jewish Century." In *Makers of Jewish Modernity: Thinkers, Artists, Leaders, and the World They Made*, ed. Jacques Picard, Jacques Revel, Michael Steinberg, and Idith Zertal, 597–612. Princeton: Princeton University Press, 2016. (Excerpt available at https://www.tabletmag.com/sections/arts-letters/articles/in-defense -of-philip-roth.)

———. "Sentient Dogs, Liberated Rams, and Talking Asses: Agnon's Biblical Zoo—or Rereading *Tmol shilshom*." *AJS Review* 28, no. 1 (April 2004): 105–35.

———. *Shlosha paytanim* [Three Poets of the Sacred Quotidian]: *Paul Celan, Dan Pagis, Yehuda Amichai*. Jerusalem: Mossad Bialik, 2020.

———. "The Shtetl and Its Afterlife: Agnon in Jerusalem." *AJS Review* 41, no. 1 (April 2017): 133–54. https://agnonhouse.org.il/wp-content/uploads/2017/05/shtetl_and_its_afterlife_agnon _in_jerusalem-1.pdf.

———. "S. Y. Agnon's Jerusalem: Before and After 1948." *Jewish Social Studies* 18, no. 3 (Spring/ Summer 2012): 136–52.

———. " 'To what shall I compare thee?' Jerusalem as Ground Zero of the Hebrew Imagination." *PMLA*, special issue, "Cities," ed. Patricia Yaeger, 122, no. 1 (January 2007): 220–34.

———. "Yehuda Amichai: paytan shel ha-yomyom" [Yehuda Amichai: Sacred Poet of the Quotidian], *Mikan* 14 (Spring 2014): 143–67.

Deleuze, Gilles, and Felix Guattari. "Kafka: Toward a Minor Literature; The Components of Expression." *New Literary History* 16, no. 3 (Spring 1985): 591–608.

———. *Kafka: Toward a Minor Literature*. Minneapolis: University of Minnesota Press, 1986.

Derrida, Jacques. *Acts of Religion*. Ed. Gil Anidjar. New York: Routledge, 2002.

———. *The Gift of Death*. Trans. David Wills. Chicago: University of Chicago Press, 1995.

Diamond, James Arthur. *Maimonides and the Hermeneutics of Concealment: Deciphering Scripture and Midrash in the Guide of the Perplexed*. Albany: SUNY Press, 2002.

Dickinson, Emily. "Some Keep the Sabbath Going to Church." In *Final Harvest: Emily Dickinson's Poems*, ed. Thomas H. Johnson, 66. Boston: Little, Brown, 1961.

Donne, John. "The Anniversarie." In *John Donne: The Conservative Revolutionary*, ed. N. J. C. Andreasen, 219–20. Princeton: Princeton University Press, 1967.

Dumper, Michael. "Muslim Institutional Development in Jerusalem: The Role of Waqfs." *Journal of Islamic Jerusalem Studies* 2, no. 1 (Winter 1998): 21–38.

Dvi-Guri, Lilian, ed. *Kurzweil-Agnon-UZG: Correspondence*. Ramat Gan: Bar Ilan University Press, 1977.

Dylan, Bob. "Highway 61 Revisited (Audio)." YouTube, March 12, 2019. https://www.youtube .com/watch?v=8hr3Stnk8_k.

Eagleton, Terry. *Sweet Violence: The Idea of the Tragic*. Oxford: Blackwell, 2003.

Eastman, Richard. "The Open Parable: Demonstration and Definition." *College English* 22 (October 1960): 15–18.

Eiland, Howard. *Walter Benjamin: A Critical Life*. Cambridge: Belknap Press, 2014.

Eliav, Z. Yaron. *God's Mountain: The Temple Mount in Time, Place, and Memory*. Baltimore: Johns Hopkins University Press, 2005.

Elior, Rachel. "The Garden of Eden Is the Holy of Holies and the Dwelling of the Lord." *Studies in Spirituality* 24 (2014): 90.

———. *Harut 'al ha-luhot: ha-mahshava ha-hasidit, mekoroteha ha-misti'im vi-yesodoteha ha-kabali'im* [Incised in the Tablets]. Tel Aviv: Misrad ha-bitahon, 1999.

Etzion, Yehuda. *'Alilot ha-mufti ve-ha-doktor: ha-si'ah ha-yehudi-muslemi be-nosei har ha-bayit'al reka' pera'ot tarpa"t* [The Plots of the Mufti and the Doctor: the Jewish-Muslim Discourse on the Temple Mount in Light of the Riots of 1929]. Beit El: Sifriyat Beit El, 2014.

Ezrachi, Elan. *Shfuya ba-halomah: ge'ut ve-shefel be-50 shnot ihud yerushalayim* [Awakened Dream: 50 Years of Complex Unification of Jerusalem]. Herzliya: Albatross, 2017.

Feldman, Yael. *The Glory and the Agony: Isaac's Sacrifice and National Narrative*. Stanford: Stanford University Press, 2010.

Felstiner, John. "Writing Zion." *New Republic*, June 5, 2006. https://newrepublic.com/article /65477/writing-zion.

Fishbane, Eitan. *The Art of Mystical Narrative: A Poetics of the Zohar*. Oxford: Oxford University Press, 2018.

Fishbane, Michael. *Inner-Biblical Exegesis: Biblical Interpretation in Ancient Israel*. Oxford: Clarendon Press, 1985.

———. Introduction to *The JPS Bible Commentary: Song of Songs. The Traditional Hebrew Text with the New JPS Translation*. Philadelphia: Jewish Publication Society, 2015.

———. *The Kiss of God: Spiritual and Mystical Death in Judaism*. Seattle: University of Washington Press, 1994.

Fishelov, David. "Amichai: A Modern Metaphysical Poet." *Orbis Litterarium* 47 (1992): 178–91.

Fogel, David. "Bintot ha-yom" [At the End of the Day]. In *Kol ha-shirim*, ed. Aharon Komem, 38. Tel Aviv: Ha-kibbutz ha-meuchad, 1998.

Follis, Elaine. "The Holy City as Daughter." In *Directions in Biblical Poetry*, ed. Elaine R. Follis, 173–84. Sheffield, UK: JSOT, 1987.

Foucault, Michel. "Of Other Spaces: Heterotopias." Trans. Jay Miskowiec, from *Architecture, Mouvement, Continuité*, no. 5 (1984): 46–49. https://foucault.info/documents/heterotopia /foucault.heteroTopia.en/.

Fox, Everett, ed. *The Five Books of Moses*. New York: Schocken, 2000.

Frick, Frank S. "Mother/Daughter (NRSV, Village) as Territory." In *Women in Scripture: A Dictionary of Named and Unnamed Women in the Hebrew Bible, the Apocryphal/Deuterocanonical Books, and the New Testament*, ed. Carol Meyers. Grand Rapids: Eerdmans, 2000.

Frye, Northrop. *Anatomy of Criticism*. New York: Atheneum, 1968.

———. *Fables of Identity: Studies in Poetic Mythology*. New York: Harcourt, Brace and World, 1963.

Frymer-Kensky, Tikva. *Studies in Bible and Feminist Criticism*. New York: Jewish Publication Society, 2010.

———. "Zion, the Beloved Woman." In *In the Wake of the Goddesses: Women, Culture, and the Biblical Transformation of Pagan Myth*, 168–78. New York: Fawcett Columbine, 1992.

Gilad, Elon. "The History of the Temple Mount: Where Gods Collide." *Haaretz*, November 19, 2014. http://www.haaretz.com/archaeology/.premium-1.627324.

Ginsberg, H. L. "Introduction to the Song of Songs." In *The Five Megilloth and Jonah*. Philadelphia: Jewish Publication Society, 1969.

Girard, René. *The Scapegoat*. Trans. Yvonne Freccero. Baltimore: Johns Hopkins University Press, 1986.

Givón, Talmy. "The Drift from VSO to SVO in Biblical Hebrew: The Pragmatics of Tense-Aspect." In *Mechanics of Syntactic Change*, ed. Charles N. Li, 181–254. Austin: University of Texas Press, 1977.

Gluzman, Michael. *Ha-guf ha-tzioni: Le'umiyut, migdar u-miniyut ba-sifrut ha-'ivrit ha-ḥadasha* [The Zionist Body: Nationalism, Gender, and Sexuality in Modern Hebrew Literature]. Tel Aviv: Ha-kibbutz ha-meuchad, 2007.

———. "Im lo tihiyeh yerushalayim: 'al *Isha boraḥat mi-besora*" [If Jerusalem Ceases to Exist: On *To the End of the Land* by David Grossman]. *Haaretz*, May 5, 2008. https://www.haaretz.co.il/literature/1.1322595.

Gluzman, Michael, Hannan Hever, and Dan Miron, eds. *Be-'ir ha-harega—Bikur me'uḥar bimlot meah shana la-poema shel Bialik* [In the City of the Slaughter: A Belated Visit on the Centenary of Bialik's Poema]. Tel Aviv-Jaffa: Resling, 2005.

Gold, Nili Scharf. *Yehuda Amichai: The Making of Israel's National Poet*. Waltham: Brandeis University Press, 2008.

Goldberg, Leah. *Lea Goldberg: Selected Poetry and Drama*. Trans. Rachel Tzvia Back. New Milford, CT: Toby Press, 2005.

———. "Tel Aviv, 1935." Trans. Adriana X. Jacobs. From "Ha-masa' ha-katzar be-yoter" [The Shortest Journey]. In *'Im ha-layla ha-ze* [With This Night]. Bnai Brak: Sifriat Poalim, 1964. http://teachgreatjewishbooks.org/resource-kits/leah-goldbergs-tel-aviv-1935#resources.

Golden, Leon. "Aristotle on Comedy." *Journal of Aesthetics and Art Criticism* 42, no. 3 (Spring 1984): 283–90. https://www.jstor.org/stable/429709?seq=1.

Goldhill, Simon. *The Temple of Jerusalem*. Cambridge: Harvard University Press, 2005.

Gosetti-Ferencei, Jennifer-Anna. "Immanent Transcendence in Rilke and Stevens." *German Quarterly* 83, no. 3 (Summer 2010): 275–96.

Gouri, Haim. *Shoshanat ha-ruḥot*. Tel Aviv: Ha-kibbutz ha-meuchad, 1960.

Grabar, Oleg, and Benjamin Kedar, eds. *Where Heaven and Earth Meet: Jerusalem's Sacred Esplanade*. Austin and Jerusalem: University of Texas Press and Yad Ben Zvi, 2009.

Greenberg, Rafi, and Yonatan Mizrahi. "Mi-Silwan le-Har ha-bayit: Ḥafirot arkhiyologiot ke-emtza'i li-shlita. Hitpatḥuyot—bi-kfar Silwan u-va-'ir ha-'atika shel yerushalayim be-shnat 2012" [From Silwan to the Temple Mount: Archaeological Digs as Means of Control. Developments in the Village of Silwan and the Old City of Jerusalem in 2012]. *Emek Shaveh* (2013). http://alt-arch.org/en/wp-content/uploads/2013/04/Frm-Sil-to-Tmpl-Mnt-English-Web-.pdf.

Grossman, David. "Amichai va-anaḥnu" [Amichai and Us]. *Haaretz*, October 22, 1999.

———. *The Book of Intimate Grammar*. Trans. Betsy Rosenberg. New York: Picador, 2002.

———. *Sefer ha-dikduk ha-penimi*. Bnai Brak: Ha-kibbutz ha-meuchad, 1991.

———. *To the End of the Land*. Trans. Jessica Cohen. New York: Knopf, 2010.

Gruber, Christiane. "Al-Buraq." *Encyclopaedia of Islam*, 3rd ed., 40–46. Leiden: Brill, 2012.

Grumberg, Karen. *Hebrew Gothic: History and the Poetics of Persecution*. Bloomington: Indiana University Press, 2019.

Gurevitch, Zali. "The Double Site of Israel." In *Grasping Land: Space and Place in Contemporary Israeli Discourse and Experience*, ed. Eyal Ben-Ari and Yoram Bilu, 203–16. Albany: SUNY Press, 1997.

———. "Eternal Loss: An Afterword." In H. N. Bialik, *Revealment and Concealment: Five Essays*. Jerusalem: Ibis, 2000.

———. *Ha-'ivrit 'al pinu* [Travels in Hebrew]. Jerusalem: Carmel, 2017.

———. *Kol Dodim: 'Al leshon ha-ahava shel shir ha-shirim* [The Sound of Love: On Erotic Language in the Song of Songs]. Tel Aviv: Bavel, 2013.

Gurevitch, Zali, and Gideon Aran. "'Al ha-makom" [On Place]. *Alpayim* 4 (1991): 9–44.

———. "The Land of Israel: Myth and Phenomenon." *Studies in Contemporary Jewry* (1994): 195–210.

Habermann, A. M. "Siḥot 'im S. Y. Agnon" [Conversations with Agnon]. In *Masekhet sofrim ve-sifrut* [On Writers and Literature]. Jerusalem: Reuben Mas, 1976.

Halbertal, Moshe, and Avishai Margalit. *Idolatry*. Trans. Naomi Goldblum. Cambridge: Harvard University Press, 1992.

Halbwachs, Maurice. "The Legendary Topography of the Gospels in the Holy Land." In *On Collective Memory*, ed. and trans. Lewis A. Coser, 193–235. Chicago: University of Chicago Press, 1992.

Halevi, Yehuda. *The Kuzari*. Trans. Hartwig Hirschfeld. London: George Routledge and Son, 1969.

———. "Ode to Zion." In *The Penguin Book of Hebrew Verse*, ed. T. Carmi, 347–48. Harmondsworth: Penguin, 1981.

———. "Zion Won't You Ask." In *Yehuda Halevi: Poems from the Diwan*, trans. Gabriel Levin, 101. London: Anvil Press, 2002.

Halkin, Hillel. Introduction to *Sholem Aleichem, Tevye the Dairyman and The Railroad Stories*, ix–xlii. Trans. Hillel Halkin. New York: Schocken, 1987.

Harnik, Raya. "I will not offer my first-born for sacrifice." In *Shirim le-Goni* [Poems for Goni], 9. Tel Aviv: Ha-kibbutz ha-meuchad, 1983.

Hasan-Rokem, Galit, and David Shulman. *Untying the Knot: On Riddles and Other Enigmatic Modes*. New York: Oxford University Press, 1996.

Hass, Amira. "Beyond the Holiness of Israel's Security Forces." *Haaretz*, February 26, 2019. https://www.haaretz.com/opinion/.premium-beyond-the-holiness-of-israel-s-security -forces-1.6965282.

Hasson, Nir. "Reclaiming Jerusalem's No Man's Land." *Haaretz*, October 30, 2011. https://www .haaretz.com/1.5204736.

———. "Temple Mount Custodian Lost Control. It's in Israel's Interest to Assist." *Haaretz*, March 12, 2019. https://www.haaretz.com/israel-news/.premium-temple-mount-custodian -lost-control-it-s-in-israel-s-interest-to-aid-it-1.7018424.

———. "Temple Mount Tensions Continue as Israeli Police Officers Refuse to Remove Shoes at Disputed Prayer Site." *Haaretz*, March 9, 2019. https://www.haaretz.com/israel-news /.premium-israeli-police-refuse-to-remove-shoes-at-disputed-temple-mount-prayer-site -1.7002612.

———. *Urshalim: Yisraelim u-falastini'im bi-yerushalayim 1967–2017* [Urshalim: Israelis and Palestinians in Jerusalem, 1967–2017]. Tel Aviv: Sifriat aliyat ha-gag, 2017.

———. "Why Israel and Jordan Are Clashing over the Temple Mount." *Haaretz*, February 24, 2019. https://www.haaretz.com/israel-news/.premium-why-israel-and-jordan-are-clashing-over-the-temple-mount-1.6962043.

Hasson, Nir, and Olivier Fitoussi. "Jerusalem Municipality Removes Dome of the Rock from Temple Mount Drawing." *Haaretz*, June 14, 2019. https://www.haaretz.com/israel-news/jerusalem-municipality-erases-dome-of-the-rock-from-temple-mount-drawing-1.7369163.

Havrelock, Rachel S. "Pioneers and Refugees: Arabs and Jews in the Jordan River Valley." In *Understanding Lives in the Borderlands: Boundaries in Depth and in Motion*, ed. William Zartman, 189–216. Athens: University of Georgia Press, 2010.

Hazan, Noa, and Avital Barak, eds. *Ha-har, ha-kipa ve-ha-mabat: har ha-bayit ba-tarbut ha-hazutit ha-yisraelit* [The Mountain, the Dome, and the Gaze: The Temple Mount in Israeli Art]. Haifa: Pardes, 2017.

Heschel, Abraham Joshua. *Maimonides: A Biography*. Trans. Joachim Neugroschel. New York: Farrar, Straus and Giroux, 1983.

Hever, Hannan. *El Ha-hof ha-mekuveh: Ha-yam ba-tarbut ha-'ivrit ha-modernit* [To the Desired Shore: The Sea in Modern Hebrew Culture]. Jerusalem: Van Leer Institute and Ha-kibbutz ha-meuchad, 2007.

———. "Perakim le-sefer ha-medina me-et Shay Agnon" [Chapters for the Book of State by S. Y. Agnon]. *Mikan* 14 (March 2014): 168–99.

Hirschfeld, Ariel. "'Ha-heder Ha-yarok shel Shir Ha Shirim" ["The Green Room" of Song of Songs]. *Haaretz*, April 11, 2017. https://www.haaretz.co.il/literature/.premium-1.4009931.

———. "'Ivut ha-merhav bi-groteska bi-*tmol shilshom*" [Distortion of Space as Grotesque in *Tmol shilshom* by S. Y. Agnon]. *Jerusalem Studies in Hebrew Literature* 2 (1982): 49–60.

———. *Kinor 'Arukh: Lashon ha-regesh be-shirat Hayim Nahman Bialik* [A Tuned Violin: The Language of Emotion in the Poetry of Hayim Nahman Bialik]. Tel Aviv: Am Oved, 2011.

———. *Likro et S. Y. Agnon* [Reading Agnon]. Tel Aviv: Ahuzat Bayit, 2011.

———. "Nafshi Yatsah Bidvaro" [How I Wanted Him When He Spoke]. *Haaretz*, April 17, 2017. https://www.haaretz.co.il/literature/.premium-1.4024012.

———. *Rishimot 'al makom* [Local Notes]. Tel Aviv: Am Oved, 2000.

———. "A Source and Oblivion—Story, Folk and Folktale in Agnon's Writing." *Jerusalem Studies in Jewish Folklore—Textures: Culture, Literature, Folklore, for Galit Hasan-Rokem* 28 (2013): 532–35.

Hoffman, Adina. *Till We Have Built Jerusalem: Architects of a New City*. New York: Farrar, Straus and Giroux, 2016.

Hoffman, Anne Golomb. *Between Exile and Return: S. Y. Agnon and the Drama of Writing*. Albany: SUNY Press, 1991.

Holtz, Avraham. "Ha-mashal ha-patu'ah ke-mafte'ah le-sefer ha-ma'asim shel Shai Agnon" [The Open Parable as Key to S. Y. Agnon's *Book of Deeds*]. *Ha-sifrut* 4 (1973): 298–333.

———. "Hitbonenut be-firtei *Tmol shilshom*" [Reflecting on the Details: *Tmol shilshom*]. In *Kovetz Agnon*, ed. Emuna Yaron et al., 178–221. Jerusalem: Magnes Press, 1994.

Hurowitz, Victor Avigdor. "Tenth Century BCE to 586 BCE: The House of the Lord (Beyt YHWH)." In *Where Heaven and Earth Meet: Jerusalem's Sacred Esplanade*, ed. Oleg Grabar and Benjamin Z. Kedar, 15–35. Austin and Jerusalem: University of Texas Press and Yad Ben Zvi, 2009.

Ibn Tibbon, Samuel, trans. *Sefer moreh ha-nevokhim*, by Moses Maimonides. Jerusalem: Monson, 1960.

Idel, Moshe. "The Land of Israel in Medieval Kabbalah." In *The Land of Israel: Jewish Perspectives*, ed. Lawrence Hoffman, 176–81. Notre Dame: University of Notre Dame Press, 1986.

Inbari, Motti. *Jewish Fundamentalism and the Temple Mount: Who Will Build the Third Temple?* Trans. Shaul Vardi. Albany: SUNY Press, 2009.

'Ir Amim. "The Separation Barrier." https://www.ir-amim.org.il/en/issue/separation-barrier. Accessed July 9, 2021.

Irshai, Oded. "The Christian Appropriation of Jerusalem in the Fourth Century: The Case of the Bordeaux Pilgrim." *Jewish Quarterly Review* 99, no. 4 (Fall 2009): 465–86.

Jackson, Rosemary. *Fantasy: The Literature of Subversion*. London: Routledge, 1981.

Jagendorf, Zvi. *Coming Soon: The Flood*. London: Halban, 2018.

Jelen, Sheila. "Bialik's Other Silence." *Hebrew Studies Journal* 44 (2003): 65–86.

Josephus, Flavius. *Antiquities of the Jews*. In *The Works of Flavius Josephus*, trans. William Whiston. Baltimore: Armstrong & Berry, 1834.

Joyce, James. *Ulysses*. Mineola: Dover Publications, 2002.

Kadari, Tamar. " 'Friends Hearken to Your Voice': Rabbinic Interpretations of the Song of Songs." In *Approaches to Literary Readings of Ancient Jewish Writings*, ed. Klaas Smelik and Karolien Vermeulen, 183–209. Leiden: Brill and University of Antwerp, 2014.

Kafka, Franz. *The Basic Kafka*. Introduction by Erich Heller. New York: Washington Square Press, 1979.

———. *Briefe, 1902–1924*. Frankfurt am Main: S. Fischer, 1966.

Kapach, Yosef ben David, trans. *Rabbeinu Moshe ben Maimon, Moreh Nevokhim, tirgem le-'ivrit bi'er ve-hikhin 'al pi kitvei yad ve-defusim*. Jerusalem: Mossad ha-rav Kuk, 1977.

Kaplony, Andreas. "635/638–1099: The Mosque of Jerusalem (Masjid Bayt Al-Maqdis)." In *Where Heaven and Earth Meet: Jerusalem's Sacred Esplanade*, ed. Oleg Grabar and Benjamin Z. Kedar, 100–131. Austin and Jerusalem: University of Texas Press and Yad Ben Zvi, 2009.

Kartun-Blum, Ruth. *Profane Scriptures: Reflections on the Dialogue with the Bible in Modern Hebrew Poetry*. Cincinnati: Hebrew Union College Press, 1999.

Kassow, Samuel. "Shtetl." In *The YIVO Encyclopedia of Jews in Eastern Europe*. http://www.yivo encyclopedia.org/article.aspx/shtetl. Accessed July 9, 2021.

Kayam, Yaelle, dir. *Ha-har* [The Mountain]. Israel, Windelov/Lassen July August Productions, 2016. https://www.imdb.com/video/vi907851289?playlistId=tt4917622&ref_=vp_rv_0.

Kedar, Benjamin Z., and Denys Pringle. "1099–1187: The Lord's Temple (Templum Domini) and Solomon's Palace (Palatium Salomonis)." In *Where Heaven and Earth Meet: Jerusalem's Sacred Esplanade*, ed. Oleg Grabar and Benjamin Z. Kedar, 132–49. Austin and Jerusalem: University of Texas Press and Yad Ben Zvi, 2009.

Kemal, Salim. *The Philosophical Poetics of Alfarabi, Avicenna and Averroes: The Aristotelian Reception*. London: Routledge, 2010.

Kierkegaard, Søren. *Fear and Trembling*. Trans. Alastair Hannai. New York: Penguin, 2005.

———. *The Kierkegaard Reader*. Ed. Jane Chamberlain and Jonathan Rée. Oxford: Blackwell, 2001.

Kirshenblatt-Gimblett, Barbara. Introduction to *Life Is with People: The Culture of the Shtetl*, ed. Mark Zborowski and Elizabeth Herzog, ix–xlviii. New York: Schocken, 1995. http://easteu rotopo.org/articles/kirshenblatt-gimblett/.

Kittay, Eva Feder. *Metaphor: Its Cognitive Force and Linguistic Structure*. New York: Oxford University Press, 1990.

Klein, Menachem. "Jerusalem's Alternative Collective Memory Agents." *Israel Studies Review* 35,

no. 1 (Spring 2020): 1–16. https://www.berghahnjournals.com/view/journals/israel-studies
-review/35/1/isr350102.xml.

Koëlle, Lydia. *Paul Celans pneumatisches Judentum: Gott-Rede und menschliche Existenz nach der Shoah*. Mainz: Matthias-Grünewald-Verlag, 1997.

Koestler, Arthur. *Promise and Fulfillment: Palestine, 1917–1949*. New York: Macmillan, 1949.

Kraemer, David. "Maimonides and Jerusalem." In *Jerusalem 1000–1400: Every People under Heaven*, ed. Barbara Drake Boehm and Melanie Holcomb, 82–84. New Haven: Yale University Press, 2016.

Kraemer, Joel. *Maimonides: The Life and World of One of Civilization's Greatest Minds*. New York: Doubleday, 2008.

Kristeva, Julia. *Tales of Love*. Trans. Leon S. Roudiez. New York: Columbia University Press, 1987.

Kronfeld, Chana. *The Full Severity of Compassion: The Poetry of Yehuda Amichai*. Stanford: Stanford University Press, 2016.

——. "The Land as Woman: Esther Raab and the Afterlife of a Metaphorical System." *Prooftexts: A Journal of Jewish Literary History*, forthcoming.

——. "My Chana." *Shofar* 36, no. 2, tribute issue for Chana Bloch (Summer 2018): 8–20.

——. *On the Margins of Modernism; Decentering Literary Dynamics*. Berkeley: University of California Press, 1996.

——. "Rethinking Biblical Poetic Intertextuality in Modern Israeli Poetry." *Prooftexts*, special issue, "Imagining Biblical Poetry," ed. Elaine James and Steve Weitzman, forthcoming.

Kurzweil, Baruch. *Masot 'al sipurei Shai Agnon* [Essays on the Stories of S. Y. Agnon]. Jerusalem: Schocken, 1962.

Kushner, Aviya. "How One Nation Mourns a Poet." *Partisan Review* 68, no. 4 (Fall 2001): 612–16.

Lakoff, George, and Mark Johnson. *Metaphors We Live By*. Chicago: University of Chicago Press, 1980.

Laor, Dan. *Ḥayei Agnon*. Jerusalem: Schocken, 1998.

——. "La'asot sefer yoḥasin le-zar'o: *Korot Bateinu* me-et S. Y. Agnon." *Haaretz*, July 13, 1979.

Laor, Yitzhak. *Shirim 1974–1992* [Poems 1974–1992]. Tel Aviv: Ha-kibbutz ha-meuchad, 2002.

Leibowitz, Yeshayahu. "Ha-geula ha-meshiḥit be-mishnato shel ha-Rambam" [Messianic Redemption in Maimonides's Thought]. In *Emuna, historia ve-'arakhim ma'amaraim ve-hartsa'ot* [Religion, History, and Values: Articles and Lectures], 89–101. Jerusalem: Akademon, 1982. http://www.leibowitz.co.il/leibarticles.asp?id=68.

——. "Ha-Rambam: Ha-adam ha-avrahami" [Maimonides: The Abrahamic Man]. *Be-terem* 211 (1955): 20–22. http://leibowitz.co.il/about.asp?id=59#_edn1.

——. "The Six Day War." In *Judaism, Jewish People, and the State of Israel*, ed. Yeshayahu Leibowitz, 404–5. Tel Aviv: Schocken, 2005.

Letteris, Ha-Levi-Meir, ed. *Mahzor kolel ha-tefilot ve-ha-piyyutim le-khol mo'adei El* [Prayerbook with Prayers and Piyyutim for All the Holidays]. Prague: Gottlieb Haase, 1847.

Levin, Hanoch. "The Akeda (The Binding)." Trans. Donny Inbar. In *Queen of Bathtub*. Tel Aviv: Cameri Theater, 1970. http://www.sjsu.edu/people/victoria.harrison/courses/JWSS111/s1/Hanoch-Levin-Binding-and-Creation.pdf.

Levinson, Jon. *The Death and Resurrection of the Beloved Son*. New Haven: Yale University Press, 1995.

Lieber, Dov. "Amid Temple Tumult, the Who, What and Why of Its Waqf Rulers." *Times of Israel*, July 20, 2017. https://www.timesofisrael.com/amid-temple-mount-tumult-the-who-what-and-why-of-its-waqf-rulers/.

Lipsker, Avidov. "Yisud Buczacz: Mofet, Kedusha Ve-ashma be-'Ir u-meloah le-Shay Agnon" [The Founding of Buczacz: Template, Sanctity, and Guilt in *A City in Its Fullness* by S. Y. Agnon]. *Maḥshavot 'al Agnon*, 1:59–96. Ramat Gan: Bar Ilan University, 2015.

Liska, Vivian. *German-Jewish Thought and Its Afterlife: A Tenuous Legacy*. Bloomington: Indiana University Press, 2016.

Long, Burke O. *Imagining the Holy Land: Maps, Models, and Fantasy Travels*. Bloomington: Indiana University Press, 2003.

Long, Gary Alan. "Dead or Alive? Literality and God-Metaphors in the Hebrew Bible." *Journal of the American Academy of Religion* 62, no. 2 (Summer 1994): 539–52.

Lorberbaum, Menachem. *Nutzaḥnu be-ne'imuto: Torat ha-elohut ke-poetikah be-yitzira ha-yehudit ha-andalusit* [Dazzled by Beauty: Theology as Poetics in Hispanic Jewish Culture]. Jerusalem: Yad Izhak Ben-Zvi and the Hebrew University of Jerusalem, 2011.

Maimonides, Moses. *Commentary on the Mishnah*, Tractate Middot, catalogue 38, fols. 294v–295. Bodleian Libraries, University of Oxford (MS Poc.295).

———. *The Guide of the Perplexed*. 2 vols. Trans. and ed. Shlomo Pines. Introductory essay by Leo Strauss. Chicago: University of Chicago Press, 1963.

———. *Letters and Essays of Moses Maimonides*. Ed. Isaac Shailat. Jerusalem: Ma'aliyot, 1987–88.

Makiya, Kanan. *The Rock: A Tale of Seventh-Century Jerusalem*. New York: Pantheon Books, 2001.

Manea, Norman. Introduction to *The Correspondence of Paul Celan and Ilana Shmueli*. Trans. Susan H. Gillespie. New York: Sheep Meadow Press, 2010.

Mariaselvam, Abraham. *The Song of Songs and Ancient Tamil Love Poems: Poetry and Symbolism*. Rome: Editrice Pontificio Istituto Biblico, 1988.

Marmur, Michael. "Heschel's Two Maimonides." *Jewish Quarterly Review* 98, no. 2 (Spring 2008): 230–54.

Meyer, Yakov Z. "Parashat Tzav / When Texts Supplant Sacrifice." *Haaretz*, March 26, 2015. http://www.haaretz.com/weekend/portion-of-the-week/.premium-1.649055.

———. "Parashat Vayakhel-Pekudei / Moses as Literary Contractor." *Haaretz*, March 12, 2015. http://www.haaretz.com/weekend/portion-of-the-week/.premium-1.646614.

Meyers, Carol. "Gender Imagery in the Songs of Songs." *Hebrew Annual Review* 10 (1986): 209–23.

Meyers, Carol L., and Eric M. Meyers, eds. *Haggai, Zechariah 1–8. The Anchor Bible: A New Translation with Introduction and Commentary*. New York: Doubleday, 1987.

Milner, Iris. "Sacrifice and Redemption in *To the End of the Land*." *Hebrew Studies* 54 (2013): 319–34.

Mintz, Alan. *Hurban: Responses to Catastrophe in Hebrew Literature*. New York: Columbia University Press, 1984.

Miron, Dan. "Bein shtei neshamot: ha-analogia ha-faustit bi-*tmol shilshom* le-shai agnon" [Between Two Souls: The Faustian Analogy in S. Y. Agnon's *Tmol Shilshom*]. In *Mi-vilna li-yerushalayim* [From Vilna to Jerusalem], ed. David Asaf, Israel Bartal, et al., 549–608. Jerusalem: Magnes Press, 2002.

———. *Bein shtei neshamot: ha-analogia ha-faustit bi-tmol shilshom le-shai agnon: ba'ayat ha-tragedia ha-modernit* [Between Two Souls: The Faustian Analogy in S. Y. Agnon's *Tmol Shilshom*: The Dilemma of Modern Tragedy]. Jerusalem: Mossad Bialik, 2020. [Expanded version of the above.]

———. "Domesticating a Foreign Genre: Agnon's Transactions with the Novel." *Prooftexts* 7, no. 1 (January 1987): 1–27.

———. "The Literary Image of the Shtetl." *Jewish Social Studies*, n.s., 1, no. 3 (Spring 1995): 1–43.

———. "Mi-mashal le-sipur toladi: petiḥa le-diyun bi-*tmol shilshom*" [From Parable to Chronicle: Preliminary Discussion of *Tmol shilshom*]. In *Kovetz Agnon* II, ed. Emuna Yaron et al., 159–87. Jerusalem: Magnes Press, 2000.

———. "Yeled tov u-malei ahava" [A Good and Loving Boy]. *Haaretz: Tarbut ve-sifrut*, October 12, 2005, 2. http://www.haaretz.co.il/literature/1.1050312.

Molinaro, Enrico. *The Holy Places of Jerusalem in the Middle East Peace Agreements: The Conflict between Global and State Identities*. Brighton, UK: Sussex Academic Press, 2009.

Namdar, Ruby. *The Ruined House*. Trans. Hillel Halkin. New York: Harper Collins, 2017.

Neuwirth, Angelika. "The Spiritual Meaning of Jerusalem in Islam." In *City of the Great King: Jerusalem from David to the Present*, ed. Nitza Rosovsky, 93–116. Cambridge: Harvard University Press, 2013.

Omer, Mordechai. *Upon One of the Mountains: Jerusalem in Israeli Art*. Jerusalem: Genia Schreiber Gallery, 1988.

Omer-Sherman, Ranen. "Yehuda Amichai's Exilic Jerusalem." *Prooftexts* 26, nos. 1–2 (Winter/Spring 2006): 212–39.

Oz, Amos. *The Silence of Heaven: Agnon's Fear of God*. Trans. Barbara Harshav. Princeton: Princeton University Press, 2000.

Pagis, Dan. *Ha-shir dabur 'al ofanav: Meḥkarim u-masot ba-shira ha-'ivrit shel yemei ha-beinayim*. Ed. Ezra Fleischer. Jerusalem: Magnes Press, 1993.

———. *Hebrew Poetry of the Middle Ages and the Renaissance*. Foreword by Robert Alter. Berkeley: University of California Press, 1991. Shortened translated version of the above.

———. *Points of Departure*. Bilingual ed. Trans. Stephen Mitchell. Introduction by Robert Alter. Philadelphia: Jewish Publication Society, 1981.

Pardes, Ilana. *Agnon's Moonstruck Lovers: The Song of Songs in Israeli Culture*. Seattle: University of Washington Press, 2014.

———. *The Song of Songs: A Biography*. Princeton: Princeton University Press, 2019.

Pedaya, Haviva. "The Divinity as Place and Time and the Holy Place in Jewish Mysticism." In *Sacred Space: Shrine, City, Land*, ed. Benjamin Z. Kedar and R. J. Zwi Werblowsky, 84–111. New York: New York University Press, 1998.

———. *Merḥav u-makom: Masa 'al ha-lo-muda' ha-teologi-politi* [Expanses: Essay on the Theological and Political Unconscious]. Tel Aviv: Ha-kibbutz ha-meuchad, 2011.

———. "Temurot ba-kodesh ha-kodashim: Min ha-shulayim la-mercaz" [Changes in the Holy of Holies: From the Periphery to the Center]. *Mada'ei ha-yahadut* [Jewish Studies] 37 (1996): 53–110.

Peri, Yoram, ed. "Changing Perspectives on the Temple Mount." Special issue of *Israel Studies* 32, no. 1 (Summer 2017).

Perloff, Carey. "Tragedy Today." *PMLA* 129, no. 4 (October 2014): 830–33.

Persico, Tomer. "The End Point of Zionism: Ethnocentrism and the Temple Mount." *Israel Studies Review* 32, no. 1 (Summer 2017): 104–22.

———. "The Temple Mount and the End of Zionism." *Haaretz*, November 28, 2014, 8–10. http://www.haaretz.com/news/features/.premium-1.628929.

———. "Why Rebuilding the Temple Would Be the End of Judaism As We Know It." *Haaretz*, November 13, 2014. http://www.haaretz.com/news/features/.premium-1.626327.

Prawer, Joshua. *The History of the Jews in the Latin Kingdom of Jerusalem*. Oxford: Clarendon Press, 1988.

Rabin, Yitzhak. "Inauguration of Jerusalem 3000 Festivities." Israeli Ministry of Foreign Affairs.

September 4, 1995. https://mfa.gov.il/MFA/MFA-Archive/1995/Pages/PM%20Rabin-%20In auguration%20Jerusalem%203000%20Festivities.aspx.

Rappel, Yoel. "Zehuto shel meḥaber ha-tefila li-shlom ha-medina" [The Identity of the Writer of the Prayer for the Safety of the State]. In *Et Shivat Tzion Hayinu ke-ḥolmim*, ed. R. Benyamin Lau and Yoel Rappel, 355–61. Jerusalem: Koren, 2013.

Rechnitzer, Haim O. "Redemptive Theology in the Thought of Yeshayahu Leibowitz." *Israel Studies* 13, no. 3 (Fall 2008): 137–59.

Reiner, Elhanan. "Destruction, Temple and Holy Place." In *Streams into the Sea: Studies in Jewish Culture and Its Context*, ed. Rachel Livneh-Freudenthal and Elchanan Reiner, 138–52. Tel Aviv: Alma College, 2001.

———. "Overt Falsehood and Covert Truth: Christians, Jews and Holy Places in Twelfth Century Zion." *Zion* 63, no. 2 (1998): 157–88.

Reiter, Yitzhak. *Contested Holy Places in Israel-Palestine: Sharing and Conflict Resolution*. London: Routledge, 2017.

———. *The Eroding Status-Quo: Power Struggles on the Temple Mount*. Trans. Amy Erani. Jerusalem: Jerusalem Institute for Policy Research, 2017.

Reiter, Yitzhak, and Jon Seligman. "1917 to the Present: Al-Haram al Sharif/Temple Mount (Har Habayit) and the Western Wall." In *Where Heaven and Earth Meet: Jerusalem's Sacred Esplanade*, ed. Oleg Grabar and Benjamin Z. Kedar, 231–74. Austin and Jerusalem: University of Texas Press and Yad Ben Zvi, 2009.

Ricoeur, Paul. *The Rule of Metaphor: Multidisciplinary Studies of the Creation of Meaning in Language*. Trans. Robert Czerny. Toronto: University of Toronto Press, 1977.

Rokem, Na'ama. "German-Jewish Encounters in the Poetry of Yehuda Amichai and Paul Celan." *Prooftexts* 30, no. 1 (2010): 97–127.

Rosen, Tova. "Kemo ba-shir shel Shmuel Ha-nagid: Bein Shmuel Ha-nagid le-Yehuda Amichai" ["As in Shmuel Ha-nagid's Poem": Between Shmuel Ha-nagid and Yehuda Amichai]. *Meḥkarei yerushalayim be-sifrut 'Ivrit*, no. 15 (1995): 106–83.

Rosenak, Avinoam. "Halakhah, Thought and the Idea of Holiness in the Writings of Rabbi Chaim David Halevi." In *Creation and Re-creation in Jewish Thought: Festschrift in Honor of Joseph Dan on the Occasion of His Seventieth Birthday*, ed. Rachel Elior, 309–38. Tübingen: Mohr Siebeck, 2005.

Rosenzweig, Franz. *Star of Redemption*. Trans. William W. Hallo. Boston: Beacon Press, 1964.

Roskies, David G. *The Jewish Search for a Useable Past*. Bloomington: Indiana University Press, 1999.

Roth, Cecil. *The Haggadah, A New Edition*. London: Soncino Press, 1959.

Roth, Norman. "Maimonides on Hebrew Language and Poetry." In *Maimonides, Essays and Texts: 850th Anniversary*, ed. Norman Roth, 109–22. Madison, WI: Hispanic Seminary of Medieval Studies, 1985.

Roth, Philip. "The Conversion of the Jews." In *Goodbye, Columbus and Five Short Stories*, 137–59. New York: Vintage/Random House, 1987.

Sadan, Dov. *'Al Shai Agnon: Masa 'iyyun ve-ḥeker* [Studies in Agnon]. Tel Aviv: Ha-kibbutz ha-meuchad, 1973.

Safrai, Samuel. "Holy Congregation in Jerusalem." *Scripta Hierosolymitana* 23 (1972): 62–78.

Sagi, Avi. "Keeping God on the Temple Mount." *Haaretz*, April 18, 2018. http://www.haaretz .com/misc/article-print-page/.premium-1.681883.

Sandbank, Shimon. "Li-va'ayat ha-shir ha-kal" [The Problem of the Simple Poem]. *Siman Kriah* 12–13 (February 1981): 331–34.

Saposnik, Arieh Bruce. "Wailing Walls and Iron Walls: The Wailing Wall as Sacred Symbol in Zionist National Iconography." *American Historical Review* 120, no. 5 (December 2015): 1653–81.

Schechter, Solomon, ed. *Avot d-Rabbi Natan*, version A. Vienna, 1887; reprint, New York: Jewish Seminary of America, 1950.

Scheindlin, Raymond P. *The Song of the Distant Dove: Judah Halevi's Pilgrimage*. Oxford: Oxford University Press, 2008.

Schley, Donald G. *Shiloh: A Biblical City in Tradition and History*. Sheffield, UK: JSOT Press, 1989, 2009.

Schmemann, Serge. "Incidents and Arguments Add to Arab-Israeli Friction." *New York Times*, September 25, 1996. https://www.nytimes.com/1996/09/25/world/incidents-and-arguments -add-to-arab-israeli-friction.html.

Scholem, Gershom. *Retzifut u-mered: Gershom Scholem be-omer u-ve-si'ah* [Continuity and Rebellion: Gershom Scholem in Conversation]. Ed. Avraham Shapira. Tel Aviv: Am Oved, 1994.

Schorsch, Ismar. "Behind God's Names." *Jewish Theological Seminary*, November 20, 1993. http:// www.jtsa.edu/behind-gods-names.

Schwartz, Avraham, and Yisroel Schwartz. *The Megilloth and Rashi's Commentary with Linear Translation*. New York: Hebrew Linear Classics, 1983.

Schwartz, Hava. "The Return to the Monument: The Looming Absence of the Temple." *Israel Studies Review* 32, no. 1 (Summer 2017): 48–66.

Schweid, Eli. "Kelev hutzot—ve-adam: 'iyyun be-*Tmol shilshom* le-Shai Agnon" [Stray Dog— and a Man: Studies in *Tmol shilshom*]. *Molad* 11 (December–January 1958).

Shabtai, Ya'akov. *Past Continuous*. Trans. Dalya Bilu. New York: Overlook Press, 1985.

———. *Zikhron Devarim*. Bnai Brak: Ha-kibbutz ha-meuchad, 1977.

Shachar, Galili. *Gufim ve-shemot: kri'ot be-sifrut yehudit hadasha* [Bodies and Names: Readings in Modern Jewish Literature]. Tel Aviv: Am Oved, 2016.

Shaked, Gershon. "Midrash and Narrative: Agnon's 'Agunot.'" In *Midrash and Literature*, ed. Geoffrey H. Hartman and Sanford Budick, 285–303. New Haven: Yale University Press, 1968.

Shalev, Meir. *Reshit* [In the Beginning]. Tel Aviv: Am Oved, 2008.

Shammas, Anton. *Arabesques*. Trans. Vivian Eden. Berkeley: University of California Press, 2001.

Shandler, Jeffrey. *Shtetl: A Vernacular Intellectual History*. Vol. 5. New Brunswick, NJ: Rutgers University Press, 2014.

Shershow, Scott Cutler. *Laughing Matters: The Paradox of Comedy*. Amherst: University of Massachusetts Press, 1986.

Shmueli, Ilana. *The Correspondence of Paul Celan and Ilana Shmueli*. Trans. Susan H. Gillespie. New York: Sheep Meadow Press, 2010.

———. *Sag, dass Jerusalem ist. Uber Paul Celan: Oktober 1969–April 1970*. Eggingen: Edition Isele, 2000.

Silk, Dennis. *Retrievements: A Jerusalem Anthology*. Jerusalem: Israel Universities Press, 1968.

Smith, Jonathan Z. *Map Is Not Territory: Studies in the History of Religion*. Chicago: University of Chicago Press, 1978.

Soja, Edward. *Thirdspace: Journeys to Los Angeles and Other Real-and-Imagined Places*. Hoboken: Blackwell, 1996.

Soker-Schwager, Hanna, ed. "Koah meshihi halash: teologia politit, dat ve-hiloniut ba-sifrut ha-'ivrit" [A Weak Messianic Power: Political Theology, Religion, and Secularism in Hebrew Literature]. Special issue of *Mikan* 14 (March 2014).

Soloveitchik, Yosef-Dov Halevi. *Ish ha-halakha—galui ve-nistar* [The Man of Halakha—Revealed and Concealed]. Jerusalem: Ha-histadrut ha-tzionit ha-'olamit, 1979.

Soulen, Richard N. "The *Wasfs* of the Song of Songs and Hermeneutic." *Journal of Biblical Litera-ture* 86, no. 2 (June 1967): 183–90. https://www.jstor.org/stable/3263272.

Spiegel, Shalom. *The Last Trial: On the Legends and Lore of the Command to Abraham to Offer Isaac as a Sacrifice.* Trans. Judah Goldin. New York: Jewish Lights Classic Reprint, 1993.

Stern, David. "Agnon from a Medieval Perspective." In *History and Literature: New Readings from Jewish Texts in Honor of Arnold Band,* ed. William Cutter and David C. Jacobson, 176–82. Providence: Brown Judaic Studies, 2002.

———. "Ancient Jewish Interpretation of the Song of Songs in a Comparative Context." In *Jew-ish Biblical Interpretation and Cultural Exchange: Comparative Exegesis in Context,* ed. Nata-lie B. Dohrmann and David Stern, 87–107. Philadelphia: University of Pennsylvania Press, 2008.

———. Introduction to "The Tale of the Menorah." In S. Y. Agnon, *A Book That Was Lost and Other Stories,* ed. Alan Mintz and Anne Golomb Hoffman, 233. New York: Schocken, 1995.

Stevens, Wallace. "Sunday Morning." In *The Collected Poems of Wallace Stevens,* 66–70. New York: Alfred A. Knopf, 1993.

Strauss, Leo. Introductory essay. In Moses Maimonides, *The Guide of the Perplexed,* trans. Shlomo Pines, xi–lvi. Chicago: University of Chicago Press, 1963.

———. *Persecution and the Art of Writing.* Chicago: University of Chicago Press, 1952.

Stroumsa, Sarah. *Maimonides in His World: Portrait of a Mediterranean Thinker.* Princeton: Princeton University Press, 2012.

———. "The Politico-Religious Context of Maimonides." In *The Trias of Maimonides / Die Trias des Maimonides: Jewish, Arabic, and Ancient Culture of Knowledge,* ed. G. Tamer, 257–65. Berlin: De Gruyter, 2005.

Theoharis, C. Theoharis. "For with God All Things Are Possible: Philip Roth's 'The Conversion of the Jews.'" *Journal of the Short Story in English* 32 (Spring 1999): 2–6.

Till, Karen. "Wounded Cities: Memory-Work and a Place-Based Ethics of Care." *Political Geog-raphy* 31, no. 1 (2012): 3–14.

Todorov, Tzvetan. *The Fantastic: A Structural Approach to a Literary Genre.* Trans. Richard How-ard. Ithaca: Cornell University Press, 1973.

Trible, Phyllis. "Depatriarchalizing in Biblical Interpretation." *Journal of the American Academy of Religion* 41, no. 1 (March 1973): 30–31.

———. *God and the Rhetoric of Sexuality.* Philadelphia: Fortress Press, 1978.

Tsafrir, Yoram. "70–638: The Temple-less Mountain." In *Where Heaven and Earth Meet: Jerusa-lem's Sacred Esplanade,* ed. Oleg Grabar and Benjamin Z. Kedar, 72–100. Austin and Jerusa-lem: University of Texas Press and Yad Ben Zvi, 2009.

Tuchner, Meshulam. *Pesher Agnon* [Interpreting Agnon]. Ramat Gan: Massada, 1968.

Tversky, Yitzhak. "Ha-Rambam ve-Eretz Yisrael: hebetim hilkhati'im, philosophi'im ve-histori'im." In *Tarbut ve-ḥevra be-toldot Yisrael bi-yemei ha-benayim: Kovetz ma'amarim le-zikhro shel Haim Hillel Ben-Sasson* [Medieval Jewish Culture and Society: Essays in Memory of Haim Hillel Ben-Sasson], ed. Reuven [Robert] Bonfil, Menahem Ben-Sasson, and Joseph Hacker, 353–81. Jerusalem: Mercaz Zalman Shazar, 1988.

Twain, Mark. *Innocents Abroad.* Hartford, CT: American Publishing Company, 1869. https://www.gutenberg.org/files/3176/3176-h/3176-h.htm.

Twersky, Isadore. "Maimonides and Eretz Yisrael: Halakhic, Philosophic and Historical Per-spectives." In *Perspectives on Maimonides,* ed. Joel Kraemer, 257–90. London: Littmann Li-brary of Jewish Civilization, 1996.

Tzaban, Yahil. "Neged Agnon: O zehu ha-matsa' shel ha-bayit ha-yehudi" [Against Agnon; or, This Is the Platform of the Jewish Home]. *Haaretz*, March 24, 2017. https://www.haaretz .co.il/literature/.premium-1.3948333.

Um Juni. Virtual Tour Kibbutz Degania Site. https://degania.org.il/en/virtual-tour/umm-juni/.

Walden, Geoff. "Würzburg, Part 2: Würzburg during the War." The Third Reich in Ruins, http:// www.thirdreichruins.com/urzburg2.htm, July 20, 2000.

Wallach, Yona. "Hebrew." In *Wild Light: Selected Poems of Yona Wallach*, trans. Linda Zisquit, 6–8. New York: Sheep Meadow Press, 1997.

Weiser, R. Meir Leibush ben Yehiel Michal [Ha-malbi'm]. *Mikra'ei kodesh*, vol. 8, *Nevi'im u-ktuvim*. Vilna: Hotza'at aḥim Re'em, 1890.

Whedbee, J. William. *The Bible and the Comic Vision*. Minneapolis: Fortress Press, 2002.

Whitman, Jon, ed. *Interpretation and Allegory: Antiquity to the Modern Period*. Boston: Brill-Leiden, 2000.

Wieczorek, Marek. "The Ridiculous, Sublime Art of Slavoj Žižek." Introduction to Slavoj Žižek, *The Art of the Ridiculous Sublime: On David Lynch's Lost Highway*, viii–xiii. Seattle: University of Washington Press, 2000.

Witztum, Eliezer, and Moshe Kalian. "The 'Jerusalem Syndrome'—Fantasy and Reality: A Survey of Accounts from the Nineteenth Century to the End of the Second Millennium." *Israel Journal of Psychiatry and Related Sciences* 36, no. 4 (1999): 260–71.

Wood, James. "Like a Prayer: The Poetry of Yehuda Amichai." *New Yorker*, January 4, 2016, 74.

Yaari, Eliezer. *Mi-pa'am le-fa'am* [Every So Often]. Photographs: Alex Levac. Hod ha-sharon: Agam Books, 2020.

Yadin, Azzan. "קול [Voice] as Hypostasis in the Hebrew Bible." *Journal of Biblical Literature* 122, no. 4 (Winter 2003): 601–26.

Yaffe, B. Abraham. *Pegishot 'im Leah Goldberg* [Meetings with Leah Goldberg]. Tel Aviv: Tcherikover, 1984.

Yehoshua, A. B. *Mar Mani*. Tel Aviv: Ha-kibbutz ha-meuchad, 1993.

———. *Mr. Mani*. Trans. Hillel Halkin. San Diego: Harcourt Brace, 1993.

———. "Mr. Mani and the Akeda." Trans. Rivka Hadari and Amnon Hadari. *Judaism* 50 (Winter 2001): 61–65.

Yeshurun, Avot. *The Syrian-African Rift and Other Poems*. Trans. Harold Schimmel. Philadelphia: Jewish Publication Society, 1980.

Young, James. *At Memory's Edge: After-Images of the Holocaust in Contemporary Art and Architecture*. New Haven: Yale University Press, 2002.

———. *The Stages of Memory: Reflections on Memorial Art, Loss, and the Spaces Between*. Amherst: University of Massachusetts Press, 2016.

Yuval, Israel. *Two Nations in Your Womb*. Berkeley: University of California Press, 2006.

Zakovitch, Yair. "The First Stages of Jerusalem's Sanctification under David: A Literary and Ideological Analysis." In *Jerusalem: Its Sanctity and Centrality to Judaism, Christianity, and Islam*, ed. Lee I. Levine, 16–35. New York: Continuum, 1999.

———. "Kol demama daka: Tzura ve-tokhen be-Malachim 1, 19:12" [A Still Small Voice: Structure and Content in I Kings 19:12]. *Tarbiz* 51, no. 3 (1983): 329–46.

———. *Shir ha-shirim, mikra le-yisrael: perush mada'i la-mikra* [Song of Songs, Israel's Scriptures: Scientific Interpretation of the Bible]. Tel Aviv and Jerusalem: Am Oved and Magnes Press, 1992.

———. *The Song of Songs: Riddle of Riddles*. Trans. Valerie Carr Zakovitch. London: T&T Clark, 2018.

Zakovitch, Yair, and Avigdor Shinan. *From Gods to God: How the Bible Debunked, Suppressed or Changed Ancient Myths and Legends.* Trans. Valerie Zakovitch. Lincoln: University of Nebraska Press, 2012.

———. *Lo kakh katuv ba-tana"kh* [Once Again: That's Not What the Good Book Says]. Tel Aviv: Mishkal-Yedioth ahronot and Chemed, 2004.

Zemach, Eddy. "Be-kefel dmut" [Doppelgänger]. *Moznaym* 62, nos. 7–8 (1988): 43–49.

———. *Kria tama: 'Iyyunim be-sifrut 'ivrit* [Readings in Hebrew Literature]. Tel Aviv: Hakibbutz ha-meuchad, 1990.

Zerubavel, Yael. *Recovered Roots: Collective Memory and the Making of Israeli National Tradition.* Chicago: University of Chicago Press, 1995.

Zierler, Wendy I. *And Rachel Stole the Idols: The Emergence of Modern Hebrew Women's Writing.* Detroit: Wayne State University Press, 2004.

Zipperstein, Steven J. *Pogrom: Kishinev and the Tilt of History.* New York: Liveright, 2018.

Zucker, David J. "Isaac: A Life of Bitter Laughter." *Jewish Bible Quarterly* 40, no. 2 (2012): 105–10.

———. "Ishmael and Isaac: Parallel, Not Conflictual Lives." *Scandinavian Journal of the Old Testament* 26, no. 1 (2012): 1–11.

Zvi Greenberg, Uri. "Bizkhut em u-vena vi-yerushalayim." In *Uri Zvi Greenberg: Kol Ketavav,* 7:57–59. Jerusalem: Mossad Bialik, 1994.

Index of Names

Index of Biblical Citations